Feminist Theatrical
Revisions of
Classic Works

Feminist Theatrical Revisions of Classic Works

Critical Essays

Edited by
SHARON FRIEDMAN

McFarland & Company, Inc., Publishers
Jefferson, North Carolina, and London

LIBRARY OF CONGRESS CATALOGUING-IN-PUBLICATION DATA

Feminist theatrical revisions of classic works : critical essays / edited by Sharon Friedman.
    p.   cm.
    Includes bibliographical references and index.

    ISBN 978-0-7864-3425-1
    softcover : 50# alkaline paper

    1. Feminism and theater. 2. Feminist theater.
3. English drama — History and criticism. 4. American drama — History and criticism. 5. Women in literature.
I. Friedman, Sharon, 1947–
PN1590.W64F46   2009
792.082 — dc22   2008034167

British Library cataloguing data are available

©2009 Sharon Friedman. All rights reserved

No part of this book may be reproduced or transmitted in any form or by any means, electronic or mechanical, including photocopying or recording, or by any information storage and retrieval system, without permission in writing from the publisher.

Cover image: Psyche with the candelabra over the blindfolded figure of Eros, with wings. *Metamorphoses*, Second Stage Theatre, New York, 2001. Photographer: Joan Marcus.

Manufactured in the United States of America

McFarland & Company, Inc., Publishers
   Box 611, Jefferson, North Carolina 28640
      www.mcfarlandpub.com

To Stephen, Danny and Joanna

Acknowledgments

This book is the result of genuine collaboration. Above all, I wish to thank the contributors for the knowledge and talent that they brought to this shared project, as well as their patience in seeing it through from its inception to its publication.

The idea for this volume grew out of several panels that I participated in at the Mid-America Theatre Conference and the Comparative Drama Conference. These in turn led to a faculty workshop, sponsored by New York University's Humanities Council, "An Interdisciplinary and Intercultural Examination of Twentieth-Century Adaptations and Re-Visions of Classic Texts." I am indebted to my co-directors, professors Carol Martin and Laura Slatkin, as well as the workshop participants— Awam Amkpa, Helene Foley, Amy Green, and Julie Malnig — who brought diverse disciplinary perspectives and personal insight to our table. Special thanks to Julie Malnig, my friend and colleague, for reading drafts of the introduction, not to mention carrying on countless conversations that provided inspiration and insight.

NYU's Gallatin School and the Stephen Golden Faculty Enrichment Grant provided indispensable financial support at various stages of this project. I was fortunate to have the assistance of two talented graduate students: Mary Caulfield, who helped collect materials for the volume, and Catherine Massey, who gave me the benefit of her skillful editing and her deep understanding of the craft of scholarship.

Heartfelt thanks to my family — my husband, Stephen Steinberg, my children, Daniel and Joanna, my mother, Sylvia Friedman, and my sister, Jacqueline Friedman —for their support and excitement for the project.

Table of Contents

Acknowledgments — vii

Introduction
    SHARON FRIEDMAN — 1

I. Classical Theater and Myth

All Is Not Right in the House of Atreus: Feminist Theatrical Renderings of the *Oresteia*
    JULIE MALNIG — 21

The Philomela Myth as Postcolonial Feminist Theater: Timberlake Wertenbaker's *The Love of the Nightingale*
    MAYA E. ROTH — 42

Mary Zimmerman's *Metamorphoses*: Storytelling Theater as Feminist Process
    ANDREA J. NOURYEH — 61

The Political Is Personal: Feminism, Democracy and *Antigone Project*
    CAROL MARTIN — 79

II. Shakespeare and Seventeenth Century Theater

Lear's Daughters and Sons: Twisting the Canonical Landscape
    LESLEY FERRIS — 97

The Feminist Playwright as Critic: Paula Vogel, Ann-Marie MacDonald, and Djanet Sears Interpret *Othello*
    SHARON FRIEDMAN — 113

Transgressive Female Desire and Subversive Critique in the Seventeenth Century Canon: JoAnne Akalaitis's Staging of *Phèdre*, *The Rover*, and *'Tis Pity She's a Whore*
    CHERYL BLACK — 135

Reconfiguring the Text and the Self: The Wooster Group's *To You, the Birdie!* (*Phèdre*)
    JOHAN CALLENS — 152

III. Nineteenth and Twentieth Century Narratives and Reflections: The Romance, the Novel, and the Essay

Outside the Law: Feminist Adaptations of *The Scarlet Letter*
    Lenora Champagne   169

Expressions of "Lust and Rage": Shared Experience Theatre's Adaptation of *Jane Eyre*
    Kristin Crouch   189

A Mystical Place Called Grand Isle: Adapting Kate Chopin's *The Awakening*
    Chiori Miyagawa   204

SITI Company's *Room*: Theatrical Performance and/as Feminist Invitational Rhetoric
    Sandee K. McGlaun   215

IV. Modern Drama

Deconstructing (A Streetcar Named) Desire: Gender Re-citation in *Belle Reprieve*
    Deborah R. Geis   237

Nora's Journey Through a Century of Feminisms to the Postmodern Stage of *Mabou Mines DollHouse*
    Amy S. Green   247

Bibliography   267
About the Contributors   279
Index   283

Introduction

Sharon Friedman

In 2007, *New York Times* theater critic Ben Brantley observed that "genre-bending, time straddling adaptation" had become an "exceptionally lively art on London's stages," and that "reconfigurations of classics are testing and stretching the traditional limits of theater in the age of cultural cross-pollination."[1] In addition to transformations of plays by Shakespeare, Molière, and Chekhov, Brantley noted visionary "morphings" of Virginia Woolf's poetic novel *The Waves* and Alfred Hitchcock's thriller *The 39 Steps*. Also in 2007, ATHE's Women and Theatre Program, a major organization for artists, teachers, and scholars, bestowed its prestigious Jane Chambers playwriting award on Australian dramatist Christine Evans for her play *Trojan Barbie: A Car-Crash Encounter with Euripides' Trojan Women*.[2] "Encounter" and "reconfiguration" are key words in contemporary adaptations of works that we know and love, and connote not only imaginative renderings of the texts but also a re-writing of culture.

Re-visioning the classics, often in a subversive mode, has evolved into its own theatrical genre in recent years, and many of these productions have been informed by feminist theory and practice.[3] The avant-garde feminist theater has become a site for imaginative re-interpretations of myth, classical and modern drama, the novel, and even the personal and philosophical essay. As feminist critics began to use historicist, psychoanalytic, and deconstructive approaches to probe constructions of gender absorbed and interpreted by dramatic works, playwrights and directors—working in this cultural milieu—have experimented with dramatic form, mise-en-scène, language, and the body to foreground and re-present images of women and gender ideology woven into canonical texts, established genres, and theater practices. These productions transcend reproduction and adaptation to become theatrical dialogues with their source texts. The aim is to "invoke that work and yet be different from it."[4]

Feminist re-visionary theater emerges from the intersections of experimental performance, the tradition of literary and dramatic adaptations of the classics, and feminist theater and theory.[5] Aesthetically, this theater engages various approaches to intertextuality—ways in which texts and performances echo or are linked to earlier renditions, whether by allusion, by assimilation of formal and thematic features, or by divergence from the classic story. Playwrights and directors, often collaborating with actors and scenic designers, continue to employ a range of strategies associated with modernist theatrical adaptation: transposing historical or geographical setting and using the skeletal plot to comment on contemporary experience (reminiscent of Eugene O'Neill's 1931 trilogy, *Mourning Becomes Electra*), or creating a more abstract setting using provocative stage imagery, choreographed movement, and acoustical techniques (such as Andre Serban's 1972–1974 *Fragments of a Trilogy*).[6] However, in her study of postmodern directorial adaptations, Amy Green argues that it is "contradiction" rather than "continuity" between a "familiar, well-established text and its all-new theatrical idiom that marks contemporary classical revival as the unique product of our specific theatrical, cultural, and historical milieu."[7] Postmodern productions do not necessarily seek analogues. In "collage style" they disassemble and reorder segments of texts to convey a sense of disconnection with the linearity and universality we have sought in historical narratives. Productions with explicitly political perspectives alter or parody a text, interject anachronistic language, and rearrange its parts to denaturalize the values we have come to associate with its iconic figures moving through seemingly inevitable destinies. In Brechtian terms, these distancing devices make the familiar strange, drawing our attention to ideology encoded in the plot, language, and structures of the dramatic or literary text as well as in performance. They demand that we consider these theatrical choices as divergent from earlier versions and historically situated. In their study of adaptations of Shakespeare, Daniel Fischlin and Mark Fortier argue that adaptations have the potential to "reshape conventions in such a way as to expose orthodoxies that support the tradition."[8]

Feminist theater, in particular, challenges the notion that the classic, having attained almost mythic stature, contains transcendent truths to be applied uncritically to ever new historical conditions and that canonical texts represent links on a cultural continuum.[9] In their creative and critical encounter with earlier texts, theater artists and audiences focus more on transformation than on preservation. Several theatrical productions place marginalized or subordinated women center stage as they uncover what critics see as the "subversive potential in reflecting [...their] confinement and oppression,"[10] and imbuing them with "subjectivity and a bodily presence that undermines flat constructions of character."[11] They often expand upon scenes in which women appear together, and the characters question their relationships to each other and to the men whose projects they thwart or abet. Other productions reclaim representations of powerful and often demonized women, question their transgressive status, and ultimately disrupt any fixed idea of woman as "object, sign, or 'other.'"[12] Theatrical re-visions sometimes probe the "unconscious" of the text, defined by Dympna Callaghan as the "reverse side" of what is written or that which is not directly presented or spoken but "operate(s) contrapuntally" with presence and speech to construct the category "woman" and to express an asymmetrical distribution of power between the sexes.[13] The theater artists often pose questions about these gaps, contradictions, and silences directly to the audience in pre-production and post-production discussion groups, publications, and program notes. The venues for these productions range from women's theater groups to regional and university theaters, and, of course, established, but continually experimental, theaters with target audiences receptive to re-visions of the classics.

Numerous feminist theatrical re-visions of classic works have been produced all over the world from the 1970s until the present, and many of these plays have been anthologized or analyzed in collections devoted to a particular period of theater or playwright that has spawned adaptations.[14] This volume differs from previous collections in that the plays discussed draw on source texts from several genres and periods. The productions represent a range of theatrical approaches and thematic concerns. The scope of this collection addresses the work of theater artists primarily in the United States, Canada, and England. Given the constraints of space, I have made no attempt to be inclusive of all writers and directors who have contributed to the revisionist stage.[15]

It is also important to note that not all of these theater texts are primarily feminist in the myriad ways in which we understand this complex idea. As several critics are quick to point out, the category "feminist" is "contested," "unstable," and certainly evolving, and it intersects with diverse political perspectives and experimental theater practices.[16] However, the premise of this collection is that feminism, in its many incarnations, has profoundly influenced the postmodern revisionist stage. Writing in 2006, Aoife Monks saw critical representations of gender and a "critique of history and the canon" in productions by a "new breed" of female directors involved in formalist experimentation, but who do not necessarily see their projects as engaging feminist issues. Monks contends that the artist's intention is not necessarily the only criterion by which to discern a feminist dimension in a work.[17] In addition, plays that are not explicitly feminist might be "layered" with "feminist strands" that are not always ascertained by critics.[18]

Several of the productions discussed here might be viewed as "postmodern feminism" or "feminist postmodernism," depending upon how the spectator interprets and weights its core themes and aesthetic approaches. As Jill Dolan has observed, the alliance of feminist criticism and postmodern style has produced a "wealth of invigorating thinking" and thought-provoking theater.[19] The contributors to this volume pose feminist questions to these plays, and, in reading for gender, illustrate the significance of historical moment, cultural ideology, dramaturgical practice, and theatrical venue for shaping a revisionist interpretation of a classic text. In the pages that follow, I present a capsule history of feminist theater theory and its intersections with postmodernist ideas and styles. My purpose is to provide a frame of reference for the issues, concepts, and terms often alluded to by these writers as they situate their analyses of the plays historically, ideologically, and aesthetically.

Intersections: Feminist and Postmodern Theater and Theory

Feminist theater has been analyzed in terms of its origins, its defining attributes, ideological predilections, aesthetic practices, political goals, and the material conditions undergirding productions and theater companies. Indeed, a body of theory has produced several critical categories informed by an array of feminisms, but these categories are not offered here as a grid to determine how a text and performance should be read. Rather, they offer us the language through which discussions and debates often take shape in book-length studies of feminist theater, theater journals, and theater companies during the period in which the plays and productions discussed in this volume were created.[20] As Geraldine Harris has argued, "Advances in performance practices may be *influenced* by theories, but are ultimately produced through the process of creating work."[21]

Theater historians situate the emergence of feminist theater in the 1970s, developing out of the radical theater of the 1960s that was committed to addressing political issues such as civil rights, ethnic and class hierarchies and inequalities, and the Vietnam War. For some groups, radical theater meant the creation of new theatrical forms. Arthur Sainer describes the aims of radical theater activity of this period: "to become 'more directly involved with life; to place the accent on the process of creation…; to establish a new kind of relationship with the spectators considered on many levels as potential creators; to insist on the actor's creativity; and to rethink the role of the director as well as the role of the playwright….'"[22] In her history of women's theater groups, Dinah Leavitt argues that feminists envisioned the concept of collectivity in the theater as a response to the hierarchical and "competitive power structure" of conventional theater. Furthermore, theatrical works were often composed collaboratively and drew from the raw material and recollection of women's experiences recounted by women, at times through the presentation of a group protagonist, and sometimes to exclusively women's audiences in a theatrical setting that resonated with the consciousness-raising groups of the 1970s.[23]

Feminist theater criticism burgeoned in the 1980s and 1990s, and theorized texts and productions that were not only coalescing into a distinct cultural form, but also attracting the attention of mainstream media. Helene Keyssar describes the early 1980s feminist theater as

> productions and scripts characterized by consciousness of women as women; dramaturgy in which art is inseparable from the condition of women as women;

performance (written and acted) that deconstructs sexual difference and thus undermines patriarchal power; scripting and production that present transformation as a structural and ideological replacement for recognition; and the creation of women characters in the "subject position."[24]

Furthermore, Keyssar observed a "contagion" between feminist theories and feminist theater criticism.[25]

Susan Steadman's comprehensive 1991 review-essay on the theoretical and historical background of feminism and theater identified two other practices associated with feminist theater: breaking "sexual taboos" in the foregrounding of women's sexuality and challenging the assumption of heterosexuality as the norm. In her survey of issues, Steadman also discusses the feminist reassessment of spectatorship in subverting the "male gaze"—the objectification of women's bodies on stage (first theorized in film criticism) as a mechanism by which the patriarchy exerts authority and power over women through the processes of looking and shaping women's aspirations to be "looked at."[26]

Several feminist theater theorists analyzed the differences between branches of feminist thought that developed in the 1980s, particularly as they informed plays as well as theater companies. Liberal, bourgeois feminism emphasized women's equality with men, and called for greater representation of women in the theater. It envisioned a humanism that includes women, and conceived of human nature as essentially unchanging and universal with each person possessing a unique "essence." In contrast, radical (or cultural) feminism focused on the need to identify sexual differences between women and men, and often exalted the particular qualities and experiences that they believed united women across other categories (race, ethnicity, class, sexuality). Materialist (or socialist) feminism claimed that cultural feminists ignored the specific conditions of history, historical processes, class, and culture in formulating transcendent categories and bonds among women. Indeed, women of color and lesbian feminists objected that their concerns were often elided in the categories that were emerging. The inclination to ignore critical differences among women in terms of race, ethnicity, and sexuality led many feminists to organize not only political groups but also theater companies around these specific identities and call attention to the heterogeneity among women.[27] In observing this trend, Elaine Aston identifies the 1990s as the decade in which feminism began to think transnationally, and theater artists sought to make "cross-border connections, resistant to the colonial 'othering' of gender, race, and nation."[28]

The rise of gender studies, queer theory, and postmodernist critical theory challenged any kind of unified, stable, or all-encompassing identity, and this stance found its way to the stage. Naomi Schor identified "around 1985" as the time when "feminism began to give way to what has been termed gender studies," although many critics do not perceive rigid distinctions between the two terms.[29] Theorists defined gender as a constellation of restrictive, socially prescribed attitudes and behaviors distinct from sex. Often building on the arguments of materialist feminists, gender studies critics argued that "masculinity" and "femininity" are reproduced through a range of mechanisms including language, culture, and institutions. For example, in *Technologies of Gender*, Teresa de Lauretis maintained that "gender ... is the product of various social technologies, such as cinema.... [It] is not a property of bodies or something originally existent in human beings."[30] Theater as an institution reproduces social practices, discourses, and norms through the "technologies" of stage conventions and dramatic texts. However, theater also has the potential to subvert those norms, represent fragmented selves, and reinterpret fixed representations of gender for each generation of viewers. Postmodern theatrical re-visions that focus on deconstructing gender in classic texts have certainly made use of cross-gender casting and masquerade.

The idea of shared experience as the basis of a unified and essential concept of "woman" was questioned by postmodern critical theorists intent on discovering how experience and identity derive from "one's personal subjective engagement in the social practices, discourses, and institutions" (including theater) that construct gender and inform our interpretation of the world.[31] In her essay "Constructing Experience: Theorizing a Feminist Theatre History," Charlotte Canning writes that "experience was no longer cast as a coherent and whole expression of the truth about women; instead it became a process that invoked a fragmented sense of self in the always shifting intersections of discourses."[32] If not entirely fragmented and unstable, identity was conceived of as plural, with overlapping or competing affiliations.

Still, in the midst of all of these theoretical debates, many postmodern feminists maintain that feminism *in practice* needs to explore "woman" as both a construct and woman as an actual subject "embodied and historically located." Geraldine Harris articulates the position that woman is "an identity category which cannot be simply transcended in one fell swoop but which is not an 'absolute' either."[33] Many feminist theater artists who re-vision classic texts continue to move women center stage and foreground the concerns of the women characters in the context of the canonical work and our contemporary understanding of its themes. Other writers and directors disrupt familiar cultural narratives that represent the concepts of "masculine" and "feminine" as immutable. In *Making a Spectacle*, Lynda Hart looked to playwrights who undermined not only narratives but also the theatrical "structures that have held women framed, stilled, embedded," in order to revoke "the forms that have misrepresented women and 'killed them into art.'"[34] The feminist postmodern revisionist stage offers a variety of approaches to create "new meanings at the site of representation."[35]

In 1994, Amy Green situated her study of postmodern classical revival in the general climate created by "critic-theorists" who argued that texts are "unstable" and "interactive" and that authors are less reliable sources of meaning than we once believed. From this perspective, theater artists no longer needed to discern the playwright's intention or the universal truths assumed to be contained in the classic text. Instead, the text "served the production as catalyst, reference point, or fertile ground from which directors and their collaborators may cultivate new theatrical works," and take the liberty to "make, rework, [and] 'rewright'" the canon.[36] Feminist playwrights and directors who assume this postmodern perspective in re-visioning the classics take the same liberty to rework texts that constitute rich sources for thinking about gender.

Theatrical Styles

Aesthetic considerations in feminist theater theory have always intersected with political concerns, and, as already noted, a range of forms are evident on the revisionist stage as well. Writing in the mid–1990s, Helene Keyssar observed "two sets of conventions or style" that seemed particularly salient: Realism and Brechtian non-realism. Reflecting on her earlier assumptions about these forms—that realism (prevalent in American feminist theater) was attached to the "exploration of women as individuals" and that Brechtian non-realism (associated with British feminism) represented "women as social and political forces"—she revised her position and asserted that these distinctions were not so easily categorized by nation or political aims. Previously, she had argued that Brechtian epic theater proved ultimately more provocative in terms of disrupting ideologies of gender relations as "natural" and therefore immutable. Keyssar and other critics of realism were concerned that this mode of representation would re-inscribe gender relations even as it critiques the system, and disguise the fact that theater, construed as a mirror to life, is actually a re-construction, an interpretation of belief-systems rather than a reflection of gender as universally conceived.[37] Critics and theater artists called for more experimental staging productions using Brechtian "epic" conventions—the alienation effect, epic (episodic) structure, and the social gest—to disrupt the spectator's expectations of gendered images and relationships reenacted on stage. In contrast to naturalistic theater in which the actor becomes the character and thereby arouses audience identification with what seems "natural" or universal, the Brechtian actor demonstrates the character in terms of historically situated social attitudes and relationships.[38]

In 1996, however, Keyssar wrote that the dichotomy between realism and Brechtian non-realism was being challenged by artists and theorists working in hybrid forms, drawing on psychoanalytic interpretations of representation, community theater, and other media. Citing Michelene Wandor, Keyssar noted that feminist transformations of realism—a "representation of recognizable settings, characters and events re-accentuated by the newness of the material to the stage"—could be a compelling mode of incorporating historical and didactic messages that shared certain goals with Brecht. Other critics, notably

Janelle Reinelt, sought a "feminist transformation of Brechtian techniques."[39] Keyssar, adapting the theory of Mikhail Bakhtin, argued for the potential of feminist drama to become more "dialogic." Rather than fuse seemingly different voices as "often disguised parts of one, authorial voice," the dialogic text would resist the easy resolution of events and the "fixing of characters."[40] Feminist theatrical re-visions of classic texts continue to use all of these aesthetic approaches and share with experimental theater a questioning attitude toward traditional means of representation and the semiotics of the stage. Geraldine Harris defines stylistic postmodernism as productions that are hybrids in terms of media and genres of visual and performing arts. "They borrow from other past texts and performances, employ irony, parody and pastiche, paradox and contradiction, while they deliberately play upon intertextuality...."[41] Clearly feminist re-visions of the past three decades are informed by this aesthetic as well. As Lynda Hart asserts, theater, in its specific uses of the body, language, and stage space, can appropriate dramatic conventions and subvert their customary usage.[42]

In describing the contours and intersections of these theoretical and aesthetic categories of analysis, I would be remiss if I did not speak to the individual artist's motivation and vision for re-interpreting a particular classic text. In "Feminist Theory and Contemporary Drama," Janet Brown invokes Monique Wittig's caveat that "since no individual can be reduced to her/his oppression we are also confronted with the historical necessity of constituting ourselves as the individual subjects of our history as well." Brown maintains that every artist "invents her own form, expressive of the individual story she relates." Even in the process of connecting with communities—artistic, political, or familial—artists are "constantly engaged in 'making ourselves up' in the creation of something new."[43] This attitude is eloquently expressed by several of the playwrights and directors discussed in this collection.[44]

A Note on Terminology: Adaptation and Re-Vision in Experimental Theatre

I have chosen to use the term "re-vision" rather than "adaptation" to stress the element of interpretation involved in the productions discussed in this volume. The artists' visions, their approach to elucidating prior texts, though certainly varied, share an awareness that we are all subject to historical contingencies, beliefs, and commitments that inform our responses and expectations. Re-vision means to see and see again. Theater artists observing, reflecting on their observations, and interrogating the underpinnings of their responses to works that have historical currency produce new texts that are layered and open-ended, inviting audiences to engage the process of interpretation.

Fischlin and Fortier discuss the "problem of naming" that has resulted in a range of labels that go beyond inventive re-productions of the classics on the contemporary stage: offshoots, spinoffs, transformations, reductions/emendations, tradaptations (foreign-language works), and even appropriations, which suggest a kind of usurpation of the authority of the originary text.[45] The authors make clear that each of these classifications is too narrow to include the many and often overlapping strategies used by artists to realize the possibilities they see in adaptation, and so they choose to retain the use of the term "adaptation." Many of the essayists in this volume do the same, or use the terms "re-vision" and "adaptation" interchangeably. As Fischlin and Fortier so eloquently explain, adaptation involves the "interpenetration of contemporary circumstances and contingencies with earlier histories and values" that may differ from our own social understandings.[46] Re-visioning a text calls attention to these differences even in the context of compelling and seemingly universal themes.

Organization of the Essays

The essays in this volume are organized into four sections according to the period and genre of the source text re-visioned:

I. Classical Theater and Myth
II. Shakespeare and Seventeenth Century Theater
III. Nineteenth and Twentieth Century Narratives and Reflections: The Romance, the Novel, and the Essay
IV. Modern Drama

Within each section, the essays are arranged chronologically in terms of the period in which the adaptations were produced, beginning in the 1980s and ending with the current decade. Each essay focuses on one or more theatrical productions, and also references earlier or contemporaneous adaptations as points of comparison in the ever expanding intertextual field surrounding an iconic figure or scenario. Some of the essays compare productions that span two decades. The logic of this framework is to give readers a better sense of the historical development of feminist theatrical re-visions in the context of the cultural moment in which particular issues and aesthetic concerns converge and seem to prevail. The theater texts discussed indicate the wide-ranging influence of feminism on the revisionist stage. Reflecting the cross-fertilization that has occurred in feminist criticism and performance, the collection includes essays by scholars and theater artists who have been engaged in a shared project to create a vibrant experimental theater of spirited inquiry.

Section I begins with Julie Malnig's, "All Is Not Right in the House of Atreus: Feminist Theatrical Renderings of the *Oresteia*," in which she compares the Women's Experimental Theatre's *Electra Speaks* (1980) and Ellen

McLaughlin's *Iphigenia and Other Daughters* (1995). Malnig argues that both productions "bear the mark of their decade," focus on different components of the myth and bring varying gender ideologies to their interpretations of the texts. The analysis demonstrates the ways that "cultural politics informs theatrical practice and how feminist theatrical aesthetics fosters cultural criticism and debate." However, Malnig also notes that what seems most productive is to "root these works in a cultural continuum rather than an oppositional model of feminist analysis." She contends that contemporary theatrical works may still draw on and incorporate earlier strands of feminist thought.

Maya E. Roth's essay, "The Philomela Myth as Postcolonial Feminist Theater: Timberlake Wertenbaker's *The Love of the Nightingale*," reflects on the significance of this play, written in 1988, during the peak of apartheid violence in South Africa. Roth argues that Wertenbaker, one of the first Anglophone women playwrights to explore global issues in the 1980s, adapts the myth to involve audiences in human rights concerns, and in doing so "continues a long-standing civic theater tradition." And while the play's critique of gendered violence is powerful, it also "pursues a critique of tyranny, violence against cultural difference, and the escalating cycles of revenge borne from silence too long endured, injustice too long sustained."

In "Mary Zimmerman's *Metamorphoses*: Storytelling Theater as Feminist Process," Andrea J. Nouryeh observes that "although women's struggle for autonomy within an unjust socio-sexual hierarchy" does not appear as a central theme in this 1998 production, the playwright, a self-proclaimed feminist, selects particular myths and interpolates female voices and bodies to tell stories that speak to her desire for autonomy and change. Nouryeh argues that Zimmerman's inventive stage rendering of a work that has "at its core the metaphor of perpetual change" undermines the notion of identity as fixed and immutable. Furthermore, this auteur-director's intensely collaborative process in working with designers and actors is reminiscent of productions developed by early feminist theater groups.

The final essay in this section is Carol Martin's "The Political Is Personal: Feminism, Democracy and *Antigone Project*," in which she analyzes this 2004 collaboration of five playwrights (Tanya Barfield, Karen Hartman, Chiori Miyagawa, Lynn Nottage, and Caridad Svich), each creating a one-act version of Sophocles' *Antigone* that favors Antigone's perspective. The plays re-situate the figure of Antigone on a beach, in the U.S. during World War I, in an archive, in an African village, and in the underworld. As the author observes, the plays interpret the narrative in the context of the political landscape of the twenty-first century, making the "political personal." Martin complicates her analysis by examining a range of feminist interpretations and adaptations of this foundational text, moving from debates among classicists, and psychoanalytic and historicist critics, to adaptations that draw on this legend to address political movements in various nations.

Section II of this volume addresses re-visions of two Shakespeare plays (*King Lear* and *Othello*) and works by seventeenth-century playwrights. In "Lear's Daughters and Sons: Twisting the Canonical Landscape," Lesley Ferris analyzes *Lear's Daughters,* produced by the London-based company Women's Theatre Group in 1987, and Mabou Mines's female *Lear,* played by Ruth Maleczeck in 1990, in terms of two major strategies that have developed in the English-speaking theater to address the dearth of roles for women. One tactic is to enlist a featured actress to perform the major role in a canonical play. Another tactic is employed by the playwright who "imagines a dramatic world in which women have some sense of autonomy and space, as in the plays of Aphra Behn." In casting Ruth Maleczeck as Lear, Lee Breuer reworked the gender hierarchy of a play that he saw as a "fundamental story about the interrelations of power and gender." In contrast, *Lear's Daughters* invents a "politicized back-story" to the play that calls attention to the absence of the mother and re-imagines the daughters' stories.

My essay, "The Feminist Playwright as Critic," argues that Ann-Marie MacDonald's *Goodnight Desdemona (Good Morning Juliet)* (1988), Paula Vogel's *Desdemona* (1993), and Djanet Sears's prequel to *Othello, Harlem Duet* (1997), transposed to contemporary Harlem, demonstrate the synergy between theater and theory in their inventive feminist re-writings of the tragedy. Casting the playwright as critic, I observe that all three dramatists incorporate contemporary critical approaches from feminist and gender studies, literary criticism, performance and cultural studies that result in a highly theatricalized drama of ideas.

In "Transgressive Female Desire and Subversive Critique in the Seventeenth Century Canon," Cheryl Black addresses director Joanne Akalaitis's "non-illusionist, visually evocative aesthetic" in her socio-political feminist interpretation of John Ford's *'Tis Pity She's a Whore* (1992), Aphra Behn's *The Rover* (1994), and Jean Racine's *Phèdre* (2002). Black argues that these works present female protagonists with transgressive sexual desires, and that Akalaitis's inventive juxtapositions of text, aural and visual imagery, casting, and performance create mise-en-scènes that foreground sexual and reproductive politics, as well as the sexual violence that lurks just beneath the surface of the plays. Black also notes the director's attention to plays that were first produced in an era that Michel Foucault identified as the "origin of 'bio' politics."

Johan Callens's "Reconfiguring the Text and the Self" analyzes Elizabeth LeCompte's intertextual method in the Wooster Group's *To You, the Birdie (Phèdre)* (2001), working from Paul Schmidt's translation of Racine's *Phèdre,* the mythical pretext, Euripides' as well as Racine's adaptations, and selected choreographies of Martha Graham. Callens notes that although "never billed as feminist takes," the Wooster Group's iconoclastic reinterpretations of canonical dramatic texts pay attention to the "disenfranchisement and stereotyping of female characters." Through a theater piece constructed as "assemblages of juxtaposed elements," combining "found materials, films and videos, dance and movement, multi-track scoring, and an architectonic approach to theatre design," the Wooster Group reframes Phèdre's story as it "exposes and undoes" the frames of genre, class, religion, and duplicitous morals that have set her up as a "deservedly punished woman."

Section III focuses on theatrical re-visions of nineteenth-century novels and Virginia Woolf's twentieth-century analytic and reflective essays. All three novels have been considered feminist by critics who contextualize the protagonist's quest for autonomy in terms of the social position of women during the time in which they were written. However, the narrative structures are interpreted for the stage by postmodern stylistic strategies to destabilize fixed identities, even for transgressive women, and foreground cues in the text that indicate the internal conflicts of characters who do not conform to gender expectations.

Lenora Champagne's "Outside the Law" examines re-visions of the *Scarlet Letter* by three playwrights: Phyllis Nagy, Suzan-Lori Parks, and Naomi Wallace. These productions span the 1990s, a period that the author sees as marked by the rise of religious fundamentalism, the culture wars over gender roles, the surveillance of sexuality, and sexual representation in the arts. Champagne characterizes these works as "explosions" of Nathaniel Hawthorne's romance that focus on the outsider as "seducer, disrupter, and voice of repressed desire in American culture" and make explicit the repressed sexuality alluded to in the text. Specifically, the analysis explores the "liminal, outlaw status" of the female characters—Hibbins, the witch, Pearl, the demon child, and Hester Prynne, the adulterous mother—who defy gender hierarchy and "reside outside the law."

Kristin Crouch's essay, "Expressions of 'Lust and Rage,'" analyzes Shared Experience Theatre's production of Charlotte Brontë's *Jane Eyre* (1997–1999), adapted and directed by Polly Teale and brought to the stage by a team of predominantly women theater artists. Crouch focuses on the split character approach, achieved through an inventive script, staging, and performance, that presents Rochester's mad wife, hidden away in the attic, as the prim governess's alter-ego as she negotiates her way through Victorian gender-based constraints. Indeed, Bertha Mason, the wife originating from the West Indies and seen by many critics as the representation of English anxiety about its sexually-taboo encounters with colonized subjects, here represents Jane's more "passionate and expressive self" trapped within Victorian norms for women.

In "A Mystical Place Called Grand Isle," playwright Chiori Miyagawa writes about her personal motivation to adapt Kate Chopin's 1899 novel *The Awakening* for the stage in 2000. Miyagawa characterizes herself as an outsider attracted to the character of Edna Pontellier because she too is an outsider. Edna resists social norms for privileged women in New Orleans at the turn of the century as she emerges from the "disturbing" psychic turbulence in which she had been engulfed. However, Miyagawa interprets the novel as a spiritual journey toward the recognition of the nature of impermanence. Deconstructing the "self/selfless dichotomy" that has informed many interpretations of Edna's dilemma, the playwright wishes instead to "obliterate the category of self" and to have Edna realize the "ephemeral nature of all existences." Through minimalist dialogue and action as well as "time breaks" in the unfolding of the scenario, Miyagawa stages the quest for eternity, the thread that links her to Chopin and to Edna, and the potential for relationships among women beyond individual identities.

Sandee K. McGlaun's essay, "SITI Company's *Room*," brings the framework of a feminist "invitational rhetoric" to bear on Anne Bogart's and Ellen Lauren's 2000 rendering of Virginia Woolf's lecture/essay *A Room of One's Own*, as well as other essays and fragments of her novels, adapted as a playtext by Jocelyn Clarke. Through the interaction of the essays, the body, and literal and metaphorical spaces, Woolf's prose becomes a twenty-first century theatrical performance that "bodies forth" an invitation to consider the self and the world that resonates with the complexities of the essays. In imagining the author's mind at work, Bogart re-conceives Woolf's famous question: "What kind of space does a woman need in order to create, and what shape does that space take today?"

Section IV addresses modern dramas reconfigured by postmodern theatrical strategies, including theatrical hijinks, flamboyant sets, cross-dressed actors, and highly stylized performances to point to the performativity of gender enacted in realistic texts that purport to be representational.

In "Deconstructing (A Streetcar Named) Desire: Gender Re-citation in *Belle Reprieve*," Deborah R. Geis notes the many "recitings" of Tennessee Williams' 1947 play from the mid-1980s through the mid-1990s, a period marked by the AIDS crisis as well as dramatic "re-interrogations" of canonical texts through the discourse of feminist and queer theories. She focuses on *Belle Reprieve* (1991), a collaborative play by Bloolips, a British, gay-identified theater group, and Split Britches, an American, lesbian-identified group, that "alters and reverses" the gender roles in *Streetcar* in a "postmodern refashioning and 'queering'" of the play that by many accounts is already about the collapse of cultural myths. The characters/performers—Blanche, played as a "man in a dress," and Stanley, played as a "butch lesbian"—draw attention to the sexual role playing in Williams's text as well as the roles that we all assume in daily life.

Amy S. Green surveys several adaptations of Henrik Ibsen's *A Doll House* to frame her in-depth analysis of *Mabou Mines DollHouse* (2002), a playful twenty-first century postmodern rendering of "gender as performance in the Helmer marriage and of Ibsen's use and defiance of melodrama and the well-made play." Collaborating with actor/dramaturg Maude Mitchell, who plays Nora, director Lee Breuer employs a series of theatrical devices (including the controversial use of large women and small men) to demonstrate the ironies in the "imbalance of power and oppression" and make explicit the "figurative masks at work" in Ibsen's play. With a Brechtian effect, the production draws upon spectator response to the characters' dilemmas, and, at the same time, critically distances the audience, inviting them to see the "artifice of gender in theatrical and everyday performance."

—⁂—

For critics and audiences who perceive these transformations of the classics as "appropriations," or even "hostile takeovers," it is comforting to remember that the source texts remain intact and, as Amy Green reminds us, "available to be read, analyzed, interpreted, and produced" for future generations.[47] The irony may be that these re-contextualizations, allusions, borrowings, citings, and parodies produce new audiences eager to engage the classics on their own terms. It is also worth remembering that the process of re-vision involves a profound engagement with these texts as well as the complex, contradictory and impassioned responses that they have evoked. For feminists, this project moves beyond the texts to the cultural narratives they have engendered. This is indeed serious play in a living theater.

Notes

1. Ben Brantley, "When Adaptation Is Bold Innovation," *The New York Times*, 18 February 2007: B9.
2. See "Women and Theatre Program, Association for Theatre in Higher Education," <http://www.athe.org/wtp/html/chambers.html>.
3. This paragraph and the following two are drawn from my article "Feminist Revisions of Classic Texts on the American Stage," *Codifying the National Self: Spectators, Actors and the American Dramatic Texts (Dramaturgies No. 17)*, eds. Barbara Ozieblo and Maria Dolores Narbona-Carrion (Brussels: Peter Lang, 2006) 87–89.
4. Daniel Fischlin and Mark Fortier, "General Introduction," *Adaptations of Shakespeare*, eds. Fischlin and Fortier (London: Routledge, 2006) 4.
5. For discussions of modernists' adaptations of myth, see John Vickery, *Myth and Literature* (Lincoln: University of Nebraska Press, 1966) and *Myths and Texts: Strategies of Incorporation and Displacement* (Baton Rouge: Louisiana State University, 1983); and Andrew Von Hendy, "The Modernist Contribution to the Construction of Myth," *Modern Myths* (Amsterdam: Rodopi, 1993) 149–188. Also see Kate Hamburger, *From Sophocles to Sartre* (New York: Frederick Ungar Publishing Co., 1969) and Angela Belli, *Ancient Greek Myths and Modern Drama: A Study in Continuity* (New York: New York University Press, 1969).
6. Robert Brustein makes a distinction between "simile" and "poetic metaphor" productions in "Re-Working the Classics: Homage or Ego Trip?", *The New York Times*, 6 November 1988: H16.
7. Amy Green, *The Revisionist Stage: American Directors Reinvent the Classics* (Cambridge: Cambridge University Press, 1994) 2.
8. Fischlin and Fortier, 17.
9. In 1969, Angela Belli asked why "any artist should feel the need to cast a backward glance and resuscitate ancient material." Belli cited T.S. Eliot's defense of James Joyce's "mythic method" in *Ulysses*. Unlike postmodern critics, Belli saw the significance of this device in its permanence, and she echoed Eliot in her conviction that our cognizance of the

mythic order underlying the new creation enables it to "reaffirm a truth ... that there is a superb continuity to our culture perceivable to those who sense in the presence within our age of the extraordinary achievements of the past. Link is joined to link" (Belli, vii.)

10. Rosemary K. Curb, "Re/cognition, Re/presentation, Re/creation in Woman-Conscious Drama: The Seer, The Seen, The Scene, the Obscure," *Theatre Journal* 37 (1985): 316.

11. Ryan Claycomb, "Re-Performing Women and Reconstructing the Audience: Paula Vogel's *Desdemona* and Post-modern Feminist Parody," *Text and Presentation* 20 (1999): 87.

12. Susan M. Steadman, "Introduction," *Dramatic Re-Visions: An Annotated Bibliography of Feminism and Theatre, 1972–1988* (Chicago: American Library Association, 1991) 14.

13. Dympna Callaghan, *Woman and Gender in Renaissance Tragedy* (Atlantic Highlands, NJ: Humanities Press, 1989) 65, 75.

14. See Marianne Novy's four books on women's adaptations of Shakespeare; Alisa Solomon, *Re-Dressing the Canon: Essays on Theatre and Gender* (London: Routledge, 1997); Julie Holledge and Joanne Tompkins, "Narrative Trajectories: *A Doll's House* and *Antigone*," *Women's Intercultural Performance* (London: Routledge, 2000) 18–55; Helene Foley, "Bad Women: Gender Politics in Late Twentieth-Century Performance and Revision of Greek Tragedy," *Dionysus Since 69*, eds. Edith Hall, Fiona Macintosh, and Amanda Wrigley (Oxford: Oxford University Press, 2004); Susan Clement and Ellen Donkin, *Upstaging Big Daddy: Directing Theater as if Gender and Race Matter* (Ann Arbor: University of Michigan Press, 1993); Lizbeth Goodman, ed. *Mythic Women/Real Women: Plays and Performance Pieces by Women* (London: Faber and Faber, 2000).

15. One major omission is the work of playwright Caryl Churchill. As Elaine Aston asserts, Churchill's theater has been enormously influential to the development of contemporary feminist theater practice and scholarship on the English stage. [Aston, *Feminist Views on the English Stage* (Cambridge: Cambridge University Press, 2003) 18.] Churchill's *A Mouth Full of Birds* (1986), written in collaboration with David Lan, has been examined as a feminist re-vision of Euripides' *The Bacchae*. See Allison Hersh, "How Sweet the Kill": Orgiastic Female Violence in Contemporary Revisions of Euripides' *The Bacchae*," *Modern Drama* 35.3 (1992): 409–423. Hersh compares Churchill's play to Maureen Duffy's *Rites* (1969), loosely based on Euripides' play. Also see Raima Evan, "Women and Violence in *A Mouthful of Birds*," *Theatre Journal* 54.2 (2002): 263–284. Evan cites numerous studies of this play by noted feminist scholars.

I would also like to call attention to Cherry Moraga's *The Hungry Woman: A Mexican Medea* (1995) published in Maria Teresa Marrero and Caridad Svich, eds., *Out of the Fringe* (New York: Theatre Communications Group, 2000) 289–364.

16. Geraldine Harris, *Staging Femininities: Performance and Performativity* (Manchester, NH: Manchester University Press, 1999) 7. Elaine Aston and Geraldine Harris observe that feminism "has always operated self-reflexively: as an evolving 'body' of political ideas and impulses." They view the "future" as a question, hence the question mark following their title. [Aston and Harris, "Feminist Futures and the Possibilities of 'We,'" *Feminist Futures?* (Houndmills, Basingstoke, and Hampshire: Palgrave Macmillan, 2006) 3.]

17. Aoife Monks, "Predicting the Past: Histories and Futures in the Work of Women Directors," Aston and Harris, 88–102. Janelle Reinelt notes that the late playwright Sara Kane knew the "themes and preoccupations of second-wave feminism" and that she satirized them in *Phaedra's Love* (1996) and at times "charted their inadequacy to capture real lives of suffering" as in *Blasted* (1995). ["Navigating Postfeminism: Writing Out of the Box," Aston and Harris, 31.]

18. Leslie Hill and Helen Paris, "Curious Feminists," qtd. in Aston and Harris, 13–14.

19. Jill Dolan, "In Defense of the Discourse: Materialist Feminism, Postmodernism, Poststructuralism ... and Theory," *A Sourcebook of Feminist Theatre and Performance*, ed. Carol Martin (London: Routledge, 1996) 97. Also see Harris, *Staging Femininities* for an extended discussion of the commonalities and differences between postmodernism and feminism. Harris observes commonalities between the two perspectives, including the "critique of historical truth and the transparency of language in order to expose the hidden and unequal power relations within belief systems...." And both put forward a concept of subjectivity

"that is constantly being produced and reproduced through competing discourses." However, many feminists believe that the feminist project cannot simply dismiss the idea of a "stable 'female subject' around which organizations gain access to privileges and rights previously denied to women even in their multiple identifications and pluralities" (10–20).

20. For example, see: Sue-Ellen Case, *Feminism and Theatre* (New York: Methuen, 1988); Jill Dolan, *The Feminist Spectator as Critic* (Ann Arbor: University of Michigan Press, 1988); Lynda Hart, *Making a Spectacle: Feminist Essays on Contemporary Women's Theatre* (Ann Arbor: University of Michigan Press; 1989); Steadman for an extensive bibliography of books, articles, theater journals, and special issues of theater journals on feminist issues; Elaine Aston, *An Introduction to Feminism and Theatre* (New York: Routledge, 1995); Brenda Murphy's bibliography in *The Cambridge Companion to American Women Playwrights*, ed. Murphy (Cambridge: Cambridge University Press, 1999); and Elaine Aston and Janelle G. Reinelt's bibliography in *The Cambridge Companion to Modern British Women Playwrights* (New York: Cambridge University Press, 2000).

21. Harris, 2.

22. Arthur Sainer, qtd. in Dinah Leavitt, *Feminist Theatre Groups* (Jefferson, NC: McFarland, 1980), 1.

23. Dinah Leavitt, "Feminist Theatre in America," in Leavitt, 1–22. Also see Charlotte Rea, "Women's Theatre Groups," *Drama Review* 16 (June 1972): 79–82; Rea, "Women for Women," *Drama Review* 18 (December 1974); Janet Brown, "Feminist Theory and Contemporary Drama," *The Cambridge Companion to American Women Playwrights*, ed. Brenda Murphy (Cambridge: Cambridge University Press, 1999), 158–159; Helene Keyssar, "Feminist Theatre of the Seventies in the United States," Murphy, 173–194.

24. Helene Keyssar, "Introduction," *Feminist Theatre and Theory* (New York: St. Martin's Press, 1996) 1.

25. Ibid., 4.

26. See Steadman's summary section, "Feminist Issues Surrounding Drama/Performance/Theatre," 12–16. Also see Teresa de Lauretis, *Technologies of Gender: Issues on Theory, Film, and Fiction* (Bloomington: Indiana University Press, 1987); Annette Kuhn, *The Power of the Image: Essays on Representation and Sexuality* (London: Routledge and Kegan Paul, 1985); E. Ann Kaplan, *Women and Film* (New York: Methuen, 1983); Laura Mulvey, *Visual and Other Pleasures* (Bloomington: Indiana University Press, 1989).

27. For studies of feminist theater companies see Leavitt; Michelene Wandor, *Understudies* (London: Methuen, 1981); Wandor, *Carry On, Understudies* (London: Routledge, 1986); Helen Krich Chinoy and Linda Walsh Jenkins, *Women in American Theatre*, rev. ed. (New York: Theatre Communications Group, 1987); Lizbeth Goodman, *Contemporary Feminist Theatres: To Each Her Own* (London: Routledge, 1993); Charlotte Canning, *Feminist Theatres in the USA* (London: Routledge, 1996). Also see Yvonne Yarbro-Bejarano, "Chicanas' Experience in Collective Theatre: Ideology and Form," in Keyssar, *Feminist Theatre and Theory*, 213–227.

28. Aston, 8.

29. Naomi Schor, "Feminist and Gender Studies," *Introduction to Scholarship in Modern Languages and Literatures*, ed. Joseph Gibaldi (New York: MLA, 1992) 275. Also see Judith Butler, *Bodies That Matter: On the Discursive Limits of "Sex"* (New York: Routledge, 1993); *Differences* 3:2 (issue on queer theory, 1991), Teresa de Lauretis, ed.; Alisa Solomon and Framji Minwalla, eds. *The Queerest Art: Essays on Lesbian and Gay Theater* (New York: New York University Press, 2002).

30. de Lauretis, *Technologies of Gender*, 2–3.

31. de Lauretis, qtd. in Charlotte Canning, "Constructing Experience: Theorizing a Feminist Theatre History," *Theatre Journal* 45 (1993): 534. Canning also cites Joan W. Scott, *Gender and the Politics of History* (New York: Columbia University Press, 1988) 4–5.

32. Canning, 534.

33. Harris, 19. She cites theorists Rebecca Schneider, Judith Butler, Diane Elam, and Susan Bordo to develop her argument.

34. Lynda Hart, 3. Hart is quoting a phrase from Sandra Gilbert and Susan Gubar, *The Madwoman in the Attic* (New Haven Press, 1979) 17.

35. Jill Dolan, "In Defense of the Discourse," 97.
36. Green, 4.
37. Janelle Reinelt, "Beyond Brecht: Britain's New Feminist Drama" in Keyssar, 35–48; Elin Diamond, "Brechtian Theory/Feminist Theory: Toward a Gestic Feminist Criticism," in Martin, 120–135; Elin Diamond, *Unmaking Mimesis: Essays on Feminism and Theater* (New York: Routledge, 1997); Dolan, *The Feminist Spectator as Critic* (Ann Arbor: University of Michigan Press, 1991) 106–117.
38. See Bertolt Brecht, *Brecht on Brecht*, ed. and trans. John Willett (New York: Methuen, 1964).
39. Keyssar, "Introduction," 4–7.
40. *Ibid.*, 8.
41. Harris, 7.
42. Hart, 3.
43. Monique Wittig, "The Point of View: Universal or Particular," *Feminist Issues* (1983): 63–69, qtd. in Brown, 171.
44. See, for example, Andrea J. Nouryeh's article on Mary Zimmerman's *Metamorphoses* and Chiori Miyagawa's essay on her adaptation of Kate Chopin's *The Awakening* in this volume.
45. Fischlin and Fortier present an extensive discussion of terminology under the heading "The Problem of Naming," 2–4.
46. Fischlin and Fortier, 18. These authors also offer an in depth analysis of the cultural and political implications of adaptation.
47. Green, 180. The terms "appropriations" and "hostile takeovers" are referred to by Fischlin and Fortier, 3.

I

CLASSICAL THEATER AND MYTH

All Is Not Right in the House of Atreus
Feminist Theatrical Renderings of the Oresteia

JULIE MALNIG

Over the past thirty years, the myths, stories, and characters that form the basis for Aeschylus's epic trilogy, the *Oresteia* (consisting of *Agamemnon*, *The Libation Bearers*, and *The Eumenides*), have been an endless source of fascination, attraction, and discovery for feminist theatrical practitioners. Playwrights and directors of many stripes are drawn to the play's grand themes: war and peace, the nature of justice, the transition from barbarism to civilization, and the excesses of power. But underlying all of these issues, and central to the world views espoused by the Greek writers who adapted the myth—Sophocles, Euripides, as well as Aeschylus—are the unmistakable tensions between women and men. As classicist Froma Zeitlin has written, "If Aeschylus is concerned with world building, the cornerstone of his architecture is the control of women, the social and cultural prerequisite for the construction of civilization. The *Oresteia* stands squarely within the misogynistic tradition that pervades Greek thought, a bias that projects a combative dialogue in male-female interactions and also relates the mastery of the female to higher social goals."[1]

Whether to argue with it, expand on it, or fill in the perceived missing gaps, feminist playwrights and directors have engaged with this influential, foundational text of the Western canon in order to revise deeply imbedded and traditionally-held assumptions about women's relationship to patriarchy, family, and society. Clearly, too, for many feminist theatrical adaptors, the attraction of these plays has to do with the force of some of the female characters themselves who, even if within the narrative framework are ultimately beaten down, won over, or defeated, nonetheless assert themselves and their desires. The sheer depth of these heroines (in particular those of Euripides) has proven irresistible to feminist interpretation.[2] That these productions were born from the theatrical avant-garde should come as no surprise, since it is pre-

cisely within the postmodern reframing of narrative and the aversion to realism that the possibility of "unforeseeable inflexions," as theatre scholar Jonathan Miller has noted, may be found.[3]

My broad goal in this essay is to compare two feminist-oriented theatrical productions of the *Oresteia* myth—the Women's Experimental Theatre's *Electra Speaks* (1980) and Ellen McLaughlin's *Iphigenia and Other Daughters* (1995)—to explore the ways in which their dramaturgical and theatrical practices intersected with and illuminated the prevailing gender ideologies and politics of their time. As Roberta Sklar, co-founder with Sondra Segal and Clare Coss of The Women's Experimental Theatre, has remarked, "Theatre does not operate in a historical vacuum. It is not pure, free of its time. It springs from a desire to recognize one's own experience, have it, value it, express it, see it flower."[4] Both productions bear the mark of their decade. Although each play focuses on different aspects of the myth and with different gender emphases, both make a compelling case for the ways that cultural politics may inform theatrical practice and, in turn, how a new feminist theatrical aesthetics may foster cultural criticism and debate.

The Feminist Continuum

Of course, to summarize the trajectory of feminism over the last thirty years would necessitate an essay of its own. But a brief discussion of some of the major strands of feminist thinking since the late 1970s is instructive in considering how pertinent feminist ideologies move in and through these works and how these same ideologies have affected the subsequent critiques of the productions. In 1986, Michelene Wandor, in *Carry On, Understudies*, was one of the first scholars to lay out a major conceptualization of feminist thought, which would eventually gain wide currency with American feminist critics. Here, Wandor outlined three major approaches or "tendencies" that she characterized as radical (also known as cultural), liberal, and materialist feminism.[5] Cultural feminism, linked to the ideologies of the 1970s and early 1980s, has operated on the premise that there are unwavering sexual differences between women and men, and that female experience has been overlooked and superseded by a universal male "we." Underlying cultural feminism is the premise that women's experience has been denigrated, overlooked, or undervalued, and as Sue Ellen Case notes, "that the patriarchy is the primary cause of oppression."[6] Liberal (or bourgeoise) feminism has been connected to the premise that

Opposite: The Chautauqua Theatre Company's 1996 production of Ellen McLaughlin's *Iphigenia and Other Daughters*; from left to right: guest artists Monica Bell as Chrysothemis and Beth Dixon as Clytemnestra, and company member Lisa Rothe as Electra. Chautauqua Theatre Company is the resident professional theatre and conservatory of the Chautauqua Institution. Courtesy Chautauqua Institution, Chautauqua, New York.

women will achieve deserved recognition and parity by participating equally in "male" culture, as demonstrated by the attempts to pave the way for women to enter social, political, and artistic realms previously dominated by men. As Jill Dolan notes, "Liberal feminism takes its cues from liberal humanism."[7] Unlike the cultural feminist stance, liberal feminism suggests that women *not* be differentiated from men, but rather that they become equal to men as a result of their eventual inclusion into traditional male spheres (such as in the arts, business, and culture).

Materialist (or socialist) strands of thought (which Sue Ellen Case notes actually encompass a range of positions)[8] broadly emphasize the political, economic, and historical forces operating in the culture that work to maintain sexual differences between women and men; materialist feminism looks to the ways that social and cultural institutions frame women's and men's experience and how ideology, class interests, and racial difference undercut the cultural or liberal feminist notion of women as a discrete and unified group. Gender is not considered innate in the materialist feminist critique, and, as Jill Dolan has noted, "it is dictated through enculturation, as gender divisions are placed at the service of the dominant culture's ideology."[9] By the late 1980s and into the 1990s, materialist theories of feminism borrowed heavily from the critiques of postmodern, poststructuralist, and psychoanalytic inquiries, which rejected the notion of an inherent, unified self, and prodded understanding of the myriad ways that social systems enforce gender distinctions.

As several scholars have pointed out, while these frameworks have been invaluable in differentiating among various kinds of feminist work, too often they become used as tools to categorize or contain, rather than, in Sue-Ellen Case's words, "as tactics to be employed when ... useful."[10] From the perspective of several dramatic critics of the late 1980s and early 1990s, the work of Women's Experimental Theatre (WET), which most agree was groundbreaking in calling attention to the way women's behaviors were largely prescribed under patriarchy, seems to exemplify the feminist politics of difference in its adherence to isolating and foregrounding women's experience as unique from men's.[11] As theatre scholar Charlotte Canning has noted, the theatrical efforts of WET, along with those of many early feminist theatre groups of the 1970s and early 1980s, have been described as exemplary of a cultural feminist aesthetic and viewed as "the necessary labor of pioneers who paved the way but had operated under naïve or simple views of women and feminism."[12] *Iphigenia and Other Daughters*, on the other hand, although it has not been subject to the same critical scrutiny as *Electra Speaks*, seems to fall more within the materialist feminist-oriented camp, particularly in its rearrangement of traditional narrative sequencing, its use of irony and anachronisms, and altered sense of time. While McLaughlin's play, however, is not centered necessarily on the ways that race, class, or broad economic structures enforce sexual divisions, as is traditionally the focus of much materialist analyses, it is in keeping with a poststructuralist-feminist theatrical sensibility that, as theatre critic Jill Dolan notes, "breaks with realist narrative strategies, heralds the death of unified characters, decenters the subject, and foregrounds conventions of perception."[13] In this type of postmodern materialism, there is a dramaturgical emphasis on the female subjects as they are represented in and by history coupled with production elements that suggest that their identities are in flux and subject to change. Yet *Iphigenia and Other Daughters*, like *Electra Speaks*, can still be "read" from more than one ideological stance; it, too, for instance, focuses on a women's world, and contains echoes of what today might be considered cultural feminist streams of thought.

What seems most productive, then, to a critical assessment of these two works is an approach rooted in a *continuum* rather than *oppositional* model of feminist analysis. Theatre scholars Charlotte Canning and Esther Beth Sullivan, drawing on the ideas of feminist theorist Teresa de Lauretis, suggest that in critiquing feminist theatrical work of the past we think in terms of "development" rather than "progression," since all too often the "dynamic" of progress, in which theoretical positions are seen as linear and goal oriented, "undercuts the possibility of grasping the sophistication specific to past moments or the way that past moments inhabit present ones."[14] They caution that adhering to a progressive understanding of feminism typically leaves the feminist scholar with no option but to perceive earlier work as "outworn, simplistic, one-dimensional, or failed."[15] Seen in light of "development," on the other hand, with its intimations of "working out by degrees," and "to make known more gradually,"[16] feminism itself may be viewed as capable of incorporating change and building on, while not erasing, previous eras of thought. Here, Canning and Sullivan advocate that feminist scholars and critics embrace both a post structural feminist analysis that challenges the notion of the stability of gender, as well as an understanding of identity politics in which individuals stake out their positions in gender, race, and class.[17] If viewed from this perspective, then, we see not only how a feminist work may inhabit more than one critical or theoretical position at once, but how the seeds contained in a historical work of one particular era may still speak to a current generation. A salient example (which I discuss at the conclusion of this essay), is a recent restaging of *Electra Speaks* at Yale University, directed by performer and writer Deb Margolin and original co-creator Sondra Segal, which, nearly thirty years after its conception, still speaks to a current generation of young women.

The Women's Experimental Theatre

Of the feminist productions I am considering, WET's *Electra Speaks* was perhaps most closely aligned with the feminism of its time. Founded in 1976 by Clare Coss, Sondra Segal, and Roberta Sklar, WET was one of the foremost women's theatrical troupes of the late 1970s and early 1980s. *Electra Speaks* was the third part of a trilogy called *The Daughters Cycle*, a trenchant theatrical exploration of the Western, patriarchal family as a deeply gendered system that devalues female experience. *Daughters,* the first piece in the trilogy, looked closely at the psychic bonds between mothers and daughters, while *Sister/Sister* confronted the relationships between the female siblings in the family dynamic, looking at the "shifting patterns of alliance and betrayal"[18] among biological sisters.

WET produced its work during a renaissance of second-wave feminist activity in this country. The feminist ideological imperatives of the era in the late 1970s and early 1980s, particularly in the realms of art and literature, coincided with WET's political and theatrical aims: to reclaim women's artistic efforts "lost" to the traditional male canon and to explore women's subjective experience unfiltered through male interpretations. In what can now be seen as an evolutionary moment in women's consciousness-raising, many feminists sought to identify those universals which could be traced to female experience as differentiated from previously accepted universals derived from the male experience. WET's aesthetic was part of the groundbreaking experimental theatre work of the late 1960s exemplified by companies such as The Performing Garage, the Open Theatre, and The Living Theatre, where actors and directors, heeding Artaud's charge for a reinvigorated theatre, coupled an expressive politics with an experimentalism that challenged conventional notions of the "text" and broke down traditional barriers between the actor and spectator. Roberta Sklar herself had been an early member of Joseph Chaikin's Open Theatre in the mid–1960s and served as co-director of several of its productions.[19] Part of the experimentalism of the period extended to an interest in breathing new life into ancient and classic texts and "revisioning" them from a contemporary perspective.[20] WET, though, was the first to engage in this type of work from a decidedly feminist perspective.

Exploding traditional myths and mythic creations was a central part of the excavation and reexamination process of 1970s feminism; theorist Teresa de Lauretis saw this project akin to a "new aesthetic," whereby feminists sought "to retell well-known stories in order to destabilize the literary and scientific myths of origin."[21] But while this emphasis on revisiting myth and ritual was in part an attempt to rethink and "reclaim" female protagonists co-opted by the patriarchy, in the case of WET, exploring the *Oresteia* represented an ingenious attempt to break open one of the bedrock sources of Western representations of women to re-examine not only the myth, but the dynamics of the Western familial structure and its Freudian implications.[22] Freudian theory, too, particularly the idea that individuality and autonomy come at the expense of the relationship with the mother, was viewed suspiciously during this time as one more type of cultural myth used to suppress women's potential. (The members of WET, in fact, were influenced by the ideas of feminist psychoanalyst Nancy Chodorow who urged consideration of the strong pre–Oedipal bonds between mother and daughter.[23]) As classicist Helene P. Foley has noted, feminists' emphasis at this time on myth and Greek sources also represented "part of a larger move in feminist psychology to restore psychic health through female archetypes."[24]

Perhaps one of the more debated aspects of WET's *The Daughter's Cycle*, from the vantage point of feminist critics of the 1990s, was the "The Matrilineage," a ritual form in which each actor recites her name, recalling her female ancestry. Enacted prior to each performance, the Matrilineage names mothers, grandmothers, and great grandmothers, paying tribute to those who may not have been recognized during their lifetime. To critics of a later generation, the Matrilineage seemed to represent an a-historical bonding of women that, as one critic noted, "naturalizes mother/daughter relationships as the primal link between women."[25] But with WET's emphasis on exploration of the female as subject, and the renewed feminist attention to validating women's experience generally, WET felt compelled to address the fact that "All women are daughters—what could this simple universal truth mean?"[26] The Matrilineage, in fact, was fueled by WET's anthropologically-based theatre-making process, in which the company held workshops often with groups of more than one hundred women, to garner women's thoughts on a variety of contemporary issues. In these quasi consciousness-raising groups (a hallmark of 1970s feminism), it is not surprising that the theme of mothers—and mothers and daughters—would loom large.[27] WET itself was never "a participatory democracy" as were many other feminist theatre troupes of the time; Sklar, Segal, and Coss wrote and shaped the final, theatrical product.[28]

Electra Speaks

In their final trilogy of *The Daughters Cycle*, WET drew on Sophocles' *Electra*, in which the title character is in obsessive mourning for her father. The entirely female cast played all of the roles, including the silent male figures, suggesting in part the malleability of sex-role construction in culture. The actors were instructed to "speak with the experience of Electra in each role and character that she plays."[29] The piece opens with a voiceover of Electra recounting the myth, or "the old story," as it is called. The accompanying performers create a series of physical and vocal images that depict the central contours of the classical myth—Agamemnon's sacrifice of his daughter Iphigenia to promote the "favorable winds of war" for his Trojan expedition; his wife Clytemnestra's murder of her husband and his war prize, Cassandra, in revenge; and the resulting death of Clytemnestra and Aegisthus, at the hands of her enraged son, Orestes. This description of the myth gets repeated successively throughout the play, but with each telling, the text becomes laden with feminist questions, opening up the story to the silences buried within:

> The mother has been at home with the children for the ten years that the father has been waging war. *What happened between them during those years?*... The mother learns of the sacrifice of her daughter. *Who tells Electra of the sacrifice of her sister?*... They say for years the younger daughter obsesses on her father's death, longing to avenge his murder but unable to act. *Does Electra want to kill her mother?* [n.p.].

A three-act play, *Electra Speaks* drew on an array of experimental theatre and acting techniques, such as short scenic compositions, direct address, commentary, visual tableaus, and pantomime, all of which attempted to create a quasi-Brechtian relationship with spectators. As Sklar and Segal have noted, "Performer and audience member became partners in a process that moved towards change on both sides of the performing line."[30] While one could argue that these non-naturalist techniques—in 1980—were in their own way "postmodern," some critics contend that the ritual nature of the production in fact encouraged an audience involvement and identification that precluded the primarily female spectators from standing back with any sort of objective stance.[31] (As I will show, *Iphigenia and Other Daughters* positions its spectators quite differently.) Yet, WET's intent, I think, whether or not it was fully realized in performance, was to create a dynamic whereby women spectators might both identify with the characters and become aware of women's historically de-valued position within the traditional Western family. Their aim was never simply to reflect women's experience, but to explore the ways that gender roles are reinforced in cultural institutions and become imbedded in women's own consciousness.

Perhaps one of the most striking examples of WET's attempts "to delineate the interaction between the psychological and social worlds"[32] is the Act One "Dumb Show," or "A History of Violence Against Women," which consciously spotlights those elements of the Greek myth that are either left out of the Aeschylian and Sophoclean plays, or routinely accepted as historical givens. To the sounds of a tambourine, the actor playing Electra catalogues a history of rapes and murders in the Greek legend (including the rape of Leda, Clytemnestra's mother, by Zeus [disguised as a swan], Agamemnon's murder of Clytemnestra's first husband, Tantalus, and their child; and his rape of Clytemnestra) as two other performers pop out their heads and hands from behind a screen burlesquing the mayhem. Behind a second screen, another performer "alternately gives the finger and raises a clenched fist to tally the rapes and murders which are punctuated with the ting of a triangle" (n.p.). In this particular sequence, WET combines humor with biting political critique. The scene probes the subtext of the myth to suggest that the two rapes and two murders by Agamemnon provide additional motivation for Clytemnestra's revenge. And, too, it speaks to the issue of male violence as a deep, societal ill.

Many feminist writers and dramatists of the 1970s and early 1980s looked to mythological and heroic female figures as models of inspiration and strength.

As a theatrical work, *Electra Speaks* doesn't necessarily glorify these figures, though, but uses them to illustrate how archetypal images have continued to permeate women's consciousness and perpetuate divisions damaging to women.[33] As the voiceover at the beginning of the play reminds us, Orestes, after carrying out the slaying of his mother and her lover, has been in exile for many years. The avenging goddesses, or Furies, torment Orestes for his matricide, but he flees to Delphi, where he is tried by a male jury. The Greek goddess of wisdom, Athena, the daughter of Zeus, breaks the tie and exonerates Orestes, thus upholding the idea of patriarchal law. In *Electra Speaks*, Athena is cast as an ambitious, male-identified trial lawyer who when pardoning Orestes also excoriates Clytemnestra: "You know, the women in this family, they have pushed this boy. His mother got rid of him. His sister pushed him to murder. And you're coming to me — telling me this court should take action against him — for murdering this woman. He did society a favor. Poor Clytemnestra. Poor Clytemnestra my ass!" (n.p.).

The idea of women working against each other and their own self interests was a prominent theme of *Electra Speaks*; how the nuclear family pits mother, daughter, and sister against one another was one of its central cultural critiques. As Coss, Segal, and Sklar asked, "Whose interests are served by the institutionalized division between women in the family?"[34] In Act II (focused on the mother-daughter bond), Electra confronts Clytemnestra and questions how she could have sacrificed Iphigenia for the sake of victory and the "favorable winds of war":

> Suppose the winds hadn't come? Suppose after he killed her winds hadn't come. Suppose he sent Electra.... What would you have done...? "Would you have pretended to believe he was just missing you? What would you have done. I hate you. I hate you for this. You would have sent me too [n.p.].

Although Electra turns against Clytemnestra, as in Sophocles's *Electra*, in *Electra Speaks*, with its emphasis on what goes unspoken between women, her motivation for the hatred of her mother stems less from rage at Clytemnestra's killing of her father (or her union with Aegisthus in her father's absence), than from her mother's seeming powerlessness in the face of male prerogative and desire. In the piece, Clytemnestra is portrayed as domineering but also as a victim of male brutality, as well. She says in reply to Electra: "Yes, Electra. I would have sent you too. I would have had to send you too. I would have had to believe your father" (n.p.).

It is the sacrifice of Iphigenia, of course, on which the entire story of the *Oresteia* hinges. WET presents her as the archetypal female martyr, the essential good girl, who unaware of her father's ruse, follows his command to visit Aulis on the pretext of marrying the Greek warrior Achilles. In one dramatic scene, the character of Iphigenia, as portrayed by actor Mary Lum, is harangued by various voices of authority pressuring her to marry. Lum spins her head from left to right, in rapid succession while chanting "get married, get married, get married, get married" (n.p.). Simultaneously, another actor speaks for Iphigenia, and fills in what goes unsaid:

> They say that she is virginal and green. They say she had to be bound and gagged. That she wept and pleaded. They don't say she was a young woman murdered by her father.... They don't say that she was shocked.... That she fought tooth and nail.... They don't say that she didn't want to die [n.p.].

The power of the scene emanates from the attempt both to humanize *and* distance Iphigenia's character so that women audiences might identify with her dilemma, yet at the same time become aware of the broader historical and material circumstances into which she has been placed. As Coss, Segal, and Sklar have said of WET's acting technique, "We see a woman in the playing space who is just herself. Then we see her enact another and also herself at the same time. We also see her comment on it."[35] In what might be described as a kind of theatricalized consciousness-raising, the idea was that personal identification might lead to greater self awareness and understanding.

The final act of *Electra Speaks* spotlights Electra and her initial attempt to take charge of her own life and "sever her ties with the House of Atreus."[36] As we were told of the "old story," at the beginning of the play, Electra was eventually confined to a loveless marriage (in Euripides' version) and in her refuge goaded others into action; while she yearns to kill her mother in retribution for her transgressions, it is ultimately her brother Orestes who completes the deed. Froma Zeitlin notes that while many heroines have populated Greek literature, "*functionally* women are never an end in themselves, and nothing changes for them once they have lived out their drama onstage."[37] But *Electra Speaks* revises this state of affairs as Electra attempts to transform herself from passive agent to active subject. In this highly psychologized feminist adaptation, Electra tries to recreate herself after years of feminine indoctrination, and becomes aware of what was previously an obedience to an essentially idealized, absent father. Autonomy and self realization, she learns, do not necessarily mean identification with the father *or* denial of the mother.

As Electra musters the will to leave and enter the threshold of a new life:

> She tugs
> She lugs
> She lurches
> She heaves
> She hauls
> . . . .
> She stands firm [n.p.].

Electra will use the confrontations with the mother and father figures to propel herself into possibility and begin to fulfill the vision of what Teresa de Lauretis would later term the "feminist subject," this newly formed being who, in Sue-Ellen Case's words, "can find self-determination, can change."[38]

Iphigenia and Other Daughters

Fifteen years later, in 1995, actor and playwright Ellen McLaughlin's *Iphigenia and Other Daughters* continued to rework the Oresteian legend, in what was now a decidedly feminist-postmodernist context. Likening herself to the Athenian playwrights, she sees herself as part of a tradition of revising and reworking these basic plots, and making them speak to contemporary audiences. As McLaughlin notes, "The stories already have a claim on us just as we have a claim on the stories."[39] In *Iphigenia and Other Daughters*, which previewed at the Classic Stage Company in New York City, the story focuses on the women characters—Clytemnestra and her daughters Electra, Iphigenia, and Chrysothemis—who have been left behind in the wake of war. In her own feminist trilogy—what McLaughlin calls "a sort of *Iphigenia*-ia"[40]—Sophocles' *Electra* is the emotional centerpiece flanked on either end by Euripides' *Iphigenia in Aulis* and *Iphigenia in Tauris*. In McLaughlin's retelling, it is the sacrifice of Iphigenia that hovers over the entire production—"the aspect of the Trojan War which everybody forgets about," says McLaughlin.[41]

While *Electra Speaks* was part of a vital feminist theatrical movement whose aims were to promote greater female presence on stage and to make women's subjective experience the stuff of theatre, McLaughlin's *Iphigenia and Other Daughters*, by contrast, spoke to and from a very different political and aesthetic milieu. In large measure, by the early 1990s, feminism was pulled in two directions between those critics and theorists wedded to the identity politics of race, class, and sexuality and those who questioned the idea of an individual's or groups' identity as an unchanging and cohesive "truth." Within feminist *theatrical* criticism, the focus shifted away from analyses of "images of women" in culture, and questions of what constituted "women's identity," to postmodern, materialist analyses suggesting that the subjective self is never fixed, but rather constructed and determined in response to changes in material culture.[42]

McLaughlin mirrored these trends through various stylistic devices and techniques (which I will expand on shortly), such as the fracturing of the text and mix of historical time periods, a poetic and vernacular pastiche of spoken style, an ironic (and often unendearing) representation of the women characters, and a foregrounding of the way history (and hence culture and ideology) has shaped their roles as tragic heroines. It is perhaps this last characteristic that most specifically marks McLaughlin's play as materialist in orientation in that McLaughlin not only portrays how her subjects have been presented in history, but allows them to speak to history, with a kind of historical consciousness, suggesting that had cultural and political conditions been different, so too might have been their lives. Similar to feminist theatrical practitioners of the 1970s who "sought to counter the andro-centric biases of Greek based myths,"[43] McLaughlin wants to present to literary history a counter-reading of these characters, but her main concern is to locate and preserve in the women's stories the grand, heroic themes of the *Oresteia* itself—honor, duty, justice, the effect of war, and commitment to the state. McLaughlin, for instance, is intrigued by the fact that:

> None of the [female] characters in these plays ever sets foot in Troy.... When you think of it though, the Trojan War lasts for ten years, the trip home can take quite a long time (in Odysseus' case, another ten years)—what *was* going on in those countries all that time the men were gone? Clytemnestra, for instance, runs her country for the duration of the war; she kills her husband within hours of his finally arriving home, then runs the country for another twenty years.[44]

She has created characters who are aware of their place (or lack of it) within the history and politics of their own society, and who consciously consider their roles as tragic.[45]

Despite its primarily materialistic and historical concerns, though, McLaughlin's work still trades in ideas from earlier eras of feminist politics in its need to recognize and affirm women's experience. Like *Electra Speaks*, *Iphigenia and Other Daughters* uses the myth to give voice to those female voices silenced or negated. It also focuses on the domestic and familial spheres and explores the tensions among women family members that are laid bare in the wake of patriarchal coercion. McLaughlin herself has said of her set of plays that they "address the margins of the epic, the footnotes to the great drama. This strikes some essential truth about women's existence for me."[46] For her, the creation of the work was also something of a consciousness-raising as she describes how each of the women depicted—Clytemnestra, Electra, Iphigenia, and Chrysothemis—represents parts of herself. Her recuperative efforts are evident in her desire "to gather stories, sift through what we can make out of the unchronicled, the lost lives, quilts, songs, anonymous poems that might have, could have been rendered by people not unlike ourselves."[47]

One way to explain these "cultural feminist" leanings in McLaughlin's rendering of the *Oresteia* is to consider the political climate of the 1990s itself. On social, political, and professional fronts, women had made many gains, but the era witnessed a concomitant backlash against women's advances, symbolized by the rise of the New Right, the conservative Bush-Reagan years, and a media bent on packaging the era as "post-feminist." The atmosphere of retrenchment underscored the need for many women dramatists and artists (as well as scholars) to continue to highlight women's experience, to further the unfinished project of "recuperating" women's texts, and in the process oppose some of the anti-feminist counterclaims.[48] McLaughlin was, in a sense, reclaiming the myth of the House of Atreus for her generation. The generally positive response to and interest in *Iphigenia and Other Daughters* suggested that audiences were ripe for such a work, which re-asserted women's primacy, albeit in a new, postmodern frame.[49]

Perhaps McLaughlin's boldest move artistically was her radical reorganization of the Greek plays themselves to emphasize the female sacrifice at the heart of the drama. Here, she was in keeping with other feminist-oriented adaptations of the *Oresteia* of the early 1990s, such as Ariane Mnouchkine's epic trilogy *Les Atrides*, and a three-part version consisting of Euripides's *Iphigenia at Aulis* and *Agamemnon* and Sophocles's *Electra* mounted by former Guthrie Theatre director Garland Wright.[50] By placing *Iphigenia in Aulis* at the beginning of her trilogy, McLaughlin dramatizes the circumstances under which Iphigenia was lured to her death and makes her sacrifice the overriding motivating force for Clytemnestra's murders. "I threw out the notion of Clytemnestra as an adulteress," says McLaughlin, "because it never really made that much sense to me."[51] It is the male drive for power, instead of women's desire for revenge that now buttresses the play.[52] This type of postmodern dramaturgical transposition has the effect of questioning the "authority" of the original Greek plays; it undermines the notion of an essential or unified "masterwork" and thus "eclipses male narratives of mythic heroism."[53] By extension, too, it suggests that women's identity itself is unstable and that different narratives may be written back into history.

While *Electra Speaks* was very much rooted in the psychological relationships among women characters, and their ultimate personal liberation (Electra, at the conclusion of the play, literally walks out of the House of Atreus), *Iphigenia and Other Daughters*, as I have noted, probes these women's stories in relationship to history and the history of the myth. As McLaughlin has said, "Clytemnestra clearly feels that she is a part of history, Chrysothemis that she is outside history, and Electra that she is history."[54] McLaughlin's characters are aware of their circumstances, even if they are powerless to change them. In response to Chysothemis's statement that "We are always at the edge of importance," Clytemnestra responds, "I was running a country. I have always been at the center of the drama. And I have never waited for anything. Except ripeness, the moment, the true beauty of the crafted event."[55] Electra tells us: "I will write on walls with my blood.... I will bang my lice-ridden head against the concrete floor and howl and howl. Narrating my history to the air, telling my one story again and again. It will all be the same to me" (43). Chysothemis, the character McLaughlin has described as "the awful voice" in her head,[56] the "realist" who possesses the most clarity about her own relegated place in culture, ruminates about what women were doing "during ... stock markets crashing, landslides, train wrecks, handshakes.... Ironing? Planning dinner? Folding sheets? While millions died, while the world came to an end, what was I up to at the time? Making a sandwich?" (57).

McLaughlin's postmodern staging, scenic design, and acting style all work toward disrupting conventional viewer expectations of the ancient myths and help provoke new, feminist materialist readings. Unlike in *Electra Speaks*, there is no "ideal" female or feminist spectator here, in part because by the mid–1990s there was already a fairly splintered women's movement, as explained earlier, with differing social and political agendas. To "identify" with McLaughlin's characters seems beside the point. The depictions of the women often verge on caricature, and these images, combined with the anomalies in speech, dress, and acting style provide a "slightly jarring aesthetic shock," as McLaughlin herself notes.[57] Helene P. Foley has remarked of the women characters in McLaughlin's play that they "are both the object of vision and (like Electra) the tortured eyes (and tongues) that witness the past and keep it alive."[58] When mother and daughter argue it is inevitably over their competing claims to history; in defending her slaying of Electra's father, Clytemnestra tells her: "You see how the inevitable holds us in her hands. So here we are. My dead against your dead, my love against your love. My history against your history, in perpetuity" (34).

In McLaughlin's opening piece, *Iphigenia in Aulis*, the production elements force a rather painful (and at times humorous) recognition of the way their different life experiences have distanced mother from daughter. The desired aesthetic, as the stage directions indicate, is one of "minimalist dance."[59] Amidst the stark, other-worldly setting — a stage strewn with pebbles, a mound of rocks to the right leading off to a cliff — the regal-bearing Clytemnestra (played magisterially by Kathleen Chalfant) paces back and forth, while Iphigenia sits in front of her curled up in a chair. Clytemnestra speaks colloquially of those "eager, beardless, ignorant hopped-up bastards" (20) waiting to kill her daughter. Iphigenia, in blank verse, refers to herself as a phantom: "I am just some spell that is cast/It is a powerless power" (21). Clytemnestra speaks from her stance as a queen who knows the outcome of her daughter's fate; Iphigenia remains virginal and innocent. In alternating interior monologues, the two women never face or speak directly to one another, but rather gaze out toward the audience whose attention becomes focused on the way that patriarchal culture, as symbolized by male prerogatives and power, has defined their fate. As critic Robert Andreach has noted of these exchanges, they expose the way the characters react to their "experience of the male world."[60]

Like *Electra Speaks*, *Iphigenia and Other Daughters* reveals how women do damage to themselves under patriarchy, but its often deliciously ironic banter works toward propelling spectators *away* from the characters, drawing us to the source of their anger (male coercion). In *Electra*, the second part of McLaughlin's trilogy, in which Electra goads on her brother Orestes to kill their mother for her transgressions, the setting now is realistic, not mythic. McLaughlin foregrounds Electra's neurotic attachment to her father and suggests that her excessive mourning and devotion to the past have made a mess of her — as the directions note she is "filthy and presumably smelly" (27). Electra appears in a large pit in the center of the stage, one end of a piece of rope attached to her boot, the other to a stake. She is metaphorically and literally bound to the earth, to her history, as the angry, grieving daughter. Clytemnestra asks what families do with such daughters as hers: "Dress them up as best we can, endure them privately ... turn down their invitations by saying, "Not feeling quite up to it, Packing for a trip abroad, Summer camp, Swiss academy..." (42). Clytemnestra refers to Electra as a "hulking, nearly middle-aged monstrosity" (42); Electra calls her mother a "sagging carcass," a "rotting beauty" and tells her that "even as you stink you stamp and flirt your pointless feathers" (30). Once again, in these presentational exchanges Electra and Clytemnestra don't "confront" each other so much as proclaim at one another, and their caustic exchanges undercut any sense of identification.

In the character of Orestes, the one male character depicted in McLaughlin's theatrical recreation, McLaughlin draws out the 1990s emphasis on the analysis of gender, which signaled a move away from "the women-centered investigations of the 1970s"[61] to a consideration of how patriarchal values confine men's as well as women's destinies. As a representative of the "new man," Orestes furthers the play's materialist concerns by suggesting that ideological frameworks shape both male and female experience and that within the history of patriarchy, men, too, have sought ways to undermine its constraints.[62] Orestes makes his entrance in the second play of the trilogy, *Electra*, in which he has returned as a World War I veteran. Of all the characters, Orestes is the one who has been *through* history, but he repudiates much of that history. McLaughlin has said of his character, "He knows he is a tragic figure, but that has no appeal to him. He did not choose this."[63] As Orestes says, "I'm tired of killing" Electra responds, "I'm tired of waiting" (51). He has fought in the "Great War," but he has come back weary and disillusioned. In the character of Orestes, McLaughlin suggests that the history of which the women are so desirous is indeed man-made, flawed, and full of violence and hatred. Electra has idealized Orestes (and by implication all male experience) when she tells him, "I pictured you in Africa, standing on a marketplace, color all around you.... Or at sea somewhere, shirt sticking to your back, watch the sky go crimson and enormous" to which Orestes replies, "It was never like that. Ditch to ditch, death to death, that's all" (53).

Orestes appears again in the final of the three plays, *Iphigenia in Tauris*, which now, as in the first play, is set in mythic time. McLaughlin depicts the contours of the myth as described in the Euripidian play: at the moment of Iphigenia's death a calf is killed in her place, and she is spirited away to the barbaric land of Tauris where, as a priestess to the goddess Artemis, Iphigenia prepares Greek captives for their sacrifice. Orestes flees to Tauris to escape the avenging Furies (for the murder of his mother) where he must return a statue of Artemis to Athens in order to ensure his survival. At Tauris, Orestes eventually unites with Iphigenia (with Athena's aid) and returns home to Greece. The stage directions describe "a mound of rocks culminating in a stone altar," as five women figures in diaphanous white dresses stand cater-cornered from one another as "stand-ins" for Artemis. In their recognition scene, there is the suggestion here of a new, redemptive future — that brother and sister will escape from this particular history together, and "pass through the stone wall of history" (74). Iphigenia and Orestes are conscious of their role in propping up this "male myth of heroism" should they continue to live out the narrative of the House of Atreus. "We are performing a legend," says Iphigenia. "And the legend is performing us," replies her brother (72). But there is the hope that they may conduct themselves differently.

Changing history will be hard-fought, McLaughlin implies, and women and men must embark on the project together. Ultimately, though, McLaughlin leaves her spectators in a state of postmodern limbo. The act of brother and sister helping one another to remake the legend, without help from Athena (as occurs in Euripides), "will be the part everyone will forget," says Iphigenia (75). Although Iphigenia and Orestes are comrades now and on the threshold of breaking through the myth, the bloodshed, and the cycles of violence, Iphigenia becomes the statue; she is rendered "visible and mute" (75). An air of ambiguity still hangs over her and Orestes' fate. While *Electra Speaks*, despite its nonlinear, experimental style, moves rather triumphantly and idealistically toward the heroine's emergence and transformation, *Iphigenia and Other Daughters* is much more muted in its outcome. In keeping with a kind of feminist postmodern refusal of closure, it suggests that rewriting the myth may be imaginable but that we are not fully equipped to change it — just yet.

A Coda: Electra and Iphigenia Look Back

In April of 2007, the acclaimed New York-based performer and writer Deb Margolin directed and produced an abridged version of *Electra Speaks* with her Theatre Studies students at Yale University. Margolin and her class were fortunate to be able to work with Sondra Segal who served as a co-director of the "revival." Margolin herself has referred to *Electra Speaks* as a "primary, vital feminist text"— and notes that bringing it to Yale was something she had "dreamed of doing for a long time."[64] Indeed, for Margolin, seeing *Electra Speaks* in 1980, as a young performer, was a transformative experience: "I never saw theatre like this. I never saw women that weren't perfect little blondes singing arpeggios.... They affirmed that women's lives have theatrically viable images."[65] For Margolin's Yale student performers, who constituted an array of ethnic backgrounds and nationalities — African American, Jewish, Indian, Haitian, and Afghani — the rehearsal process, conducted with Segal was a revelatory one. They wrote short, weekly papers in response to the script; discussed and debated the works of feminist writers, such as Adrienne Rich and Mary Daly; and created "family sculptures" that depicted iconic scenes or moments from their own family life. To accommodate the number of women who wanted to perform in the piece (the original *Electra Speaks* was performed by five actors) each of the female characters was played by several women. The students became so invested in the work, says Segal, that they felt as if they had written the play themselves.[66]

Despite being performed in an entirely different cultural, social, and political milieu, outside of its original feminist context, the work clearly struck a chord with these young women. For most of them, *Electra Speaks* represented a profound anti-war play, a theme made all the more pressing by the ongoing war in Iraq.[67] Much of the passion and poignancy revealed in the finished production was a result of the students' own personal experiences of a male-dominated culture. Rape, sexual molestation, incest, and sexual harassment were all issues that surfaced in the students' preparatory work for the show. One student coined the phrase "the artifice of equality" to describe a campus climate in which women are accepted but still feel inhibited to speak freely in class. The difference between then and now, as Segal sees it, is that these brilliant, talented, ambitious women are now equipped for a "new world," but that world is not always there for them.[68] The success of the piece — measured not only by the audience response but what it meant in the lives of the performers — suggests, of course, that the feminist work begun over thirty years ago is not complete. The spirit of the original production lives on in these contemporary Electras and Iphigenias who continue to "perform the legend" and revise the "old stories" as they seek their own feminist truths.

This essay is dedicated to the memory of Judy C. Rosenthal, a feminist pioneer, with whom I collaborated on our 1993 essay on *Electra Speaks*.

Notes

    1. Froma Zeitlin, *Playing the Other: Gender and Society in Classical Greek Literature* (Chicago and London: The University of Chicago Press, 1996) 88.
    2. In an interesting 1999 exchange in an Electronic Seminar Series Archive on "The Reception of the Texts and Images of Ancient Greece in Late Twentieth-Century Drama and Poetry in English," several classics scholars debated Sue-Ellen Case's charge, in her 1988 book, *Feminism and Theatre*, to disengage from producing the Greek classic plays because of their sexist underpinnings. In this online dialogue, Lorna Hardwick and Marianne McDonald served as responders to Mary-Kay Gamel's short piece "Staging Ancient Drama: the Difference Women Make." While, as Gamel argues, "revisions of ancient drama with masculinist agendas often pass without notice," she and others endorse engaging with these texts, but through a feminist reframing of them. Hardwick argues for a kind of contemporizing that would link concerns from the time of play to modern ones. Gamel concludes that "feminist productions can participate in the patriarchal subtext of ancient dramas not in order to confirm that subtext, but to examine and question it." Given that this exchange occurred ten years after *Feminism and Theatre* was published, and with several feminist-inspired theatrical productions behind it, Case herself might not have been in disagreement with these positions. (http://www2.open.ac.uk/ClassicalStudies/GreekPlays/e_archive/1999/May.htm.) See Sue-Ellen Case, *Feminism and Theatre* (New York: Methuen, 1988) 5–27.
    3. Jonathan Miller, *Subsequent Performances* (New York: Viking Penguin, Inc., 1986) 34–35.
    4. Sondra Segal and Roberta Sklar, "The Women's Experimental Theatre," *The Drama Review (TDR)* 27.4 (Winter 1983): 75.
    5. See Jill Dolan, *The Feminist Spectator as Critic* (Ann Arbor: UMI Press, 1988) 3–11;

Charlotte Canning, *Feminist Theaters in the U.S.A.: Staging Women's Experience* (London and New York: Routledge, 1996) 4–6; and Case, *Feminism and Theatre*, 62–95.

  6. Case, *Feminism and Theatre*, 64–5.
  7. Dolan, *The Feminist Spectator*, 3.
  8. Case, *Feminism and Theatre*, 82.
  9. Dolan, *The Feminist Spectator*, 10.
  10. Case, *Feminism and Theatre*, 131; Canning, *Feminist Theaters*, 5.
  11. Esther Beth Sullivan, "Women, Woman, and the Subject of Feminism: Feminist Directions," *Upstaging Big Daddy: Directing Theatre as if Gender and Race Matter*, eds. Ellen Donkin and Susan Clement (Ann Arbor: University of Michigan Press, 1993) 17–18.
  12. Canning, *Feminist Theaters*, 5.
  13. Jill Dolan, "In Defense of the Discourse: Materialist Feminism, Postmodernism, Poststructuralism ... and Theory," *Presence and Desire: Essays on Gender, Sexuality, and Performance* (Ann Arbor: University of Michigan Press, 1993) 88.
  14. Charlotte Canning and Esther Beth Sullivan, introduction, *Stages in Feminism: The Daughters Cycle of the Women's Experimental Theatre*, unpublished manuscript, 12.
  15. Ibid.
  16. Ibid.
  17. Canning and Sullivan, quoting Teresa de Lauretis who states that feminism "is a developing theory of the female-embodied social subject that is based on its specific, emergent, and conflictual history," conclude that "implicit in her description is the idea that feminism is moving and changing, and that it is not the same set of ideas, theories, and practices now in 1992 that it was in 1972 or in 1982. But also implied is the assertion that we need ways of addressing the complex and sometimes idiosyncratic developments of feminism that can not be accounted for in relation to progress" (*Ibid.*, 13). The de Lauretis article from which Canning and Sullivan quote is "Upping the Anti (sic) in Feminist Theory," *Conflicts in Feminism*, eds. Marianne Hirsch and Evelyn Fox Keller (New York: Routledge, 1990) 256.
  18. Roberta Sklar, "*Sisters* or Never Trust Anyone outside the Family," *Women and Performance* 1.1 (Spring-Summer 1983): 61.
  19. Roberta Sklar, for instance, worked alongside Joseph Chaikin at The Open Theatre in the early 1970s and served as co-director of some of that company's major ensemble works including *The Serpent, Terminal*, and *The Mutation Show*; she also directed Beckett's *Endgame*. See Cornelia Brunner, "Roberta Sklar: Toward Creating a Women's Theatre," *The Drama Review (TDR)* 24.2 (June 1980): 23. Although Sklar acknowledges the pivotal influence of The Open Theatre on her own directorial and creative work, she eventually left as she became painfully aware of the inherent sexism at work in the company. As Sklar has noted of her break with The Open Theatre, "I worked much the way women did in the peace movement and in the student movement: We did a lot of the work, got little of the credit, and didn't realize that there was a major section missing in the political analysis—the section that was about us" (Brunner, "Roberta Sklar: Toward Creating," 30). Also see Julie Malnig and Judy C. Rosenthal, "The Women's Experimental Theatre: Transforming Family Stories into Feminist Questions," *Acting Out: Feminist Performance*, eds. Lynda Hart and Peggy Phelan (Ann Arbor: University of Michigan Press, 1993) 202.
  20. Theatrical revisions of the classic Greek plays dates back to the late 1960s with notable productions such as Jonathan Miller's *Prometheus Unbound*, in 1967; Andre Gregory's *The Bacchae*, in 1969; Richard Schechner's *Dionysus in '69*; and Andre Serban's *The Trojan Women*, in 1973. See Amy Green, *The Revisionist Stage: American Directors Reinvent the Classics* (Cambridge, UK, and New York: Cambridge University Press, 1994) 42–46.
  21. Teresa de Lauretis, *Feminist Studies/Critical Studies* (Bloomington: Indiana University Press, 1986) 10–11.
  22. As its creators note, *Electra Speaks* was also "an analysis of the ways in which the lines of demarcation are drawn in the patriarchal family." Clare Coss, Sondra Segal, Roberta Sklar, "Notes on the Women's Experimental Theatre," *Women in Theatre: Compassion and Hope*, Karen Malpede (New York: Drama Book Publishers, 1983) 240–41.
  23. Nancy Chodorow argues that it is society and culture that has devalued these bonds

between mother and daughter. As she notes, "The difficulties that girls have in establishing a 'feminine' identity do not stem from the inaccessibility and negative definition of this identity, or its assumption by denial (as in the case of boys). They arise from identification with a negatively valued gender category, and an ambivalently experienced maternal figure, whose mothering and femininity ... are accessible, but devalued." "Gender, Relation, and Difference in Psychoanalytic Perspective," *The Future of Difference*, eds. Hester Eisenstein and Alice Jardine (Boston: G.K. Hall and Co., 1990) 14.

24. Helene Foley, "Bad Women: Gender Politics in Late Twentieth-Century Performance and Revision of Greek Tragedy," *Dionysius Since 69: Greek Tragedy at the Dawn of the Third Millennium*, eds. Edith Hall, Fiona Macintosh, and Amanda Wrigley (New York: Oxford University Press, 2004) 99. For more on the uses and appeal of myth and ritual in 1970s feminism see Gayle Kimball, *Women's Culture: The Women's Renaissance of the Seventies* (Metuchen, New Jersey, and London: The Scarecrow Press, 1991) 8.

25. Dolan, *Feminist Spectator*, 94.

26. Sondra Segal and Roberta Sklar, "The Women's Experimental Theatre," *Women in American Theatre* [revised and expanded], eds. Helen Krich Chinoy and Linda Walsh Jenkins (New York: Crown Publishers, 1987) 307.

27. Sondra Segal and Roberta Sklar, interview by the author and Judy C. Rosenthal, 1 February 1991, New York City. These workshops were held at Margot Lewithin's Women's Interart Theatre in New York City, where WET was in residence for most of its producing life.

28. Some of the collectively run feminist theater troupes of the period that also relied on techniques from consciousness raising included It's All Right to be Woman Theatre (New York City), Lilith Theatre (New York City), Thank-You Theatre (Los Angeles), and At the Foot of the Mountain Theatre (Minneapolis). See Canning, *Feminist Theaters*, 34–36, 68–73.

29. Clare Coss, Sondra Segal, and Roberta Sklar, *Electra Speaks*, unpublished play manuscript, 1980. Additional references in the text.

30. Segal and Sklar, "The Women's Experimental Theatre," 306.

31. See Dolan, in *The Feminist Spectator*, who argues that "the text breaks with the mystifying conventions of fourth-wall realism, but constructs in its place ritual systems that demand a similar suspension of disbelief" (90).

32. Segal and Sklar, "The Women's Experimental Theatre," 306.

33. See Canning, *Feminist Theaters*, 124–7, on the uses of ritual in women's theater of the 1970s and 1980s.

34. Clare Coss, Sondra Segal, and Roberta Sklar, "Notes on the Women's Experimental Theatre," 241.

35. Ibid., 236.

36. Segal and Sklar, "The Women's Experimental Theatre," 307.

37. Zeitlin, *Playing the Other*, 347.

38. See Sue-Ellen Case, "Toward a Butch-Femme Aesthetic," *Making a Spectacle: Feminist Essays on Contemporary Women's Theatre*, ed. Lynda Hart (Ann Arbor: University of Michigan Press, 1989) 282–3. Case expands on de Lauretis's concept of the feminist subject outlined in her essay "Technologies of Gender," *Technologies of Gender: Essays on Theory, Film, and Fiction* (Bloomington: Indiana University Press, 1987).

39. Ellen McLaughlin, *The Greek Plays* (New York: Theatre Communications Group, 2005) xv.

40. Ibid., xiii.

41. McLaughlin quoted in Randy Gener, "Angel at the Atreus Table," *The Village Voice*, 21 February 1996.

42. For further discussion on the poststructuralist stance see Sue-Ellen Case, *Performing Feminisms: Feminist Critical Theory and Theatre* (Baltimore: The Johns Hopkins University Press, 1990) 7–13.

43. Canning, *Feminist Theaters*, 127.

44. McLaughlin, *The Greek Plays*, 14.

45. Classicist Helene P. Foley points out that in actuality women in Greek society "are

both more embedded in the social system and marginal to its central institutions." They did indeed hold substantial positions of responsibility and authority within the family household and religious and civic rituals. Foley continues that "[r]ecent critics, myself included, have hypothesized that female characters are doing double duty in these plays, by representing a fictional female position in the tragic family and city and simultaneously serving as a location from which to explore a series of problematic issues that men prefer to approach indirectly and certainly not through their own person" [*Female Acts in Greek Tragedy* (Princeton and Oxford: Princeton University Press, 2001) 4].

46. McLaughlin, *The Greek Plays*, 14.

47. *Ibid.*, 4.

48. An example was the widely heralded *Vagina Monologues*, Eve Ensler's graphic celebration of women's sexuality; although its message about demystifying the female body seemed more akin to 1970s feminism, its immense popularity suggested that the project of consciousness raising was not complete.

49. See Gener, "Angel at the Atreus Table;" Ben Brantley, "Good Girl in a Bloody Greek Legend," *The New York Times*, 11 February 1995; Greg Evans, "Iphigenia and Other Daughters," *Variety*, 13 February 1995; and Richard Morin, "Two Feminist Retakes of Greek Legend," *Seattle Weekly*, 2 May 2007.

50. Ariane Mnouchkine's *Les Atrides*, presented at the Brooklyn Academy of Music in 1992, prefaced the Aeschylian *Oresteia* (*Agamemnon, The Libation Bearers*, and *The Eumenides*) with Euripides's *Iphigenia in Aulis*. This highly celebrated production featured a totally multinational cast, and according to classicist Marianne McDonald, "adopts what one might call a postmodern collective geopolitical perspective." See "The Atrocities of *Les Atrides*: Mnouchkine's Tragic Vision," *Theatre Forum* 1.1 (Spring 1992): 13. While space does not permit a fuller exploration, *Les Atrides* can be seen as representative of a strand of transnational feminism also emerging in the 1990s. The work of cultural and literary theorist Gayatri Spivak was particularly influential in this regard. See Elaine Aston, *Feminist Views on the English Stage: Women Playwrights 1990–2000* (Cambridge, UK, and New York: Cambridge University Press, 2003) 8–9. For more on *Les Atrides* see Sarah Bryant-Bertail, "Gender, Empire and Body Politic as Mise en Scène: Mnouchkine's *Les Atrides*," *Theatre Journal* 46.1 (March 1994): 1–30. Garland Wright's production appeared at the Guthrie Theatre in Minneapolis in 1992. Also in 1992, The Actors' Gang, in Los Angeles, presented its adaptation of *The Oresteia* consisting of *Agamemnon* by Charles Mee, Sophocles's *Electra* by Ellen McLaughlin, and *Orestes* also by Charles Mee.

51. Gener, "Angel at the Atreus Table."

52. In Euripides, the queenly Clytemnestra is literally brought to her knees in despair at her realization that instead of marriage her daughter faces death.

53. Sharon Friedman, "Feminist Revisions of Classic Texts on the American Stage," *Codifying the National Self: Spectators, Actors, and the American Dramatic Text*, eds. Barbara Ozieblo and Lola Narbona (Brussels: Peter Lang, 2006) 84.

54. McLaughlin, *The Greek Plays*, 5.

55. Ellen McLaughlin, "Iphigenia and Other Daughters," *The Greek Plays* (New York: Theatre Communications Group, 2005) 53, 35. Additional references in the text.

56. McLaughlin, *The Greek Plays*, 8.

57. *Ibid.*, 14.

58. Helene P. Foley, "Iphigenia and Other Daughters," rev., *Didaskalia* 2.2 (April 1995): 3.

59. McLaughlin, *The Greek Plays*, 3.

60. Robert J. Andreach, "Ellen McLaughlin's *Iphigenia and Other Daughters*: A Classical Trilogy from a Contemporary Perspective," *Comparative Literature Studies* 35.4 (1998): 380.

61. Elaine Showalter, ed., *Speaking of Gender* (New York and London: Routledge, 1989) 2.

62. As feminist critic Elaine Showalter notes, "For those materialist critics who prefer the term 'gender' however, talking about 'sexual difference' implies both a belief in the inevitability of the social relations between the sexes, and a downgrading of history and social

process in favor of psychic and linguistic determinants" (3). For an overview of the move from feminist to gender-oriented analyses of the 1980s and 1990s, and some of the controversies, see Showalter's introduction to *Speaking of Gender*, 1–11.

63. McLaughlin, *The Greek Plays*, 9.

64. Program notes, *Electra Speaks*, Yale University, Whitney Humanities Center, 26–28 Apr. 2007.

65. Deb Margolin, interview by author, 12 May 1991, New York City.

66. Sondra Segal, interview by author, 7 September 2007, New York City. I attended the production on Thursday, April 26, 2007, and Sondra Segal kindly agreed to meet and speak with me after the production about her experiences in revisiting this work. Overall, it was a thrilling experience for her to see what new readings these young women brought to the text.

67. *Ibid.*

68. *Ibid.*

The Philomela Myth as Postcolonial Feminist Theater
Timberlake Wertenbaker's *The Love of the Nightingale*

MAYA E. ROTH

> *Why is the world in the hopeless state it is and what can we do to change it?*
> —Timberlake Wertenbaker[1]

> JUNE: *We show you a myth.*
> ECHO: *Image. Echo.*
> —Female Chorus, *The Love of the Nightingale* (sc. 20, 62)[2]

The Love of the Nightingale, Timberlake Wertenbaker's acclaimed play based on the ancient Philomela myth—which premiered at the Royal Shakespeare Company's The Other Place in Stratford-upon-Avon—profoundly engages both classical traditions and postmodern theater practices to interrogate the violence of silencing. Written and premiered in 1988, during the peak of apartheid violence in South Africa, this mythic play draws audiences into an interactive space of political witnessing and active inquiry about dispossession, body politics, and escalating cycles of violence. In its adaptation of myth to involve audiences in human rights concerns, Wertenbaker continues a long-standing civic theater tradition—practiced by ancient Greek tragedians no less than Shakespeare, Brecht, or late twentieth-century feminist playwrights—of re-shaping classical myths to speak to audiences of one's day. A classicist by training, who has since translated extensively from ancient Greek to English (eg. Sophocles' *Theban Plays*, RSC, 1991; Euripides' *Hecuba*, American Conservatory Theatre, 1995) as well as an acclaimed playwright of original works, Wertenbaker stages self-reflexive polyphonic dialogues with received cultural mythologies, and live audiences, in *The Love of the Nightingale*.

Wertenbaker's depth of knowledge of ancient works makes *The Love of the Nightingale* one of the most erudite and intertextual of modern adaptations of myth in recent decades, as exemplified by her placing the Philomela myth in constellation with the ancient tragedies of *Hippolytus* and *The Bacchae*. Like the playwright's 1985 *The Grace of Mary Traverse*, a female-centered re-imagining of the Faustian legend; her recent radio play *Dianeira* (1999), based on the ancient myth; and *The Ash Girl*, her multicultural re-visioning of the Cinderella fairytale premiered in 2000, *The Love of the Nightingale* intricately layers myth, feminism, and politics.³ Written during her second wave of production, when she was much courted by major British theaters, *The Love of the Nightingale* first appeared in the same year as Wertenbaker's most widely celebrated play, *Our Country's Good* (1988), which also investigates dispossession/s in post-colonial registers.⁴ These plays' vivid interactive dialogues with specific canonic works interrogate the gendered politics of representation as well as ideologies of difference, rights and power. In that, they work within historian Joan Scott's definition of gender as "a primary field within which or by means of which power is articulated."⁵

A "dark meditation on violence" and its legacies, as Susan Carlson has described the play, it is also, as Wertenbaker points out, about "love," language and loss that ultimately queries what kind of future we will pass on to our children.⁶ Through its structure and content, *The Love of the Nightingale* investigates how to transform social relations, as well as our psyches, so entrenched in inequalities and binary conceptions. At the heart of this postmodern classic is a complicated feminist consciousness that interrogates gender and language, refracted through class, country, and culture, exposing how discourses of otherness themselves produce social and psychic violence. While its critique of gendered violence hits hard, the play more broadly pursues a critique of tyranny, violence against cultural difference, and the escalating cycles of revenge borne from silence too long endured, injustice too long sustained.⁷ Wertenbaker was among the forefront of Anglophone women playwrights exploring global concerns in the 1980s, echoing the interests of material feminists more broadly.

Commissioned by the Royal Shakespeare Company to write a play, any play, Wertenbaker gravitated toward Ovid's *Metamorphoses*, and then found herself "caught up" in the myth of Philomela. In correspondence, she explains that working with myth provides a kind of freedom: "you can invent the language" and follow "imagination." "You can be more poetic than with a history play," less bound to historical specificities, which she rigorously researches when setting a play in the past.⁸ Importantly, Wertenbaker has emphasized elsewhere that myths, like history plays, allow her to foreground themes more than topicalities, to "free ... people's prejudices" about themselves and the world.⁹ Unlike history plays, however, myths encourage the narrative voice, enacted through male and female choruses in *The Love of the Nightingale*. Wertenbaker taps these choruses for meta-commentary in and outside the dramatic action, for self-reflexive mirroring of the audience's own roles, and for rapid reframing of the story and its stakes in different contexts—bridging the distance to

The Love of the Nightingale stages the psychic and embodied violence of Philomele's loss of voice. Emma Matthews is shown here in the acclaimed world premiere of *The Love of the Nightingale* opera in 2007. The music is composed by Richard Mills with libretto by Timberlake Wertenbaker in an award-winning collaboration by West Australian Opera and the Perth International Arts Festival, directed by Lindy Hume. Shot by Bridget Elliot from the wings of His Majesty's Theatre in Perth.

today, yesterday, long ago, and some place else, even for a moment.[10] By choosing a lesser-known ancient myth, the playwright imagined the play might provide "a kind of jolting," jarring consciousness more effectively than a familiar story might, a strategy that echoes Brecht's goals for estrangement. Indeed, dislocations—of tradition, of space and time, of character perspective and forms of address, of genres and cultures—emerge in *The Love of the Nightingale*, as in other Wertenbaker plays, as a defining theatrical strategy, facilitating critical engagement for audiences and stirring more complex inquiry of human and social experience as well as ethics.

The ancient myth centers on the rape, maiming, grief, and ultimate revenge of Philomela, an Athenian princess, sent as a companion for her beloved sister Procne, who misses their Athens home after being married to the Thracian King, Tereus.[11] While escorting Philomela to his wife, Tereus desires his young sister-in-law and rapes her; he cuts out her tongue to cover his brutality and imprisons her for later visits, then returns to his palace where he tells Procne that Philomela died on the voyage. In Ovid's version, Philomela, full of grief, sews the tragedy into a tapestry which she sends to Procne, leading Procne to kill her son, Itys, in retribution against his father. Together she and Philomela then serve the butchered boy to Tereus to eat; on his discovery of these horrors, Tereus chases Philomela and Procne with rage until the gods turn all three into birds to prevent more violence—a mythic metamorphosis. Procne is turned into a swallow, a migratory bird; Philomele a nightingale, a nocturnal bird renowned for its mournful song; and Tereus a hoopoe, a bird that buries its head under sand.[12]

Wertenbaker's adaptations reveal feminist and civic as well as theatrical impulses. She creates a large cast of characters, specifying class and cultural range, thereby reinforcing the social dimensions of the story, not only interpersonal ones, for a contemporary mixed gender audience. She transforms the muted Philomele's method of revelation to Procne, from sewing and sending a tapestry, marked feminine and domestic, to the public, embodied activity of street performance, marked feminist by "making a spectacle" of it for an onstage community of women.[13] While retaining the infanticide near play's end, Wertenbaker makes Philomele Itys's murderer, echoing aspects of *The Bacchae* where the young royal spies on the drunken bacchantes and is then killed by his aunt and mother on threatening them; Wertenbaker omits the cannibalism. Perhaps most creatively, Wertenbaker places the myth of Philomela in dialectical tension with *Hippolytus*, (the chaste youth desired by his stepmother) parodied in a play-within-the-play and engaged throughout the text. As Joe Winston asserts in "Recasting the Phaedra Syndrome: Myth and Mythmaking in *The Love of the Nightingale*," the most famous violent incest narrative in Western drama is shown to efface and displace the far more frequent pattern of male-to-female sexual abuse, creating little space for helping women to make sense and speak of their experiences of rape, incest, and sexual harassment.[14] This highly theatrical addition also helps to highlight, and reflect on, various onstage (and offstage) audience responses to theater, character choices, and the "cultural centrality" of shaming women for sex, including rape. Wertenbaker's play, in contrast, establishes a positive perspective on female desire through Philomele as early as scene two, differentiating rape from women's sexuality. By triangulating the Philomela myth with the Phaedra myth and *The Bacchae*, Wertenbaker suggests that ancient and contemporary discourses of sexual and cultural otherness can feed violence, even as she deepens the focus on the complex relationship of women to violence through this dialogic constellation of myths.[15]

The play advances through a panoramic series of complex juxtapositions: of male and female experience, of Athens and Thrace, of dispossession and power, of story and performance. Indeed, during its ninety minute playing time (when performed, as written and premiered, without intermission), *The Love of the Nightingale* moves to more than a dozen locations, crossing years in the mythic narrative and reaching explicitly forward, anachronistically, to contemporary times through the chorus ("Why are races exterminated?/Why do white people cut off the words of blacks?/...Why are little girls raped and murdered in the car parks of dark cities?") (sc. 20, 62). Thus guided by the principles of feminist adaptation and postmodern storytelling rather than ancient tragedy's unities, Wertenbaker's dramaturgy connects seemingly disparate experiences, exploring the dispersal of power and hierarchies of difference. She also mixes poetry, cool distance, harrowing violence, and parody, thereby both evoking and deconstructing a reverence for ancient myths and classical styles. The play's spare efficiency and constant motion of settings slows in the play's middle, lending special emphasis to a series of scenes on the beach, where the grief, tyranny, and trauma at the center of this myth about rape and brutal silencing unfold. Here the play reveals its emotional center, an excavation of the psychic and social tolls of violence and dispossession — not only for Philomele, but also for others, including Procne, whom we see waiting at court with the chorus of women, feeling exiled, displaced from her home culture, language, and family.

Though widely recognized as one of Wertenbaker's most explicitly feminist works, *The Love of the Nightingale* is also one of her most popular plays, an intriguing observation given the relatively conservative climate for feminist plays in professional theater in the past two decades. Indeed, *The Love of the Nightingale* has been in near-continuous production since its writing, undoubtedly in part because it can easily fit into a classic "slot" at professional theaters, where classics tend to draw cache — and thus audiences. Winner of the 1989 Eileen Anderson Central Television Drama Award, the play was most recently adapted as an opera, with Wertenbaker writing the libretto, for premiere by the West Australian Opera for the Perth International Arts Festival in 2007. Similarly, universities are drawn to its feminism and/or its classical engagement. The play's feminist ethics emerge in part from its talks back to, and with, classical traditions in mainstream spaces, helping to make audiences conscious of received patterns of representation, reception, and social formation, which the play deconstructs through parody, direct address, and interrogative structures. As Alisa Solomon observes in her analysis of other contemporary adaptations, through a complex metatheater, a play can also be seen to "self-reflexively consider its own embeddedness in cultural institutions," such as theater, and in "historical moments," such as the postmodern one in which this play was written.[16] Importantly, Wertenbaker's critical intervention of received stories, venues, and forms, such as refracting ancient Greek tragedy through feminist problematics and intercultural rhythms of dispersal, equips audiences with poly-focal critical vision to interpret not only this play in performance, but also to bring to encounters with other "classics" staged in those very same theaters in the future. In this, she achieves a new tradition of civic theater based in profound dialogue with received sources, engaging feminist as well as postcolonial ethics.

Staging Post-Colonial Feminism: Bodies, Voices, Dispossession

> What is a myth? The oblique image of an unwanted truth, reverberating through time....
> — Male Chorus, The Love of the Nightingale (sc. 8, 31)

In the middle of *The Love of the Nightingale*, Timberlake Wertenbaker provides an unrelenting image of rape, one of the atrocities at the center of the ancient Philomela myth. In scene thirteen, the audience hears Philomele's screams from just out of sight, King Tereus having dragged her, his sister-in-law, away (offstage) to "have" her when she will not return his love. Our focus stays on Philomele, for it is her screams we hear echoing from nearby, subjectifying her experience even while the play displaces the narrative action by disrupting its locus, moving it offstage. If Wertenbaker seems to echo the ancient Greek prohibitions on staging rape/violence onstage, a prohibition flouted in the play's first parodic scene of war, this staging more importantly refuses any scopophilac desire and/or festishization of violence against women that an array of feminist critics have theorized in other contexts.[17] Repeatedly, this "realistic" performance moment in *The Love of the Nightingale* is singled out by reviewers and audience members for its harrowing impact.[18] The human violation at the center of the Philomela myth literally echoes throughout the space of the theater, in the here and now of performance.

This staging functions on several levels at once. It creates an immediacy that ruptures the representational frame — a key strategy of political, and feminist, theater. It activates auditory space, like ancient Greek theater, compelling audiences to listen to painful truths: one of the play's primary injunctions, theatrically heightened here.[19] At the same time, the trope of violation, excavated from the myth, foregrounds (em)bodied politics, a cornerstone concern of feminist, civil, and human rights movements.

This staging works powerfully in performance because it is both visceral and creative, investing and enmeshing the audience directly in the myth's "unwanted truth reverberating through time." By disrupting the onstage presentation of events and continuing the traumatic event audibly, Wertenbaker pulls audience members into the action, theatrically compelling us to participate in making meaning of the action as it happens, in effect subjectifying us in performance.[20] As much as we are active participants in the theatrical meaning-making, however, we are also complicit in our inaction, one of the recurrent critiques of this play about doing and saying nothing when people are abused.[21] We stay in our seats, obeying the rules of this social order (here, the theater) while screams for help in the social, not just representational, space go unaided. We become yet another in the string of witnesses (chorus members, soldiers, companions) who in Wertenbaker's rendering of the myth do nothing, say nothing, to stop the chain of violence they see in motion.

This striking nodal action is complexly layered, highly theatrical, haunting, and humane, all at once. It is also distinctly political, not only because Tereus is a king, but also because its emotional force reminds us of the human costs of injustice, evoking empathy and social concern. While the rape unfolds offstage, Niobe, one of Wertenbaker's invented figures, speaks, onstage, of the brutality of rape and war while Philomele calls for her help. Inserted into the re-telling of the myth and cast as Philomele's nurse and chaperone, Niobe is a slave, a survivor of the ravages of war. With cynical pragmatism, Niobe addresses the audience directly, like a third chorus, advising us that Philomele should acquiesce, that her pain will be even greater if she resists:

> She should have consented. Easier that way. Now it will all be pain. Well I know. We fought Athens. Foolish of a small island but we were proud. The men — dead. All of them. And us. Well — we wished ourselves dead then, but now I know it's better to live [sc. 13, 44ff].[22]

In this complicated mix, we glimpse the post-colonial ethic that infuses Wertenbaker's re-visioning of the classic myth. Unexpectedly, *The Love of the Nightingale* evokes the war crime of rape, a strategy of cultural or group degradation as ancient as the myth and as contemporary as Argentina's Dirty War that erupted in the decade prior to the play's writing (1976–83) or indeed the government-sanctioned rapes and genocide in Darfur today (2003–2007). Niobe's direct address to the audience unfolds with cynicism, yet also exilic force, compelling the audience to engage critically: "Power is something you can't resist.... Oh dear, oh dear, she shouldn't scream like that. It only makes it worse. Too tense. More brutal." Do we agree with her? Are we too complicit; isn't she? Political concerns overlay the raw violence, heightening the connections and disjunctures between Philomele's and Niobe's violations. Rather than allowing the audience to sympathize solely with a single figure, the character of Philomele, *The Love of the Nightingale* insists in its defining moments that we recognize rape as a social weapon, historicizing a ubiquitous violence that echoes from ancient to contemporary times, brutalizing individuals, families, and whole cultures, too often dismissed. And still, in the theater, Philomele screams; no one helps.

As encapsulated in its double staging of rape and war-survivor testimony, *The Love of the Nightingale* also stages their complicated connections — linking local and global traumas. Philomele's personal experience of tyranny — her rape, her subsequent maiming, her imprisonment as a sexual slave ("my caged bird") — connects to the brutal tactics of repressive regimes: isolation, murder, the disappearance of witnesses, censorship, intimidation, sexual humiliation, and deceit. "(T)he first meaning of danger," explains Hero in the women's chorus as they sense imminent doom for Procne, Philomele, and Tereus's soldiers, their husbands, "is the power of a lord or master" (sc. 9, 32).

Three techniques intersect in the staging of the rape, which illuminate Wertenbaker's distinctive poetics and a vibrant model of (feminist, post-colonial) civic theater. Geo-political sites of contention connect: violence against the smallest sites of contention — the body, a vagina — connect to the largest sites of contention — a country, a homeland.[23] In addition to enacting a feminist (em)bodied politics, seeing interconnections between personal and political concerns, this theatrical technique explicitly links domestic and international civics. Secondly, affective and critical perspectives intermediate here, both compelled as necessary and *sometimes conflicting* modes of moral response; in effect, audiences are cast as thinking, feeling subjects who are "jarred" to make sense of shifting, complicated perspectives in a search for justice. Thirdly, through direct address and mirroring of the audience function, audience members are implicated, theatrically, in the action, and hailed as participants in the theatrical world as well as an historicized social world.

As the rape staging exemplifies, the force of Wertenbaker's play comes from its surprising mix of raw intensity and sharp logic. By juxtaposing Philomele's immediate shrieks of violation with Niobe's harsh, even ironic acceptance of the status quo, the play also invokes both reflection and empathy simultaneously, so that both faculties problematize — and extend — each other. The scene makes audiences profoundly uncomfortable, a mode which Wertenbaker finds highly productive.[24] This unsettling layering of emotion and social critique is equally powerful in other nodal moments of this complex feminist play, including the mutilation scene, the activist street theater scene, and, subsequently, Philomele's killing of Itys. Thus our encounter with the trauma of rape, and its chain of connections (enabling conditions, direct and indirect victims-survivors, political consequences, emotional realities) stays vivid, vital, in need of ongoing processing beyond the scene, beyond the frames of the play.

Simultaneously, *The Love of the Nightingale* develops a subtle argument about war, the play's first word, developing a materialist critique: "War is the inevitable background, the ruins of the distance establishing place and perspective," as the male chorus explains (sc. 1, 9). Theatrically and politically, the two sisters' trajectories remain intimately, inextricably linked with war, fomented by the (masculinist) culture of conquest and violence: Procne feels exiled in Thebes, a warprize bride to Tereus, the warrior whose troops came to excel in brutality. Philomele's body and spirit is pillaged, her tongue ripped out by Tereus to silence her testimony, and so, after years of domination, she seeks vengeance against his son. Niobe is a displaced refugee of a country decimated by war, a hardened survivor of injustices too many to name whose ribald pragmatism girds her underclass passage. The soldiers fight and follow orders, knowing to look the other way when state or officer violence trespasses civil bounds and thus refuse responsibility. The choruses, Itys, and Tereus are all saturated in a system of hierarchies and difference enforced by violence if not consent, of institutionalized might as right. When, toward play's end, Itys bursts into the women's Bacchanalia, wielding childish threats of war that echo

Pentheus in *The Bacchae*, Philomele, too, responds with the language of war, killing him with his father's sword as the women's chorus circles round, like Procne, all complicit. The chain of reciprocal violence that Wertenbaker stages — of violence rather than communication — not only brutalizes the oppressed, but indeed spreads, impelling mistrust and destruction. The stakes? "The future."

Since war is the "inevitable background" to Wertenbaker's re-telling of Philomele, Procne, and Tereus' story, war emerges as a feminist issue, and silencing a global one. Rather than pegging the horror of violence on a single individual, a great hero deranged or plagued by desire or the gods' curse, as the ancient myth suggests, issuing moral sanction against intense desire — and incest — (or women traveling without a blood relative), this play instead casts Philomele's rape and mutilation by Tereus as part of a larger cycle of violence perpetuated, and historicized, by a culture that embraces war and silences questions, difference, and critique.[25]

Quoting Eavan Boland's injunction to listen as epigraph to the play, Wertenbaker activates auditory space through silence, speech, rhythm, and sound/s. From its beginning, the play's emphasis on storytelling, its spare poetic language, and the sharp intellect articulated by its trio of primary female figures — Philomele, Procne and Niobe, each so different from the other — compels its audience to *listen*. While the male chorus frame myth as "public speech" and call themselves objective reporters of events, the female chorus urge Procne to listen to the silences in between their words — to hear the imagery in their rounds of warnings, to sense their meaning in poetry, as they feel dispossessed from language itself. ("Without the words to demand./Or ask. Plead. Beg for./Without the words to accuse./Without even the words to forgive./The words that help to forget./ What else was there?" they ask in a choral round in scene twenty before Philomele kills "the future," Itys.) As Jennifer Wagner observes, the audience learns to hear the female chorus's "other way of talking" more acutely precisely because no one onstage hears them, Procne missing the Thracian "inflections" which rattle her Athenian directness.

Both Geraldine Cousin and Christine Dymkowski note that characters ask questions repeatedly, making this play "interrogatory" in form and pattern.[26] Indeed the play's last line is a question: "Didn't you want me to ask questions?" (sc. 21, 66). Meanwhile, Philomele's cries for help when she is raped, her song at play's end, her calling out Tereus' abuses before he brutally silences her: all of these pleas attune audiences to listen more closely, with sensitivity and readiness. The play's structure of language, sound, and questioning urges audiences not only to listen, speak, and inquire, but moreover to *hear*, offering in that practice some hope for reconciliation, an antidote to violence, a process for building understanding across gender and cultural differences, for moving through griefs and oppression.[27]

In *The Love of the Nightingale*, Tereus's cutting out of Philomele's tongue is a climactic brutality, a violation even worse than rape. "Now truly I pity Philomele," says Niobe, her sympathies compelled as Philomele crouches in a pool of blood, voiceless, although she had savored Philomele's social fall immediately after the rape.

> Now she is silent. For good. Of course he could have killed her, that is the usual way of keeping people silent. But that might have made others talk. The silence of the dead can turn into a wild chorus. But the one alive who cannot speak, that one has truly lost all power [sc.16, 51].

Indeed, Tereus's brutal silencing of Philomele, presented centerstage, is the play's defining action, signaling Wertenbaker's primary concern with the aggression of silencing — and the violence bred from it. This scene exemplifies how, as Susan Bassnet suggests, "Wertenbaker is representative of the postcolonial writer, calling upon us to consider the ways in which power relations in the world have been shaped by the language" — and silences — "imposed by the dominant power."[28]

The mutilation scene occurs two full scenes after the rape (and one scene after Tereus returns to Procne with blood on his hands). When Tereus comes to violate her again, while Philomele tries to have Niobe wash out the violence of the rape, she challenges him. In an extraordinary monologue, Philomele moves from "victim" — lost in a semiotic cesspool of confusion and self-blame, asking Tereus for explanation — to a resistor upon realizing that he, not she, is responsible, a discovery elicited by her own series of questions and self-response. Overwrought and in pain, she nonetheless retains her intelligence and stamina, ultimately realizing: "My body bleeding, my spirit ripped open, and I am the cause? No, this cannot be right, why would I cause my own pain?" (sc.15, 49). Charging him unfit for leadership — a tyrant "filled with violence" — she promises to expose him to his subjects, making the theater space double as an imagined town square. Then, there, when she will not stay quiet about his violence and proposes that her sister rule, when she mocks him and imagines a new social order, he cuts out her tongue.

"Myth," Wertenbaker's male chorus offers the audience, "is an unwanted truth reverberating through time" (sc. 8, 31). Myth is also, they explain, "public speech" — what we may recognize, like the Greeks, as civic exchange. *The Love of the Nightingale* engages myth as an act of cultural resistance and political testimony from the margins, opening up ancient stories so that different "unwanted truths" may reverberate. So that we can hear difficult speech — of bodies, taboo topics, oppressed cultures, human need and injustice — to create a social, civic space for rethinking ethics and politics.

Engaging Myths

> Listen. This is the noise of myth. It makes the same sound as shadow. Can you hear it?
> — Eavan Boland, *The Journey* (epigraph to *The Love of the Nightingale*)

The Philomela myth has captivated imaginaries for millennia, influencing works by Ovid (*Metamorphoses*, 8 C.E.), Shakespeare (*Titus Andronicus*, 1594), Sam Shepard (*Silent Tongue*, 1994), and Naomi Iizuka (*Polaroid Stories*, 1997–99), to name a select few. For contemporary female writers, in particular, the haunting myth of incest rape, silencing, tyranny, and revenge resonates strongly. Martha Cutter notes that contemporary American women writers of color, for example, seem to invoke the myth frequently, in novels such as Alice Walker's *The Color Purple* (1982), Toni Morrison's *The Bluest Eye* (1970), and Gloria Naylor's *The Women of Brewster Place* (1983).[29] Post-colonial artists and critics such as Emma Tennant, Graham Huggan, and Elissa Marder, have also found resonance in Philomela's resistance and creative testimony about her abuse — her rising from voiceless/mute to witness/survivor/activist through non-linguistic channels such as song, artwork, or, in Wertenbaker's version, street performance.[30]

One can see Wertenbaker's work with and through myth in this play as a way to engage moral debate and to reflect on both the human condition and current events, a parallel gesture to the ancient Greek tragedies whose forms she explodes and whose chauvinisms she estranges. Bassnet suggests that this return to myth allows Wertenbaker to present particularity and generality simultaneously, and "reinforces the notion of hybridity since myths transcend national boundaries, and become part of a shared inheritance" across cultures and times.[31] *The Love of the Nightingale*'s invocation of traditional cultures, rooted in myth and gendered spheres of experience, layer with its post-colonial poetics — characterized by intercultural dislocations, tropes of exile, and interconnected local and global experiences — to create a multiply situated dramaturgy. Indeed, the play has traveled exceptionally well internationally, performed in myriad Anglophone cultures and translated into languages as different as German and (Egyptian) Arabic.[32]

In correspondence, the playwright advises performers to "go for the reality of it," and not get "lulled by the poetry." "The danger is when people think 'Myth! Greek! Flowing Robes!'...."[33] She voices her wish to see the play performed by an African company — perhaps in part because of the living legacy in Africa of using ancient myths to involve community in urgent moral discussions that feed contemporary theaters of testimony. Furthermore, the playwright cautions against "shy(ing) away from the killing of Itys onstage" because it "unbalances the play and lets the women off." Resisting the celebratory impulse of cultural feminism that assumes superior "feminine" values, she insists that, "(v)iolence is shared equally in the play." Wertenbaker advocates for a complicated social and psychic chain of events that, unlike the scenarios of Greek myth, subject to the whims of gods and fate, are presented as avoidable, if profoundly challenging, at every juncture.

Wertenbaker was not the only Anglophone female theater artist to springboard from parts of Ovid's *Metamorphosis* in recent decades. Naomi Iizuka (*Polaroid Stories,* 1999) and Mary Zimmerman (*Metamorphoses,* 2001), both working in America, developed quite different postmodern plays, which featured a panoply of myths more akin to Ovid's in contrast to *Nightingale*'s relative depth of focus on the Philomela-Procne-Tereus myth.[34] Although Iizuka incorporates the Philomela myth ("Philomel's Story: fucked-up love song"), her metamorphic depiction of contemporary American street culture—a maze of drug-kings and lost souls each told in a snapshot—contrasts with Wertenbaker's approach to challenging political and social abuses head-on. Both plays give voice to the dispossessed in part through alliance with classical figures, and invite audiences to consider the traumas of human relationships amplified through mythic allusion, Iizuka's anchored in the plight of America's homeless youth. However, Iizuka's tone toward the audience seeks creative and human connections in the theater space, modeled by characters' choral self-namings for the audience, offered as a seeming antidote to the traumas that she stages. A comparison of the two works points to how Wertenbaker's intertextual theater of testimony foregrounds dialectical inquiry to expose and, together with audiences, interrogate relationships based on power. Her civic theater interrogates ethics using legal language—charges, queries, evidence, and debate.

Like her haunting "childlike" song that opens *Polaroid Stories* in darkness, Iizuka's Philomele is a cipher, a "fragment of an old song" amid the din of urban blight. Her rape and maiming is only implied by the blood spilling out of her mouth when she opens it to sing. This is a nightmarish image of Innocence Violated, unmoored from any text. She touches the blood and it smears everywhere, then blossoms, techno music building, creating a dreamlike, almost hallucinatory world of sound and image. The gaping mouth mute and then transformed serves as an emblem of the playwright's symbolic poetics. When next she appears, Philomele warbles without a tongue, her sound unintelligible, but "filled with nostalgia and longing," the transcendent image reverberating as hope from pain, yearning from bleakness, alternately enchanting and haunting.

In Wertenbaker's treatment, the psychic and material realities of rape, silencing, and dispossession unfold graphically; we see and hear who enacts it, from Tereus directly, to all who "did nothing" though they recognized the signs, could have warned Philomele or alerted Procne and forged community. Moreover, as Jennifer Wagner points out, "the passivity of each Chorus" in key moments of urgency in the drama is "interestingly particularized according to gender, and a discrimination of their respective behaviors" as male and female communities "lays before us an uncomfortable familiar reflection on the relationship of gender and social power."[35]

Philomele's mutilated mouth, first bloodied by Tereus' silencing of her vocal resistance and years later offered as bodily testimony, signifies Wertenbaker's driving ethics as well as theatrics. Procne's response to her homeless sister when she opens her mouth, muted and scarred, testifies to the veracity of Philomele's speaking body, affirms the violence her activist street theater claims, and reveals the unrelenting dispossession she has suffered even as it facilitates Procne's feminist awakening and search for justice: "Is this what the world looks like? (*Pause*) Justice. Philomele, the justice we learned as children, do you remember? Where is it?" (sc. 18, 58). Furthermore, Philomele's public revelation of her abuse underscores her resistant, feminist subjectivity, earlier evidenced in her bold questions, laughter, argument, and social transgressions.

The Love of the Nightingale also uses myth and epic in the framework of feminist theater practices—such as female-centered stories that incorporate feminist awakenings; denaturalization and parody of received ideologies of representation, gender, and power; emphasis on linguistic, psychological, and social structures that shape gender experiences (both male and female), understood in diversity; performances that move between the frames of the dramatic and social worlds to incite audience participation and moral conscience; thematic focus on body politics and silenced "voice;" and scenic rhythms that place personal and political lives in reciprocal relation — in order to activate a space of epistemological inquiry and feminist critical concern.

Transforming Myths

> We have a choice of how to tell the story. We have a choice of whom to make the hero, how to name the demon, how to chart the journey. And the choice matters more than I can say.
> —Naomi Iizuka, What Myths May Come[36]

Wertenbaker's active and frequently metatheatrical negotiation of source materials creates part of the essential dynamism in performances of her plays and makes a significant contribution to contemporary theater practice. *The Love of the Nightingale*'s self-reflexive mechanisms—mirroring of action and audience members, doubling of scenes from different perspectives, direct address to audience members about both the play and its devices— position theater as a site of social praxis, a space where cultural memories may and must be re-negotiated to imagine more just, diversified, and feminist futures. Tellingly, these meta-theatrical devices emerge in core moments of the play, such as in the (very funny) palace scene when Philomele's family and Tereus watch *Phaedra*, helping us to interrogate, through parody, its politics and the characters' limited critical inquiry; in the rape and mutilation scenes when Niobe stands in for the onstage audience, making us complicit; and in the activist street theater scene when Philomele performs her abuse "in a grotesque and comic way" with hand-made puppets, creating transgressive space with and for the audience structured through a women-centered theatrical circuit of representation. As Geraldine Cousin suggests, this last example is pivotal, situating theater as a prospective forum for the dispossessed; it culminates in the onstage audience of women using the puppets to act out their own experiences of abuse, thereby evoking therapeutic and/or testimonial use of dolls to show, and release, "unspeakable" incest and sexual abuses.

The title of Sophocles' lost play *Tereus* suggests that the Thracian King was its tragic hero. In Rubens' painting *Tereus Confronted with the Head of His Son*, the painter places emphasis on the moment of Tereus' intense loss, his horrified grief as Procne and Philomela present his son's head to him on a platter. In Shakespeare's macabre tragedy *Titus Andronicus*, there is little more for Lavinia, the beautiful victim inspired by Philomela, to do other than die once she reveals her rapists to Titus, for her brutal maiming causes such shame and grief to her father as well as herself; Titus, Shakespeare's protagonist, then pursues the fiends with mad vengeance, performing a vendetta of cruelty and destruction (including feeding the flesh of the violent teens to their mother) to degrade and trump the Goths who conceived such terrors.

In Wertenbaker's play, as the spatial rhythms indicate, Philomele and Procne share centerstage. At the same time, the play's dual narrative structure, following the sisters' individual and divergent scenarios, is de-stabilized by repeated interventions from the male and female choruses as well as Niobe, all of whom speak from both inside and outside the narrative. They shift focus from theatrical to theater space and from onstage action, situated critically and in changing diversity, to audiences in the social world. In this "post-feminist" moment, or rather this period of backlash against feminism, Wertenbaker's theater of female subjectivities, polyphony, dislocations, and global identities remains relevant, both explicitly feminist and impatient with identity politics that over-determine gender: "This (play), you will say, watching Philomele watching Tereus watching Philomele, must be about men and women.... You will be beside the myth," cautions the chorus in scene eight. "If you must think of anything, think of countries, silence, but we cannot rephrase it for you. If we could, why would we trouble to show you the myth?" (sc. 8, 31).

Contrary to its pointers to "think of countries, silences," as well, this play has been read in performance almost exclusively in gendered terms.[37] As Susan Carlson discusses in "Issues of Identity, Nationality and Performance," Wertenbaker's *The Love of the Nightingale* disarmed many male theater reviewers used to the intense "emotionalism" and "phallocentrism" of ancient tragedies; even as they commended its wit, theatricality, and poetic force when the play premiered, they were taken aback by its contemporary references and feminist critiques. One can also detect their discomfort with female voices and/or women's issues engaging at the center of public discourse about human rights and, in effect, politics. In an interview with Wertenbaker, for instance, John L. DiGaetani exposes defensive anger about the play's allying rape and male-to-female violence with "more significant" patterns of social injustice, rejecting the play's presentation of rape as a social issue instead of isolated individual crimes.[38] With time, *The Love of the Nightingale*'s feminist social critiques have gained added authority as waves of recent testimonies emerge from a range of wars in the past century (World War II, Korean War, Balkans Wars, Ugandan Civil War, Argentina's "Dirty War," the Iraqi War) about the use of rape, gendered humiliation, and sexual servitude to humiliate and colonize other cultures; Wertenbaker's civic engagement in local and global registers was prescient and activist, for finally in 2001 rape and sexual slavery became recognized as war crimes, in the wake of ethnic cleansing campaigns in Bosnia.[39] At the same time, the women's murder of Itys resonates with the violence perpetuated by dispossessed communities against innocents, whether enacted by suicide bombers in the Middle East and Europe, terrorist cells in America and South Asia, or resistance movements and individuals across the world who respond to immoral social orders with violence.

In Wertenbaker's version, justice becomes so degraded — "without even the words to ask" — that in the penultimate scene the women cannot imagine a future, asking the audience: "What else was there?" "We can ask: Why did Medea kill her children? Why do countries make war?" (sc. 20, 62). Five years since her rape and maiming, five years dispossessed from Tereus' violence, five years as the King's sexual servant and "caged bird," Philomele kills the boy, Itys, when he rages into the women's community. Instead of the ancient myth's cannibalism after infanticide, Wertenbaker then stages conversation between Tereus and Procne, trying to process the traumatic past and "what love is." Not yet knowing Itys is dead but only that Philomele has found Procne, Tereus explains his infamy as "beyond words" and yet, when pressed, he claims his fair privilege as King and a man who loves his country, complaining that he has pressures and justifying his actions with the delusion that he loved Philomele. Then Procne reveals Itys, murdered while she "did nothing," and she holds Tereus directly responsible for his son's death and his "blood(ying) the future." In horror Tereus rages, and the women's chorus shifts into narrative mode, explaining that in the myth the gods transformed Philomele, Procne, and Tereus into birds.

Wertenbaker practices a different kind of metamorphosis than the myth: she imagines social transformation from a bleak cycle of violence. *The Love of the Nightingale* ends simply, with a child onstage and three birds — often represented by screen projections, sometimes puppets. Aunt and nephew, all their losses restored, consider what has happened in the/ir story. After showing the dangerous alternatives, *The Love of the Nightingale*'s brief coda performs a call to stay engaged with each other, imagining ways to hope and act in the world through inter-relation and inquiry across differences, even in the harshest of times. Although Philomele acknowledges that she doesn't much like being a nightingale, she explains to Itys that a change of perspective, and relationships, was necessary: "We were all so angry the bloodshed would have gone on forever. So it was better to become a nightingale. You see the world differently" (sc. 21, 65). As Carlson, Cousin and David Ian Rabey have observed, scene twenty-one explores how other systems of relation — other models of learning and justice — might emerge out of this cycle of violence.[40] With Philomele's voice restored and Itys resurrected as a live presence, Wertenbaker moves the play and audience away from dramatic pains to consider how we cultivate a moral future. The play's ending aspires to diversified community across genders, generations, and cultures, joined by our asking difficult questions together. The final moment is a beautiful song, at last, as Itys's penultimate question hovers for the audience, invoking a younger generation's query of older and preceding ones: "What is right?"

Notes

1. Quoted by Marina Cantacuzino, "Why Writing Came Second," *Sunday Times* (London), 6 April 1986.
2. Timberlake Wertenbaker, *The Love of the Nightingale* (London and Melbourne: Dramatic Publishing, 1990). As the play's episodic structure-twenty-one short scenes to be performed in a single act-is important to the play, all my references include scene number. Additional references in the text.
3. *The Grace of Mary Traverse* premiered at the Royal Court Theatre, while Wertenbaker was writer in residence there. Dianeira was first broadcast by BBC Radio Three, which has also broadcast Wertenbaker's *Hecuba*. *The Ash Girl* premiered at Birmingham Repertory.
4. Wertenbaker's first wave of production, as an emergent playwright, was tied to smaller theaters, many of which, like the Women's Theatre Group and Shared Experience, were explicitly feminist. While Wertenbaker's "new" works of the nineties-*Three Birds Alighting on A Field* (1992), *The Break of Day* (1995), *After Darwin* (1998)-were all set in an explicitly postcolonial England, rendered in relation to a changing Europe and global economy, all also invoked foundational cultural myths as analogies. Her most recent plays have re-imagined female-centered sources for performance: *The Ash Girl* (2000), *Galileo's Daughter* (2004), and *Jenufa* (2007). Her feminism blends materialist and humanist strands, refuting the celebratory impulses and essentialism of cultural feminism.
5. Joan Scott, "Gender: A Useful Category of Historical Analysis," *Gender and the Politics of History* (New York: Columbia University Press, 1999) 42, 28-52.
6. Susan Carlson, "Issues of Identity, Nationality and Performance: The Reception of Two Plays by Timberlake Wertenbaker," *New Theatre Quarterly* 9.35 (1993): 267, 267-89. Timberlake Wertenbaker, interview with the author, 14 September 2006.
7. In the introduction to her first anthology of plays, Wertenbaker writes that the subjugated Basques' political violence inspired her even more specifically than the prospect of gendered rebellion, explaining that *The Love of the Nightingale* was motivated by "the violence that erupts in societies when they have been silenced for too long. Without language, brutality will triumph" [*Plays One* (London: Faber and Faber, 1996) viii].
8. Timberlake Wertenbaker, personal correspondence, 12 September 2006.
9. Heidi Stephenson and Natasha Langridge, *Rage and Reason: Women Playwrights on Playwriting* (London: Methuen Drama, 1997) 143.

10. See Jay Gipson-King on the play's historiography, discussing how the choruses' fracturing of narrative helps to expose the ideological investments of different acts of telling, or not telling. Forthcoming in Maya Roth and Sara Freeman, eds. *International Dramaturgy: Translations and Transformations in the Theatre of Timberlake Wertenbaker* (Brussels and London: Peter Lang).

11. Ovid, *Metamorphoses*, trans. A.D. Melville (Oxford: Oxford University Press, 1988) 6.587ff and Robert Graves, *The Greek Myths* (London: Penguin, 1993) 166-8.

12. Ovid switches the birds for Philomele and Procne, whereas some ancient versions cast Tereus as a hawk (a predatory bird, a raptor). Wertenbaker follows Graves' pairings.

13. Jennifer Wagner, "Formal Parody and the Metamorphosis of the Audience in Timberlake Wertenbaker's The Love of the Nightingale," *PLL Papers on Language and Literature* 31.3 (1995): 243, 227-54.

14. Joe Winston, "Re-Casting the Phaedra Syndrome: Myth and Morality in *The Love of the Nightingale*," *Modern Drama* 38.4 (1995): 510-19.

15. Not coincidentally, all three of these ancient stories end with mothers killing their sons in some fashion (Phaedra indirectly), surfacing an atavistic cultural fear of women's sexuality, which Wertenbaker rebukes.

16. Alisa Solomon, Re-Dressing the Canon: *Essays on Theatre and Gender* (London and New York: Routledge, 1997) 3.

17. See, for example, Laura Mulvey's influential film theory in "Visual Pleasure and Narrative Cinema," *Screen* 16.3 (1975): 6-18. Key feminist theater theory responses include Elin Diamond, "Mimesis, Mimicry and the True-Real," *Modern Drama* 32 (1989): 58-72 and Jeanne Forte "Focus on the Body: Pain, Praxis and Pleasure in Feminist Performance," *Critical Theory and Performance*, eds. Janelle Reinelt and Joseph R. Roach (Ann Arbor: University of Michigan Press, 1992) 248-61. The dominating male gaze Tereus has enacted (his name means "one who watches," notes Graves) moves offstage, to assure audiences do not join it, just as earlier the play disrupts identification with his scopophilia by having others note its danger-making that desiring gaze an object of inquiry rather than primary conduit of audience identification.

18. See Nehad Selaiha, "Theatre, Women and Violence," rev. of *The Love of the Nightingale*, *Al-Ahram Weekly Online*, dir. Dalia Baisouny, Women & Memory Research Centre, Cairo, Egypt, vol. 379, 28 May–3 June 1998, http://weekly.ahram.org.eg/1998/379/cu1.htm, and Carlson's analysis of the premiere's reception, for example.

19. Alice Rayner articulates the significance of auditory space in the phenomenology of ancient Greek theater in the excellent essay "The Audience: Subjectivity, Community and the Ethics of Listening," *Journal of Dramatic Theory and Criticism* 7.2 (1993): 3–24.

20. Significantly, this staging direction may ease the performer's own violation, for she is not asked to perform the violent subjugation of Philomele physically — rather to perform it audibly, giving her relative performance agency in a scene of rape. The character gains representational force, the performer agency. See Elaine Aston for discussions of feminist staging challenges and strategies explored by British feminist theater artists in dealing with "the male gaze," including when staging violence against women: Elaine Aston, *Feminist Theatre Practice: A Handbook* (London: Routledge, 1999) 56–62.

21. When I saw Georgetown University's production, for instance, I was caught in the visceral echo of hearing other such screams coming from a nearby space (the street, a neighbor's home), feeling I should help in the immediacy of rape or abuse. During the post-show talkback, jointly sponsored by Mask & Bauble Dramatic Society and Take Back the Night, others responded similarly, caught by the creative "realism" of the staging. *The Love of the Nightingale*, dir. Tom Huddleston, Poulton Hall, Georgetown University, 12 November 2004.

22. This representational layering echoes Wertenbaker's staging of Mary Traverse and Mrs. Temptwell commenting onstage about Mr. Manners' offstage rape of Sophie, whose cries we hear in 1.3 of *The Grace of Mary Traverse*. Both Niobe and Mrs. Temptwell display cynicism that challenges audience empathy, exposing social indifference as they double for the audience.

23. To read more about the structuring of gender, space and transnations, see Alison Blunt and Gillian Rose, eds. *Writing Women and Space: Colonial and Post-Colonial Geographies* (New York: Guilford Press, 1994).

24. In a lecture I hosted at Georgetown University, Wertenbaker elaborated on the importance of "uncomfortable" theatrical representations of human nature and society, as exemplified by selected ancient Greek tragedies, Shakespeare, Shaw and Brecht, because their "uncomfortable"-ness provokes audiences to think and question — an ethic incompatible with reviewers working under deadline pressures, she wryly observed. Wertenbaker, "The Importance of Being Uncomfortable," Gonda Theatre, Davis Center, Georgetown University, Washington, D.C., 14 April 2006.

25. In the rape scene, Tereus does invoke his desire, and the rape, as the gods' will when Philomele refuses him, for example; yet the gods' visible absence from the play, Philomele's innocence, and the self-serving manipulation of this tactic become visible as a consequence of its ironic repetition, including by the soldiers who likewise invoke the gods' will on seeing Itys' murder.

26. Wagner 242. Geraldine Cousin, *Women in Dramatic Place and Time: Contemporary Female Characters on Stage* (London: Routledge, 1996) 114–21; Christine Dymkowski, "'The Play's the Thing': The Metatheatre of Timberlake Wertenbaker," *Drama on Drama: Dimensions of Theatricality on the Contemporary British Stage*, ed. Nicole Boireau (New York: St. Martin's Press, 1997) 121–35.

27. In that, the play anticipated forums such as the South African Truth and Reconciliation Commission (started in 1995), which publicly documented the violence and atrocities committed by all parties during apartheid in order to acknowledge and weigh grievances. The Commission hoped that by recognizing atrocities in a public forum, the divided country might move together, across differences, toward reconciliation and re-educate cultural values.

28. Susan Bassnet, "The Politics of Location," *Cambridge Companion to Modern British Women Playwrights*, eds. Elaine Aston and Janelle Reinelt (Cambridge, UK: Cambridge University Press, 2000) 79.

29. Martha Cutter, "Philomela Speaks: Alice Walker's Revisioning of Rape Archetypes in *The Color Purple*," MELUS 25.3/4 (Autumn-Winter 2000): 161–180.

30. Elissa Marder, "Disarticulated Voices: Feminism and Philomela," *Hypatia* 7.2 (1992): 148–66. Also Graham Huggan, "Philomela's Retold Story: Silence, Music and the Post-Colonial Text," *Journal of Commonwealth Literature* 25 (1990): 12–23.

31. Bassnet 78.

32. To read more about the Egyptian translation, see Sara Freeman, "Nightingale on the Nile: An Interview with Dalia Basiouny," in Roth and Freeman, eds., *International Dramaturgy*.

33. Wertenbaker, personal correspondence, 12 September 2006.

34. Please see Andrea J. Nouryeh's article "Mary Zimmerman's *Metamorphoses*: Storytelling Theater as Feminist Process," published in this volume.

35. Wagner 237.

36. Naomi Iizuka, "What Myths May Come: Can We See the Future in the Mirror of Our Storied Past?" *American Theatre* (September 1999): 18.

37. The play's reception betrays familiar critical and audience bias to encountering representations of women's experience as representative of human experience rather than specifically gendered experience — a trend ably documented by the New York State Council on the Arts Report on the Status of Women in Theatre. Suzanne Bennett and Susan Jonas, "Status of Women in Theatre: A Limited Engagement?" NYSCA, 20 January 2002.

38. John L. DiGaetani, "Interview with Timberlake Wertenbaker," *A Search for a Postmodern Theater* (New York: Greenwood Press, 1991) 265–73.

39. See "Sexual Violence," *The New York Times* 24 February 2001, A24. "The conviction this week by the Hague war crimes court of three Bosnian Serbs for rape and sexual enslavement marks the first time an international tribunal has convicted defendants exclusively for sexual violence or prosecuted sexual slavery at all. The decision shows the progress

that women's issues have made in international justice, which used to ignore mass rape, considering it a natural occurrence in war. The tribunal's verdict should also encourage individual nations to treat sexual violence more seriously."

40. David Ian Rabey, "Defining Difference: Timberlake Wertenbaker's Drama of Language, Dispossession and Discovery," *Modern Drama* 33.4 (1990): 518–28.

Mary Zimmerman's Metamorphoses
Storytelling Theater as Feminist Process

ANDREA J. NOURYEH

In an attempt to define feminist theater, Loren Kruger writes: "There is a saying that women have always made spectacles of themselves. However, it has been only recently, and intermittently, that women have made spectacles themselves. On this difference turns the ambiguous identity of feminist theatre."[1] Taking Kruger's notion that feminist theater has an ambiguous identity, we might choose to define a production as representative of feminist theater not only by the play's story and subject matter but also by the manner in which the piece is created or staged. Has the director abandoned an auteur position for a non-hierarchical directorial style that was the hallmark of many early feminist troupes of the 1970s and for some to the present day? Has the production been in some way collectively scripted? Is the play a non-linear, "mosaic," ensemble piece, rejecting traditional realism and inventing new performance contexts?[2] Are the creative artists involved with the production primarily women or at least committed to gender equity? Do the script and performance illuminate socio-economic inequities and socio-political concerns of women and other disenfranchised groups? And does the re-vision of a canonical text resist and subvert pejorative images of women and the fixed construction of gender? Gayle Austin argues that by examining images of women in these works a theatrical production can serve as "a laboratory in which to reconstruct new, non-genderized identities" and, as a result, question the assumptions embedded in these works.[3]

The author/director Mary Zimmerman asserts that her adaptations that reshape classical texts include more women and center more on women, though none of this has been particularly conscious on her part.[4] Where, then, does one place Mary Zimmerman's 1998 adaptation of Ovid's *Metamorphoses*[5] based upon David R. Slavitt's translation along the spectrum of feminist theater if it does not explicitly focus on the gendered nature of Ovid's work or the subjugation of women in particular myths? After examining Zimmerman's script, her essay on strategies of composition, and her electronic correspondences to multiple interviewers in which she shares her intentions and, in the course of these exchanges, comments on her feminism,[6] I do not find the answer to this question readily apparent or perhaps useful to interpreting the production. In fact, her *Metamorphoses* presents a series of tales about love, death, loss, desire, and the problems of greed that are decidedly "humanist" rather than feminist. By Zimmerman's own admission, she states that she is drawn to "material that speaks in a fundamental way about what it is to be a person: to know you are going to die" and to "really smart ideas about loss and change."[7] Her goal is primarily to make beautiful theatrical pieces whose images and verbal messages resonate with her audiences' experiences.

In what ways, then, do we see this expectation — Zimmerman's proclivity to give women center stage, informed by her experience as a woman and a self-proclaimed feminist — take shape in her production? And what significance do these identities have for her interpretation of Ovid's rendering of the myths? Rather than question if Mary Zimmerman's *Metamorphoses* is a feminist play, I choose to ponder the myriad ways in which her adaptation is informed by aspects of feminist aesthetics that have developed and changed over the past three decades and that have been influenced by postmodern theater. Pat Schroeder argues in her defense of critical pluralism that the "variety of available theatrical forms is one of the strengths of the contemporary theatre, and feminists can and should take advantage of this variety."[8]

Although women's struggles for autonomy within an unjust socio-sexual hierarchy do not emerge as a central theme in Zimmerman's play, nor does the social production of gender appear to be exposed through alterations to the source text, Zimmerman's attraction to a work that has at its core the metaphor of perpetual change, fluidity as both a thematic concern and a theatrical strategy, has produced a theater piece that undermines fixed notions of gender and the concept of an immutable identity. Furthermore, the playwright's appropriation of a canonical text, her selections and omissions based, in part, on the representation of women, and the interpolation of female voices and bodies to tell stories that speak to her desire for autonomy and change may be seen as aspects of feminist theatrical strategies that have retained their significance in postmodern theater. As Janet Brown observes in productions of the 1990s, "A new perception of the act of speech itself has emerged ... performance is perceived as a political gesture, not merely a psychological or spiritual one...; it is public and therefore political in nature...; and it operates in circular fashion, reaching backward in time to give speech to silenced forebears, and extending into the future, nurturing the next generation."[9] In this sense, Zimmerman has chosen to "make the personal political" and through an inventive adaptation, given herself a sense of agency. Her representation of women as speaking subjects through words, the body, spectacle, and movement within a re-framing

Felicity Jones as Psyche, with candelabra, approaching the blindfolded figure of Eros, with wings, played by Doug Hara. Mary Zimmerman's *Metamorphoses*, The Second Stage Theatre, New York, 2001. Photographer: Joan Marcus.

of mythical stories expands the notion of authorship as it reshapes the canon. And although Zimmerman retains her position as auteur-director, her approach to developing the performance text is intensely collaborative, open, and respectful of all the talents of her performers and designers, a quality reminiscent of productions developed by early feminist theater groups.

Why Ovid and Why These Stories?

By her own account, Mary Zimmerman acknowledges that her decisions about adapting classical works for the stage often come from books that were formative during her childhood. One such text was Edith Hamilton's *Mythology: Timeless Tales of Gods and Heroes* (1942) with vivid illustrations by Steele Savage whose "pen and ink drawings [were] engraved on [her] heart."[10] It is in this text that we find nearly all of the specific stories that are reenacted in Zimmerman's award winning play *Metamorphoses*. While Zimmerman went directly to Slavitt's translation for her writing and it is certainly a source text which provided several of the play's poetic passages, a comparison of the play's scenes with Hamilton's choices for her anthology of classical mythology leads the critic to see Zimmerman's selections as a personal response to the power of the myths and the artistic images that accompanied them: Hamilton's "Stories of Love and Adventure" include Apuleius's Cupid and Psyche, along with Ovid's versions of Orpheus and Eurydice, Ceyx and Alcyone, and Baucis and Philemon; "The Less Important Myths" include the stories of Midas, Erysichthon, and Pomona and Vertumnus. Zimmerman also includes the story of Phaeton from the section entitled "Four Great Adventures" as well as glimpses into the stories of Pandora from "How the World and Mankind were Created," Atalanta from "The Great Heroes before the Trojan War" and Narcissus from the "Flower-Myths."[11] In Hamilton's *Mythology,* Ovid is pared down to the tales that she wanted to transmit to her young, high-school-aged students in the 1940s and 1950s. Stories of divine caprice, rape, and incest are decidedly absent while tales of lovers, of women — mortals and goddesses— wronged or scorned who took revenge, of heroic and independent women, and of men who learn hard lessons are favored. Thus, a woman teacher with a didactic agenda that eschews the Ovidian stories of lust and violence spoke to and influenced the young Zimmerman whose sense of the Greco–Roman world and its literature was formed by Hamilton's perspective. In this way, Ovid became transformed in the psyches of both his interpreter and her reader, and his stories became theirs. They appropriate the classical text, "becoming in Claudia Herman's phrase, *voluses de langue,* 'women thieves of language' (or of the tongue), taking myths and re-seeing them."[12]

The potency of the myths is clear from Sara Mack's assessment of Ovid as a "masterful story teller with an eye for the kind of detail that brings people alive and creates scenes never to be forgotten."[13] In fact, selections of his poems were performed on stage during his lifetime.[14] It, therefore, makes sense that Zimmerman, a student of performance studies interested in turning non-dramatic work into plays, would be drawn to the drama found in his epic. She states that the stories have proven themselves, that as oral texts they are essentially performance texts, and "when you encounter them on the page they have an inherent, unreleased theatrical element."[15] Thematically, Ovid creates a work that transcends the expected heroic tales of military exploits. His *Metamorphoses* is, according to Galinsky, "a veritable anthology of human conflicts and depiction of the whole range of human nature" by providing stories that treat love and hate, fear, jealousy, desire, shame, pride, recklessness, lust, anger and betrayal.[16] The myths, therefore, provide a myriad of possibilities for creating an adaptation with a contemporary feel. Ovid even presented portraits that appear to be quite modern "case studies of abnormal personalities:"[17] those of neurosis as exemplified by Phaeton, self-love as in Narcissus, compulsive greed as in Erysichthon, and incest as in the story of Myrrha.[18] All of these psychological problems find their way into Zimmerman's play.

While driven by the effect these stories had on her as a girl, Zimmerman is neither a slave to Hamilton's choices, nor to their originals. That she restores the myth of Myrrha who desires her father and tricks him into having sex with her, which Hamilton would never have allowed to surface in her book, is only one indication that the choices of the stories in her play are her own. Excising whole swathes of Ovid's epic, Zimmerman creates her own arrangement of episodes which develop the shape of her play organically. The order that she developed "musically or perhaps rhythmically," follows what she calls "an emotional score" that grew out of experiments with juxtapositions of scenes when she was not certain what scene should follow another.[19]

Giving Space to Female Voices

While she maintains Ovid's narrative device of telling stories within stories, Zimmerman does not feel obliged to deal with his choice of narrators[20] and does not hesitate to assign them to female storytellers. This choice, in effect, expands the space given to women in the *Metamorphoses*. Ovid's representation of gender and sexuality, as interpreted by Alison Sharrock, might further explain the affinity Zimmerman had for *Metamorphoses* as well as her decision to frame her play with female narrators:

> More than any other non-dramatic ancient poetry, male authored as it overwhelmingly is, Ovid's work gives space to a female voice, in however problematic a manner, and to both male and female voices which reflect explicitly on their own gendered identity. It is also driven by a troubled relationship with the purveyors of Roman masculinity — the army, politics, Augustus, epic and so on. Moreover, the poet — par excellence — of the fluidity of identity clearly provokes a gendered reading.[21]

The interpolation of women's voices is foregrounded by the fact that her play begins with lines spoken primarily by two women taken from the first 85 lines of Book I in Slavitt's translation.[22] An unidentified woman kneels by the side of the pool and peers at her reflection before she looks up and addresses the audience. She shares her own concerns with transformation: "Bodies, I have in mind, and how they can change to assume new shapes—I ask the help of the gods, who know the trick: change me, and let me glimpse the secret and speak, better than I know how, of the world's birthing, and the creation of all things, from the first to the very latest."[23] Zimmerman's female performer assumes Ovid's narration, displacing his authority without violating his vision. It is her body we see with the first uttered word, "Bodies," and it is her voice that we hear asking for the story of creation.

Neither the poet nor the gods answer her. Instead a woman scientist continues the story about an earth in chaos, where neither the sun nor the moon shed its light, where there was no differentiation between land and sea, and no order, "until at last a god sparked, glowed, then shone like a beam of light to define earth and the heavens and separate water from hard ground" (6). Her distillation of the Ovidian description of creation summons the god Zeus who appears in the sky lighting a cigarette—that beam of light, perhaps. The great patriarch, although aloft, is hardly godlike, and the anonymous and presumably ordinary woman interrupts his efforts to insinuate himself in the narrative:

> ZEUS: A paradise, it would seem, except one thing was lacking: words.
> WOMAN: And so
> [Midas enters through the doors.]
> WOMAN: man was born.
> [Midas comes forward and steps into the water.]
> WOMAN: He was born that he might talk [6].

Trying again to assert his right to define the world and exercise his power, Zeus challenges her insistence on the power of human speech, the very power that she has wrested from him and has not yet given to Midas who has already entered the stage. He offers: "Some say the god perfected the world, creating of his divine substance the race of humans" (7). He is silenced and not allowed to continue. Instead the woman scientist counters his argument and completes Ovid's worldly thought: "others maintain that we come from the natural order of things" (7).[24] As the scientist continues her narrative role, the anonymous woman disappears and Zeus is, in effect, banished from the stage.

The fluidity of metamorphosis articulated and embodied in the play's first lines is illustrated when the scientist removes her lab coat and transforms from the hierarchical position of a professional with expertise to that of a lowly laundress who, like the other two joining her on stage, begins washing linens in the pool. These three women are the principal storytellers and first contemplate what it would be like to be rich. In response to their focus on the money none of them has, one begins the story of Midas which comes alive before the audience. It is not until she names the anonymous figure we have seen standing in the pool as "a certain King, named Midas. Net worth: one hundred billion" that he is allowed to speak (8). Thus, Zimmerman not only gives the poet's words to women, but she gives these women the power to control who gets to talk as well as what is heard and when. Ovid's masculine narrative is thus interpreted by lower class women whose reasons for telling this tale clearly illustrate the perspective of those whose backbreaking labor makes the rich and luxurious life of wealthy capitalists possible and whose life experiences allow them to reinvent the story's lesson. In the original, when Bacchus grants Midas his wish to have the power to turn all he touches into gold, the king does not realize the folly of this request until his next meal when everything that comes up to his lips or that his fingers touch turns into metal. In the version told by the laundresses, the lesson is more poignant as well as parodic. It reflects the need for intact familial relationships rather than merely the problems of self absorption and greed.

Not only does Zimmerman have the women introduce the story of Midas, but she also uses anachronism, a common postmodern device, to help her redefine the myth in feminist terms. As Amy Green argues, "The interjection of anachronistic references" contributes to the deconstruction of the "formidable edifice of received meaning."[25] The king is now a contemporary corporate executive who wields his economic power with a sense of enlightened authority and thus tries to justify his wealth and to convince his listeners — the audience — that all of his hard work and material goods have been acquired for the family. However, he can't remember this important fact and falters each time he tries to articulate benevolence as his primary objective. In fact, he gets increasingly annoyed with his daughter whose playing distracts him. Yet, he is stricken with guilt and grief when she jumps into his arms and is turned into an inanimate, golden statue. His search for the river that will remove this curse and restore his daughter's humanity becomes his discovery of his love for his child and a shift in his priorities. Zimmerman's laundresses tell this contemporary version of the myth that effectively illustrates the fluidity of identity that Sharrock claims is endemic to Ovid's epic. In her discussion of the unstable gender categories related to Roman sexuality and masculinity, Sharrock notes: "A man, to be a man, must be *durus* (hard), but love (for which he needs to be *durus*) will make him *mollis* (soft)."[26] In Zimmerman's scenario, in order for Midas to become healed and whole in his own eyes, he must move from being *durus* (hard) to loving — impenetrable and in control — to a love that will make him *mollis* (soft) and a better father.

Another example of Zimmerman's use of anachronism and family drama is found in the staging of Phaeton's story of seeking the truth of his paternity and discovering that he is the son of Apollo the Sun God, his exalted, yet distant father. This is a story of a troubled youth whose lack of a father figure cripples his maturing process and whose adolescent folly and proud demand to take his father's place as the driver of the Sun chariot, a feat for which he is unprepared, lead to destruction. This myth resembles a Jungian dream told to a therapist where Phaeton's neurosis can lead him to grave consequences— he is an example of a youngster who will not survive parental neglect intact. Here again, the expert scientist, the therapist, is a woman, and her analysis and interpretation of the boy's "dream" at the end of the session derives from the work of Joseph Campbell, Carl Jung and Sigmund Freud. She articulates the playwright's sense that myths are "the earliest forms of science" (67). Thus Zimmerman not only alters the received meaning of the myth but also gives a woman the responsibility for explaining its significance as a cautionary tale about parent/child relationships to her audience.

In her staging of the tale of Orpheus and Eurydice, Zimmerman uses the fluidity of Ovid's storytelling strategy to render a female character's subjectivity. Rather than merely have a male actor narrate the Ovidian tale which focuses on Orpheus' mourning, his powerful attempt to reclaim his love, and his fatal uncertainty that Eurydice is, in fact, following him, Zimmerman repeats it— staging it a second time— using Rilke's version told from Eurydice's perspective and narrated by a woman. Eurydice, the object of Orpheus' desire, is now so fulfilled with death that she is "deep within herself," unable to see that the man in front of her is her husband and that the path on which she walks is her ascendance to life (46).[27] In having a woman retell the tale giving Eurydice agency, the story becomes much more than a tribute to the power of the musician Orpheus and his song, despite his inability to ignore the God's admonition that he not look back.[28] We hear Eurydice's voice. It becomes equally compelling and provides a sense that she remains, even in death, her own person capable of speaking her own desire.

Transforming the Self through Crafting the Play

Clearly, Zimmerman found stories that reflect her own thoughts and experiences in the poet's focus on the power and autonomy of the goddesses and the desires of mortal women to choose their own lovers or a path to independence where their spirituality transcends their physical desires. In addition, the lessons about change, about love lost, about moving on and being transformed by the loss contained in the myths spoke directly to Zimmerman's life experiences at the moment she began working on the piece. She had lived with someone from the time she was twenty years of age and then, after seventeen years, he left her. She related that the emotional upheaval was devastating and "change felt so soul destroying and ... I was so frightened of what was going to come. And I couldn't sort of stand the state I was in; I wanted to be through it ...

through the moment of metamorphosis [which] is so excruciating but then it can produce something new."[29] This personal crisis in her life became the creative engine for her play and explains why the playwright was drawn to stories and language that often center on the transformation that occurs when one finds or loses love — of a parent, of a lover, of a child, of one's self.

It is as if the development and writing of *Metamorphoses* became the vehicle through which Zimmerman, herself, came through to the other side of her pain and was, thus, changed and reborn. There are a number of tales in which we see rebirth manifested. In Myrrha's prayer to the gods after she runs from her father's horror at her tricking him into an incestuous relationship, "change me, make me something else, transform me entirely; let me step out of my own heart," one can read Zimmerman's prayer about her own sense of loss at the time and her need to escape the prison of an immutable self (60).[30] In the story of Alcyone and Ceyx,[31] a couple who have lived in "a monotony of happiness,"[32] but are separated when Ceyx is drowned at sea, one might find Zimmerman's discovery about why her own relationship faltered. In death, the couple is reunited but as kingfishers. Every year, there are seven days of calm upon the ocean — the halcyon days — when these two seabirds who have mated and reared their young can tend to a new nest on the gentle water. The playwright reflects that the couple had been too interdependent, too lost in each other, "not individuated enough"; but as birds they became a team where they are freer to drift apart and come back together and therefore have a more mature relationship.[33]

In the story of Vertumnus and Pomona, Zimmerman explores the nature of love and transformation at the heart of her play. Fearing that Pomona will not return his affection, the shy Vertumnus disguises himself multiple times and makes no impression upon her. He even dresses up as an old woman who speaks on his behalf, admonishes her for ignoring Aphrodite, and attempts to warn her about the folly of her actions with the sad story of Myrrha who is cursed with an unquenchable physical desire for her father because she refused to fall in love and thus spurned the powers of the goddess. While none of these ruses work, Pomona tells him to take off the disguise. It is the narrator who assures the audience that "When at last the god revealed himself just as he was, much to his surprise, he had no need of words. Little Pomona was happy with what she saw, unadorned and undisguised" (62). What Zimmerman shows in this tale is her own transformation from despair about lost love to hope for finding love again. Her lesson is that in order to love and to be loved in return, we have to remove our disguises and our defenses and have faith that the qualities that we possess are loveable enough.

The final two tales in Zimmerman's play become healing rituals in contrast to Ovid's concluding paean to the wondrous leadership of Caesar and Augustus. The myth of Eros (love) and Psyche (the soul), found in Hamilton but not in Ovid, is beautiful yet elusive. In her effort to uncover the message of this story she found so compelling, Zimmerman admits to "stealing wholehandedly" from an essay about Eros by Jungian James Hillman in his collection *A Blue Fire*.[34] In this myth Psyche fails to trust in her feelings about the blindfolded husband whose face she has never seen and thus injures him and drives him away. His mother Aphrodite, jealous of the girl's exquisite beauty and angered when she realizes that her son had wedded Psyche rather than make her fall in love with a monster as he had been commanded, compels the girl to undergo innumerable impossible tasks as punishment. His love and her persistence in the face of adversity convince Zeus to intervene and unite the lovers despite Aphrodite's wishes. Although it is never clear why the myth centers around the notion that the soul can never be allowed to look upon love, Zimmerman ponders what it means for the soul to find love blindly: "I just have faith that if you allow yourself to be trusting, to sort of forget about your past hurts, your past wounds, that's the chance at which you will find love."[35] Her method of telling the story through a series of questions and answers allows the myth to maintain its mystery, deferring any fixed meaning of love while conveying a message of hope in the quest to all those who have loved and lost:

> A: The soul wanders in the dark, until it finds love.
> And so, wherever our love goes, there we find our soul.
> Q: It always happens?
> A: If we're lucky. And if we let ourselves be blind.
> Q: Instead of watching out?
> A: Instead of always watching out [76–77].

This penultimate story in her play sets the tone for the final tale of healing: that of Baucis and Philemon who are extremely generous to the deities Hermes and Zeus who visit them disguised as destitute beggars. Though far poorer than those who unknowingly have turned the gods away with nothing, this older man and wife treat these strangers like honored guests and share their meager meal. The gods reward them not only with riches, but grant them their wish that they die at an old age, together. Their goodness and their love become the play's final redemptive moment in which we hear their prayer — "let me die the moment my love dies; let me not outlive my own capacity to love; let me die still loving, and so, never die" — a desire which all in her audiences share (83). In fact, in the final moments of the play, she brings the audience full circle to the laundress's story of Midas. He has at last found the river, washes himself clean of the curse, and is reunited in an embrace with his daughter who has returned to life.

The message at the heart of Zimmerman's text, love that hurts is also that which cures and restores, significantly transforms Ovid's poem and results from what its feminist creator insists "is undoubtedly the unconscious and conscious impulses of my own personality in dialogue with the original text: how I read its story, how I can best give that story a body, what I am drawn to, what I feel is beautiful, what formal consideration I value, what I am obsessed with. In other words, my own taste."[36] Begun as "Six Myths," the original production was announced for the season at Northwestern University in 1996, but Louise Lamson remembers that Zimmerman had not yet selected which six myths she would include: "She ended up picking six that focused on the transformative power of love and then during the rehearsal process wanted to add one more — Baucis and Philomen — and that became the coda of the show."[37] When the show was done professionally, Eros and Psyche was added to the original seven, and Zimmerman used mere glimpses of other myths — Atalanta running around the stage, Narcissus looking at himself in the water, and Pandora opening up the box — as transitional moments that helped move the play fluidly when an actor needed time for a costume change or a member of the cast needed to get from one side of the stage to another.[38] These glimpses also foreground Zimmerman's choices — what has been expanded and what has been glossed over as they allude to Ovid's more expansive text.

The pool of water as a setting is both a metaphor and a physical site of change and mutability. As she explains, "water is an ancient and cross-cultural symbol of transfiguration. It is an element that transforms almost anything left in it too long, and is itself subject to change: it can easily freeze into a solid or evaporate as steam."[39] The pool transforms into the river bank where laundresses wash clothes, the pond where Narcissus sees his reflection, the pool on Midas's property, and the stormy ocean in which Ceyx drowns. This use of water is further augmented by its capacity for evoking visual metaphors of emotions and physical states — despondency, grief, drunkenness, rapacious appetites, and sensual pleasure. In searching for unique ways to use the pool, she discovered that she could stage the myth of Phaeton as if he were a teenager lying on a therapist's couch floating on an inflated raft. The scene that resulted from rehearsal has the actor stretched out on the raft with the therapist sitting poolside taking notes as he relates what had happened when he went to confront his father. She also found that the pool could be the very object of Erysichthon's insatiable hunger as well as serve to become the place of his mother's captivity and rescue when he sells her into slavery for coins to buy him the endless supply of food he is driven to desire. "The fact of the water changed the original stories: an angry father tries to drown his daughter rather than strangle her; a woman sleeps by the edge of the sea instead of in her bed as she awaits the return of her husband; in her grief a girl literally dissolves into tears instead of turning into a bush."[40] It not only becomes the realm of Hades from which Eurydice begins to ascend, it becomes the incestuous bed of Myrrha and her unwitting father where the sounds of the water help create the tension between its sensuality and the transgression depicted in it. With this scenic device Zimmerman truly reinvents the way an audience understands the central themes of her source text.

The play's movement from tale to tale and from stories narrated to those embedded within them allows Zimmerman to keep the spirit of her source text while it echoes a strand of feminist aesthetics. With its multiple climaxes and its cyclical frame, her script rises and falls in waves, or ripples, like the surface of the water in the pool around and in which the action takes place. At the same time, this non-linear structure follows a fluid and meandering quality that Ovid himself used in weaving the threads that create the fabric of his poem. Zimmerman's *Metamorphoses* pays homage to as well as revises Ovid's stories of transformation through her choice and arrangement of narrative and scenic elements. It becomes a reworking of Ovid's stories and words as forged through the crucible of Zimmerman's sensibilities, her emotions and experiences, as well as her directorial eye. Both its structure and visible trope of transformation are invitations to creative artists and their audiences to imagine other *Metamorphoses* that will no doubt challenge and unsettle the canon, redefine its limits and yet allow them to draw upon it for inspiration.

Zimmerman's Collaborative Process

Although theater by its very nature is a collaborative art form, it is feminist theater that has worked most consistently toward eschewing the hierarchical structures of mainstream theater where, as Michelene Wandor wrote, "writers are temperamental flowers, actors are intellectual zombies, and directors are martinets."[41] While some companies worked toward creating theater pieces using a democratic and collective decision making process, others found that they could best achieve their artistic goals by relying on a process that was collaborative but emphasized the skills specific to each of the company's members. Where Zimmerman fits within this continuum is somewhat difficult to ascertain, particularly since she is both the writer and the director of her pieces. Yet, when examining her process and listening to her actors and designers speak about how scripts are written and staged, it becomes clear that Zimmerman's method of working depends upon all of the skills as well as the creative impulses of her cast and production team.

Adapting large non-dramatic texts that are episodic in nature is Zimmerman's artistic signature as a writer/director. For these plays, she must make choices as to what parts of the source text — what episodes or stories — she will stage, not unlike a screenwriter determining what aspects of the narrative of a novel will be transformed into the screenplay. Obsessed quite often with these books since childhood, she begins with an image which these stories have evoked in her, "the spark that ignites the creative process."[42] While the starting impulse may begin with an extremely personal response to the source texts, she reveals that her choice of materials is often derived from discoveries that surface in the pre-rehearsal discussions and rehearsal process. She likens this to an archeological dig: "...the piece is made and shaped by the digging itself: it is both unpredictable and utterly preordained. It is made by who we are, who we are together, the circumstances of production, and the conditions of the world as they exist and change throughout our rehearsal process. We can't know what the piece will become, but it is inescapable."[43]

Certainly the creative impulses for these plays are Zimmerman's, yet her design team is crucial for a script to manifest itself. What makes her method of writing unique is the fact that she writes her plays during the course of the rehearsal period while she is in production. Preparation before rehearsal has little to do with setting the dialogue and characters; instead it consists of lengthy discussions with her designers who read the original text that will be adapted and then talk with her about what draws her to the text, what parts of the text she will probably be using, why she wants to do this adaptation now, and perhaps what preliminary visual ideas she has for it. Once the set design is determined, it helps generate the script of the play: "The original story is the mother of the set, but the script of that story is in part the child of the design."[44]

In the case of *Metamorphoses*, she wanted to stage the myths in water, the basis for Greco-Roman maritime culture that depended upon the sea for commerce, travel, and as a food source; is a purifying and corrupting element; and is the source of and agent of transformation. The pool of water and its deck, designed by Daniel Ostling, had to be as flexible as a level, open stage floor to represent multiple locations, allow a great deal of physical movement, and yet not overwhelm the actors—"It must have, or be, a character, but a character that is pliable and modest, able almost to disappear. Most of all it must contain things for which I don't as yet have any use, but for which the cast eventually will. It must dare me to find a way to exploit all of its talents and possibilities."[45] Since the first two and a half weeks of rehearsal had to be conducted on dry land until the set was built and the cast could be in the pool, it was essential that her designers were continuing presences as each scene developed.

Her organic and integrated writing and directing process allows for arresting images to be found collaboratively. One such example is the banquet that Baucis and Philemon prepare for their guests, the disguised Zeus and Hercules. The designer helped Zimmerman arrive at the use of illuminated candles in wooden bowls to become the plates of food that the peasants serve. In performance, these float on the pool's surface as if on top of a huge table. The entire space is transformed from the poor simple cottage to a "glittering marble-columned temple" with its gold roof and carved gates (82). As the audience is invited by the narrator to contemplate walking down the street at night alone and hear Baucis and Philemon's prayer stirring in the branches of trees above them, the stage picture becomes a kind of mirror-image of a starry sky, the canopy of night reflected in the water, before the company blows out the candles and thus ends the play. With this final moment, the four elements of life for the classical world—fire, water, land and air—are brought together into the production.[46]

Zimmerman's actors also are collaborators in the shaping process of the text and the production. They must have a multiplicity of skills, an ability to fill out her ensemble and a willingness to play whatever roles come up in the as-yet-unwritten script that will be written, if you will, on their bodies. "Who I cast may well end up determining which of the hundreds of potential roles in the original text will end up on stage."[47] Her openness to possibilities embedded within the source text without preconceived notions about the specific scenes and specific actors to play the roles prior to rehearsal is unusual. It asks the performers to trust her implicitly, while permitting her to tailor the play to her cast members' movement capabilities and their interactions with each other. After initial discussions with her cast about the text, she might ask them to do some physical improvisations that allow her to see whether what the text has evoked in her imagination is possible. They discover how to create these images. The next day she brings in bits of textual material for the cast to work on and starts the process of assigning roles. Each night after rehearsals, she writes more text and casts the new episodes and scenes in her head, "the most agonizing part of devising" for her[48] and what she terms "a huge chess game."[49] She stays merely one step ahead of the cast each day, building on the work of the previous day's rehearsal and the discoveries that were made. "Bit by bit, day by day, the text and images are built together.... Each day's rehearsal makes the next day's. As [they] go along, more and more decisions are made, fewer and fewer options are available."[50]

Working on a play composed in this collaborative manner allows emotional and physical solutions for the actors to surface as they discover ways of realizing Zimmerman's emerging script and answer questions about how to tell the story, what makes the story compelling, what central idea of the story emerges and what makes it so moving or funny. The work uncovers something much larger than the director, the designers and the performers: "It takes over ... it arrives in the room. Everyone feels it."[51] The rehearsal environment is playful and creative; it fosters an ensemble of trust and a feeling of safety despite the fact neither the director nor the cast know where the show is going from day to day.[52] While she might be extremely directive and offer definitive ideas about how she wants a scene played, there are times when Zimmerman takes the explorations found through improvisation and distills them, finds the clarity within the physical and vocal skills that they have and bring to rehearsal, and crafts her piece with their talents foremost on her mind.[53] One might say that her actors are her most important artistic materials, and that her designers provide her with the canvas for her text. Thus all of her collaborators bring gesture, lighting, costumes, and sound that help build the layers of texture and color for the piece that are determined as she applies the "paint" of words and storytelling to it.

Conclusion

At the end of his epic, Ovid wrote of his own immortality in the poems he had created:

> And now is my poem finished, which not even Jupiter's rage, or fire and sword, or even the greedy gnawings of age shall ever undo. I await my death at some random hour, but all it can take is my body. Over this, it shall have no power. My work, my fame, will continue, ascending as high as the sky, and among the stars the name of Ovid shall never die but twinkle on forever — wherever the eagle has spread its wings and as long as the Latin language is written and read. If the words of poets have any truth or worth they give this hope to me, who wrote them — that I shall become them, and live.[54]

While the Latin of the poet is no longer written, it is certainly still read two millennia later and its myths continue to haunt us. Ovid's work has lived on, as he predicted, but is now remade by Mary Zimmerman to fit our times. Unlike Ovid, Zimmerman does not claim immortality for her vision or complete authority over her text. Rather, her adaptation of these classic tales encourages collaboration between herself and other theater artists as well as audiences to pry open the text for perpetual transformation, echoing the stories connected by this theme. This open-ended approach to composition is consistent with postmodern theatrical strategies, but also resonates with the feminist aesthetics developed in experimental theater companies of the 1970s.

The story that the playwright/director tells by creating a collage of tales from Ovid's *Metamorphoses* and the narratives derived from other authors significantly alters the canonical work to reflect a feminist as well as humanist sensibility. Her play avoids tales that look at women's use value, at the traffic in women — specifically their exchange from father to husband — or as objects of subjection and rape and thus reshapes the source text it adapts.[55] Women are the story tellers, women often initiate the scenes, and women provide as much, if not more, analysis of the actions throughout the narrative than men. By staging her own emotional and psychological connection to the stories of this canonical work, Zimmerman shares what she believes is important to know about the world and communicates this personal view to her audiences. In so doing, she has created a re-visioning of Ovid for the stage that is informed by her feminism, where myth is not bound by gender and has the power to transform.[56]

Notes

1. Loren Kruger, "The Dis-play's the Thing: Gender and Public Sphere in Contemporary British Theatre," *Theatre Journal* 42.1 (March 1990): 27.
2. Patricia R. Schroeder, "American Drama, Feminist Discourse and Dramatic Form: A Defense of Critical Pluralism," *Theatre and Feminist Aesthetics,* ed. Karen Laughlin and

Catherine Schuler (Madison, NJ: Fairleigh Dickinson University Press, 1995) 75. Dinah Leavitt, in her work *Feminist Theatre Groups,* lists the following qualities used to describe feminist drama in the 1970s that seemed to have " rejected traditional 'male' forms, which are built on a hierarchical dramatic structure: plotless, circular rather than linear, layered, poetic, choral, lyric, primal, ritualistic, multi-climactic, surreal, mosaic or collage-like, and non-realistic." She also argues that "no other experimental/political theatre has so extensively relied on collective playwriting" (Jefferson, NC: McFarland 1980) 98, 101.

3. Gayle Austin, *Feminist Theories for Dramatic Criticism* (Ann Arbor: University of Michigan Press, 1990) 19.

4. Mary Zimmerman, e-mail correspondence, 28 July 2006. (Zimmerman accumulates her e-mail correspondence with students and scholars and shares their questions and her responses with others.)

5. The world premiere of *Metamorphoses* was produced by Lookingglass Theatre Company, Chicago, October 25, 1998, at the Ivanhoe Theatre; The New York City premiere was by the Second Stage Theatre, September 2001; The Broadway production opened at Circle in the Square, New York, March 4, 2002. *Metamorphoses* received the Drama Desk and Lucille Lortel Awards for Best Play.

6. Zimmerman, e-mail correspondence. Zimmerman sees herself as a feminist, one who, in her own words, in college "was a lie-awake-at-night feminist" and who has been a feminist all of her life.

7. Ibid.

8. Schroeder 79.

9. Janet Brown, "Feminist Theory and Contemporary Drama," *The Cambridge Companion to American Women Playwrights,* ed. Brenda Murphy (New York: Cambridge University Press, 1999) 157.

10. Bill Moyers, "Transcript: Bill Moyers Interviews Mary Zimmerman," *Public Broadcasting Station: Arts and Culture,* 22 March 2002 <http://www.pbs.org/now/transcript/transcript_zimmerman.html>.

11. Edith Hamilton, *Mythology: Timeless Tales of Gods and Heroes* (Boston: Little, Brown & Company, 1942) vii–ix.

12. Quoted in Amy Richlin, "Reading Ovid's Rapes," *Pornography and Representation in Greece and Rome,* ed. Amy Richlin (New York: Oxford University Press, 1992) 161.

13. Sara Mack, *Ovid* (New Haven, CT: Yale University Press, 1988) 28.

14. Ibid, 1.

15. Zimmerman, e-mail correspondence.

16. Karl G. Galinsky, *Ovid's Metamorphosis* (Berkeley: University of California Press, 1975) 45.

17. Mack 1–3.

18. Phaeton, the son of mortal woman Clymene and Apollo the Sun god, insisted on driving his father's chariot into the heavens. When he lost control and the horses went wild, nearly destroying the Earth, Jove threw a thunderbolt and destroyed him. Erysichthon, having cut down a tree sacred to Ceres, incurs the goddess's wrath; she curses him with the presence of Famine from whom he develops an insatiable appetite. He is driven first to sell off his daughter (his mother in Zimmerman's version) multiple times and then devours himself. Myrrha, refusing all suitors, tricks her father with the help of her nurse into several sexual encounters. When he discovers her identity, he comes after her with a sword. Escaping his wrath, she prays to the gods and is transformed into a bush.

19. Zimmerman, e-mail correspondence.

20. For example, Ovid has Orpheus relate the tale of Myrrha and Vertumnis tell Pomona the tale of Iphis, the female raised as a male and rescued from her lesbian love of Anatarete when Isis transforms her into a man. Zimmerman drops the story of Iphis, focuses on Orpheus' tragic loss of Eurydice, and gives Vertumnis the tale of Myrrha as a way to teach Pomona a lesson about spurning love. In this way she prevents the story of Myrrha from diluting the pain of loss that Orpheus experiences and allows her, instead, to concentrate on juxtaposing his sense of the ascent from Hades and his fatal looking back with Eurydice's desire

to remain in the realm of the dead. Yet, by substituting the Iphis tale with that of Myrrha, Zimmerman is able to use the impact of a tale of a young woman's forbidden heterosexual but incestuous desire for her father and the consequential rejection of all potential suitable mates as an appropriate cautionary tale for Vertumnis to use in trying to win Pomona's affections.

21. Alison Sharrock, "Gender and Sexuality," *Cambridge Companion to Ovid* (Cambridge, UK: Cambridge University Press, 2002) 95.

22. David Slavitt, trans., *The Metamorphoses of Ovid* (Baltimore: Johns Hopkins University Press, 1994) 1–3.

23. Slavitt 1; Mary Zimmerman, *Metamorphoses: A Play* (Evanston: Northwestern University Press, 2002) 5. Additional references in the text.

24. Slavitt 3.

25. Amy Green, *The Revisionist Stage* (Cambridge, UK, New York: Cambridge University Press, 1994) 3.

26. Sharrock 97.

27. The Rilke portion of "Orpheus and Eurydice" is from Stephen Mitchell's translation of Rainer Maria Rilke's "Orpheus. Euridyce. Hermes," in *The Selected Poetry of Rainer Maria Rilke* (New York: Random House, 1987). It is interesting to note that, in this case, a member of the cast suggested the Rilke poem, which Zimmerman did not know. By incorporating this suggestion she was able to "blend voices ... look at something one way and then another" (Zimmerman, e-mail correspondence).

28. Note that Sarah Ruhl has taken up this same theme in her play *Eurydice*, reviewed by Charles Isherwood in *The New York Times* 3 October 2006 and 19 June 2007. In 2006, Isherwood observed that the "mixture of visual allure, playfulness and emotional clarity recalls" Zimmerman's *Metamorphoses*.

29. Moyers.

30. Ibid.

31. Very much in love, Ceyx, the king of Thessaly, and his wife Alcyone are separated only when he goes off by sea to consult an oracle. He dies in a storm but his body returns to shore where she finds him. They are transformed into birds and are thus reunited.

32. Moyers.

33. Ibid.

34. Zimmerman, e-mail correspondence. See James Hillman, *A Blue Fire: Selected Writings* (New York: Harper & Row, 1989).

35. Moyers.

36. Mary Zimmerman, "The Archaeology of Performance," *Theatre Topics* 15.1 (2005): 25–26.

37. Louise Lamson, e-mail correspondence, 16 July 2006.

38. Lamson, e-mail correspondence; Daniel Ostling, personal interview, August 2006, New York City.

39. Zimmerman, "The Archaeology of Performance," 27.

40. Ibid.

41. Quoted in Elaine Aston, *Feminist Theatre Practice: A Handbook* (New York: Routledge, 1999) 29.

42. Zimmerman, e-mail correspondence.

43. Zimmerman, "The Archaeology of Performance," 25.

44. Ibid., 27.

45. Ibid.

46. Ostling, personal interview.

47. Zimmerman, "The Archaeology of Performance," 32.

48. Ibid.

49. Jonathan Arbarbanel, "Stage Persona: Mary Zimmerman," *PerformInk: Chicago's Entertainment Trade Paper* <http://www.performink.com/archives/stagepersonnae/2000/Zimmerman>.

50. Zimmerman, e-mail correspondence.

51. Ibid.
52. Lamson, e-mail correspondence.
53. David Catlin, personal interview, August 2006.
54. Slavitt 330–331.
55. She had intended to include the myth of "Leda and the Swan" but she couldn't find a place for it in the play's structure or the ideas for staging it were not feasible (Zimmerman, e-mail correspondence). If it had been staged, I certainly could not have made this claim. What it illustrates, however, is that Zimmerman works organically on her play in rehearsal using a very personal response to the images and the narratives rather than from a desire to send her audiences a fixed message about her source text.
56. Moyers.

The Political Is Personal
Feminism, Democracy and Antigone Project

CAROL MARTIN

Now we may weep, indeed.
Now, if ever, we may cry
In bitter grief against our fate.
Our heritage still unappeased.
In other days we stood up under it,
Endured it for his sake,
The unrelenting horror. Now the finish
Comes, and we know only
In all that we have seen and done
Bewildering mystery.

— Sophocles' *Antigone*[1]

Antigone Project (2004)[2] is the collaboration of five playwrights each creating a one-act version of Sophocles' *Antigone*. The plays in the project, first conceived and developed by the theatre company Crossing Jamaica Avenue in collaboration with Chiori Miyagawa and Sabrina Peck, situate Antigone in vastly different contexts: a beach, the U.S. during World War I, an archive, an African village, and the underworld. *Hang Ten* by Karen Hartman, *Medallion* by Tanya Barfield, *Antigone Arkhe* by Caridad Svich, *A Stone's Throw* by Lynn Nottage, and *Red Again* by Chiori Miyagawa all squarely favor Antigone's point of view or at least what feminist theatre practitioners have interpreted as Antigone's point of view: Antigone acts in the public sphere in ways that today seem ethical and heroic. Antigone's willingness to act upon her beliefs makes her an archetype of secular individualism, a paradoxical position in relation to Sophocles' *Antigone* because in his play Antigone's beliefs and actions privilege religion over government. As a woman, Antigone represents the voice of the oppressed of which "woman" is an unchallenged archetype.

Joey Collins as General Carlton and April Yvette Thompson as Antoinette Thebes in *Medallion* by Tanya Barfield, directed by Dana Iris Harrel at Women's Project and Productions, New York, autumn, 2004, as part of *Antigone Project*. Photographer: T. Charles Erickson.

Sophocles' Antigone *and* The Antigone Project

Sophocles' *Antigone* is a foundational Western text that pits Antigone, a young virgin woman, and Creon, a new king, against one another. Although not part of an extant trilogy like the *Oresteia*, the story of Antigone is part of a much larger narrative that begins well before the events portrayed in the short time period of the play. In brief, Sophocles' Antigone presents the conclusion to the fall of the House of Labdacus, the original patriarch of the Oedipal clan.[3] The play "completes" the Oedipus story by following the curse into the next generation. Oedipus has unwittingly killed his father, King Laius, and married his mother, and in assuming the throne in Thebes he has disgraced the community he intended to redeem. His exile and the events that ensue comprise the Antigone narrative. Antigone is famously faithful to her father Oedipus and her brother Polyneices; she defies her uncle and king, Creon (successor to Oedipus), on account of his refusal to allow the burial of Polyneices whom Creon, with good reason, considers an enemy of the state. Of course this part of the story is also complex. Polyneices wars against Thebes because his brother, Eteocles, has denied him his fair share of the kingship. The curse upon the family that Laius will die at the hand of his own son extends to the next generation where, in a double murder, Eteocles and Polyneices each die at the hand of the other.

The braided knot of the relationship between Antigone and Creon includes the individual strands of male and female, uncle and niece, sister and brother, daughter and father, state and religion, obedience and freedom, fate and self-determination, and passive compliance and active moral consciousness. As head of state and as Antigone's uncle, Creon's dual patriarchal position makes him demand of Antigone obedience in the form of passive compliance to his laws. As a virgin niece, Antigone upholds her religious duty to bury her brother by invoking the freedom to follow her conscience and the laws of religious practice.

Feminist readings of *Antigone* center on her willingness to act, to reject passivity even as a strategy for survival, and to assert her own point of view even at the risk of her own life as her beliefs privilege religion over the state.

> For me it was not Zeus who made that order,
> Nor did Justice who lives with the gods below
> mark out such laws to hold among mankind.
> Nor did I think your orders were too strong
> That you, a mortal man, could over-run
> the gods' unwritten and unfailing laws.[4]

Antigone chooses to obey the gods' laws as the higher order no matter the consequences. She also fears the gods' punishment were she not to follow their laws. Revisions of *Antigone* typically situate her consciously electing to die in order to do what is ethically right in honoring her brother, have a voice in the history of events, and to take a stand for social justice. This is the way in which we (many readers in the U.S.) tend to understand Sophocles' *Antigone* today.[5]

All of this is recontextualized in *Antigone Project*. Antigone's plight and her determination are resituated from the polis in ancient Greece to women in the third world and other sites, and address the mechanisms of history, the future, civil rights, individual freedom, and national security. All of the plays cast Antigone as the female moral and ethical protagonist of the play and Creon or the world he represents as the rigid, power hungry antagonist. The mission of the Women's Project underscored this perspective and the company's historical association with feminism in producing female playwrights. When in 2004 she became artistic director of the Women's Project, Loretta Greco wrote:

> I do believe the Women's Project has a very particular point of view, which is informed by our mission of developing and producing women artists, in addition to the unique themes that intrigue us and the unique way we create work. The Women's Project [founded in 1978 by Julia Miles] aims to honor its rich legacy by investigating the female artists who came before us, by celebrating the legends among us, and by mentoring a new breed of women artists and delivering them to the front line where they will continue the vital tradition of telling stories and revealing voices that would otherwise remain unheard.[6]

Greco's statement is a politically informed strategic understanding of female theatre artists. The plays that comprise *Antigone Project* resurrect the legend and align the story with the political landscape of the early twenty-first century.

Other Readings of Sophocles' Antigone

The significance of Antigone's gender for opposing the state's entrenched patriarchy has not always been interpreted as 21st century Western readers might think. Even within the field of classic studies, as Helene Foley points out, there are diametrically opposed readings of how audiences in ancient Greece may have viewed *Antigone* in its original context.[7] Christiane Sourvinour-Inwood, for example, argues that when one takes Attic ideology into consideration, Antigone is a "bad woman" who we first meet outside the house (not the proper place for women) and in the dark planning to defy the law of the king and undermine the unity of the polis. In this reading, Creon's actions exemplify the way men were supposed to control women and sons.[8] On the other hand, drawing evidence from Greek funerary topoi, Larry Bennett and Blake Tyrrell point out that "Antigone's actions exactly parallel those in the funerary topos..." and that from this perspective "Antigone's actions are noble as she sacrifices herself for her brother — just as warriors sacrifice their lives for the city and its causes — whereas Creon is simply impious for exposing the corpse."[9]

Although it is beyond the purview of this essay to document all the many versions of Antigone, it is important to note the longevity and scope of this practice. European translations and adaptations (including operas) focusing on Antigone and Creon date back to at least the 1530s.[10] Revisions of *Antigone* in the twentieth century are most germane to this paper and often resituate Antigone in specific political movements. Most notable is Anouilh's *Antigone* (1944), first produced in Nazi-occupied France. In the Turkish playwright Kemal Demirel's *Antigone* (1966) Polyneices is imprisoned rather than killed and Antigone tries to release him because she feels he would make a more humane king than Eteocles.[11] South African versions of *Antigone* include most famously Athol Fugard's *The Island* (1973) set in apartheid South Africa and based on real events occurring in the Robben Island prison. Griselda Gambaro's *Antigone Furiosa* (1986) looks at Argentinean violence in light of Argentina's political structure. Slovak playwright Peter Karvas's 1961 *Antigone a tí druhí* (*Antigone and the Others*) is set in a concentration camp where Antigone is part of a group of inmates who try to organize against the Creon Kommandant. Nikos Koundouros created *Antigone: A Cry for Peace* that was performed at the border of Greece and the former Republic of Yugoslavia during the Balkan war in 1994.[12] His film *The Photographers* (1998) set the themes of *Antigone* in an imaginary Islamic country where western news reporters rush in and become just as much a spectacle as the oppressive warlords.[13] Different people use the scenes of violence the media depicts for both western visual consumers and the promotion of Islamic fundamentalism. There are two choruses: A chorus of photographers always ready to photograph the dead and dying and a chorus of women who look on in silence. Antigone's act of burying her brother is an act against "the spectacle of male cruelty set up by the Islamic despot for the consumption of western journalists and spectators."[14] In the U.K. Cathy King has written a version of the Antigone story entitled *Gone*. The American actor, writer and director Judith Malina translated and directed *Antigone* through the lens of Brecht and Artaud's theories, and the Living Theatre first performed the play in 1967 in Europe. More recently, in 2001 the experimental playwright Mac Wellman wrote an adaptation of *Antigone* of the same title.

Feminist Interpretations of Antigone

Greek tragedy in general and *Antigone* in particular occupy both a troubled and hallowed place among feminist theater theorists. Contemporary adaptations of Greek tragedy have often been in tandem with feminist and gay movements. These revisions typically give female characters more prominent roles, more assertive personalities, and more sympathetic motivations.[15] As Steve Wilmer notes in "Women in Greek Tragedy Today: A Reappraisal," feminist scholars have continued to address the complexities of Greek tragedy because female characters in Greek tragedy often hold a moral [and ethical] stance that is different from their male counterparts, creating the opportunity for strong female roles in the service of reflecting upon the consequences of obeying edicts driven by [male] hubris. About Antigone, Wilmer writes, "In recent years productions throughout the world have used the play to call attention to oppressive conditions in different countries, almost inevitably stressing the rectitude of Antigone's stance."[16] Contemporary perspectives have come full circle from an ideological position that Greek tragedy is a misogynist form of theater that needs to be rejected to a broad spectrum of engagement with the genre employing methodologies that include a variety of feminisms inflected with the fields of psychoanalysis, theater studies, and performance theory.[17]

An early American feminist adaptation (winter 1975–1976) of *Antigone* used the narrative as a means to personal development. Susan Suntree discusses the formation of the Women's Ensemble of the Berkeley Stage Company in terms of the members' relationship to the Antigone myth. "We came to see Antigone not as a person blinded by pride but as a woman accepting a restorative role in her culture. Most importantly, she chose herself by putting forth her belief in her own values and experiences.... Her courage was reborn in us as we struggled to actualize our liberation."[18] The result was *Antigone Prism* that used some parts of Sophocles' *Antigone* in order to confront what the group understood as the central question posed by the Antigone story: "Will you act to create yourself?"[19]

Front and center in many adaptations of *Antigone* is the heroine's rejection of waiting in the antechamber of history. Antigone acts. For many playwrights who have written adaptations of *Antigone* this is her cause celeb. Antigone has outsized fate—the fate of the House of Labdacus—and has the personality to meet that fate head on. In saving her family's honor by burying her brother Polyneices, Sophocles' Antigone both defies the state and upholds the sanctity of one of its basic units—the domestic sphere of the family with its codes of loyalty and religious obligation. Antigone rebels against the state in order to honor her family and the gods. Although Antigone's moral stance is the aspect of her character that has most compelled theater artists, it is also important to observe that, in honoring her family, Antigone observes her domestic obligations only to a degree. At the same time she honors her family she forfeits her family's future by choosing death and refusing to produce the next generation, clearly a violation of gender norms.

Peggy Phelan reads Sophocles' *Antigone* via Lacan in terms of the difficulty of staging a new theater of lesbian desire. That a war has just occurred and Antigone addresses the agents of war with a political act that defies the rule of law does not figure as much in Phelan's reading as a psychoanalytic assessment of Antigone's tragic choice to die. According to Phelan, "Sophocles' play is a meditation on the ways in which dying reproduces and multiplies death."[20] The ultimate interest of *Antigone* for Phelan is not about justice as much as it is about the desire to go beyond "the law of the father" precisely because Antigone expresses her subjectivity by placing herself outside the reach of Creon via her suicide.[21] Phelan poses a crucial question: "is it that women's desire for anyone or anything always already (re) produces death within the masculine Imaginary?"[22] Citing Lacan, Judith Butler points out, "Lacan's concern with the play is precisely with this rushing by oneself to one's own destruction, that fatal rushing that structures the action of Creon and Antigone alike."[23] As she focuses on the questions the play raises about kinship and the political, what strikes Butler about Lacan and Hegel's reading of Antigone is the way in which she is understood as "one who articulates a prepolitical opposition to politics, representing *kinship as the sphere that conditions the possibility of politics without ever entering into it.*"[24]

For many theater practitioners, however, it is Antigone's political act of burying her brother in the face of an edict from the state that she deems unjust. From twentieth and twenty first century perspectives, which are informed by if not the rise of feminism then certainly new discourses on women and their place in public life, being prepared to die for what she deems a morally correct action makes Antigone a virtuous character. But virtue, as we often learn in

Greek tragedy, is not necessarily without hubris. Sophocles' Antigone not only buries her brother, she taunts Creon by insulting him: "if you think my acts are foolishness, the foolishness may be in a fool's eye."[25] What is taunting a king if not hubris? Sophocles' Antigone publicly disobeys the king, insults him, and forbids her sister Ismene from participating in burying Polyneices because Ismene did not respond on Antigone's timetable. Still, Antigone acts according to her beliefs. She honors family before the state, the gods above humans, the sacred over the secular. She is willing to die alone "unwept and unwed" for her convictions. Mostly ignored in scholarly analyses and artistic adaptations is the fact that Haemon, Creon's son and Antigone's betrothed, is willing to die for Antigone. (Neither Haemon nor Creon are included in Butler's index.) Haemon tries diplomacy before he turns against his father. He is the counterpart to Creon, just as Ismene can be read as the counter part to Antigone. As Foley observes, "The gendering of ethical positions permits the public exploration of moral complexities that would not otherwise have been possible."[26] Certainly Creon and Antigone can be understood as confined by ethical positions that are gendered in a way that Haemon is able to avoid. But in adaptations the opposition between Creon and Antigone is typically not tempered by the ways in which Haemon and Ismene provide different strategies and moral reasoning, and the conflict is waged between King and female subject — uncle and niece.

The Antigone Project

The five playwrights who wrote plays for *Antigone Project* all focus their narratives on Antigone rather than shift the focus to Creon as Sophocles does for the final third of the play. Miyagawa's contribution to *Antigone Project*, *Red Again*, is specifically in response to the war in Iraq and the demise in civil liberties encoded in The Patriot Act. Her play is generally in response to the political climate after 9/11. "I looked at the ways human atrocity gets repeated in history. With the invasion of Iraq and the problem in human rights both in the U.S. and in Arab countries, I wanted to write about the cyclical nature of history. From this perspective, the events at Abu Ghraib became inevitable."[27] *Red Again* is about a larger notion of history that is beyond individuals and a specific time period:

> I'm reporting a double suicide. My sister Antigone hanged herself, and her boyfriend Harold found her body and then stabbed himself. My name is Irene. I live in Manhattan. Please hurry. We are being evacuated. All people of Japanese descent received notice to relocate in forty-eight hours. I'm packing my life into two suitcases that I can carry. I can't carry two dead bodies. I can't carry my sister. I can't carry her. I have to carry linen and silver and our family curse. Antigone is dead. Forever. I can't carry any more. I'm being sent far, far away from home. Somewhere called Treblinka. Do you know where it is? I think it's

> in Bosnia. Or Cambodia. Please. I need help. I'm reporting a broken heart, broken bodies, broken humanity.[28]

The disintegration of history as a series of distinct occurrences with unique qualities is a device Miyagawa uses in other of her plays, especially *America Dreaming*.[29] In *Red Again*, Miyagawa flattens the temporal depth of history into an eternally recurring present making it seem like we are being swallowed by the violent and unjust repetitions of history. Miyagawa's Antigone is both burdened with and hopeful about history. History's stories repeat themselves even as there is the possibility of something new being written on the white pages of the future.

> I know right now it feels like all violent acts and atrocities in human history are converging and happening in one instant. I know it feels like that instant is a loop and it plays and plays and never stops. Red, again, and again. But there is white in these books. Irene, please hear me.[30]

The ashes and blood of history and the possible purity of a future yet to be written comprise the continuum of hope and despair for Antigone in *Red Again*.[31] *Red Again* takes place in the underworld where Antigone and Harold (Miyagawa's renamed Haemon character) find themselves in beautiful blue lights and the air has the sweet odor of the salt ocean. They are both dead but together. Sometimes they hear Irene (Miyagawa's Ismene character) in the world above reciting tragedies—murdered children, a mushroom cloud, mustard gas, and war rationing, economic sanctions—and trying to get someone to help her. But the books in the underworld that still have blank pages at the end consume Antigone and Harold's attention. They even find all the tender things they have written about one another. Their future, however, is not to remain in the underworld but to return to that other world to go "back to Red again" where they will live out their own destinies, where history is saturated with blood, constantly staining human actions red again and again. That Antigone is female, that her actions take enormous courage, that she risks her own life, and that she is finally recognized as being right when Creon loses everything makes the basic narrative about both despair and hope.[32] Nothing changes, yet political acts remain important.

In *Hang Ten* by Karen Hartman, Antigone and Ismene are sitting at the beach watching the waves crash on the shore. The endless cycle of waves is dotted with male surfers who are the subject of the sisters' gaze throughout the play. "I can't watch another boy fall," comments Antigone as she catalogues the way young men in the flush of life prep to take on the sea.[33]

> It's sick. He tries with all his might, he works his pecs in his mom's garage, he pumps iron from a catalogue so he can hold up the board, paddle out, paddle, paddle. He goes to a beach where he knows no one: he kneels, he bites it, he kneels, he holds it, he stands, he bites it, he stands, he holds it, he stands, he stands, he stands. He's ready to come to his home beach and ride waves in front of us, in front of girls.[34]

As she holds him in her sight, Antigone sees the young man, all young men, as physically ripe for waves and war. "He gets hard little muscles down his skinny front ... he is a buttfuckable Hellenic god.... But how will it end? How does it end no matter how worthy, how pretty, how ready the boy? Waves crash one way, into coast, into rock. I can't look."[35] Ismene wants not only to stay out of trouble but also to rewrite her story so that she can get out of the tragic narrative and enjoy the muscled boys in jams on the beach.

> There once was a girl named Ismene. She had parents and siblings. They were not the same people. She was an exiled princess surviving a war. Her brothers fought on different sides. That's okay. Families split and that is okay. That is how humans move on, the capacity to love new people. The rules changed. The ruler changed. And everyone forgot about Princess Ismene's rotten family. Such that she got a really good job with full benefits and two-hour lunches in a seaside town and watched surfers all afternoon. She hired the surfers to do odd jobs for her, washing walks or clipping flora. They wear little pants called jams. These jams expose the hipbones and unlace below the navel. Ismene was a lucky princess.[36]

As Antigone and Ismene sit in their beach chairs watching the horizon dotted with the endless spectacle of young men riding the waves, falling and getting up again, a pernicious view of men emerges. "Boys spring fresh from the waves every day," Ismene comments in an attempt to ameliorate Antigone's desolation at the loss of her brother.[37]

Boys and men are not only expendable; they are the pleasure of sex and war. They are their bodies provocatively unclothed for easy availability and killing. Ismene confesses that she is loyal to no one, to nothing, except change. She is a survivor without moral gumption and doesn't want Antigone to bury Polyneices precisely because it will make life difficult for her. A Surfer approaches the women, confesses his love for Antigone and proposes marriage. Then he asks which of the women is Antigone and Ismene responds, "I am Antigone." Just as young men ride the waves (of power and war) that will take them under, young women are interchangeable vessels for lust and progeny. Ismene responds so quickly because she knows that she must create a new future and, for her, marriage is the only way to do that.

In *Hang Ten* Hartman pits moral conscience against survival. The cycle of waves and boys bobbing in the sea is its own seduction that makes risking everything to bury a dead man look like naïve folly. The foolishness is Antigone's and by extension anyone who risks everything for moral conviction. Hartman makes Ismene look smart but vapid. Ismene doesn't care, she lies, but she survives because she delimits her accountability as a matter of freedom of choice. This is Hartman's critique of democracy: freedom for all, for anything, anytime, anywhere according to whatever mood. Democracy includes the choice of total self–interest.

Medallion by Tanya Barfield marks the absence of the dead in the physical form of a telegram held by a black laundress, Antoinette (Antigone), as she sits in the office of General Carlton (Creon), a white officer at the close of World War I. We hear a telephone operator recite part of General John Joseph Pershing's message to the French military about the inferior status of black American troops:

> ...We must not eat with blacks, must
> not shake hand or seek to talk or meet with them outside
> the requirements of military service. We must not
> commend too highly the black American Troops,
> particularly in the presence of white Americans....[38]

As history bleeps into the background Antoinette confronts General Carlton with the command, "Give me my brother's body." The General relents and listens to Antoinette's plea for something of her brother's to bury: the Medal of Honor the French awarded him. With nothing at all left of her brother, Antoinette requests that the U.S. government award him a medal of honor. General Carlton huffs: "Mrs. Thebes, the French may award Croix de Guerre to the Negroes, but we do not."[39] Antoinette responds with a litany of the equality of suffering of those who go to war:

> Squattin'in the rotted rat-filled trenches, ear ripped by
> Machine fire, burnt by shells, squalid smell of blood,
> Knee deep in a wasted land of water....
> ...
> Rats feedin' off the flesh of fresh cadavers,
> Eatin' the eyes, stealin' the sight....
> ...
> gassed for mother-land....
> ...
> lost hand in battle....
> ...
> twisted and barbed by wire, continued to fight.[40]

The General has also lost both his father and brother in war. He screams at her to shut up and keep in mind that she is only a colored woman, and he can dismiss her without so much as a thought. There is no body to bury and no honor to award.

Barfield makes the ritual act of burial at the center of Sophocles' *Antigone* impossible. There are no remains; there is no body, so there can be no act that blankets mourning. Antoinette's litany of the wages of war, its toll on the bodies of young men, underscores her realization that she must live without closure. The war continues at home in race relations that will not allow the recognition of common grief or of compassionate listening. No action can be taken. Resisting the ethos of a corrupt and immoral state is beyond both Antoinette and the General for entirely different reasons. They are in the same room but exist in different spheres. The play ends with the General turning on the radio as a way to sonically erase Antoinette's presence as he turns his attention away from her. She is condemned to forever live a war without conclusion.

A Stone's Throw by Lynn Nottage takes place in Africa where Antigone has defied the law by becoming pregnant out of wedlock. When Antigone confides to Ismene that her period has not come, Ismene cautions, "God is merciful, but the law is not."[41] The crime was seduction with the character Man telling Antigone he wants to carry her basket, to look at her, to know her name. He promises that Antigone will come to know the road to his house as a bride. When Antigone refuses to yield, the Man makes his case:

> Miss, I don't know why I'm still standing here. But I am.
> I'm a simple man, a poor man from a village with nothing to recommend it.
> I'm a good farmer with arid land, that is me today.
> But it may rain tomorrow and everything will be different....
> Or it may not rain for a year and I'll continue to sift dust for a family.
> I'll have to walk past you at the marketplace and shut my eyes.
> Miss, it may take me a year, to think so, to properly woo you away from your family.
> To earn the right to stand here by law. One long year.
> I'm telling you this, because I stand here disgracefully and hopefully wanting desperately to know your name.
> And I'll walk away now and work for a year for your dowry, if that is what you want.
> But it is too long to wait for one kiss.[42]

Nottage makes the Man's love seem innocent even though he knows only Antigone will suffer the consequences of their tryst. Antigone doesn't respect the law and insists that she did nothing wrong. While not exactly about Islam's Sharia law that governs everything from politics, banking and business to sexuality and hygiene, Nottage places Antigone's story in the context of females suffering legal consequences that males do not. The law in Nottage's version of Antigone and Ismene's world prosecutes some but protects others for the same act. The Man in *A Stone's Throw* is not like Haemon, as he doesn't come to Antigone's rescue. Antigone insists to Ismene that she did nothing wrong and she is not ashamed. Both Ismene and Antigone know that, as some African Sharia laws demand, Antigone will be stoned to death for her action. Ismene shows Antigone the size of the stones that will be hurled at her even as Antigone asserts that for a woman to have sex with a man is not wrong. But even as both sisters know that what Antigone says is true, they also know that she will die for her action.

In the twenty-first century, Antigone and feminism resonate with one another more in the realm of the political than the personal. Taken collectively, the plays in *Antigone Project* resist the ethos of a corrupt and immoral state and extricate the Antigone story from the complicated twine of religion and politics. It is curious that with fundamentalism and its literal reading of texts like the Old and New Testaments, the Koran, and the Torah — all texts that propose legal systems in various ways and demand different degrees of observance — that none of the playwrights engaged the conflict of two systems: of the state and that of religion. If the rise of Greek tragedy is closely associated with Athenian democracy, then one reading of Antigone can surely understand her as a "moral agent" who listens to the voice of the political right. She prefers the old law of the gods to the new law of the city-state. True, Creon is neither just nor wise but that can be said about many so-called leaders in all areas of life. This does not necessarily send us running to religious texts. Or does it? What is at the core of Antigone's story? The failure of the law? Of leadership? Or of ethics? Or all three intertwined? These are each very complex questions and, taken together, they present extremely complex sets of questions and possibilities. The plays of the *Antigone Project* do not address these issues as such. They do address the ways in which we repeat ourselves in history, the ways governments enact racism even in the face of the sacrifice of one's life to defend the country, legal systems that discriminate against women, and abiding self–interest in the face of the need for ethical actions. These concerns do not exclusively belong to feminism, but they have all been the subject of feminism in the U.S. since the nineteenth century when, while working for abolition, women became aware of their own lack of personal, political and legal rights. Rather, the playwrights find it more important to start with the feminist position that Antigone is a woman who acts against the role assigned to her by history and/or society: she acts in the public sphere and as such justly challenges the ways in which the public sphere is still governed by males, sexism, and racism. Powerfully, in all these plays when Antigone takes a moral action, it is for the benefit of everyone, not women alone. She is a woman acting as a woman but for the "general good" and for the protection of the individual. Antigone is written as both female and universal agent, a view that owes much to humanist feminism. It is this move, to align the female voice and story not with women alone but with a universality that speaks to the human condition by portraying the circumstances of female characters that sets these plays apart from the cultural feminism seen in productions such as *Antigone Prism* of the 1970s.[43]

Like Greek tragedy, feminism and democracy reveal structural tensions when placed in relation to each other. According to Harvard historian Nancy Cott, feminism's goals can be contradictory in the way they seek to extend to women both the clout of the group and the privileges of individualism. Women are asked to recognize their unity in order to implement a project that stands for diversity. Feminism asks for sexual equality by pointing out sexual difference, yet assumes a unity based on gender.[44] As a movement, feminism is very much like modern adaptations of Antigone: it is devoted to the individual voice, which always acts in the context of the collectivity of history. If we understand feminism to be a complicated ideological endeavor not without contradictions, Antigone becomes an exquisite feminist hero.[45]

One play among these five adaptations sets *Antigone* in the future. Caridad Svich places the story of Antigone in an archive where an historical Antigone is pitted against a digital one. The remains of Antigone in *Antigone Arkhe*—a hemp belt, silk dress, a lock of hair, and even Antigone's body—remain sealed behind glass unyielding to analysis implying that we continue to hear Antigone say what we would like to hear. History keeps operating beyond the archive. As the Archivist comments on exhibitions, Historical Antigone continues to speak from a place no one seems able to hear:

> Awakening the ever-new lament
> In your death you have undone my life
> The day-star's sacred eye watches me.
> Oh city of my fathers in the land of Thebes.[46]

In spite of the archive, history is still a blur, memory a form of chaos, words fragmented, and artifacts immaterial to knowledge.

Sophocles' *Antigone* takes place before the birth of secular individualism and the *Antigone Project* comes after; hence it is often read as a philosophical-literary-theatrical document proclaiming individualism, its glories and its penalties. Individualism in the twenty-first century, however, is under great pressure both from religious fundamentalists and from increasingly comprehensive surveillance systems. Antigone as the steadfast individual facing all the bound up powers of patriarchy and the state is an endangered species. The plays that comprise *Antigone Project* are to varying degrees aware of this. It is no longer a question of understanding the ways in which personal oppression results from political systems but of understanding the ways in which political systems create the experience of the personal, of understanding the ways in which "the political is personal." Individuals—cherish the illusion of self-determination while actually being part of various systems—national, legal, commercial, religious—that forms not only actions and meaning but also self-consciousness. Whether Antigone is brave or brazen, acting according to religion to defend family honor, or proclaiming agency, she can be understood as "personal" or "political" according to context. Hence, in these plays, Antigone is active during World War I, during 9/11, she is at the beach, she is in Africa challenging patriarchal law, and she is in the archive. But what we make of her is also always a part of what we make of ourselves in history and in the rapidly changing landscapes of national cultures.

Notes

1. Sophocles, *Antigone*, trans. Elizabeth Wyckoff (Chicago: University of Chicago Press, 1970).
2. *Antigone Project* with one-act plays by Tanya Barfield, Karen Hartman, Chiori Miyagawa, Lynn Nottage, and Caridad Svich was produced by the Women's Project under Producing Director Loretta Greco in association with Crossing Jamaica Avenue. The production

premiered October 13, 2004, at the Women's Project's Julia Miles Theatre. *Hang Ten* was directed by Anne Kaufman, *Medallion* by Iris Harrel, *Antigone Arkhe* by Anne Dorsen, *A Stone's Throw* by Liesl Tommy, and *Red Again* by Barbara Rubin. Chiori Miyagawa selected the playwrights based on friendships and racial and stylistic diversity. All of the commissioned plays were required to be political expressions and to have an Antigone character.

3. *Antigone* takes place after many disasters of tragic proportions. Laius, the pedophile son of Labdacus and father of Oedipus, stole Pelops' young son Chrysippus and ravished him by force. When Pelops found his son dangling from death's noose strung up out of shame, he cursed Laius to die at his own son's (Oedipus) hands. A catholic (or should I write Catholic) guilt of pedophilia damns the whole family line. Laius receives an oracle warning him of his impending doom. When Oedipus is born, Laius binds his ankles and passes him to a shepherd who is supposed to leave him to starve to death. The back-story, all that family history, desire, intrigue, betrayal, fealty, and murder is as important as the back-story in Aeschylus' trilogy although it is not often alluded to either in contemporary analyses of the play or adaptations. Bloodguilt was the way of the ancient world. Punishment for an unlawful act is visited upon the culprit as well as his/her descendants. Even in the bible "...the guilt of the parents upon the children, upon the third and upon the fourth generations...." (Exodus 20:5; cf. 34:7; Numbers 14:18).

4. Sophocles 174.

5. In *Greek Tragedy on the American Stage: Ancient Drama in the Commercial Theater, 1882–1994*, Karelisa V. Hartigan points out that different political realities during the same period of time make audiences more or less receptive to the meanings both the original and adaptations of Greek tragedy produce. Writing about *Antigone*, Hartigan observes, "At the 1946 staging of this [Anouilh's] *Antigone*, most [American] drama critics were reluctant to recognize the possibility that an ancient play could have modern political meaning. While both brave and relevant to a French audience under Nazi occupation, Antigone's protest had no meaning to an American audience never held by a foreign power and free of military concerns [(Westport, CT: Greenwood Press, 1995) 113].

6. Loretta Greco, "Statement from Loretta Greco: Artistic Director of Women's Project and Productions," unpublished mission statement, 2004.

7. Helene Foley, "Tragedy and Democratic Ideology: The Case of Sophocles' *Antigone*" in Barbara Goff, ed., *History, Tragedy, and Theory* (Austin: University of Texas Press, 1995) 131.

8. Christiane Sourvinour-Inwood qtd. in Ibid., 132–134.

9. Larry Bennett and Blake Tyrrell qtd. in Ibid., 141.

10. Operas focusing on Antigone and/or Creon have been written by: Baldassare Galuppi (1751), Giovannie Batista Casali (1752), Guiseppe Scarlatti (1752), and Ferdinando Gasparo Bertoni (*Antigone in 1756 and Creonte* in 1776) among others.

11. In a January 2, 2008, email correspondence the young Turkish scholar Serap Erincin wrote, "In the play, where Antigone saves her brother not because of kinship but because he will serve the people better, Demirel talks about the injustice in the contemporary materialistic world and reinforces the idea that every individual is responsible for every other. (In the beginning of the play the king is Eteocles, who has imprisoned Polyneices. Antigone tries to save Polyneices from the prison since she believes he will create humane living conditions for the people of Thebes....) Demirel reinforces the idea that laws set by people are not permanent, but what people have done for humanity will never be forgotten.

12. Pantelis Michelakis, "Greek Tragedy in Cinema: Theatre, Politics, History" in Edith Hall, Fiona Macintosh, and Amanda Wrigley, ed., *Dionysus Since 69: Greek Tragedy at the Dawn of the Third Millennium* (Oxford: Oxford University Press, 2004) 210–11.

13. Ibid., 210.

14. Ibid., 211.

15. Foley, "Bad Women: Gender Politics in Late Twentieth-Century Performance and Revision of Greek Tragedy," in *Dionysus Since 69*, 77–79.

16. Steve Wilmer, "Women in Greek Tragedy Today: A Reappraisal," *Theatre Research International* 32.2 (Chicago: Cambridge University Press, 2007) 107–108.

17. Sue Ellen Case infamously skewered the Greeks and their theater in a 1985 essay entitled, "Classic Drag: The Greek Creation of Female Parts" [*Theatre Journal* 37.3 (1985): 317–327] in which Case points out that despite strong female characters (and roles) such as Clytemnestra, Medea, Antigone, Hecuba, etc. the representation of women in Greek tragedy does not necessarily have anything to do with lives of women in ancient Greece. Aristotle's views on women largely reflect their legal status at the time. Women had legal standing first only through their father, then their husband or nearest male relative. Women were always under the protection of a man who could represent them in the public sphere in matters of consequence. Women were prominent subjects in art and theater but almost totally absent as authors of their own stories. We know what men said about women and how they represented them. In her book, Case proposes a significant reading strategy: "The feminist reader can, however, discover the methodology and assumptions of patriarchal production." And this approach just might lead feminist scholars and artists to "...decide that such plays do not belong in the canon-and that they are not central to the study and practice of theatre" [*Feminism and Theatre* (New York: Routledge, 1988) 19].

18. Susan Suntree, "Women's Theatre: Creating the Dream Now" in Gayle Kimball, ed., *Women's Culture: The Women's Renaissance of the Seventies* (Meteuchen, NJ, and London: Scarecrow Press, 1981) 111.

19. Ibid.

20. Peggy Phelan, *Mourning Sex: Performing Public Memories* (London: Routledge, 1997) 13.

21. Ibid., 14.

22. Ibid., 15.

23. Judith Butler, *Antigone's Claim: Kinship Between Life and Death* (New York: Columbia University Press, 2000) 46.

24. Ibid., 2.

25. Sophocles 174.

26. Foley, *Female Acts in Greek Tragedy* (Princeton: Princeton University Press, 2001) 172.

27. Chiori Miyagawa, interview with the author, 10 June, 2007.

28. Miyagawa, Red Again, unpublished playscript (2004), 62.

29. Miyagawa, *America Dreaming*, in Carol Martin and Saviana Stanescu, ed., *Global Foreigners* (London, New York, and Calcutta: Seagull Press, 2006) 261–288. Also see Miyagawa's discussion of her artistic choices in her play, *Awakening*, discussed in this volume.

30. Miyagawa, *Red Again*, 68.

31. Ibid., 61.

32. Miyagawa, interview.

33. Karen Hartman, *Hang Ten*, unpublished manuscript (2004), 3.

34. Ibid., 3.

35. Ibid., 3–4.

36. Ibid., 5.

37. Ibid., 9.

38. Tanya Barfield, *Medallion*, unpublished playscript (2004), 15.

39. Ibid., 19.

40. Ibid., 19–20.

41. Lynn Nottage, *A Stone's Throw*, unpublished playscript (2004), 44.

42. Ibid., 55.

43. Western universalism is built upon valuing the unique voice, the singular artist, and liberty in relation to the law, capitalism, and religion. It is also important to remember that when Hellenistic universalism (different from democratic Athens) began spreading it was not a friendly form of enlightenment. Greek armies and colonists poured into Asia and what we now call the Middle East and forced the Hellenization of everyone with whom they came into contact. It was a cultural renaissance with a noose waiting for those who resisted. Populations with their own form of law and practice, such as the Jews, were persecuted for following their halakah (religious Jewish law). For a discussion of Hellenization and the Jewish

people see Paul Johnson, *A History of the Jews* (New York: Harper and Row, 1987.) The relationship between religious law and secular law, capitalist democracy and egalitarian social well-being that guarantees equal human access to education and health, and the oppression of women and the world's poor are new versions of a very, very old conflict.

44. Nancy Cott, *The Grounding of Modern Feminism* (New Haven and London: Yale University Press, 1987) 5.

45. Individualism takes many forms, and its causes have been debated. Martin Luther was among the first to rebel against the Roman Catholic Church to say that individuals could have direct access to God. There was no need for priests, bishops, cardinals, or the pope. This idea went hand-in-glove with emergent capitalism, which asserted that individuals could amass wealth to do with as they pleased. These two ideas, direct access to the divine and a person owning the fruits of his own labor (women were excluded for a long time from this emergent system of liberty) led to "democracy" in the modern sense. The overall idea is that each individual person is inherently equal to every other person and should have the same opportunities.

46. Caridad Svich, *Antigone Arkhe*, unpublished playscript (2004), 25.

II

SHAKESPEARE AND SEVENTEENTH CENTURY THEATER

Lear's Daughters and Sons
Twisting the Canonical Landscape

LESLEY FERRIS

In a *New York Times* essay about theater adaptation, Ben Brantley states: "Surely no single body of work has been subjected to the metamorphoses and mutilations that the Shakespearean canon has undergone over the centuries. Shakespeare presented without novelty would be the only true novelty in Shakespeare productions these days." Brantley's piece, filed from London in February 2007, discusses a variety of adaptations, including those created by Edward Hall and his Propeller Company. While Brantley champions the absence of novelty, he is oddly admiring of Hall. Hall is known for his all-male productions of Shakespeare and Brantley characterizes Hall's *Taming of the Shrew* as "domestic brutality serv(ing) up a knuckle sandwich." Such exclusive male casting apparently gives Hall the "license to pull no physical punches" and Brantley comments on the sadistic elements found in Hall's "rousing, bruising" work.[1] Brantley seems to suggest that the male actors can really go to the guts of the violence because they are men. If a woman played the role of Kate, the audience would just witness another woman being fictionally brutalized as part of a long tradition of misogynistic, shrew-taming tales. As his comments are headed under the title of "When Adaptation is Bold Innovation," is it safe to assume that Brantley sees the all-male violence as "bold" and innovative?

I cite Brantley and Hall as high profile cultural commentators—critic Brantley who celebrates adaptation without questioning its gender-specific content and Hall as a director who perpetuates a false sense of Elizabethan "authenticity" with his all male productions because they represent for me contemporary examples of what I would describe as the "default" position of male theatrical supremacy. Since the beginning of Western theater, for centuries, theater making was male only. This history makes it possible for Hall to revive a problematic performance tradition while allowing Brantley to "neutrally" report it. Yet questions are raised and continue to be raised by many women who work in the profession. As Sue Parrish, artistic director of The Sphinx Theatre,[2] states:

The Fool, played by Hazel Maycock, in *Lear's Daughters*, first performed by the Women's Theatre Group in 1987, London. Photograph courtesy of Sue Parrish, Artistic Director of the Sphinx Theatre. Photographer: Ute Klaphake.

> The "rock" of the male tradition is incarnated in "the canon," reinvented and reinforced through the continuous revivals which form the staple fare of every theatre programme: male writers, male directors, and male characters—men, centre stage. Women are enduringly inscripted as a minority, enduringly represented as "the other," stereotyped as virago, Madonna or whore: and generally seen as passive beings, exemplifying John Berger's seminal dictum in *Ways of Seeing* that "men act and women appear."[3]

"Continuous revivals" of canonical plays, as Parrish notes, are for women actors the unfortunate bedrock of contemporary theater, which replicates the historical imperative of male dominance. It is with this disparity of women's roles in mind that we turn to a particularly challenging Shakespeare play: *King Lear*.

Of all of Shakespeare's plays, *King Lear* has accrued perhaps one of the most robust and controversial production histories. Notorious for its rewritten happy ending by Nahum Tate in 1681 (which held the British stage for 150 years), scorned by Charles Lamb as unplayable, unstageable, derided by Tolstoy as full of inconsistencies, the play continues to provide theatrical fodder for many productions.[4] Fischlin and Fortier claim that the second half of the last century can be compared to the Restoration as a "highpoint in the theatrical adaptation of Shakespeare"[5] while some critics argue that *King Lear* was one of the most popular of Shakespeare's plays to be produced in the twentieth century.[6] A look at the recent North American production scene, demonstrates that this attention clearly extends into the first decade of the new century. There are a significant number of productions, and I will name but a handful: Shakespeare and Company's production directed by Tina Packer (2003); Christopher Plummer in the title role under the direction of Jonathan Miller at Lincoln Center (2004); Shakespeare festivals in Utah and Idaho (2005); Robert Falls' direction of the play for Chicago's Goodman Theatre with Stacy Keach (2006); La Mama E.T.C.'s production with Alvin Epstein (2006); Brian Bedford who both directed and played the title role at Stratford Shakespeare Festival (Canada, 2007); the Public Theatre with Kevin Kline directed by James Lapine (2007); and the Royal Shakespeare Company's tour directed by Trevor Nunn with Ian McKellan (2007).

This random sample of ten productions provided thirty roles for women (Lear's three daughters) compared to well over 100 roles for men (a minimum of ten male roles with doubling). In an article published in 1994 on the role of women at the Royal Shakespeare Company, the actor Jane Lapotaire discusses the difficulty for women in the profession, citing the fact that "men outnumber women by eight to one."[7] This then is the reality that women actors face on a day-to-day, audition-to-audition basis.

Since women began acting professionally in English-speaking theater in 1660, they have developed strategies to address, however marginally, this disparity in occupational numbers. Two tactics evolved: a featured actress would perform the major role in a canonical play, such as Hamlet; or in contrast, a playwright would imagine a dramatic world in which women have some sense of autonomy and space, as in the plays of Aphra Behn.[8]

The tradition of female Hamlets appears to begin with Sarah Siddons, the great tragic actress of the English stage, who first performed the role in 1776.[9] By the middle of the following century it was commonplace for a leading actress to have a selection of acceptable Shakespearean male roles in her repertoire and the popularity of Hamlet and Romeo prevailed. Both these roles are young men and both are riven by emotions and volatility, thus confirming the stereotype of "woman" that was acceptable to a wide, public audience.

While the role of King Lear has been off limits to women in the past, recently several notable productions have cast women in the play's title role. Lear does not fit the Hamlet/Romeo youthful stereotype and, in stark contrast, aging actors consider the role the crowning achievement of a long and distinguished career. As the actor/director Brian Bedford states in a video interview, "One of the consolations of getting older is the supreme honor of playing King Lear."[10] The British actor Oliver Ford Davies played the role at the Almeida Theatre in London in 2002 and followed with a book documenting the experience entitled *Playing Lear*, which recounts his life-long encounter with the part. Davies states that "Lear has been part of my mental landscape for most of my life," and that "It's like standing in the Louvre and staring again at the *Mona Lisa* after a lifetime of seeing it at a distance in reproduction and mangled cartoon form."[11] The difficulty of the role is legendary: "No actor can claim Lear lies within his range, it doesn't lie within anyone's range. Paul Scofield once suggested that the heights of the play must be reached by parachute rather than by mountaineering."[12]

Any woman tackling this role would face a variety of hurdles, not least of which is the acknowledged difficulty of the role. In May 1990, Robert Wilson cast the 80-year-old actress Marianne Hoppe as King Lear in Frankfurt. A significant feature of the casting choice is that Hoppe did not attempt to create the illusion of masculinity by disguising herself as a man, and the text did nothing to alter the references to the king as male. Another more recent example is Helena Kaut-Howson's decision to choose Kathryn Hunter to play the role at the Leicester Haymarket and then transfer to the Young Vic in London in 1997. Hunter was applauded for her exceptional work as well as derided. Statements that gender was not a central issue in the casting decision became part of the publicity surrounding both productions. Robert Wilson claims he spent years searching for the right actor to play the commanding eponymous role and only felt confident moving ahead after he met Marianne Hoppe, one of Europe's most highly regarded performers. Hoppe stated that "When Bob first asked me to do Lear, I laughed. The idea was so outrageous. But soon its absurdity began to appeal to me.... I will not try to play a man, but I will forget I'm a woman."[13] Echoing Wilson's reason for casting Hoppe, Kaut-Howson said that she cast Hunter because she was the best actor for the role: "We cast Kathryn Hunter because I believe the part is about old age and not about gender."[14] Hunter and her director both denied that the project was feminist and in an interview with Elizabeth Schafer director Kaut-Howson stated, "Both Kathryn Hunter and myself were adamant about it being *nothing* to do with feminism at all."[15] While I want to celebrate these two examples of women playing Lear, it is difficult to do so when Hoppe, Hunter, and Kaut-Howson are blind to the implications of gender in such a choice. To claim that such a casting decision is "not about gender" betrays an ignorance of the historical significance of gendered performance and women's enforced absence from the public stage for centuries.

Mabou Mines: Lear

In contrast to these two examples of the single central role selected for cross-gender casting, Mabou Mines' production of *Lear*, which opened in New York City in 1990, attempted to rework the gender hierarchy of the play. Indeed, director Lee Breuer "saw *Lear* as a fundamental story about the interrelations of power and gender."[16] Breuer and his company Mabou Mines worked collectively over a three-year process to develop their version of the play. Early workshops in Atlanta convinced them to stick with a southern locale and the play was set in 1950s Georgia. The major alteration was gender: Lear was a southern matriarch with three sons, instead of three daughters, and the text was changed to address this switch. The impetus for this change came from Ruth Maleczech, co-founder with Breuer of the company, and acknowledged as its leading actor. As this was the first time the company decided to produce a Shakespeare play, Maleczech had not previously had the opportunity to play Shakespeare. She described the astonishing effect the role of Lear had on her: "When a man has power, we take it for granted. But when a woman has power, we're forced to look at the nature of power itself."[17] As scholar Iris Smith states, "Not interested in playing Lear as a man, Maleczech was following a desire that had no model."[18] In considering Maleczech's desire to play the role as a woman, Lee Breuer said:

> It took me a while to understand that there were certain political imperatives inherent in that desire. What's one of the first things you see? That Lear's story, at least in part, is about the relationship between power and love. A man can be powerful and still be loved, but its rare to see a woman loved for her power — women must be powerless. So as women gain power in our society, they also find love more difficult to attain.[19]

The collective workshop process developed by Mabou Mines made it possible for several writers to publish pieces on the work-in-progress before it opened in New York. As Iris Smith observes, the messages articulated by various interviews demonstrate the different sensibilities at work:

> While Breuer and Maleczech seem to feel that they hold similar views of the play, I submit that their perspectives are far apart. For Breuer gender is one of many possible analogies; for Maleczech gender has been the material obstacle between her and the chance to play Lear, and became, once the production was underway, the elemental link between Shakespeare's words and (her) contemporary American experience.[20]

Maleczech's performance, then, embodied her personal position as a female actor in a male role. In acknowledging this, she created a Lear that was uniquely her own. As Smith says, "The wonder of Maleczech's performance lies in its self-contained understatement: the assumption that this matriarch's power, personal and economic, is the most natural thing in the world."[21] Playing the role as "the most natural thing" exposes it for what it is — the most unnatural thing — a woman with autonomy and economic power.

While Mabou Mines' production is clearly an adaptation of a classic script,[22] and one that interrogates issues of gender, the work that is the focus of the remainder of this essay invents a world of women from Shakespeare's play, and thus serves as an example of the second strategy for addressing women's roles on contemporary stages: re-imagining a world where women are present and active.[23]

Women's Theatre Group: Lear's Daughters

In the same year (1987) that Mabou Mines began working on their version of *King Lear*, the Women's Theatre Group (WTG), a London-based company founded in 1973, produced a small-scale touring production entitled *Lear's Daughters*. One of several women's companies from the politically engaged, post–1968 period in British theater, WTG committed itself to developing a collective theater-making process, a means for opposing the "traditionally paternalistic structures within mainstream theater, wherein the director ... was the authority figure who shaped the performance as a product of his own vision."[24] The collaborative nature of the group extended to the writing of the scripts. It was often the case that the plays themselves were created through a series of developmental workshops with company members. Most of the early work by the company was group written and had a focused political agenda addressing such issues as contraception, equal pay, and sex discrimination. While the collective nature was maintained, the company began to hire freelance designers and directors in 1977 and in the following year started to commission writers.[25] By 1987, when the decision was made to do a reworking of the canonical Shakespeare play, the company commissioned Elaine Feinstein to work with the actors and produce a script. After the first version of the play was presented to the company, the actors revised the script in workshops. This version is now credited as written by the Women's Theatre Group and Elaine Feinstein. The published version in the Fishlin and Fortier anthology lists all the cast members involved in the creation of the work. These include Adjoa Andoh, Janys Chambers, Gwenda Hughes, Polly Irvin, Hazel Maycock, Lizz Poulter, and Sandra Yaw.[26] The production toured widely and WTG scheduled a second tour (with some cast changes) in 1988.[27]

Lear's Daughters is more than an adaptation, it is a reinvention, a politicized back-story to Shakespeare's play that calls attention to the absence of the mother, and re-envisions the daughters' stories. *Lear's Daughters* is given multiple viewpoints from a variety of women not the least of which is the collective of theater makers themselves. Coppélia Kahn speaks about the "conspicuous omission" of the mother in Shakespeare's play and goes on to say that this absence "articulates a patriarchal conception of the family in which children owe their existence to their fathers alone; the mother's role in procreation is eclipsed by the father's, which is used to affirm male prerogative and male power."[28]

I would like to pause here a moment to consider Kahn's reading of the play — a reading that connects to the very beginnings of a gendered Western drama. In the final play of Aeschylus' trilogy *The Oresteia*, the playwright stages a trial in which Orestes is accused of killing his mother, Clytaemnestra. Athena presides as judge; Apollo, in the role of Orestes' defense lawyer, states:

> The mother is not the true parent of the child
> Which is called hers. She is a nurse who tends the growth
> Of young seed planted by its true parent, the male....[29]

The trial ends in favor of Orestes, and he is exonerated from matricide precisely because his mother is *not* considered the "true" parent. This notion of the biological superiority of the father rippled through the centuries as scientific fact.[30] While Aeschylus's play celebrates the idea of the supremacy of the father, Shakespeare's *Lear*, according to Kahn demonstrates "the failure of a father's power to command love in a patriarchal world and the emotional penalty he pays for wielding power."[31] And while Shakespeare's play does indeed examine Lear's "emotional penalty" and his failure as a father, *Lear's Daughters* rethinks this failure in startling ways: the multi-vocal script imagines the daughters' point of view and also considers the absent/present mother.

Lear's Daughters reinstates the mother as a ghostly presence in the daughters' lives. The play questions the role of women within the cultural and historical framework of a dominating, and essentially dangerous, male authority. Escape from the patriarchy is always a tantalizing, but in this case, impossible option. Indeed the play puts forward the short-lived attempt of the Queen to leave with the children. This Nora-like door slamming tested the King's power and on the Queen's return to the castle "no-one ever left again except by his say-so."[32]

The play, running at a short ninety minutes in contrast to the three plus hours of Shakespeare, consists of fourteen scenes with five characters: the three daughters (Cordelia, Regan, Goneril), the Fool, and the Nurse/Nanny. Women play all the roles. The Fool assumes the role of storyteller and commentator on the events that transpire. Such commentary functions in stark contrast to the "way in which the authority of the narrator is traditionally understood" (216). In *Lear's Daughters* the narrator is highly visible rather than a presence behind the scenes, so to speak, and not only recounts but orchestrates the dramatic action. The Fool in Shakespeare's play is the King's conscience and he stands for "worldly common sense."[33] In contrast, the Fool in *Lear's Daughters* is a constant mischievous presence, the conscience of the play itself, not its eponymous hero. This Fool reminds the audience, in a Brechtian manner, that theater *is* theater, a constructed social activity and not the Aristotelian mirrored reflection of "life." Thus *Lear's Daughters*' Fool is a materialist trickster invention that undermines Shakespeare's authorial power. Such a dramatic strategy gives the audience the opportunity to rethink history as the Fool intervenes, as we shall see, by drawing attention to themes of commerce and gender.

The story is a prequel to the events in Shakespeare's play; Lear has not yet decided to divide his kingdom; and none of the daughters is married. At the start of the play the daughters are young children and by the end they are women. The Fool begins the play by reciting a limerick with missing parts of its text filled in with nonsense singsong sounds that call attention to the gaps in the narrative and the impossibility of rendering the mother's and daughters' stories through Lear's:

> There was an old man called Lear
> Whose daughters, da da da da, fear,
> The Queen was their mum,
> Da da da da son,
> Da da da da da dada here [217].

The only recognizable words in these nonsensical lines are the daughters' "fear," a "son" and "here." It is for the audience to link this fear not only to the mother's absence but also perhaps to the mysterious presence/absence of a son, a male heir.

Jokes, fairy tales, rhymes, and children's games infuse the text with energy and rhythm and provide an oppositional counterpart to Shakespeare's poetic language. Such gaming gives the Fool multiple opportunities to look directly at the audience and comment on the action. A game of blind man's bluff under the Fool's control, (alluding, of course, to Lear's metaphorical blinding on the heath), introduces the three daughters. Each in turn — when tagged as part of the game — has a first person monologue of adolescent longing that is distinctive to them: thus Cordelia speaks about her love of words, Regan her passion for touch, Goneril her delight in color. Scene Two introduces the Nurse who tells the three girls stories about their births. The birth stories have a Grimm's Brothers, fantastical quality to them: Goneril was born under a comet, Regan's birth occurred with a volcanic eruption, and Cordelia experienced a hurricane. The three girls follow the stories with curiosity and delight. Their responses to these stories provide yet another layer of information to understanding the daughters. Feminist scholars Griffin and Aston discuss the ways in which this revision of *King Lear,* laced as it is with fairy tales, provides a depth of character for the three sisters unavailable in Shakespeare's play.[34] Such characterization fills in the gaps, answers questions and "presents a radical alternative to the way in which audiences have come to expect the telling of Lear's story..." (Fischlin and Fortier 216). The daughters as dramatically represented in *King Lear* are depicted in the classic binary of good and evil: Cordelia the good vs. Goneril and Regan the bad. One considerable difference in *Lear's Daughters* is the distinct characterization of all the daughters. Traditional analyses of *King Lear* discuss Goneril and Regan as the monstrous sisters, equally evil, twinned with little murderous difference between them. *Lear's Daughters* counters that depiction with the elder sisters having distinctly different qualities. Seeing these girls as children, observing the ways in which they deal with their familial roles and their relationship to their parents and each other, cracks the binary stranglehold that is the legacy of Shakespeare's play for the women characters.

The ghost presence of the Queen is reinforced by the fact that she exists only as a performed memory: the Nurse tells the daughters stories about their mother but more pointedly the Fool performs the Queen. Such doubling exemplifies another means of narrative subversion by linking the two characters dramatically to a single body. Juliet Dusinberre makes a connection between the Fool and women in Shakespeare's plays by articulating his depiction of a "particular sympathy between his Fools and his heroines."[35] The Queen in *King Lear* is only an absent, offstage figure, but linking the Queen to the Fool in *Lear's Daughters* is a narrative strategy that destabilizes Shakespeare's telling of the story. The first instance of this Fool/Queen doubling is Scene Three, titled "The Fool is the Queen." It begins with the Fool sitting on a box (standing in for a throne) and arranging a veil on her head (to indicate her role as Queen). The Fool alternates between playing "Fool" and "Queen" throughout the scene as the Nurse talks with the Queen about her health, accounts, taxes, and her children. While the stage directions make it clear that the Fool plays the Queen, there is an intriguing elision of roles here. Is the Queen a fool? Is the Fool a queen? Both manage things: the Queen manages the kingdom, the Fool manages the play.

The second half of the scene has the three daughters speaking short monologues about their encounters with their father, which involves descending a staircase to discover a moment of troubling kingly behavior. Each of the girls' stories interweaves feelings of awe and fear. Goneril sits on Lear's throne to test it out; Regan spies him "singing, banging his fist on the table, not quite in tune, not quite in time. And his arm is around Mother's neck. I think it's Mother. He has a hand inside her dress, holding her breast" (220). Cordelia recalls being very small and being picked up by him, establishing her as the youngest, favored one.

These three early scenes institute a variety of motifs and themes that continue throughout the play. First, the Fool is a stage manager of the action, of the storytelling. The Fool's role is meta-theatrical, referring to a moment as an act of make-believe, of theater. For example at the end of Scene Three, the Fool looks at notes, which is described in the script as "the running order," and lists out loud moments of the play that have already passed. The Fool's work is often playful, pointing at or touching the individual sisters when it is their turn to speak, a kind of child's game of tag put to use for telling the story. The Fool, unlike the other characters, often addresses the audience directly. In contrast to the sister's interior monologues about going downstairs to meet their father, for example, the Fool looks at the audience and states, "The first time I went downstairs I was pushed. And it bloody hurt" (220). While the games and fairy tales capture a certain light, child-like enthusiasm, they also conjure abrupt, sudden shifts in tone. The Fool's insertion of being pushed downstairs augurs a sense of brutality and mean-spiritedness and identifies the Fool's position in the social classes of Lear's kingdom.

A second issue that infuses *Lear's Daughters* centers on the Fool's ambiguous gender. Marilyn French in her groundbreaking work *Shakespeare's Division of Experience* explains that with *King Lear* (and other Shakespeare plays) "gender roles are absolute, but only for women." French goes on to explain that when women start to act like men, make decisions like men (such as Goneril and Regan) in Shakespeare's play, such action "topples the natural order and plunges the world in chaos."[36] In contrast to Shakespeare's gender absolutism, the Fool in *Lear's Daughters* flaunts sexual ambiguity. While the actor playing the Fool is a woman, the script goes out of its way to never use "she" or "her" in stage directions or dramatic speech. At one point Cordelia asks the Fool: "Are you a man or a woman?" The Fool responds: "Depends who's asking." And later: "It's all the same to me." Goneril follows by asking "How can you be so ... accommodating?" And the Fool replies, "It's what I'm paid for" (221). In Scene Five, entitled "Lear returns triumphant from a sporting tournament," the Fool states, "It practiced smiling in the mirror ... and put on its man's man suit" (221). Thus the character refers to itself as "it"—maintaining a deliberate sense of androgyny, a chameleon-like existence which plays on the male/female duality of the Fool's role in Shakespeare's play. While ostensibly "male" (called 'boy' by Lear), the Fool in *King Lear* exhibits a variety of "feminine" characteristics. As Germaine Greer states, "A fool is 'natural,' simple as we say, and by extension, still in a state of nature."[37] According to Juliet Dusinberre, in Shakespeare's world "Women, Fools and rustics" are all linked by their low status and links to "nature."[38]

Scholars and actors alike have debated the ambiguous position of the Fool—he is a comic trickster, and a teller of misfired jokes that are often laced with hard-hitting truths. The actor Antony Sher writes about the challenges of playing the Fool in *King Lear* in his autobiography. For Sher "the role of the Fool only works in relation to Lear. The Fool is the King's sidekick, his whipping boy, his pet, his shadow."[39] There is also a tendency, according to Kenneth Muir, for many critics to sentimentalize this shadowy figure. Muir argues against critical interpretations of the Fool's jesting as a strategy to take the King's mind off his older daughters' ingratitude: "Nothing could be further from the truth. Nearly everyone of his jests reminds Lear of the sorrow that is gnawing at his heart."[40] Far from sentimentalizing the Fool, *Lear's Daughters* represents this character as often abrupt, occasionally abrasive, conspiratorial, and a wily presence. As the production's stage manager, the Fool controls events and demonstrates the imperviousness of outside forces. The Fool's ambiguity is highlighted by its malleable gender. However, the fact that a woman actor performs the part of a traditional male role underscores the position of the actress in theater's history. Far from refusing this history, as was the case with Hoppe and Hunter's playing the King, the role of the Fool and its cross-gender casting embraces it. But the role of the Fool in *Lear's Daughters* is also a provocation, a metatheatrical device of a different order that functions as a sign, an index in the semiotic sense, pointing to the instability of gender and the many attempts to stabilize it in our culture.

One of the often-cited scholarly speculations about casting in the original Renaissance production is that the actor who played the Fool doubled as Cordelia. Since the two roles are not on stage at the same time, this is plausible. In Shakespeare's script, as King Lear holds the body of Cordelia in his arms in the final act, he murmurs, "And my poor fool is hang'd" thus linking the two in his mind.[41] In more recent contemporary productions, some directors have cast women in the role. The Fool as 'it' in *Lear's Daughters* references these casting choices while serving as a constant reminder about gender. Juliet Dusinberre makes a further connection between the Fool and women:

> To be permanently providing light relief to serious men, to be in essence a symbol of that light relief in one's very being, allies women with professional Fools, as Shakespeare perceived when he depicted particular sympathy between his Fools and his heroines—Celia and Touchstone, Viola and Feste, and Cordelia and the Fool in *King Lear*.[42]

The Fool's sense of doubleness (stage manager/character, master/servant, male/female) is echoed in the role of the Nurse/Nanny. The double character name is telling: Nurse to the Queen, Nanny to the daughters. Even though the Fool "plays" the Queen, the Nurse is the paid mother of the children as the script makes clear. The Fool says, "Three daughters. With two mothers—one buying, one selling. One paying, one paid" (219). Later the Fool states, "Three sisters, playing in the nursery, with the mother who sells, but not the mother who buys" (222). The Fool's insistence on monetary transactions underscores the capital dynamics of the monarchy. In this world, the Queen, the biological mother and manager of the household, must buy another woman to be mother to her children.

It is through the role of the Fool that a dominating concern of the play develops, that of class and money, their inseparability and their intersection in gender relations. The Fool is a mere onlooker to royal privilege and its many manifestations, and makes this apparent in recounting its own birth narrative directly to the audience:

> When I was born, nothing happened. There was no bright star, no hurricane, no visitors came from afar. Obviously my parents hadn't read the right books so my arrival was completely overlooked [220].

Kicked downstairs, and without a birth story, the Fool, like the women in *King Lear* who understand the importance of inheritance, knows there is only one route for survival: money. At the end of Scene One, the Fool turns to the audience and says, "I like money. And myself. And money" (218). At other points in the play the Fool counts money, jingles the coins in its pocket, and holds out its hand for coins.

Lear's Daughters puts forward a world that operates through the power of the monarchy to buy and sell. In Scene Ten, entitled "Investment," money relentlessly underscores the multiple narrative threads, supplying the missing parts of the women's stories. The scene begins with the Fool reading out a scene summary, a checklist of its stage management duty to keep the production on track. When the Fool arrives to the present scene it states:

> Investment is .... Money, cash, dosh, lolly, crinks, ackers, makes the world go round, doubloons, duckets, crowns, pieces of eight, much, and brass. Money — Investment. (puts coin down front of skirt. Mimes rubbing tummy.) Nest egg, pension, taken care of, rainy day, looked after, old age [227].

Following this incantation of investment, the Fool wriggles and squirms, then lifts its skirt, reaches between its legs and pulls out a "fool doll." In this eerie ghosting of the Queen giving birth, the Fool cradles the doll child and says, "Investment. Three princesses all grown older, thinking about their father and counting the cost" (227).

The Fool's theatrical birthing of a doll child is also a birthing of the play's devastating center in which the three daughters learn the price of being a female member in a royal household. Following the Fool's treatise on "investment," each daughter takes over the investment "portfolio." Cordelia dances with her father (played by the Fool) in a scene that plays out Lear's control over his youngest when he makes her dance against her will. The scene calls to mind other dancing scenarios from Nora's desperate dancing for Torvald to Salome's seven veils. Here Lear treats Cordelia like a toy demanding that she "spin" like a top; the Fool as Lear: "Spin! (Cordelia picks up her skirt.) Gather round gentleman, please. Show them Lear's baby" (227). In Regan's investment moment, she asks the Nurse what happened the night the Queen died. The Nurse attempts various evasions to her probing demands for the truth. Finally the Nurse gives in and supplies the missing parts of the narrative that link the Queen's disappearance to the King's demand for a male heir: "Alright. I used to hear him in the room below, whining on at her to let him fuck her. He wouldn't give up on her having a son" (228). The Nurse explains to Regan that although the Queen brought a significant dowry to the match, she had three miscarriages that failed to produce an heir to the throne and ultimately lead to her death. The daughters' story also reveals their vulnerability to the demands of the King. Goneril, the eldest, talks with the Nurse about going to the castle cellars with her father when she was small. Down below, in a narrative that hovers over an eerie possibility of incest, Lear shows Goneril his wealth: "crowns, coins, breastplates, gold bars, all glowing in candlelight." In reported speech Goneril tells the Nurse that the king "shut the door and bent down to me and whispered, 'When you are Queen, this will be yours. This will be our secret — just you and me — and you musn't tell'" (228). Each of the sisters' stories encapsulates a dramatized moment of the father's power bound up with capital. Cordelia dances on demand in front of the King's men; Regan learns about the Queen's substantial dowry that made the royal marriage possible and the specter of her mother's miscarriages in fulfilling her assigned role to produce a male heir; and first born Goneril is promised her father's wealth, in exchange for the "secret" of his incestuous advances.

Shakespeare's play is known for its opening scene in which the aging Lear asks his children which daughter loves him most, so he can divide his kingdom accordingly. The reward for the performance of love is quantifiable, indeed marketable. Brian Rotman in his book *Signifying Nothing: The Semiotics of Zero* analyzes *King Lear* from the point of view of the mathematical sign zero entering Western consciousness as a major disruption of Medieval stability. The play with its reverberating line "Nothing comes out of nothing" centers for him on the commodification of love with Lear's act detonating a series of events that render his world obsolete and shattered. As Rotman says:

> [Lear's] demand of "most" for "largest," the maximum amount of love for a ceremoniously measurable portion of the kingdom, reveals that it is in the one-dimensional language of quantity—arithmetic—that Lear has constructed his deal. It is a deal that treats love as a commodity, something to be bought and sold by suitably formulated speech ... speech that had internalised the principle of the deal to become the language of commerce.[43]

This reading of Shakespeare's play illuminates and underscores the buying and selling of love, a theme often overlooked or minimized by Shakespeare scholars. For Rotman:

> Lear is not a pagan folk king mythologised by Shakespeare, nor some trans-historical figure of nihilism, nor the hero of a Christian epic of Job-like redemption, nor the universal Old Dying Man Goethe took him to be, he is the embodiment of a contemporary, historically unique, social and cultural event. Lear registers, he acts out, he is, the rupture in the medieval world brought about by transactions of Renaissance capitalism.[44]

While Rotman opens up *King Lear* as a terrifying meditation on monetary transactions and a commodities market that buys and sells love, Coppélia Kahn explores the absent mother in the play iterating the work's essential connection to gender. These two analytical strands—commerce and gender—come together in the wedding ceremony in which the dowry reflects the gendered, transactional nature of the exchange. In Shakespeare's play there is one offstage marriage (Cordelia to France), while in *Lear's Daughters* there are two onstage simultaneous weddings: Regan and Goneril. Marriage is the focus of the final scenes in the play—marriage as escape from the Lear household (for Regan and Goneril) and as a necessity to maintain the male line. In Scene Twelve the two older sisters discuss their weddings. The scene opens with Goneril reading a ledger, an accounts book, bequeathed to her after her mother's death. The women closest to Lear, first the Queen, then the eldest Goneril, keep track of the money, but have no say over its use or spending. Functioning as a bookkeeper, an accountant, Goneril responds to Regan's questioning about marrying:

GONERIL: It's our job. It's what we're here for. To marry and breed.
REGAN: Like dogs?
GONERIL: Like dogs. Valuable merchandise. I can show you the figures here if you like [229].

The brutality of the numbers, the account book, is counterpoised with the brutality of an abortion: Regan is two months pregnant prior to her marriage and must abort in order to maintain her worth in the economy of gender. The Nurse and Goneril hold the screaming Regan after she drinks an abortificant. The double wedding of the two sisters follows Regan's collapse on the stage.

The concluding scene begins with the Nurse's dismissal by the King, as the daughters are grown they no longer need a nanny — an alternate mother. Each sister has a short concluding statement that foreshadows specific events in Shakespeare's play. Goneril (who as a child loved colors) expresses deep-seated anger at her controlling father and laces this anger with references to the color red ("Red in my eyes. Red on my hands" [232]), which presage the gouging of Gloucester's eyes. Regan's childhood fascination was with touch, the texture of wood and her love of carving. Her final words disturbingly connect her carving knife to her father's dismissive treatment of her mother. Cordelia's final words mirror, in some cases exactly, her first words in Scene One: "Words are like stones, heavy and solid and everyone different." She continues: "When I'm silent I'm trying to get them right" (217, 232). Cordelia's love of words and her declaration of the importance of silence for her foreshadow her famous refusal to tell her father publicly how much she loves him.

Following these monologues, the Fool throws a crown up in the air and "the sisters all reach up and catch it" (232). For Fischlin and Fortier this gesture — three female hands holding the crown — provides a "vision of a potential solidarity and the symbolic empowerment associated with grasping the crown [which] radically remake[s] Shakespeare" (216). As the sisters freeze grasping the crown, the Fool has the final moment by holding out its hand for money. This is both an "ending," as the Fool says, and as we know "a beginning" — this telling sets in motion the venerated play by Shakespeare. Renaissance scholar Stephen Greenblatt in his book *Will in the World* summarizes Shakespeare's *King Lear* as follows: "The tragedy is his greatest meditation on extreme old age; on the painful necessity of renouncing power; on the loss of house, land, authority, love, eyesight, and sanity itself."[45] At the center of this meditation is also the loss of "male prerogative and male power."[46] *Lear's Daughters* initiates a dialogue between the past and the present that exposes the ramifications of this power for the daughters who apprehend their vulnerability at an early age. Metatheatrically — the production is the site of something else. Just as the Fool intervenes in *Lear's Daughters* to remind us of the link between gender and money, so too does Women's Theatre Group intervene in theater making to deliver new insights into the vexed and troubling "roles" for women.

Notes

1. Ben Brantley, "When Adaptation is Bold Innovation," *The New York Times*, 18 February 2007: B9.
2. The Sphinx Theatre is the new name of The Women's Theatre Group. The name changed in the early 1990s. The Sphinx Theatre website is http://www.sphinxtheatre.co.uk.
3. Sue Parrish, "Forward: The Power of Tradition," *The Glass Ceiling* (London: The Sphinx, 1991) 4.
4. See Kenneth Muir, "Introduction," *The Arden Shakespeare: King Lear* (London: Methuen, 1969) xliv-xlv; Daniel Fischlin and Mark Fortier, eds., *Adaptations of Shakespeare: A Critical Anthology of Plays from the Seventeenth Century to the Present* (London: Routledge, 2000). Lamb's essay on *King Lear* is discussed in John I. Ades, "Charles Lamb, Shakespeare, and Early Nineteenth Century Theater," *PMLA* 85.3 (May 1970): 518. In 1906 Tolstoy published *Shakespeare and the Drama*. George Orwell takes on Tolstoy's critique of *King Lear* in "Lear, Tolstoy, and the Fool," *Polemic* 7 (March 1947). Maynard Mack, *King Lear in our Time* (Berkeley: University of California Press, 1965) provides an excellent overview of the controversy in the first chapter.
5. Fischlin and Fortier 2.
6. See Grace Ioppolo, ed., *A Routledge Literary Sourcebook on William Shakespeare's King Lear* (London: Routledge, 2003) 69-70 for a discussion of the play's popularity.
7. Clare Bayley, "Women in Shakespeare," *Royal Shakespeare Company Magazine* (Spring 1994): 19.
8. Aphra Behn (1640-1689), considered the first professional woman writer in England, was a prolific and popular playwright. The Women's Playhouse Trust, in 1984, revived *The Lucky Chance* (first produced in 1686) at the Royal Court Theatre. The play centers on young wealthy women forced into arranged marriages with elderly men. *The Rover*, her most popular work during her lifetime, features a range of fascinating women characters.
9. Lesley Ferris, ed., *Crossing the Stage: Controversies on Cross-Dressing* (London: Routledge, 1993) 2.
10. Brian Bedford, "Interview: Playing Lear," Stratford Festival, 9 Feb. 2007 <http://www.stratfordfestival.ca/video/#07_lear_bbedford>.
11. Oliver Ford Davies, *Playing Lear: An Insider's Guide from Text to Performance* (London: Nick Hern Books, 2003) 5.
12. Ibid., 3.
13. Arthur Holmberg, "*Lear* Girds for a Remarkable Episode," *The New York Times*, 20 May 1990: 7.
14. Elizabeth Klett, "'O, How This Mother Swells Up Toward My Heart': Performing Mother and Father in Helena Kaut-Howson's Cross-Gender *King Lear*," *Shakespeare Bulletin* 22 (September 2005): 53.
15. Elizabeth Schafer, *Ms-Directing Shakespeare: Women Direct Shakespeare* (New York: St. Martin's Press, 2000) 141.
16. Iris Smith, "Mabou Mines's *Lear*: A Narrative of Collective Authorship," *Theatre Journal* 45 (1993): 281.
17. Ross Wetzsteon, "Queen Lear: Ruth Maleczech Gender Bends Shakespeare," *The Village Voice* 30 (January 1990): 40.
18. Smith 285.
19. Wetzsteon 40.
20. Smith 285.
21. Ibid., 288.
22. See Alisa Solomon's essay on the process of creating this production in *Re-Dressing the Canon: Essays on Theater and Gender* (London: Routledge, 1997) 130-144.
23. For a comparison between *Lear's Daughters* and Howard Barker's *Seven Lears* see Graham Saunders' essay "Missing Mothers and Absent Fathers," *Modern Drama* 42.3 (Fall 1999): 401.

24. Lizbeth Goodman, "Womens' Alternative Shakespeares and Women's Alternative to Shakespeare in Contemporary British Theatre," *Cross-Cultural Performance: Differences in Women's Re-Visions of Shakespeare*, ed. Marianne Novy (Urbana: University of Illinois Press, 1993) 55.

25. Michelene Wandor, *Carry On, Understudies: Theatre and Sexual Politics* (London: Routledge, 1986) 65.

26. Fischlin and Fortier 217. Goodman documents the difficult problem identifying the author/s of collectively created work. She examines the issue with the original production of *Lear's Daughters* in *Contemporary Feminist Theatres: To Each Her Own* (London: Routledge, 1993) 97–100. As a coda to that detailed account, I would add that The Sphinx Theatre website <http://www.sphinxtheatre.co.uk> (2007) credits Elaine Feinstein as the single author.

27. Research for this essay revealed a 2003 production of the play by Yellow Earth Theatre, a London-based touring company founded by five East Asian performers in 1995. (See http://www.yellowearth.org.) It is rare for collectively created scripts to be published, let alone produced by others. The reviews of the production discuss the diverse casting of the women, a strategy that was also a crucial component of the original production. See Goodman, "Women's Alternative Shakespeares," for a full discussion of this.

28. Coppélia Kahn, "The Absent Mother in *King Lear*," *Rewriting the Renaissance: The Discourses of Sexual Difference in Early Modern Europe*, ed. Margaret Ferguson, Maureen Quilligan, and Nancy J. Vickers (Chicago: University of Chicago Press, 1986) 33–36.

29. Aeschylus, *The Oresteian Trilogy*, trans. Philip Vellacott (Harmondsworth: Penguin, 1983) lines 656–57.

30. Ferris, *Acting Women: Images of Women in Theatre* (London: Macmillan, 1990) 112–116. See Julie Malnig's "All is Not Right in the House of Atreus: Feminist Theatrical Renderings of the *Oresteia*" in this volume.

31. Kahn 36.

32. Women's Theatre Group and Elaine Feinstein, *Lear's Daughters*, Fischlin and Fortier, 228. Additional references in the text.

33. Muir lxiii.

34. Gabriele Griffin and Elaine Aston, eds., *Herstory: Plays by Women for Women*, vol. 1 (Sheffield: Sheffield Academic Press, 1991) 24.

35. Juliet Dusinberre, *Shakespeare and the Nature of Women* (London: Macmillan, 1985) 114.

36. Marilyn French, *Shakespeare's Division of Experience* (London: Abacus, 1983) 233.

37. Germaine Greer, *Shakespeare: A Very Short Introduction* (Oxford: Oxford University Press, 1986) 103.

38. Dusinberre 153.

39. Antony Sher, *Beside Myself: An Autobiography* (London: Hutchison, 2001) 164–165.

40. Muir lxiii.

41. William Shakespeare, *King Lear*, The Arden Shakespeare, ed. Kenneth Muir (London: Methuen, 1969) 217.

42. Dusinberre 114.

43. Brian Rotman, *Signifying Nothing: The Semiotics of Zero* (Stanford: Stanford University Press, 1993) 79.

44. Rotman 86.

45. Stephen Greenblatt, *Will in the World: How Shakespeare Became Shakespeare* (New York: W.W. Norton, 2004) 356.

46. Kahn 36.

The Feminist Playwright as Critic
Paula Vogel, Ann-Marie MacDonald, and Djanet Sears Interpret Othello

Sharon Friedman

The Desdemona plays of Paula Vogel and Ann-Marie MacDonald, and Djanet Sears's prequel to *Othello*, transposed to contemporary Harlem, demonstrate the synergy between theater and theory in their inventive feminist rewritings of Shakespeare's tragedy. Theatrically, these playwrights employ many of the conventions of feminist adaptation of classic texts established by the late 1980s in women's theater groups and other experimental companies. They foreground the women's plight, depict female relationships, and refocus plot to reveal the "high cost of patriarchal values" that several feminist scholars see embedded in Shakespeare's tragedies.[1] Sears's text explores the intersections of race and gender through the subjectivity of a black woman suffering rejection by her husband, Othello, who seeks inclusion in the prevailing culture through an interracial relationship. The plays reflect Carol Neely's observations that feminist adaptations of Shakespeare often alternate "between anger and empowerment, between critique of patriarchal culture and the creation of alternatives to it." These revisionist writers enlist Shakespeare's texts to "enable their critique," and in the process "transform his scripts into their own."[2]

All three playwrights play freely with Shakespeare's *Othello* to stage a counter universe at the same time that they evoke our memories (or associations) with the play. Using postmodern theatrical strategies, Vogel and MacDonald disrupt and transform familiar scenes and imagine alternate scenarios. Both MacDonald and Sears insert new protagonists, and Sears invents an entirely new history for her contemporary Othello as a prelude to the "updated" version that we anticipate. Furthermore, all three dramatists incorporate contemporary critical approaches from feminist and gender studies, literary criticism, and performance and cultural studies that result in a highly theatricalized drama of ideas. In the process they become feminist critics who resist, revise,

J. Smith-Cameron (Desdemona), Fran Brill (Emilia), and Cherry Jones (Bianca) in Paula Vogel's *Desdemona*, 1993, performed at the Bay Street Theatre Festival, New York. Photograph courtesy of the Bay Street Theatre, Sag Harbor, New York. Photographer: Michael Gravel. The world premier of *Desdemona* was presented by Bay Street Theatre, Sag Harbor, New York, in association with Circle Repertory Company, New York, New York, June 1993.

and produce new meanings in their dialogue with the Bard, as well as the critical traditions and cultural institutions that have canonized his works.[3]

Feminist Theater and Theory

Several theorists have commented on the interplay of criticism and creativity in theater. Helene Keyssar notes that the decade of the nineties saw a proliferation of diverse writings in feminist criticism and theory that she interprets as a "response to the maturation and continuation of feminist theatre itself" and the emergence of this theatre as a recognized "cultural form."[4] Indeed, Jill Dolan casts the "feminist spectator as critic," the title of her book and the inspiration for this essay. As she argues, "denaturalizing the position of the ideal spectator as representative of the dominant culture enables the feminist critic to point out that every aspect of theatrical production, from the types of plays and performances produced to the texts that are ultimately canonized, is determined to reflect and perpetuate the ideal spectator's ideology."[5] The feminist spectator, therefore, is "subversive by nature," resisting identification with "alien" or "offensive" representations. This active viewer scrutinizes the "performance frame" for depictions of her gender and/or race, class or sexual preference, dissecting and exposing ideologies in any "critical or creative act," with the recognition that ideology re-presented in theater is a "force that participates in creating and maintaining social arrangements."[6]

Gayle Austin sees the potential in "practitioners being theorists and theorists being practitioners," and in the process, "asking what they can learn from each other." She even imagines theory as a dramatic text — a "theory play" that performs, in striking new ways, insights drawn from anthropology, psychology, literary criticism, and film theory. Eschewing the pitfalls of didacticism, Austin describes the passion she experiences in responding to texts and performances through a feminist lens as an "erotics of theory."[7] Borrowing film critic Tania Modleski's anthropological terminology, she views interpretation as a "gift" in the "symbolic exchange between the critic [read playwright] and the women to whom she talks and writes." Furthermore, as Modleski articulates it, feminist criticism may "'have a performative dimension — i.e., to be *doing* something beyond restating existent ideas and views.'"[8]

Perhaps the most active spectator/critic in the theater is the playwright who dialogues with a canonical text through a substantially altered but recognizable version of its source text that calls attention to the interpretative element in any adaptation. The assumption in this form of intertextuality is, as Judith Still and Michael Worton phrase it, that every "writer is a reader of texts ... before she/he is a creator of texts," and the repetition of texts can take many forms, including "the most conscious and sophisticated elaboration of other poets' work."[9] In the case of the playwright who employs postmodern theater devices to destabilize the authority of the canonized text as well as any fixed notion of gender identity perpetuated by the universalism associated with the classics, the repetition can also be "oppositional."[10] It often takes the form of parody, deconstruction, and transposition, not only from one locale (or period) to another in search of parallels between past and present, but from one subject position to another (e.g. Desdemona assumes Emilia's or Othello's stance) to "disarticulate the past" and the presumption of continuity and universality.[11] In order to effect these transformations, productions experiment with time, space, language, and the body. Theatrical devices function not only as "aesthetic radicalism," but as interventions with the aim of demystifying the discourse, images, and myth inscribed in the text and through which "ideal spectators" are encouraged to experience themselves.[12]

Theorizing and Re-visioning Shakespeare

Several critics have commented on the astounding number of re-productions, adaptations, and radical revisions of Shakespeare's plays, particularly in the late twentieth century when literary and dramatic criticism expanded the concept of text. Shakespeare scholarship informed by Marxist, historicist, and feminist criticism views literary texts as cultural texts, and this perspective has found its way to the stage. In *Performing Nostalgia*, Susan Bennett quotes Jean E. Howard and Marion O'Connor in an epigraph to her section "Shakespeare, Agent of Power": "'Probably more than any other figure in western culture, Shakespeare has been used to secure assumptions about texts, history, ideology, and criticism.... He functions, in many quarters, as a kind of cultural Esperanto.'"[13] Analyzing the "nostalgia" that often motivates these performances, Bennett argues that Shakespeare is a "signifier," and for some "the ultimate pinnacle" of cultural elitism, patriarchy, and colonial imperialism, with which to explore the past in the present.[14] Clearly, several feminist playwrights take this attitude and embark on theatrical revision as a "weapon in the struggle for supremacy between various ideologies, various poetics."[15] However, many critics argue that Shakespeare does question the prevailing ideas of his culture and dramatizes the anxieties that emanate from the exercise of power.[16] Whether we see Shakespeare's plays re-inscribing or questioning patriarchal attitudes toward women, the discourses surrounding gender relationships based on power encoded in his texts are available for contemporary playwrights to put in motion. These playwrights challenge the terms by which women are defined, the theatrical spaces to which they have often been relegated — "backroom, bedroom, balconies,"[17] and open up myriad interpretations of the Shakespeare play that inspired their transformations.

Marianne Novy is the most prolific critic to examine women's rewritings of Shakespeare. In a series of volumes, she has explored the directions and dimensions of essays, novels, and theater works from historical and cross-cultural perspectives.[18] She observes that these writers, particularly during the period of second-wave feminism beginning in the 1960s, often incorporated into their responses to Shakespeare a critique of "colonialism, race, class, nationalism, militarism, environmental issues and sexuality." Novy also observes that using fiction as a form of criticism, these works grew out of an "interpretive community" of writers, scholars, and performers. Especially germane to this paper is Novy's assertion that *Othello* has been given particular attention by feminist critics concerned with its depiction of gender issues.[19] Her comparative article on Vogel's and MacDonald's Desdemona plays, "Saving Desdemona and/or Ourselves," argues that both writers are intrigued by the shift in Shakespeare's Desdemona from "adventurer" to "victim," and ponder "whether women can escape tragedy." However, her close examination of their parodic transformations suggests that they were guided by "different feminist ideas." MacDonald demonstrates the potential in positive images of "female strength and authority," and Vogel eschews role models to present an analysis of "male power, the ideologies and structures that maintain it, and the exploitative possibilities in relationships between women of different classes."[20]

Ric Knowles's "Othello in Three Times," also takes a contextual approach in his comparative article on Canadian adaptations of *Othello* that include MacDonald's *Goodnight Desdemona* and Djanet Sears's *Harlem Duet*. He interprets these revisionist plays produced between the 1970s and the 1990s, from the perspective of changing attitudes toward "'Shakespeare'" and the "construction of gender, race, ethnicity, and class" in Canada. His reading of MacDonald's *Goodnight Desdemona* notes its "second-wave feminist focus on the relationship between gender and genre," particularly the view that the tragedies, unlike the comedies, restrict women's agency. Her protagonist alters the power relations between the men and women in Shakespeare's text and, in the process, recognizes the subordination she has enacted in her own unexamined life. Knowles observes that in creating a "hybrid form," MacDonald turns tragedy into comedy, her tragic women into comic heroines, and reclaims Shakespeare's texts for women.[21]

Knowles observes that in *Harlem Duet*, Sears carves out a "revisionist intervention" that focuses attention on black women's experiences. Furthermore, she dramatizes the intersection of race and gender in the "central fact of *Othello*" often ignored in prior adaptations: a black man in relationship with a white woman. Knowles perceives Sears's play as participating not only in a counter-canonical tradition forged by black women playwrights, but also a 1990s effort to "redress the imbalances" of a feminist movement that elided race in seeking gender-based alliances among women.[22] Sears's "rhapsodic blues tragedy" is also a hybrid form that situates her "vexed relationship to Shakespeare, to Othello [the moor often played by white actors], and to high culture" in her rendition of Black history, its traditions and theoretical debates about achieving freedom and equality. At the same time that the play tries to "exorcise" *Othello*, it "makes claims" on the text as a site for the negotiation of cultural values. And like MacDonald's "generic in(ter)vention," it stages a "trope of self-rebirth" for its protagonist.[23]

Building on analyses by Novy, Knowles, and other critics who discern ideological discourses woven into these plays, this essay will also examine the resonance between literary and performance theories and the playwrights' inventive staging of these discourses. The passion in this kind of theorizing emanates not only from the dialogue between the artist and her audience, but also from the "hedonistic" acts of reading and writing back to Shakespeare in an intimate exchange (recounted by the playwrights themselves in prefaces, interviews, and in letters to the audience). Susan Bennett draws a link between Roland Barthes' notion of reading "in a hedonistic mode" that "unsettles the reader's historical, cultural, psychological assumptions, the consistency of his tastes, values, memories" and Artaud's call to abolish masterpieces by establishing a theater of "immediate physicality."[24] The plays under discussion invite audiences to respond intellectually, emotionally, and viscerally, and to reflect upon their unsettled responses in light of their experiences and expectations of the Shakespeare text reconsidered.

Paula Vogel's Desdemona: A Play about a Handkerchief[25]

In the premiere of *Desdemona* (1993), Paula Vogel included in the program notes a brief synopsis of *Othello*, followed by her letter to the audience in which she reveals her implicit dialogue with Shakespeare and traditional criticism surrounding the play.[26] She begins by sharing her memories of earlier readings, when she had wept for the Moor, who "goaded to desperation by the innuendos of cuckoldry that [his ensign] Iago manufactured, [and] believing his virginal bride to be the harlot coupling with his lieutenant Cassio, gives in to homicide," strangling "pure, blameless Desdemona" in her bed. At the same time, however, and despite Vogel's admiration for Shakespeare's "fantastic verse," she began to question the critical assessment of Desdemona as a "fully dimensional heroine." The woman that she reads is an abstraction played by "gawky male adolescents." Furthermore, Vogel raises two provocative questions regarding conduct in a text which, though naturalized through the ages, in her mind bears questioning:

> Had Desdemona been sleeping with the Russian Navy [that is, the Venetian garrison], would Othello have been justified in his self-pitying act of murder? [And] why did Emilia [wed to the treacherous Iago] steal the handkerchief Othello had given his wife, if she was such a devoted servant to Desdemona? ["A Letter from the Playwright"].[27]

This self-reflexive reading of *Othello*, reveals the playwright as a feminist spectator turned critic. In a deconstructive parody that dramatizes her own questions, Vogel rewrites the scene between Desdemona and Emilia, expands it to become the entire play, and places Othello's drama offstage so as to focus the action on the women's intrigues and motivations. Her raucous Desdemona undermines the conventional wisdom of a critic such as Alvin Kernan, who asserts that "In Desdemona alone do the heart and the hand go together: she is what she seems to be."[28] Vogel's Desdemona is not "of spirit so still and quiet" (I.3.95). Rather, she is Othello's worst nightmare, the transformation of Iago's pretence into reality. Though still naïve, Desdemona is no longer the innocent—unselfish in her love, forgiving of all transgressions against her. She is sexually adventurous as she works for Cassio's harlot, Bianca, in her brothel, seemingly voracious in her appetites, manipulative of anyone who can feed them, and anything but loyal in her relationships with women or men.

One might ask how this ignoble depiction transcends the abstraction that Vogel resists? Clearly, the playwright brings a close reading to the text and relies on dramatic irony as she reaches back through the critics to Shakespeare in order to fashion a more sexually transgressive Desdemona out of his subversive cues. After all, Brabantio, Desdemona's father, warns Othello that his daughter might betray him as she has betrayed her father by marrying a Moor without his consent. Furthermore, Othello reveals that Desdemona had been aroused by listening to his dangerous exploits:

> She'd come again, and with a greedy ear
> Devour up my discourse.
> [...]
> She wished she had not heard it:
> Yet she wished that heaven had made her such a man [I.3.148–162].

Vogel transposes this "greedy ear," into a greed for conquest and sexual adventure that Desdemona associates with male freedom. She explains to the scornful Emilia her desire to break out of her "narrow world" and to see the "other worlds" that married women, "bridled with linen, blinded with lace" never get to see (19).

Composing and directing the first staged reading of the play while a graduate student at Cornell in 1987, Vogel, no doubt, was aware of new critical approaches to "old" texts. She employs deconstruction and cultural criticism to her reading, moving beyond the character, beyond Shakespeare, to the culture he interprets. She probes the "unconscious" of the text — the anxiety behind the Renaissance ideal of pure and passive femininity, guardian of masculine sexuality, that all women, descendants of Eve, are responsible for the sin of human sexuality regardless of what they do or do not do, articulated by both Othello and Iago. Jyotsna Singh insightfully observes: "To label *Othello* a 'tragedy of jealousy' has almost become a critical commonplace. What has less frequently been specified is a crucial aspect of his male jealousy — namely the fear that wives can turn into whores or, put another way, that wives and whores are indistinguishable."[29] And it is this anxiety, rooted in the struggle for a secure masculine identity, that Vogel stages in her parodic revision in which Desdemona "acts out" sexually one night a week in Bianca's brothel. What if Desdemona were all that Othello fears? Would this justify his murderous deed? Either way — as faithful wife or cuckolding "whore," she is brutally punished.

Indeed, Vogel does not attempt to celebrate the purportedly "womanly" virtues — the "flexibility, compassion, realism" attributed to Shakespearean heroines.[30] She does not perceive in the women's intimacy a "mutual affection" or even a kind of female "subculture" apart from the man's world, associated with cultural feminist theory.[31] Nor does her revision function as an intervention to correct and revise the restrictions that so obviously oppress the women and inform the men's destructive fantasies of betrayal. In her analysis of *Desdemona* Novy contends that Vogel's feminist concerns focus on "structures of oppression" that shape and maintain institutions and ideologies of male power as well as conflicts between women based on class[32] — a stance often termed material feminism. Furthermore, Vogel's play marks an important shift in the feminist critical perspective in drama as characterized by Lynda Hart in her collection of essays on contemporary women's theater: "The shift ... from discovering and creating positive images of women in the content of the drama to analyzing and disrupting the ideological codes embedded in the inherited structures of dramatic representation."[33] In my view, Vogel stages her deconstruction of the discourses surrounding romantic love and women's sexuality woven through Shakespeare's text to reveal gender relations based on patriarchal power enacted in the family and the state. Furthermore, she does so through attention to dramatic conventions, stage space, iconicity, the body, and audience — all crucial elements of the performance text innovated by writers and directors and theorized in performance studies.

Vogel dislodges and magnifies the convention of the intimate scene between women in Shakespeare's theater that scholars have interpreted as representing a "counter universe" to the "increased oppression of the outside world."[34] In de-centering the tragic hero, she foregrounds and enacts the threat of female transgression — the construction of female desire — the anxiety-ridden fantasy that incites the tragic action of the play. Situated in the backroom of the palace, Emilia's workroom is filled with tools, baskets, leather bits, dirty laundry, objects that represent her subordinate social position in relation to Desdemona. The women use bodily presence and ribald language in place of whispering asides, delicately expressed confidences and plaintive ballads (e.g. Desdemona's song of lament in the willow scene). These familiar female characters, central to our most cherished narratives, speak in a forbidden language about male organs and copulation, and body forth their disruption of the categories they are intended to represent — the twin images of the virgin/whore dichotomy and the faithful handmaiden — linked to gender and class status. As in women's performance art, "the position of the female subject talking back throws that position into process, into doubt."[35]

Vogel also rearranges plot and stage space to bring the prostitute, Bianca, from the streets into the backroom of the palace, now center stage, and juxtapose her with Desdemona and Emilia. Vogel's "counter-universe" becomes anything but a safe haven. It is fraught with differences among the women and contradictions within each character. Their world is presented as inextricably intertwined with all that surrounds it to reveal the hierarchy and the intersection of gender and class relationships that might explain Emila's careless but fatal betrayal of Desdemona by confiscating the handkerchief that indicts her. In *Othello*, it is Emilia who punctures the ideal of women's purity and of unwavering faithfulness to husbands. When Desdemona asks her "Wouldst thou do such a deed for all the world?" Emilia replies: The world's a huge thing; it is a great price for a small vice" (IV.iii.70). She imagines fashioning a world that would make her wrong a right, and her cuckoldry would make her husband a monarch. In *Desdemona*, Vogel reverses the women's respective stances and gives Desdemona Emilia's lines. It is Desdemona, with the haughtiness of the desirable noblewoman, who tries to remake the world — not for her husband's gain, but for her own power: Her Emilia is unwilling to take chances, intimating that her position in the social order is vulnerable enough. Emilia's "vice" is to steal the handkerchief to aid her husband. Still clever, she explains:

> For us in the bottom ranks, when a man and wife hate each other, what is left in a lifetime of marriage but to save and scrimp, plot and plan? I says to him each night—I long for the day you make me a lieutenant's widow [13].

Vogel produces multiple and shifting identities as she dramatizes a whoring Desdemona, a spiritually monogamous Bianca devoted to Cassio, and a sassy Emilia who does not understand or always support the lady she serves. The subtext of this subversion of stereotype and depiction of difference is that women do not constitute a monolithic body or unified stance.

In *Othello* the handkerchief given to Desdemona by Othello to ensure his fidelity is confiscated by Emilia and placed by Iago in Cassio's possession—only to end up in the hands of his strumpet Bianca to become proof of Desdemona's alleged betrayal. It also functions as a powerful metaphor for the proprietary attitude toward women's sexuality and status as objects of exchange between men. Whoever possesses the handkerchief possesses the woman. The iconic identity of the handkerchief in Vogel's play—visible in a lit corner of the stage as the play opens—retains its power to convict Desdemona. However, we also see it as a mere contrivance—a "snot rag" in Desdemona's contemptuous language. The women become the "ocular proof" that Shakespeare's Othello yearns for to justify his accusation and revenge (III.iii.357). Their formidable presence functions iconically to represent their threatening sexuality, purported emasculating power, duplicitous nature, and exchange value that had only been treated symbolically in *Othello*.

Amidst all of her daring and bravado, Desdemona's fate is sealed in the cultural code reflected in the punishment of death for betrayal that she is to receive from Othello, even in Vogel's revision. The final scenes of the play constitute this tragic recognition shared by two women. Vogel, once again, dislodges a generic convention associated with tragedy—the moment of recognition that signals self-knowledge for the male protagonist. Together Desdemona and Emilia discover that Othello's gathering up of the wedding sheets from her bed, "like a body," breathing it in "like a bouquet," isn't love (45). It is surveillance.

As spectators producing meaning in our interaction with Shakespeare's text and with Vogel's production simultaneously, we might resist her disturbing representation as we long for a Desdemona free of Othello's conception of her, pure or vile, and revisioned as more tragically heroic. Yet, we feel Othello's conception more powerfully in his absence. And when this Desdemona addresses the audience directly, without the mediation of the male protagonist, spectators might, in a Brechtian sense, become "alienated" from their "habitual perceptions" of a character made strange by this shift in viewpoint.[36] Indeed, Vogel makes use of Brechtian techniques in an episodic structure of thirty short scenes punctuated with flashes of light and percussive music that invites spectators to interpose judgment between the acts and alternatives to the course of events. The audience, presumably grappling with their varied responses to the revisions of the source text, might also become aware of what does *not* change. The female world, though presented more subjectively, is still performing under a watchful scrutinizing eye. For all of Desdemona's maneuvers, she is forever confined within Othello's gaze. Spectators, however, distanced from Othello's drama, might recognize this gaze and resist its compelling vision.

Ann-Marie MacDonald's Goodnight Desdemona (Good Morning, Juliet)

Like Vogel, Ann-Marie MacDonald staged the first version of her play in 1988, though to a much wider audience. Commissioned and produced by Nightwood Theatre in Toronto during what Ric Knowles calls its "second mandate" to concentrate on the creation of "women-centred work," the play was subsequently revised in 1990 to tour nationally with Nightwood, and received the Governor-General's Award for Drama.[37] MacDonald, too, reveals herself as a spectator/critic in her implicit dialogue with the Bard, as her protagonist explicitly dialogues with his characters through her disruption of scenes and verses. In interviews, MacDonald recounts her experience as an actress facing a legion of roles in which women were "'representatives of vulnerability and instability.'" As a playwright she "'opened up a trunk that used to be filled with instruments of torture'" and "'turned [them] into toys,'" mischievously using Shakespeare "'in the same way he used everyone else as a source.'"[38] Beverly Curran links MacDonald's experiences in the theater to her observation that although MacDonald acknowledges Shakespeare in her "Notes on the text" ("The Bard is immanent, and beyond thanks"), the play is "dedicated to you, gentle reader" and that "its process" of "re-reading and re-writing" is an "intimate collaboration with the woman viewer/reader."[39] Ric Knowles observes that "the play is a theoretically sophisticated enactment of resistant reading,"[40] theorized by Judith Fetterley as reading against the ideologies of fictions that ask a woman reader to identify with a "selfhood that defines itself in opposition to her."[41] In this context, MacDonald's play challenges the institutional power of the theater to reproduce stereotypical roles for women, and the authority of the academy to perpetuate and naturalize these roles with interpretive strategies that preclude personally and politically engaged readings.

Indeed MacDonald's protagonist is an outcast academic, the beleaguered assistant professor and eternal "ABD," who finds herself in the midst of Shakespearean scenes that pique her scholarly imagination. Through Constance Ledbelly, MacDonald inhabits Shakespeare's plays as they have inhabited her, and stages a theatrical romp with hilarious consequences unintended by the character. Act I begins with Constance sequestered in her office with green plumed fountain pen and her "copious dog-eared" doctoral thesis "handwritten in green ink on foolscap," perhaps signaling the "green world" she is about to create. She is unaware of the Chorus of one who has just foreshadowed, in alchemic metaphors, her psychic quest. Her scholarly ruminations are transformed into a fantastic farcical journey through time as she moves in quantum leaps from one play to the next, replete with Shakespearean devices of mistaken identities and cross-dressed lovers. (MacDonald italicizes Shakespeare's lines.) Constance's discoveries, of course, are facilitated by her interactions with an adventurous Desdemona and a flirtatious Juliet, perhaps projections of feminine archetypes that MacDonald, a Jungian, plays with in Constance's dream-like escapade. However, like Vogel, MacDonald calls attention to the contradictions in Desdemona's character, shifting from what one critic sees as a "powerful voice, trumpeting her love for Othello to the world" to her gradual "self-erasure" by play's end.[42] Constance's journey becomes an intervention as she disrupts pivotal scenes (such as Iago's arousal of Othello's jealous fears revolving around the spotted handkerchief) that spell death for her heroines. Furthermore, she assigns familiar speeches to other characters, and redirects their desires to fulfill her unconscious wishes for Desdemona and Juliet that fuel her imaginative life.

Through the timid Constance, MacDonald conveys both a reluctance and a will to challenge cultural and institutional authorities. Constance is betrayed by her mentor, Claude Night, and deemed the laughing stock of the faculty because of her endless hermeneutic translation of an arcane manuscript. The manuscript, she believes, would produce evidence to challenge authorship and canonical criticism of Shakespeare's tragedies and, by implication, the tragic fate of the women. Prying open the plays, she contemplates the impending disasters, and, instead, sees "flimsy mistakes — a lost hanky, [and in the case of Juliet] a delayed wedding announcement" — that might easily be "set right" and that lead her to seek a source beyond Shakespeare for the answers to her questions. As Constance thinks aloud:

> In neither play do the supposedly fate-ordained deaths of the flawed heroes and heroines, seem quite inevitable. Indeed, it is only because the deaths do occur that they can be called inevitable in hindsight, thus allowing the plays to squeak by under the designation "tragedy." In both plays, the tragic characters, particularly Romeo and Othello, have abundant opportunity to save themselves. The fact that they do not save themselves tends to characterize them as unwitting victims of a disastrous practical joke. Insofar as these plays may be said to be fatalistic at all, any grains of authentic tragedy must be seen to reside in the heroines, Desdemona and Juliet [8].

Constance, an awardee of the dead languages prize — in other words, stuck in the past — searches for clues in the Gustav Manuscript that "when finally decoded will prove the prior existence of two comedies by an unknown author

... that Shakespeare plundered and made over into ersatz tragedies" (15). These comedies, she argues, were preserved and yet suppressed by Gustav, the alchemist and an elderly friend of Shakespeare, who would "shrowd them in an arcane code" (17). In MacDonald's play, of course, the code, much like the characters, is not so much cracked as deconstructed to reveal the "tragic tunnel vision" of Desdemona and Juliet as they play out the roles assigned to them by patriarchal institutions and by the conventions of the tragic genre: to die for the honor of her Lord or to die for love. Eventually, Constance instructs her characters to see beyond these prescriptive categories; at the same time, she reveals the unconscious desires of the reader in the text. Like Fetterley's resisting reader, Constance refuses identification with Othello and against herself. She moves literary criticism from a "closed conversation to an active dialogue" questioning the fear of women's sexuality, the sexual desire that, plot-wise, leads to death, and the unexamined theme of love and power.[43]

Arrested by the inscription on the manuscript to "discover your own identity and find who the author be," Constance is released from her temporal boundaries—"screeching wind," music, "warp effects" and all, to find herself in the midst of Shakespeare's scenes in which she plays out her fantasies. She leaves her existence as a scholar in search of arcane texts and attributions to seek the wise fool, who she believes was present in the comic sources and will corroborate her interpretation. In the course of the play, of course, she becomes that insightful fool and ultimately the author of her own text and life.

As Constance "falls into" the plays (speaking blank verse, of course), she discovers aspects of their characters that corroborate not only her reading of genre but also gender. Furthermore, she observes the constraints of genre on gender in tragedy's glorification of male valor at the expense of women who are "marginalized or victimized" within its conventions.[44] Constance transforms tragedy to comedy, the form in which, as Susan Snyder asserts, "ascendancy goes to the clever ones who can take advantage of sudden openings, contrive strategies, and adapt flexibly to an unexpected move from the other side."[45] She appears in Othello's citadel at Cyprus as Othello and Iago "reprise the end of the handkerchief scene," the point at which Iago ignites Othello's jealousy and fear of cuckoldry, and undermines his trust in Desdemona's fidelity. Constance hears the echoing refrain between the two, suggesting that Iago and Othello share the cultural assumption that women are by nature distrustful and require discipline and punishment:

> IAGO: *Tell me but this:*
> *Have you not sometimes seen a handkerchief*
> *spotted with strawberries in your wife's hand?*
> OTHELLO: *I gave her such a one; 'twas my first gift.*
> IAGO: *I know not that; but such a handkerchief–*
> *I am sure it was your wife's— did I today*
> *See Cassio wipe his beard with.*

OTHELLO: *It it be that—*
IAGO: *If it be that, or any that was hers,*
   It speaks against her with the other proofs.
[CONSTANCE's head peaks out from behind the arras]
OTHELLO: *Had Desdemona forty thousand lives!*
   One is too poor, too weak for my revenge. Damn her, lewd minx. I will
   chop her into messes! Cuckold me! [23–24].

Constance lays claim to Desdemona's fate as she "plucks" the handkerchief "hanging from the back of Iago's hose" and hands it to Othello. She not only reverses the course of events, but unwittingly reveals the ideological underpinnings of Othello's all too easy acceptance of Iago's "ocular proof." Constance's intervention — let's call it the "hankie in the hose"— emerges from her determination to show what has been "obvious" to her all along: Iago's deception — a highly cruel "practical joke"— has been invisible to the noble but misguided Othello because above all he fears sexual dishonor. He readily believes Iago's dictum — willingly suspends his disbelief as we do when we interpret him as a tragic victim of his noble passions rather than a base misogyny — that all wives are whores.

Constance's active reading, however, does not rest with Iago and Othello. It is the unruly Desdemona that enters MacDonald's farce and gives bodily presence to the heroic aspects of her character that the intimidated Constance wishes to uncover. Desdemona: "O valiant general and most bloody lord. That I love my lord to live with him, my downright violence and storm of fortunes may trumpet to the world; my sole regret — that heaven had not made me such a man; but next in honor is to be his wife. And I love honor more than life" (27). Constance "discovers" that Desdemona is not what she seems to be, yet Constance's ludicrous plea to Othello to save Desdemona's life points up the critical need to preserve her as the icon of gentility even in the presence of textual cues that might complicate her character: "The divine Desdemona, despite her fascination with violence and her love of horror stories, and aside from the fact that she deceived her father to elope with you, [Othello], is the very embodiment of purity and charity" (9).

Amid the myriad turn of events spawned by Constance's intervention, suffice it to say that Desdemona assumes Othello's role in relation to Constance, but loves her for her courage rather than modesty. By further twists of plot, the unrelenting Iago stirs Desdemona's jealousy by insinuating that Constance has betrayed her with Othello. Each character, in dizzying rotation, comes to occupy a new subject position, detached from her or his traditional role. Iago, however, is constant in his misogyny, and pilfers Constance's manuscript as if it were her handkerchief.

Escaping Cyprus with her skirt "speared into Desdemona's sword," Constance finds herself in Romeo and Juliet's Verona at a pivotal moment in a Shakespeare play. Minus her skirt and wearing just her "longjohns, boots and tweed jacket" she interrupts the sword fight between Tybalt and Mercutio. "I couldn't let you kill each other for, young Juliet and Romeo have wed: and by th'untying of their virgin-knot, have tied new blood betwixt you cousins here" (50). The unintended consequence of unraveling this plot is that both Romeo and Juliet, their youthful passion for each other already cooled, fall instantly in love with Constance — or rather Constantine — the Greek boy as she comes to be known in her new costume. The star-crossed lovers continue to search for transgressive love at first sight — the suppressed desire that emerges in Constance's dream reading. Romeo has homoerotic urges and Juliet thinks the cross-dressed Constance a most endearing man. Constance reluctantly responds to both of the characters she has loved. As we can well imagine, MacDonald parodies the balcony scene — with Juliet playing Romeo and Constance playing Juliet. Juliet wants to die for love, but Constance still quests for self that means more to her than "love or death" (71).

In the final scene — the crypt in the boneyard — Constance releases the characters, entombed in Gustav's Manuscript and swirling around her revisionist dreamscape, to live their own lives. Indeed, she gives up her quest for positive images, offers no corrective to their scenarios, but continues to challenge theatrical representations that have frozen their characters into symbols. Dissatisfied with the characters her revision has generated — a Desdemona as gullible and violent as Othello and a Juliet "in love with death" — the enlightened Constance instructs her characters to recognize the complexities of life. Moreover, as a self-reflexive critic, she calls into question her own project: "I must have been a monumental fool to think that I could save you from yourselves" (86–87). As the resistant reader, Constance ultimately discovers that she has rewritten their destinies to author her own, free of prescriptions for gender and genre. The iconicity of the crypt might be seen as a metaphor for the hermetically sealed text or the unconscious mind. In the end, the crypt is transformed into a textual field of quotations uttered by Desdemona and Juliet as they play out the final lines (not necessarily their own) of the dramas that Constance has attempted to decipher. Instead, her text exists, as Barthes would say, "only as 'discourse'; it is '*plural,*' and 'expressed only in an activity, a production'" — in response to "'an explosion, a dissemination that commands the reader's active collaboration to confer meaning.'"[46] Desdemona learns to "live by questions, not by their solution," and Juliet concurs: "To trade our certainties, for thy confusion" (87). The crypt, no surprise, is magically turned back into Constance's office, and her pen turned to gold.

Djanet Sears's Harlem Duet

Like *Goodnight Desdemona,* Sears's *Harlem Duet* was produced by Toronto's Nightwood Theatre Company and also won the Governor General's

Award (though almost a decade later in 1997).[47] As Ric Knowles points out, in 1989, Nightwood instituted an anti-racist mandate and began to give attention to women of color. In the period following Sears's *African Solo* (1990), the first play published by a Canadian of African descent, black theater artists had come to the fore in Toronto in the context of racist incidents and responses from the black community.[48] Sears refers to the "efforts of African Canadians across the country to form a theatrical tradition" in her introduction to *Testifyin*, her volume of contemporary Canadian Black drama.[49] Her adaptation of *Othello*, as Knowles asserts, is "*all* about race" in relation to nation, class, history, and, most pointedly, gender.[50]

In her foreword to *Harlem Duet*, "Notes of a Coloured Girl," Sears also reveals herself as critic, declaring her resistant reading of *Othello* and her determination to write a play in her effort to "exorcise this ghost" and explore "the effects of race and sex on the lives of people of African descent." More specifically, she points to the minstrelsy in the play's production history that represents the predicament of its protagonist: "...*Othello* had haunted me since I first was introduced to him. Sir Laurence Olivier in black-face. Othello is the first African portrayed in the annals of western dramatic literature."[51] Her Othello functions as a parvenue performing blackness in the halls of academe. He is a professor at Columbia University, about to leave for Cyprus with Mona, his colleague turned lover, to teach his department's courses (read civilization). Abandoning his black wife Billie and their Harlem apartment, he is in the process of becoming an "American," telling Billie that "liberation has no color" (300).

Peter Dickinson points out that *Harlem Duet* might be analyzed comparatively with Vogel's *Desdemona* and MacDonald's *Goodnight Desdemona* as a feminist "re-vision" of Shakespeare. Like MacDonald, Sears underscores the ramifications of production history and theatrical conventions for representing race and/or gender; MacDonald uses cross-dressing, and Sears calls attention to the practice of blackface and the "politics of racial casting."[52] Like Paula Vogel, Sears gives attention to the material conditions that constrain lives and shape desires. And like Vogel, she marginalizes the play, *Othello*, situating his drama offstage, to focus on its implications for women.

The drama center stage is situated in Billie's apartment as she struggles with the loss of her husband. Sears's critical rendering of a contemporary Othello in the context of his personal history within a black community is clearly a meaningful absence in Shakespeare's play. Critic Mark Fortier observes the possibilities in plundering the Shakespeare text for its "'gaps and blind spots'" and probing those spaces to see what "lurks there for us."[53] In *Othello* we know little of the protagonist's background other than his "travel's history" through "battles, sieges, fortune" and his tales of dangerous forays among Cannibals and "insolent foe" (I.3.129–144). As Stephen Greenblatt argues, "His identity depends upon a constant performance ... of his 'story,' a loss of his own origins, an embrace and perpetual reiteration of the norms of another culture."[54] Karen Newman perceives Othello's narrative as a "rehearsal of his origins," rather than a loss, moving "from his exotic tales of monstrous races to the story of the handkerchief's genealogy in witchcraft and Sibylline prophesy"—"ascriptions of European colonial discourse" that link him, in Desdemona's eyes, with Africa and "its legendary monstrous creatures."[55] In contrast, Sears imagines a history for her Othello, recited by the woman he leaves behind. In her mythic narrative, free of monstrous bestiality, she recounts their arrival in Harlem on the very day that Nelson and Winnie Mandela came to speak, and to the home they created at the intersection of boulevards named for Malcolm X and Martin Luther King. *Harlem Duet* becomes Billie's story of embracing her homeland, Harlem (real and imaginary), sometimes in concert with Othello, but more often accompanied by the voices of her women friends in their plea to sustain lasting relationships with black men.

The play explores Billie's subjectivity fraught with cultural discourses that percolate in her consciousness and shape her attempt to comprehend Othello's desire for Mona, his need to "enter the whiteness" (310). Each scene is framed by voiceovers uttering the speeches of black leaders, all male, confronting racism; oratory is accompanied by musical fragments of the blues played on cello and bass, suggesting both the tension and possibilities of collaboration between Afrocentric and Eurocentric cultural forms. Most importantly, Billie's story underscores the intersections of race and gender in her struggle toward re-birth in the presence of political discourse, cultural memory, and personal history.

Billie, like Ann Marie MacDonald's Constance, is also an undervalued academic who brings a critical perspective to her own predicament. A student of the psychology of race, she has put her education on hold to support Othello's career and to give herself time to recover after he leaves. With insight into the profession and the ideas it values (e.g. funding for studies of racial inferiority), she uses her study of rage and "dysfunction" that emanate from the binary of superior/inferior to comprehend Othello's desires and, more pointedly, her own. The result, as she articulates and ultimately enacts it, is a complex of "Obsessions. Phobias. Delusions," disorders that are "systematically supported by the larger society" (299). Even the "functional," she says, suffer from this societal disease. As Othello prepares to move out of their apartment, their emotionally charged debates about how to function in a racist environment become a duet. At one moment their voices come together in their recitation of Martin Luther King's "Dream" speech that sparks a renewed intimacy between them. Ultimately, however, they voice dissonance and confusion. Billie begins to adapt King's dream of racial harmony to her vision of time when "a Black man and a Black woman might find.... Where jumping over the broom was a solemn eternal vow that.... I ... Let's.... Can we just get this over with?" (300). The ellipses suggests that she can no longer sustain this dream or imagine what it would look like. Othello, on the other hand, castigates Black feminism (represented by Billie) for undermining his manhood.

The tensions between Billie and Othello are contextualized by the voiceovers expressing a range of political strategies within the black community: King, Malcolm X, Marcus Garvey, Jesse Jackson, and Louis Farrakhan. Paul Robeson remembers the "blood" of his forbears "in the American soil" and his inability to get decent acting roles in the U.S. (302). Later, he expresses pleasure in being able to play *Othello* in England as he covers his face in black grease paint (316). In Billie's story, Othello recedes, becoming a trace of Shakespeare's noble Moor, a signifier for blacks who perform for a hegemonic white culture, trapped in their difference and alienation. Billie says that she, too, is "trapped in history" (313). However, like MacDonald's Constance, she is aware of the mire of voices that she has internalized and must act upon to save herself.

These voices are also represented in two historically situated and fragmented scenarios of Othello/Billie like couples that intersect with and mirror exchanges between Billie and Othello. The prologue is set in a dressing room of a theater in 1928, signaling the Harlem Renaissance; the second scene is set in 1860 on the steps to a blacksmith's forge on the eve of the Civil War. The conflict between each set of lovers is identified as an aspect of black history doomed to repeat itself.[56] The Othello character leaves his black lover for a white woman who offers him status and security (theater director and slave mistress). In the theatrical milieu of the 1928 dressing room he is required to don "black face" in order to perform Shakespeare. However, in each of these depictions Othello's choice leads to his demise, whether by lynching or the revenge exacted by his black lover, an ironic reversal of Othello's vengeful act in Shakespeare's drama. In her introduction to *Harlem Duet*, Leslie Sanders points to the connections between race, gender, and sexuality that link these scenes:

> In each era, he falls in love with whiteness, craving the gaze of the white woman as affirmation of his manhood. First she is the slave mistress who relies on him. Later, she is the stage director who gives him his big break, elevating him from minstrel to Shakespearean actor.... Finally, she is an academic colleague, whose acceptance seems to cement his stature in the white world outside the Harlem apartment he has shared with Billie, which overlooks the Apollo Theatre, at the centre of the African diasporic world.[57]

As spectators anticipating some version of Shakespeare's play, we are asked to imagine the tale not only from the perspective of a black woman but also from the perspective of a community of black women discomforted by a man who makes his way in the world by obliterating his history and reinventing himself.

Like Vogel and MacDonald, Sears uses the iconicity of the handkerchief as a powerful metaphor for sexual infidelity. However, it no longer functions as a measure of Desdemona's purity. Instead, it becomes an instrument of revenge associated with Billie's, rather than Othello's, anger at betrayal. It might also serve as a motif for the potentially enabling and/or self-destructive act of adapting uncritically the emblems associated with cultural memory. Reclaiming and transforming the handkerchief's Egyptian origins and the metaphysical properties that Shakespeare gives it in his depiction of Othello's exoticism, Sears prefaces her play with the Shakespeare passage describing its "feminine" powers:

> ...That handkerchief
> Did an Egyptian to my mother give.
> She was a charmer....
> There's magic in the web of it.
> A sibyl ... in her prophetic fury sewed the work [*Othello*, 3.4.57–74].

Billie, originally named Sybil by her father, spends a good part of the play plotting Othello's demise by poisoned handkerchief (passed down by Othello's mother and given to her in marriage). In Shakespeare's play, the silken web is intended to magically subdue a man's wandering eye, (the silk dyed in "mummy which the skillful Conserved of maidens' hearts."). Sears's epigraph elides the passages that describe its seductive powers. Revisioning the exotic as alchemical (or folkloric) remedy, Billie imagines that by soaking the handkerchief in a lethal mixture of herbs and potions, and giving it to Othello on his wedding day, she can turn seduction into torture. Of course, she also fears its effects upon her lest she accidentally contaminate herself in the process, becoming a victim of the magic that she wishes to re-define on her own terms.

Karen Newman, sees the handkerchief in Othello as a "snowballing signifier" gathering "myriad associations and meanings," as it is handed down, both literally and critically. She also interprets the handkerchief's associations with the "mother, witchcraft, and the marvelous," as representing the "link between femininity and the monstrous which Othello and Desdemona's union figures in the play."[58] In *Harlem Duet,* the handkerchief remains with Billie, and the monstrous seems to reside in her fear of losing herself in her efforts to punish Othello. The obsessions and paranoia she referred to in her analysis of racism as a social malady come to haunt her. Indeed, the last scene of the play depicts Billie in the visitors' lounge of the psychiatric ward of Harlem Hospital, reciting childhood rhymes as she attempts to heal through exorcism, repossession, and as sister-in-law, Amah, says, self-possession.

Just before Billie's hospitalization, the music that frames each scene becomes cacophonous, and the words of the orators inchoate; they "loop and repeat the same distorted bits of sound over and over again" as if anticipating Billie's entrapment in her own history (310). Sears's protagonist, like MacDonald's Constance, must ultimately author her destiny, free of prescription, in Billie's case, for separatism, integration, revenge or forgiveness. She, too, must collaborate with the discourses intersecting her text in order to confer meaning upon them.

Sears's project as the playwright/critic mirrors Billie's healing to achieve self-possession. She "exorcises" (reads against the grain of) *Othello* as it has been produced and critiqued, and at the same time interprets the narrative strands that continue to speak to her in the present. In effect, she creates the stage for this productive encounter.

Vogel, MacDonald, and Sears all engage the process of "confrontation and collaboration" that Mark Fortier observes in the politics of adaptation.[59] Drawing on Walter Benjamin's argument that in every age we must "wrest tradition" away from the "conformism" that threatens to "overpower it," Fortier sees a critical space where the playwright might insert herself, take hold of the past, not as something to be preserved or mystified as timeless, but as it exists in the present.[60] To collaborate with Shakespeare, to create plays in dialogue with his, encourages active viewers to participate in that conversation as well. Indeed, the feminist playwright as critic offers us the gifts of both hindsight and foresight: To revision powerful cultural symbols identified with gender inscribed in canonical texts and, at times, petrified in production and criticism, and to know that we cannot contain the meanings that we ascribe to them even in the present moment.

Notes

1. Carolyn Ruth Swift Lenz, Gayle Greene, and Carol Thomas Neely, eds., *The Woman's Part* (Urbana: University of Illinois Press, 1980) 6.
2. Carol Thomas Neely, Epilogue, "Remembering Shakespeare, Revising Ourselves," *Women's Re-Visions of Shakespeare: On the Responses of Dickinson, Woolf, Rick, H.D., George Eliot and Others*, ed. Marianne Novy (Urbana: University of Illinois Press, 1990) 243–244.
3. Randi S. Koppen defines the feminist spectator as a viewer who "resists, revises, and produces new meanings" in response to the "text's own promptings." "'The Furtive Event': Theorizing Feminist Spectatorship," *Modern Drama* XXXV.3 (September 1992): 379.
4. Helene Keyssar, introduction, *Feminist Theatre and Theory*, ed. Helene Keyssar (New York: St. Martin's Press, 1996) 2–3.
5. Jill Dolan, *The Feminist Spectator as Critic* (Ann Arbor: University of Michigan Press, 1991) 1.
6. Ibid., 1–2, 15–16.
7. Gayle Austin, *Feminist Theories for Dramatic Criticism* (Ann Arbor: University of Michigan Press, 1990) 10, 95.
8. Tania Modleski qtd. in Ibid., 95.
9. Judith Still and Michael Wortin, "Introduction," *Intertextuality: Theories and Practices* (Manchester: Manchester University Press, 1990) 1.
10. Marianne Novy refers to Ann Rosalind Jones's use of the term "oppositional" when, as Jones says, the "ideological message and force of the reigning code ... is pulled out of its dominant frame of reference and subversively inserted into an 'alternate frame of reference.'" Ann Rosalind Jones qtd. in Marianne Novy, "Introduction," *Transforming Shakespeare: Contemporary Women's Re-Visions in Literature and Performance* (New York: Palgrave, 2000) 3.
11. In considering the "plethora of 'vandalized' Shakespeares," Susan Bennett asks whether a "new text by way of dislocating and contradicting the authority of tradition produces a 'transgressive knowledge' which would disarticulate the terms under which tradition gains authority." *Performing Nostalgia: Shifting Shakespeare and the Contemporary Past* (London: Routledge, 1996) 12.

12. Dolan, 15–16.
13. Jean E. Howard and Marion O'Connor qtd. in Bennett, *Performing Nostalgia*, 25.
14. Bennett, *Performing Nostalgia*, 21. Bennett is quoting language from an advertisement for "Multicultural Shakespeare," the theme for the Annual Shakespeare Institute at the City University of New York.
15. Andre Lefevere's perspective on "rewriting" in general qtd. in Introduction, *Adaptations of Shakespeare: A Critical Anthology of Plays*, eds. Daniel Fischlin and Mark Fortier (London: Routledge, 2000) 5.
16. Coppelia Kahn argues that "in unacknowledged ways [patriarchy] ... conceded to women, who were essential to its continuance, the power to validate men's identities through their obedience as wives and daughters." *Man's Estate* (Berkeley: University of California Press, 1981) 12. According to Madeline Gohlke Sprengnether, male fantasies of betrayal stem from fears of being weak or "feminine" in relation to a powerful woman. "The feminine posture for a male is that of the betrayed, and it is the man in this position who portrays women as whores." See "'I Wooed Thee with My Sword': Shakespeare's Tragic Paradigms," in William Shakespeare, *Othello*, ed. Alvin Kernan (New York: Signet Classic, 1998) 193.
17. Linda Hart, introduction, *Making a Spectacle: Feminist Essays on Contemporary Women's Theatre*, ed. Lynda Hart (Ann Arbor: University of Michigan Press, 1989) 8. See also Nancy S. Reinhart, "New Directions for Feminist Criticism in the Theatre and the Related Arts," *A Feminist Perspective in the Academy: The Difference It Makes*, eds. Elizabeth Langland and Walter Gove (Chicago: University of Chicago Press, 1981) 42.
18. Marianne Novy, ed., *Women's Re-Visions of Shakespeare*; Novy, ed., *Cross–Cultural Performances: Differences in Women's Re-Visions of Shakespeare* (Urbana: University of Illinois Press, 1993); Novy, *Engaging with Shakespeare: Responses of George Eliot and Other Women Novelists* (Athens: University of Georgia Press, 1994); Novy, ed. *Transforming Shakespeare: Contemporary Women's Re-Visions in Literature and Performance*.
19. Novy, Introduction, *Transforming Shakespeare*, 1, 3, 5.
20. Novy, "Saving Desdemona and/or Ourselves," *Transforming Shakespeare*, 67.
21. Ric Knowles, "Othello in Three Times," *Shakespeare in Canada: 'a world elsewhere'?*, eds. Diana Brydon and Irena R. Makaryk (Toronto: University of Toronto Press, 2002) 372, 377, 378, 380. Knowles states that Ann-Marie MacDonald has "resisted a feminist label for the play," preferring to think of it as a "humanism through a woman's point of view." MacDonald qtd. in Knowles, 380.
22. Ibid., 384–386.
23. Ibid., 385, 391. Knowles asserts that these adaptations, might be construed not only as "cultural interventions" resisting "dominant normative subjectivities" represented by Shakespeare re-productions, but also as "cultural affirmations" that "renew 'Shakespeare'" at the same time that they transform the texts, 372.
24. Roland Barthes qtd. in Susan Bennett, *Theatre Audiences: A Theory of Production and Reception* (London: Routledge, 1990) 64.
25. This analysis of *Desdemona* is drawn from my article, "Feminist Revisions of Classic Texts on the American Stage," *Codifying the National Self: Spectators, Actors and the American Dramatic Text* (Dramaturgies No. 17), eds. Barbara Ozieblo and Maria Dolores Narbona-Carrion (Brussels: Peter Lang, 2006) 95–99.
26. *Desdemona* was first produced in association with Circle Repertory Company by the Bay Street Theatre Festival, Sag Harbor, NY, in July 1993, then by the Circle Repertory Company, New York in Fall 1993, and was published by Dramatists Play Service, New York, 1994. Additional references to *Desdemona* in the text.
27. Paula Vogel, "A Letter from the Playwright," program insert, *Desdemona: A Play about a Handkerchief*, Bay Street Theatre Festival, Sag Harbor, NY, July, 1993.
28. Alvin Kernan, introduction, Shakespeare, *Othello*, ed. Alvin Kernan (New York: Signet Classic, 1998), lxiv.
29. Jyotsna Singh, "The Interventions of History: Narratives of Sexuality," *The Weyward Sisters: Shakespeare and Feminist Politics*, eds. Dympna Callaghan, Lorraine Helms, and Jyotsna Singh (Oxford: Blackwell, 1994) 46.

30. Neely 243.
31. Lenz, Greene, Neely 5.
32. Novy, "Saving Desdemona and/or Ourselves," 67.
33. Hart 4.
34. Carole McKewin, "'Counsels of Gall and Grace': Intimate Conversations Between Women in Shakespeare's Plays," in Lenz, Greene, and Neely, 118–119.
35. Jeanie Forte, "Women's Performance Art: Feminism and Postmodernism," *Performing Feminisms: Feminist Critical Theory and Theatre*, ed. Sue-Ellen Case (Baltimore: Johns Hopkins University Press, 1990) 254.
36. Bertolt Brecht, *Brecht on Theatre*, ed. and trans. John Willett (New York: Methuen, 1964) 192.
37. Knowles, 371, 393 n. 7. *Goodnight Desdemona (Good Morning Juliet)* was first produced by Nightwood Theatre in 1988 at Toronto's Annex Theatre. The revised play was toured nationally by Nightwood Theatre in 1990 to Great Canadian Theatre Company, Northern Light Theatre, Vancouver East Cultural Centre, and the Canadian Stage Company and directed by Banuta Rubess. The play was published by Grove Press, New York, 1990. The text combines prose and blank verse; direct quotes from Shakespeare are italicized. Additional references to *Goodnight Desdemona* in the text.
38. Marianne MacDonald, qtd. in Beverley Curran, "Mingling and UnMingling Opposites: Bending Genre and Gender in Ann-Marie MacDonald's *Goodnight Desdemona (Good Morning Juliet)*," *He Said, She Says: An RSVP to the Male Text* (Madison: Associated University Press, 2001) 215, 218. See also Judith Rudakoff, "Interview" with Marianne MacDonald, *Fair Play: Twelve Women Speak: Conversations with Canadian Playwrights* (Toronto: Simon & Pierre, 1990) 127–143.
39. Curran 211.
40. Knowles 378.
41. Judith Fetterley, "Introduction," *The Resisting Reader: A Feminist Approach to American Fiction* (Bloomington: Indiana University Press, 1978) xii.
42. Edward Pechter, *Othello and Interpretive Traditions* (Iowa City: University of Iowa Press, 1999) 120.
43. Fetterley xxiii, xxiv, xxv.
44. Philip C. Kolin, "Introduction," *Shakespeare and Feminist Criticism: An Annotated Bibliography and Commentary* (New York: Garland, 1991) 35–36. Kolin refers to criticism by Marilyn French, Kathleen McLuskie, Ann Thompson, Marianne Novy, and Carol Thomas Neely among others to make this point.
45. Susan Snyder, "Beyond Comedy: *Romeo and Juliet*," in William Shakespeare, *The Tragedy of Romeo and Juliet*, ed. J.A. Bryant, Jr. (New York: Signet Classic, 1998) 174. Snyder observes that both *Romeo and Juliet* and *Othello* use the world of romantic comedy as "a point of departure...." (171). Constance sounds very much like Snyder when the latter discusses the "evitability" of comedy and the "irrevocability" of tragedy (173).
46. Roland Barthes, summarized and qtd. in Gerald Rabkin, "Is There a Text On this Stage: Theatre/Authorship/Interpretation," *PAJ 26/27* IX.2 and 3 (1985): 151–152. See Roland Barthes, "From Work to Text," *Image, Music, Text* (New York: Hill & Wang, 1977) 155–164. Ric Knowles also draws on Barthes's terms when he observes that Constance's entry into theater characters' worlds, "reconstructs" Shakespeare's texts as "writerly rather than readerly...." (379).
47. *Harlem Duet* was workshopped at the Joseph Papp Public Theater in New York City, and received its premier at the Tarragon Theatre's Extra Space in Canada. It was then remounted at the Canadian Stage Theatre in 1997 by Nightwood Theatre (Fischlin and Fortier, 275). The play is published in Djanet Sears, *Testifyin': Contemporary African Canadian Drama*, Volume I (Toronto: Playwrights Canada Press, 2000) 561–632. It is also published in Daniel Fischlin and Mark Fortier's *Adaptations of Shakespeare*, 289–317. Additional references in the text refer to the Fischlin and Fortier publication of the play.
48. Knowles 380–381.
49. Djanet Sears xi.

50. Knowles 381.

51. Sears, "Notes of a Coloured Girl: 32 Short Reasons Why I Write for the Theater," *Harlem Duet* (Winnipeg: Scirocco Drama, 1998) 14, qtd. in Fischlin and Fortier, 285–286.

52. Peter Dickinson, "Duets, Duologues, and Black Diasporic Theatre: Djanet Sears, William Shakespeare, and Others," *Modern Drama* 45:2 (Summer 2002): 192.

53. Mark Fortier, "Undead and Unsafe: Adapting Shakespeare (in Canada)," Brydon and Makaryk, 352. Fortier is referring to Susan Bennett's assertion that "We can best salvage the Shakespearean text when we savage it, when we plunder it for its gaps and blind spots" (*Performing Nostalgia*, 149).

54. Stephen Greenblatt, *Renaissance Self-Fashioning* (Chicago: University of Chicago Press, 1980) 245.

55. Karen Newman, "'And wash the Ethiop white': Femininity and the Monstrous in *Othello*," *Shakespeare Reproduced*, eds. Jean E. Howard and Marion O'Connor (New York: Methuen, 1987) 150, 152.

56. Peter Dickinson argues that the structure of the three parallel plotlines dramatizes the point that "dysfunction gets repeated and replayed throughout history, not just between but within cultural groups" in "Duets, Duologues, and Black Diasporic Theatre: Djanet Sears, William Shakespeare, and Others," *Modern Drama* 45:2 (Summer 2002): 200.

57. Leslie Sanders, "Othello Deconstructed: Djanet Sears' *Harlem Duet*," Testifyin,' ed. Sears, 558.

58. Newman 156.

59. Fortier 348.

60. Walter Benjamin, "Theses on the Philosophy of History," *Illuminations*, ed. Hannah Arendt, trans. Harry Zohn (New York: Shocken Press, 1969), qtd. in Fortier, 348.

Transgressive Female Desire and Subversive Critique in the Seventeenth Century Canon
JoAnne Akalaitis's Staging of Phèdre, The Rover, and 'Tis Pity She's a Whore[1]

CHERYL BLACK

JoAnne Akalaitis, currently Director of Theater at Bard College, co-founder of Mabou Mines, and former artistic director of the New York Shakespeare Festival, is one of America's preeminent interpreters of classical works. In addition to a non-illusionistic, visually evocative aesthetic generally identified as "avant-garde," "postmodern," and/or "deconstructive," Akalaitis is recognized for what one artistic associate characterized as "a socio-political-feminist approach to the classics."[2] Akalaitis's feminist consciousness has manifested itself most clearly in plays concerned with sexual politics, and the seventeenth century, an era identified by Michel Foucault as the origin of a "bio-politics" involving the regulation and supervision of the biological processes of the human body, has proved particularly fertile ground.[3] Akalaitis's directorial repertoire includes three masterworks from the era: John Ford's 'Tis Pity She's a Whore, first produced circa 1630 and staged by Akalaitis at the New York Shakespeare Festival's Public Theater in 1992; Aphra Behn's The Rover, first produced in 1677 and staged by Akalaitis at the Guthrie Theater in 1994; and Jean Racine's Phèdre, first produced in 1677 and staged by Akalaitis at the Court Theatre in 2002. In addition to historical contexts, these works share the presence of female protagonists with transgressive sexual desires, ranging from incest and adultery to rebellion against forced marriage or mandated celibacy. The presence of transgressive desires, of course, does not necessarily result in

Val Kilmer as Giovanni and Jeanne Tripplehorn as Annabella in *'Tis Pity She's a Whore*, Director, Joanne Akalaitis, Scenic Designer, John Conklin. Presented by the New York Shakespeare Festival, and performed at the Public/Newman Theater, New York, 1992. Photographer: Martha Swope.

feminist critique of the prevailing sexual and gender ideology. Many critics question the degree of political subversion present even in Behn's female-authored text, let alone that in the works of Ford and Racine. Akalaitis's staging, however, mines these texts for subversive potential and finds them far richer than most of us have previously imagined. Through inventive juxtapositions of text, aural and visual imagery, casting, and performance, she creates *mise-en-scènes* that accentuate sexual and reproductive politics, bringing to the surface implicit themes of sexual violence and sexual double standards. Her provocative interpretations capture the dynamics of gender relationships within our cultural institutions, revealing both the dominating forces and women's resistance to such forces.

'Tis Pity She's a Whore

Very little is known of John Ford, who began writing plays in the reign of James I and died, circa 1640, during the last few years of the reign of Charles

I. The ideology of patriarchy was promulgated during the reigns of these two monarchs, who promoted themselves as the "fathers" of their subjects, an ideology defended and extended as a standard for family life in *Patriarcha*, written in 1640.[4] Ford resisted such cultural imperatives by remaining unmarried.

No previous source for Ford's tragedy has been clearly identified, although scholars have noted its similarities to *Romeo and Juliet* (star-crossed lovers, friar, nurse, and Italian Renaissance setting). Lisa Hopkins has recently argued that *'Tis Pity* "virtually rewrites" Shakespeare's tragedy and that Ford may be deliberately subverting his era's gender ideology:

> One reason why Ford himself seems to treat Annabella more favorably than he does Giovanni may arise from his grasp of the fact that his own society would have made precisely the opposite decision ... There certainly seems to be little reason for the inclusion of Philotis in the play except to reinforce the point that the constraints on women are far greater than those on men....[5]

Ford's characters include representatives from the most powerful social institutions: the family, the state, and the church. Akalaitis adds the military, changing Grimaldi, "a gentlemen" in Ford's text to "Lt. Grimaldi," a military officer. The play's central action, the incestuous relationship between the young gentlewoman Annabella and her brother, Giovanni, provides opportunities to reveal how each of these institutions works to regulate sexual and domestic relations, especially female sexuality. Although Ford dutifully metes out punishment and restores social order by play's end, subversive critique of these institutions is strongly evident. His tone betrays a cynical awareness of the injustice. His title (also the last line of his play) is heavily ironic.

Remaining essentially faithful to Ford's text, Akalaitis's *mise-en-scène* presented an interpretation that highlighted Ford's complicitous critique, focusing attention on the coercive aspects of culturally-prescribed sexual roles and the control and commodification of women's bodies. The primary visual influence of the scenic design by John Conklin is Surrealist painting and photography, including the works of Yves Tanguy, Georgio de Chirico, Lee Miller, Alberto Martini, and particularly, Man Ray. Although there is much disagreement among art critics as to whether surrealists used the female body as object or subject, there is general consensus that surrealists obsessively *featured* the female body.[6] The choice of surrealist representation, therefore, is explicitly appropriate to focus attention on female corporeality and sexuality. The use of fascist iconography, the second significant visual influence, connects personal to political oppression and increases the contemporary social relevance of this production. Generally, the imagery evokes Mussolini-era Italy, with some suggestion of Nazi "will to power." As outlined by historian Victoria De Grazia, fascist reproductive policies (*Dio, patria, famiglia*) bear a striking resemblance to America's current ideology of "Family Values" and current debates over abortion, stem cell research, and same sex marriage:

To pursue its population politics, fascism sought to establish more control over female bodies, especially female reproductive functions, at the same time that it sought to rehabilitate older patriarchal notions of family and paternal authority.[7]

Before a line of dialogue is heard, Akalaitis focuses attention on the objectified female body. The program cover features a reproduction of Lee Miller's *Nude*, the nude back of a kneeling woman. The first visual image on the stage is a projected enlargement of Man Ray's *The Prayer*, which features a nude woman in a kneeling and prostrate position, her hands reaching from underneath her body in a protective gesture. The images, similar in composition, suggest vulnerability to manipulation and control.

The incestuous relationship, as outlined by Ford and staged by Akalaitis, unequivocally reveals Annabella as a desiring subject, rather than merely the object of Giovanni's desire. In Ford's text, Annabella is not seduced or coerced by Giovanni, but freely enters into their taboo relationship: "...what thou hast urged, My captive heart had long ago resolved." Akalaitis underscores the active nature of Annabella's desire by adding several brief, silent scenes, located in Annabella's room, showing Annabella and Giovanni naked, making love, drinking wine, playing cards. During these moments, Annabella's nakedness (the absence of clothes), contrasts significantly with the nudity (to be seen naked by others as an object) of the Man Ray and Lee Miller representations.[8]

Pre–nuptial negotiations between Annabella's father, Florio, and prospective suitors Donado and Soranzo for Annabella's hand in marriage illustrate the control and commodification of women's bodies. Akalaitis accents the violent implications of such negotiations by furnishing these scenes with images of dismemberment and bondage: a sculpture of a woman's armless torso; a painting of a woman's face with distorted and dislocated features (based on a painting by Alberto Martini) and a chair and loveseat, covered in fabric and wrapped with rope.

Much of the *mise-en-scène* works to present women's culturally prescribed roles in a sinister light. Two dominant visual images, the production's backdrop, inspired by the paintings of Yves Tanguy, and a column unit based on the paintings of Georgio de Chirico, establish a haunting psychological environment. Wavy lines in the yellow backdrop suggest a sea in which float tail-bearing sperm-like globules. In addition to an evocation of reproductive sexuality, Tanguy's "inscapes" typically convey a sense of eeriness and alienation: "Tanguy's universe is one of unsurpassed strangeness... we have been led into a disconcerting world which, but for Tanguy, we should never have visited at all."[9] Like that of Tanguy, de Chirico's world evokes "a sinister realm," depicting "haunted piazzas" and "inexplicable cityscapes."[10] The association of images of fertility and reproduction with strangeness and alienation suggests the frightening aspects of "natural" female functions.

Other elements of the *mise-en-scène* which critique women's culturally prescribed roles include images based on paintings of infants by Philip Otto Rungé and the staging of the wedding scene. Art historian John Canaday characterizes Rungé as an artist who "put his faith in innocence, in nature, and in love."[11] Akalaitis placed 4' × 4' enlargements of Rungé's babies' faces on platforms stage left and right. By allowing the monstrously enlarged babies' faces to loom over the proceedings, Akalaitis makes "nature" and "innocence" grotesque. Akalaitis makes similar use of a huge cutout of a Rungé baby's arm, used by two male characters to give Annabella's companion, Putana, a sly nudge, a less-than-subtle reminder of her reproductive function.

In the wedding scene, the pregnant Annabella fulfills her familial/social duty by marrying Soranzo, her father's choice. A 4' × 4' enlargement of Man Ray's *The Hair Net* overlooks the proceedings. In the photograph, a woman's unsmiling face, tightly wrapped in a hair net, suggests entrapment. Fascist iconography proliferates during this scene. Banners bearing the fascist slogan *Dio, patria, famiglia* drop between the de Chirico columns. A troupe of young girls bring on the fascist eagle banner and then perform a Riefenstahl-esque Olympian routine. Part nightmare, part political rally, Annabella's wedding ruthlessly exposes bio-politics at work.

One of the most violent episodes of the performance demonstrates both the specifically corporeal nature of gender oppression and women's resistance to such oppression. Soranzo beats Annabella to discover the name of her lover against a background of five photographic reproductions (various sizes) of a nude and kneeling woman's back. In Akalaitis's ruthlessly realistic staging, Soranzo kicks and drags Annabella across the stage, then repeatedly slams her against a blood-red wall. Annabella's actions, as outlined in Ford's text and realized in Jeanne Tripplehorn's performance, are defiant. She refuses to name her lover, taunts Soranzo, and *sings* as he beats her. This juxtaposition of the *representation* of Woman as silent, passive, and immobile with the *reality* of a woman physically and vocally resisting abuse challenges the inevitability of gender oppression and emphasizes the dynamics of the struggle.

Visual imagery intensifies emotionally as the action of the play progresses. The use of monstrous cartoon baby arms is not without humor; as the violence of the play escalates, however, the imagery of the production gets grimmer. As the production nears its end, Akalaitis displays a reproduction of Man Ray's *Tears*. Here Akalaitis borrows a staple from the horror film repertoire, "the wide staring eyes of a victim,"[12] to stress both the horror and vulnerability of Annabella's situation. The message is explicitly pertinent as the only woman left alive at play's end is confined to a convent.

Akalaitis prefaces Annabella's murder with an added attraction for the men at Soranzo's banquet. Seated at a table draped in white linen, Soranzo and his guests watch a grainy porno film as Giovanni stabs Annabella and "plows up her fruitful womb" in a context that is unmistakably sexual. Then, with her blood, he paints the word CUNT in large red letters above her bed. Replacing metaphor ("woman"/"whore") with metonym ("woman"/"cunt"), Akalaitis returns our attention to the body, focusing on woman's sex as the "fundamental sign of her otherness."[13]

The Rover

Playwright Aphra Behn, born the year Ford died (1640), reached adulthood as Charles II restored the monarchy to England after nearly twenty years of Puritan rule. The Restoration ushered in a brief era of hedonism and sexual libertinism which was reflected in the witty and risqué plays penned by Charles's courtiers, by, for, and about themselves. Although the new ideology of libertinism promised sexual freedom, only men were in a position to benefit from it. Women in Restoration England had no social or legal status apart from wife, mother, daughter, or the enviable autonomy of widowhood, a status Behn claimed with dubious entitlement.[14] It was a riotous time, and its sexual politics, led by its libidinous monarch, supported a rape culture in which the Earl of Rochester could, with impunity, abduct a woman of considerable fortune and beauty to coerce her into marriage.[15] Behn's era was also a transitional one, in which rumblings of rebellion against both regal and patriarchal hegemony were heard. By the end of the century, England had instituted a constitutional monarchy, and pioneering feminists like Mary Astell and Margaret Cavendish had protested in print the social and sexual subjugation of women.[16]

In the theatrical subculture of the Restoration, women were actresses, actresses were whores, and Behn introduced the female playwright as a kind of "newfangled whore."[17] Although Behn enjoyed rare popular success, she also angered misogynist critics, like the anonymous writer who decreed that "as her works had neither wit enough for a man, nor modesty enough for a woman, she was to be look'd on as an Hermaphrodite...."[18] *The Rover*, the most frequently produced of Behn's "comedies of intrigue," is a genre-defying depiction of romantic and sexual escapades among three English cavalier expatriates (including the eponymous Rover), three spirited Spanish heiresses, and a highly-priced courtesan in Spanish-owned Naples during Carnival season. The heiresses pursue the rakish Cavaliers rather than submit to their brother's plans for arranged marriage or the convent, a plot complicated by competition for the Rover's affections from the beautiful courtesan, Angellica Bianca. Although Angellica would seem a formidable rival (a critic once described her as "a whore with a mind of steel rather than a heart of gold"),[19] she is no match for the virtue or fortune of the heiresses. In addition to wrangling lovers, the play is replete with pimps, bawds, clowns, masked revelers, music, dance, duels, several attempted rapes, and the obligatory "happy ending" of multiple weddings.

Although Behn borrowed the essential plot and major characters from Thomas Killigrew's semi-autobiographical *Thomaso, the Wanderer*, she significantly strengthened the female characters.[20] Because of Behn's rebellious female characters and proto-feminist dialogue ("Is there no difference between leave to love me and leave to lie with me?"), *The Rover* is now largely heralded a feminist classic and Behn herself a feminist pioneer. Dissenting critics view Behn as an apologist for Stuart patriarchy and aristocratic male privilege who stocks her plays with tantalizing spectacles of female flesh for male spectators.[21] For both critical camps, however, Behn's conclusion is problematic. As Katharine Rogers asserts, "The Rover is a bully, a drunkard, and an unabashed exploiter of women. But Behn suggests no criticism of his behavior, and rewards him with Hellena, the most desirable of the women, who brings him a fortune of 200,000 crowns."[22]

Akalaitis, however, detects in Behn a decidedly critical attitude toward the sexual politics she portrays, insisting that "in *The Rover*, maybe in spite of herself, you can see Behn's anger towards men emerge.... Her female insights and wiles and her pure female feeling get to me and move me. I feel a sisterhood across the centuries."[23] Although Akalaitis took somewhat greater liberties with Behn's text than with Ford's, she retained all important characters and events. As with *'Tis Pity*, she underscored the feminist critique implicit in Behn's play through extra-textual means, beginning with pre-production publicity materials, which unequivocally located the play in a context of feminist rhetoric and attempted to instill in audiences a critical attitude toward the play's events.

The production study guide included excerpts from seventeenth century feminist writing, a discussion of Behn's historical significance from Virginia Woolf's *A Room of One's Own*, and an essay on sexual politics in Restoration England by Behn scholar Angeline Goreau. Included in its list of discussion questions are questions on sexual behavior, gender relations, sexual double standards, and the "mini-skirt defense" for rape.[24] The production program similarly included quotes from Woolf, Goreau, Margaret Cavendish, and Simone de Beauvoir, and an Associated Press article on the Florida rape case that established the "mini-skirt defense."[25] Before the show, audience members in the lobby could pick up red telephone receivers labeled "Aphra's hotline" and hear recordings of Behn's poetry and miscellaneous writings on female sexuality and sexual double standards.

Quoting restoration conventions, the production included two sections of audience seating upstage, accommodating about fifty spectators who were also furnished with ruffs and red robes. Actor Christopher Bayes (Blunt, the country bumpkin who accompanies the Cavaliers) delivers an engaging comic prologue, inviting the audience to interact and warning them of the swordfights, hydraulic traps, smoke, and other dangers awaiting them. No sooner has Bayes set a highly comic mood with this routine, however, than a throbbing flamenco rhythm breaks it, and the entire company, dressed in black, performs a sensual Spanish dance, which ends with the men exiting and the women following in pursuit. Shifts in mood from light to dark continue throughout the performance, underscoring the genre ambivalence in the text and unsettling audience expectations.

Akalaitis fully exploits the subversive potential of Behn's carnival setting, which distinguishes the play from the typical drawing room interior of restoration comedies and provides an ideal context for "unruly" sexual adventure.[26] The masks and revelry of the carnivalesque inverts social hierarchy and challenges dominant visions of authority, identity, and sexuality. Akalaitis includes four distinct "levels" of carnivals, progressively darker in tone. The first, most festive carnival projects the omnisexual ambiance of Mardi Gras or Gay Pride parades. Masked performers in body suits with attached male and female genitalia embrace, dance, flirt, and fondle, representing a wide array of gender and sexual identities, at the same time highlighting the notion of such identities as performative and illusory.

Akalaitis extends an evocation of homoeroticism by suggesting a lesbian relationship between Angellica Bianca and Moretta, effected by a few shared embraces. In Behn's text, Moretta is clearly a bawd past her prime, but Akalaitis's Moretta is young and chic, sporting tailored business attire, a brisk, authoritative manner and a cell phone. Angellica's bravoes (here represented as dark-suited, bodyguard types) are also seen in romantic embrace. Latent homoerotic content may be detected in some of the play's homosocial horseplay, for example, in the farcical but titillating moment when Blunt demonstrates the "taste of [Lucetta's] balmy kisses" by kissing Frederick. Homoeroticism would likely have been read as such by Restoration audiences, as Restoration libertinism embraced sexual experimentation. Behn's long time lover, John Hoyle, was once indicted for sodomy, and her fellow poet and playwright John Wilmot, Earl of Rochester, penned a special paean to sodomy in his play *Sodom or the Quintessence of Debauchery*. Both Hoyle and Rochester have been cited as models for Willmore.[27] Behn herself was noted for depicting romantic bonds between women that would fall somewhere on a lesbian continuum:

> The bonding of women in female friendship is most clearly stated by Behn in her explicitly lesbian love poem, "To the fair Clarinda, who made Love to me, imagin'd more than Woman." ... in it Behn shows how important to her were those androgynous qualities for which she herself was praised.[28]

Another intriguing feature of Behn's play is the presence of the "Common shore" (sewer) running underneath the streets of the city, into which Blunt is tricked into falling by the prostitute Lucetta, and from which he "creeps out" "all dirty," with revenge against women foremost in his mind. This literal subterranean nastiness is directly analogous to the subtextual undercurrents of male domination and sexual violence in this "comedy" of sexual intrigue. Bringing this idea to the surface, Akalaitis renders "Blunt's chamber" as, literally, a men's room, complete with grungy toilets, urinals, and sinks. This setting remains in place for most of the second act, providing a repulsive backdrop to the attempted gang rape of Florinda as well as the wedding scene.

Excepting the "men's room" décor, the scenic design by George Tsypin is spare and non-illusionistic. A few prominent features, abstract in design, may be read as provocative signs of male and female sexuality. During carnival scenes, a flowing red scrim swoops from the back of the stage to the front, separating the space in a serpentine wave, forcing actors to leap back and forth through slits in the fabric, and spectators to see action from differing viewpoints. Susan Carlson's characterization of the scrim's ovoid openings as "vaginal slits" is an intriguing reading that seems in keeping with the use of disembodied pink neon lips as a sign for Angellica Bianca.[29] If we may read the scrim as suggestive of enticingly intrusive female sexuality, the production provides a striking visual counterpoint at the end of the first act, when three huge fabric penises emerge from traps and remain in place throughout the intermission and into the first scene of the second act. The penises tower over the proceedings, a grotesque reminder that women's desires and actions are still subject to masculine and patriarchal domination.

In keeping with Behn's carnival theme and plot complications dependent on mistaken identities, costumes are plentiful and powerful signs that function to blur boundaries between historical and cultural contexts and to highlight the constructed nature of identity, specifically of gender and sexuality. Costumes by Gabriel Berry primarily evoke the late-twentieth century, with some obvious pop culture references (the pimp Sancho looks like an Elvis impersonator) and some quotation of Restoration fashions (the occasional ruff or line of the Spanish noblemen's costumes). Long-haired, leather-clad, open-shirted, and tattooed Cavaliers, described by Akalaitis as "tough biker guys" manifest over determined masculinity, a hyper-heterosexuality that doubles back on itself and reminds us that "leather-clad biker guys" is also a gay archetype.[30]

Following Behn's stage directions, the three sisters, Florinda, Valeria, and Hellena, appear in a variety of costumes, most of them over determined images of femininity. Hellena, for example, appears as a novice, gypsy, harem girl, messenger boy and bride. Dressed in shades of white in their opening scene, Akalaitis highlights performed femininity by their quick, stylized assumption of demure poses with fans on the entrance of their brother, and their immediate dropping of the pose to sneak cigarettes after he leaves. Their go-go girl wedding outfits, short white skirts, veils, and boots parody traditional bridal attire.

Akalaitis's casting of leading roles serves to enhance the strength of the women's roles and may also provide additional critical commentary. A certain physical similarity among the Cavaliers (in dress, height, general body build, hair length, and color) provoked one critic's comment that they looked "almost as much alike as those bearded guys in ZZ Top."[31] One of the effects of this physical interchangeability is to comment on male attitudes regarding the interchangeability of women—any woman will do to slake Willmore's sexual appetite when Hellena eludes him, and any woman will do to avenge Blunt's anger when Lucetta humiliates him. This casting may also work to diminish Willmore's star power. By contrast, the Royal Shakespeare Company's casting of Jeremy Irons in 1986, or Williamstown Theatre's casting of Christopher Reeve in 1987, increased audience sympathy for the character and pleasure at the outcome.[32]

Behn's two leading female characters, Hellena and Angellica Bianca, are strong, independent women who aggressively pursue their desires, and Akalaitis's casting reinforces these attributes. Hellena, the boldest and wittiest of the heiresses, is portrayed by Elizabeth Marvel as a long-limbed, short-haired androgyne with a strong clear voice and brazen charm. As Angellica Bianca, African American actress Viola Davis strides across stage, a tall, proud figure with dark hair in a severe geometric cut and a powerfully rich, deep voice. Frequently appearing in shades of gold, once with a gold headband suggesting a coronet, Davis is a regal presence who knows how to handle a man (she lifts Willmore by his buttocks) and a gun (she threatens Willmore but ultimately spares him "to show my utmost of contempt, I give thee Life—"). Both women, in boots, are taller than Willmore.

Violence occurs with excessive frequency in this play, and in staging these moments Akalaitis fulfills her expressed intention to bring out the "mean-spirited brutality and the sexuality at the center of [the play]."[33] In the first scene, Belville intervenes to prevent Willmore from stealing a woman from another reveler: "use no violence here. I would not have you at your old tricks in carnival."[34] In the same scene, Sancho pressures Lucetta into pursuing Blunt, threatening to beat her if she refuses. That night, Willmore attempts to rape Florinda in a garden, deterred only by Belville's appearance, and offering the restoration version of the mini-skirt defense: "why art thou thus attired at midnight in a garden but to lure men?"[35] Later that same evening, a masked Florinda runs into Blunt's chamber (the "men's room") and is threatened with rape not only by Blunt, but the three other men who wander in, including her own brother. Both these scenes have been played for laughs, but Akalaitis stages them realistically, demonstrating male physical aggression (as the men grab, manhandle, and wrestle Florinda to the ground) and female resistance (as Florinda screams and struggles to escape). Scenes of sexual abuse are ironically juxtaposed with scenes of men brawling or dueling over their rights to women.

The denouement follows the attempted gang rape of Florinda. Disguises are dropped, misunderstandings cleared up, and the women "win" their desires—marriage to the Cavaliers. Baroque music begins, the brides appear, giddy in their go-go bridal regalia, and join hands with their grooms. At this moment, Akalaitis, perhaps taking a cue from the script's dark undercurrents or from her own sense of Behn's sublimated anger, seriously undermines the "happy" ending. After two steps in minuet rhythm, the couples abruptly halt.

An ominous sound cue, like thunder, is heard. The couples separate, walk away from each other, and freeze, eying each other warily from a distance. Black-caped figures appear bearing tall candles. Carnival is over, and Lent has begun.

Phèdre

In addition to a portrayal of transgressive female desire, Jean Racine's *Phèdre* shares with Aphra Behn's *The Rover* its premiere date (1677), and a certain indebtedness to earlier source material. Sources for Phèdre include Euripides' *Hippolytus*, Ovid's *Heroides*, Seneca's *Phaedre*, and Nicolas Boileau's rendering of Sappho's *A l'aimee*.[36] The character Phèdre shares with Ford's Annabella an incestuous desire, although, in Phèdre's case, the incest is a legal and social, rather than biological, issue.

Compared to the relative instability of seventeenth-century England (whose subjects beheaded one king and deposed another within the space of fifty years) France was rigidly unified under one king, one god, and one aesthetic standard. The position of women in France during Racine's era was, if anything, slightly more restricted than that of their sisters in England. According to historian Wendy Gibson, women were excluded from succession to the crown, husbands had complete control over their wives' property and person, and brutality against women was rampant. Interestingly, at about the time *Phèdre* was first produced, a wave of reactionary violence by women erupted in Paris, with alarming increase in shockingly unfeminine behavior: black masses, abortions, infanticides, poisonings—and, toward the end of the century, actual and attempted murders by wives of husbands.[37] In this context, Racine's decision to center a play on a woman's incestuous and adulterous desire takes on fascinating symbolic significance, especially given the fact that, like Ford in his creation of the incestuous Annabella, Racine's Phèdre (possibly created for his mistress, the actress La Champmeslé) was, and has been, largely viewed as a sympathetic creation. As one scholar affirmed: "All readers of *Phèdre* know, however, that they inevitably sympathize with the protagonist; that is, when confronted with the situations and events, they generally adopt her point of view and emotionally identify themselves with her...."[38]

Critic John Campbell recently articulated the need to liberate *Phèdre* from three centuries of critical commentary that have rendered it nearly impossible to see or read with fresh eyes: "...too often viewed as a kind of Rolls Royce of world literature ... it has generated its own myth, and comes freighted with ideals and expectations."[39] According to the myth, the significance of *Phèdre* lies in its aesthetic perfection, as exemplar *par excellence* of French neoclassicism and as the purest expression of Racine's tragic vision. Another problem noted by Campbell is the deterministic way in which *Phèdre* is often viewed, linked to ideas like "necessity," "destiny," and "fatality." For these critics the play is "a funeral ceremony in which, from the beginning, the victim has been condemned without appeal."[40]

Phèdre's origins and subsequent metamorphoses through several male-dominated traditions (from ancient Greece to Louis XIV's France), have proved problematic for many feminist critics, who have viewed the character and the work as products of misogynist imagination—false projections of male fantasy or patriarchal gender codes. Joan DeJean specifically challenges Racine as a male writer "who appropriated the right [from female literary artists]" to articulate female passion.[41] If that is the case, Akalaitis is one of several women theater artists who seem to be currently involved in a counter-appropriation to reclaim Phèdre's story and reveal it through female and feminist sensibilities. In addition to Akalaitis's staging, *Phèdre* has recently been adapted by feminist playwright Timberlake Wertenbaker and by the late, savage goddess of postfeminism, Sarah Kane. Perhaps *Phèdre* has aroused such interest because, as Mary Jo Muratore has observed, she is "triply transgressive: [her passion for Hippolytus] violates moral (incestuous), sexual (adulterous), and political regulations (he is ineligible to share the throne because his mother is foreign-born)."[42] Or, as Wertenbaker expressed her admiration of classical heroines in general, "These women are terrible and they have the courage of their horror."[43]

In a published interview with Court dramaturge Celise Kalke, Akalaitis expressed her admiration for the play and the artistry of Racine, at the same time stating her desire to make the play more relevant and accessible to a contemporary audience, explaining that "the *Phèdre* story occurs in real life."[44] Her choices regarding text, casting, and the aural and visual elements of the *mise-en-scène* worked to fully exploit the horror and courage of Phèdre's subversive sexuality and to undermine traditional preconceptions of character or play.

For a performance text, she chose Paul Schmidt's streamlined, modern translation, which she described as "very speakable."[45] Although Schmidt deviates considerably from Racine's poetic style, he avoids obvious anachronisms and retains the general structure, events, characters, and tone of Racine's original. To this text, Akalaitis made minor cuts and changes, occasionally restoring lines from Racine that Schmidt had deleted. Several of these re-insertions highlight the sexual politics and sexual double standards at play in these events. For example, Akalaitis restored early references to Theseus's seduction and abduction of Phèdre (abandoning her sister Ariadne to do so) and also restored Theseus's final line naming Aricia, the captive Athenian princess, as his heir.[46] This action is significant in that it rewards, rather than punishes, a transgressing female character (Aricia loved Hippolytus despite Theseus's edict that she never marry or bear children).

In keeping with Schmidt's text, actors' speech in the performance is standard American enunciation, with a few notable exceptions. In moments of great emotional intensity, Phèdre, and later, Theseus, break out in Racinian French. This choice intensifies such moments emotionally in the same way that music does—invoking response on a subconscious level. In addition, when Phèdre uses French speech during her famed *aveu* of love to Hippolytus, the evocation of French neoclassicism calls attention to Phèdre's subversion of aesthetic, as well as moral, law. As Muratore explains:

> Phèdre casts herself as Hippolytus's subordinate, an inversion of the courtly love tradition that Hippolytus's confession of love to Aricia exemplifies. The typical courtly lover is of course a male ... who serves as 'vassal' to a woman of superior rank ... Phèdre's improperly submissive salutation to Hippolytus (whom she thrice calls her "Seigneur") [in Schmidt, translated as "Prince"] ... inverts this paradigm.... The role of the heroine is limited to inspiring passion, generally platonic ... Phèdre's sexual aggressiveness ... defies all expectations for female behavior.[47]

Phèdre commits an even more blatant transgression when she invites Hippolytus to commit a violent act—to slay her with his sword—on stage.[48] Akalaitis has Phèdre use Racine's language for this moment: "*Voila mon coeur ...*" a moment that metatextually resonates with Annabella's appeal to Giovanni to "love me or kill me, brother."

The contemporary, lean language of the text matches the generally sleek and modern look of the production, although fleeting classical references may be detected—for example, in the simple, flowing gowns; wide, golden arm bands; and sandals of Oenone and Ismene.[49] Signs of masculinity and privilege mark the opening scene between Hippolytus and Theramenes, located in a workout room where Hippolytus jumps rope, lifts weights, refreshes himself with chilled Perrier, and enjoys a neck massage from Theramenes. Akalaitis blurs class distinctions among characters: Theramenes (a tutor in Racine's text) appears here as a rather elegant personal assistant. As in '*Tis Pity* Akalaitis transforms the classic nurse character. Oenone, played by a young, vibrant actress, is Phèdre's best friend, unequivocally supportive but never subservient—she drinks, smokes, and occasionally shouts at Phèdre.

The aura of reverence surrounding this play has led to a tradition in casting Phèdre as the crowning achievement in the careers of distinguished and mature performers, who have tended to approach the role with what Akalaitis has called "the grande dame" notion. "I wanted to get away from [that] because it makes the play less approachable and human."[50] Akalaitis's Phèdre, thirty-three year old Jenny Bacon, embraced her character as a sexual and social outlaw: "Her love transcends the boundaries of the socially responsible and it challenges the fabric of society."[51] From her first entrance, hooked up to an I.V., to her ostentatious death scene, Bacon dominated the stage in a mesmerizing performance remarkable for lack of vocal or physical restraint. Seemingly propelled by the passions raging inside her breast, she whispers, shrieks, sobs, laughs, writhes on the floor, springs to her knees, flings her arms in wild abandon, caresses her body in a fever of repressed longing, and collapses in a dead faint. Virtually all reviewers testified to the power and originality of Bacon's performance.[52]

Just as Akalaitis thwarted audience expectation by exploring the dark undercurrents in Behn's comedy, she manages, primarily through Bacon's performance, to inject humor underlying Phèdre's tragic situation. At unexpected moments, Bacon elicits laughter with wry delivery of a line like "I hate my life," the harsh and cynical tone of "the gods won't help! I know this," and the mocking, drawn-out enunciation of Aricia's name when Phèdre discovers that she has a rival. Oenone too adds wry humor to unlikely moments, most strikingly at the news of Theseus's death: "well, this changes everything, doesn't it?" For a moment we see Phèdre's dilemma in a remarkably new light — after all, she is not biologically related to Hippolytus. As Oenone declares, "nothing holds you back! You love Hippolytus? Why shouldn't you?" Interestingly, Oenone evokes laughter again, several scenes later, with her bitterly ironic disclosure that Theseus is alive after all. Phèdre's tragedy is not just her obsession for her stepson but also the tragedy of an unwanted marriage from which she cannot escape except through death. These startlingly original line interpretations challenge audience preconceptions about the character, the play, and the inevitability of its outcome. Is a different conclusion possible? Desirable?

Rejected by Hippolytus and fearing dishonor, Phèdre agrees to Oenone's plan to accuse Hippolytus of rape. Despite Hippolytus's lauded chastity, Theseus, a serial rapist himself, has no problem believing Oenone's story. Theseus's reaction to his "betrayal" and "dishonor" suggests his perception of rape as more an assault on his honor than on Phedre's person. In the play's final scene, Phèdre, having caused the deaths of her stepson and her best friend and dishonored her sovereign husband/king, commits a final transgression, heightened by Bacon's performance. Denying the gods or her husband the privilege of punishing her, she takes her own life, enlisting the aid of another transgressive female to do so — the poison Phèdre takes was brought to Greece by Medea. Moreover, Phèdre dies *onstage*, refusing to surrender the stage to the King in the play's final moments, a further violation of neoclassic decorum. Bacon delivers Phèdre's confession calmly, quietly, with a faint smile on her lips. There is no hint of apology or request for forgiveness in the lines, nor in Bacon's delivery of them. Critic Wendy Arons noted Bacon's "detached, unconcerned" air, her lack of shame, and her "astonishing lack of compassion for those she has harmed," adding, "It's a revelatory interpretation."[53]

Akalaitis's staging of these three plays demonstrates the rich possibilities for feminist critique inherent not only in these works, but the classical canon in general, especially those plays which feature strong female protagonists. Her interpretations reveal how a female and feminist sensibility can break through centuries of "ideals and expectations," allowing us to see and hear these stories as if for the first time. More traditional interpretations, faithful to the text's chronological and geographic boundaries, and reverent of the generic and aesthetic codes embedded in their legacy, may safely relegate their sexism, heterosexism, and misogyny to a bygone era. Akalaitis's chronologically and geographically displaced visions allow no such complacency. By rendering sexual oppression explicitly visible and explicitly immediate, these revisionings not only enhance our understanding of the sexual politics of the seventeenth century, but also illuminate the striking similarities between that era and our own time, giving these productions significant contemporary relevance.

Notes

1. I would like to thank *Theatre Studies* editor Beth Kattelman for permission to incorporate portions of a previously published essay in this chapter. See Cheryl Black, "A Visible Oppression: JoAnne Akalaitis's Staging of John Ford's '*Tis Pity She's a Whore*," *Theatre Studies* 40 (1995): 5–16. Research for this study was partially funded by a grant from the Center for Arts and Humanities at the University of Missouri.

2. David Leong, interview with Deborah Saivetz. Deborah Saivetz, *An Event in Space: JoAnne Akalaitis in Rehearsal* (Hanover, NH: Smith and Kraus, 2000) 153. Leong has served as fight director for numerous Akalaitis productions.

3. Michel Foucault, *History of Sexuality: Volume One* (New York: Vintage Books, 1990) 139.

4. Sir Robert Filmer, "Patriarcha," *Constitution Society*, <http://www.constitution.org/eng/patriarcha.htm>.

5. John Ford, "Introduction," *'Tis Pity She's a Whore*, ed. Lisa Hopkins (London: Nick Hern Books, 2003) xiii–xiv.

6. See Rosalind Krauss, *L'Amour Fou* (New York: Abbeville Press, 1985); Susan Suleiman, *Subversive Intent* (Cambridge: Harvard University Press, 1990).

7. Victoria De Grazia, *How Fascism Ruled Women: Italy 1922–1945* (Berkeley: University of California Press, 1992) 9.

8. John Berger discusses the distinctions between nakedness and nudity in *Ways of Seeing* (London: BBC and Penguin, 1972) 53–54.

9. J. H. Matthews, *Eight Painters: The Surrealist Context* (Syracuse: Syracuse University Press, 1982) 67. See also Yves Tanguy (New York: Acquavella Galleries, 1974) 1–2.

10. Matthews 459.

11. John Canaday, *Mainstreams of Modern Art* (Chicago: Holt, Rinehart, and Winston, Inc., 1981) 35.

12. Carol Clover, *Men, Women, and Chainsaws: Gender in the Modern Horror Film* (Princeton: Princeton University Press, 1992) 192.

13. Annette Kuhn, *The Power of the Image* (London: Routledge, 1985) 39.

14. See Derek Hughes and Janet Todd, *The Cambridge Companion to Aphra Behn* (Cambridge: Cambridge University Press, 2004) xii.

15. See John Adlard, ed., *The Debt to Pleasure: John Wilmot, Earl of Rochester, in the Eyes of His Contemporaries and in His Own Poetry and Prose* (Cheshire, UK: Carcanet Press Ltd., 1974) 31–34.

16. See, for example, Patricia Demers, *Women's Writing in English: Early Modern England* (Toronto and Buffalo: University of Toronto Press, 2005).

17. Janet Todd, *The Secret Life of Aphra Behn* (New Brunswick, NJ: Rutgers University Press, 1996) 135.

18. Quoted in Hughes and Todd 9.

19. Frank Rich, rev. of Williamstown Theatre production of The Rover, *New York Times*, 27 July 1987: C18.

20. For a detailed discussion of Behn's adaptation of Killigrew's original, see Jones DeRitter, "The Gypsy, The Rover, and The Wanderer: Aphra Behn's Revision of Thomas Killigrew," *Restoration* 10 (1986): 82–92.

21. For a concise discussion of this debate, see W.R. Owens and Lizbeth Goodman, eds., *Shakespeare, Aphra Behn and the Canon* (London: Routledge, 1996).

22. K.M. Rogers, *Feminism in Eighteenth-Century England* (London: Harvester Press, 1982) 98–9.

23. Mike Steele, "Feminist Provocateurs of Their Eras: Director Feels 'Sisterhood' With Playwright Aphra Behn," *Minneapolis Star Tribune*, 10 June. 1994: E5.

24. Michael Lupu and Belinda Westmaas Jones, eds., *The Rover Study Guide* (Minneapolis: The Guthrie Theater, 2004). I am grateful to Jo Holcomb and Carla Steen at the Guthrie Theater and to Barbara Bezat of the Performing Arts Archives, University of Minnesota, for assistance in obtaining materials related to this production.

25. *The Rover* Production Program (Minneapolis: Guthrie Theater, 2004).

26. For a fascinating discussion focusing on the carnivalesque in Akalaitis's production, see Susan Carlson, "Cannibalizing and Carnivalizing: Reviving Aphra Behn's *The Rover*," *Theatre Journal* 47, 4 (1995): 517–539.

27. See, for example, Dolors Altaba-Artal, *Aphra Behn's English Feminism* (Selinsgrove, PA: Susquehanna University Press, 1999) 84.

28. See Arlene M. Stiebel, "Aphra Behn," *GLBTQ: An Encyclopedia of Gay, Lesbian, Bisexual, Transgender & Queer Culture* <http://www.glbtq.com/literature/behn_a.html>.

29. Carlson 530.

30. "Essay," *Queer Cultural Center*, <http://www.queerculturalcenter.org/Pages/HalPages/Gaysemi_2.html>.

31. Nancy Franklin, "Bawdy Night," *New Yorker* 1 Aug. 1994: 73.

32. Irons, especially, seemed to dominate the RSC production with charm and star power. See reviews in *The Rover* clipping file, Billy Rose Theatre Collection, New York Public Library for the Performing Arts, Astor, Lenox and Tilden Foundations.

33. Steel, E5.

34. "The Rover Production Text," Guthrie Theater Archive, Performing Arts Archives, Manuscripts Division, University of Minnesota Libraries, Sc. 1, p. 4.

35. Ibid. 63.

36. See Joan DeJean, "Fictions of Sappho," *Critical Inquiry* 13, 4 (1987): 800.

37. Wendy Gibson, *Women in Seventeenth-Century France* (New York: St. Martin's Press, 1989) 197–207.

38. Francesco Orlando, *Toward a Freudian Theory of Literature with an Analysis of Racine's Phèdre*, trans. Charmaine Lee (Baltimore and London: The Johns Hopkins University Press, 1978) 11.

39. John Campbell, *Questioning Racinian Tragedy* (Chapel Hill: University of North Carolina Press, 2005) 217.

40. Ibid. 222.

41. DeJean 788.

42. Mary Jo Muratore, *Expirer Au Féminin: Narratives of Female Dissolution in French Classical Texts* (New Orleans: University Press of the South, 2003) 107.

43. Timberlake Wertenbaker, interview with Robin Pogrebin, *New York Times*, 29 Sept. 1998: E1; *Phèdre* clippings file, Billy Rose Theatre Collection.

44. JoAnne Akalaitis, interview with Celise Kalke, "Insights," 3, 1, *Court Theater*, <http://www.courttheatre.org/home/plays/0203/phedre/director.shtml>.

45. Kalke interview. Schmidt's adaptation is available online at *Project Muse*, <http://muse.jhu.edu/journals/theater/v030/30.1racine.html#authbio>.

46. I am grateful to Patrick Hoffman, Curator of the Theatre on Film and Tape Archive of the New York Library of the Performing Arts for allowing me generous access to the tape of this production, which enabled me to make precise notes regarding Akalaitis's minor alterations of Schmidt's text.

47. Muratore 110.

48. Ibid. 111.
49. Scenic design for this production was by Gordana Svilar and costume design by Kaye Voyce.
50. Kalke interview.
51. Jenny Bacon, interview with Celise Kalke, "Viewpoints," *Court Theatre*, <http://www.courttheatre.org/home/plays/0203/phedre/images/magazine/PhedreMagazine>.
52. See, for example, Michael Phillips, "Court Theatre's *Phèdre* Captivates," *Chicago Tribune*, 17 Sept. 2002; Mary Houlihan, "Ancient Greek Tragedy *Phèdre* Remains Fresh," *Chicago Sun Times*, 16 Sept. 2002: 46; Wendy Arons, rev. of *Phèdre*, *Theatre Journal* 55, 2 (2003): 323–5.
53. Arons 325.

Reconfiguring the Text and the Self
The Wooster Group's To You, the Birdie! (Phèdre)

Johan Callens

Introduction

The Wooster Group is well known for its iconoclastic reinterpretations of canonical dramatic texts, from *Hamlet* and *Phèdre* through *The Emperor Jones, The Hairy Ape*, and *Long Day's Journey into Night* to *Our Town, The Cocktail Party*, and *The Crucible*. In the words of their website's self-presentation, their "theatre pieces are constructed as assemblages of juxtaposed elements," combining "both modern and classic texts, found materials, films and videos, dance and movement, multi-track scoring, and an architectonic approach to theatre design." While never explicitly billed as feminist takes, these productions by director Elizabeth LeCompte have quite systematically paid attention to the male canon's disenfranchisement and stereotyping of female characters, as evidenced in Ophelia's victimization, women's polarization as virgins and whores in O'Neill, the repression of sexuality in Wilder's middle-class small-town, Eliot's sacrificial, class-based dramaturgy, or Miller's historical portrait of hysterical "witches." Among the texts LeCompte has tackled so far, Stein's *Doctor Faustus Lights the Lights* appeared to form an exception, one favored by the twentieth-century avant-garde and written by a proto-feminist, had it not been for the patriarchal bent of the Faust tradition from its inception. Small wonder that LeCompte's staging, *House/Lights* (1998), aided by Stein's revisionist dramaturgy, again interrogated gendered constructions of the self. The same patriarchal bias that suffuses the Faust tradition can be discerned in Phaedra's mythical story, a bias compounded in the classical and neoclassical dramaturgies represented by Euripides' and Racine's versions of the material.

The turn of the current century saw several stage productions in which

To You, the Birdie! (Phèdre): Directed by Elizabeth LeCompte, and staged at St. Ann's Warehouse, Brooklyn, New York, 2001). Pictured: Kate Valk. Photograph courtesy of the Wooster Group and Photographer: Mary Gearhart.

women artists reconceived the gender constructions in this story, beginning with Susan Yankowitz's *Phaedra in Delirium* (1998, dir. Alison Summers), co-produced by Women's Project and Productions and the Classic Stage Company in New York. This was followed by Liz Diamond's *Phaedra* (1998), produced for the American Repertory Theatre in Cambridge, Massachusetts, LeCompte's *To You, the Birdie! (Phèdre)* (2001) staged at St. Ann's Warehouse in Brooklyn, New York, and JoAnne Akalaitis's *Phèdre* (2002) at Chicago's Court Theatre.[1] Yankowitz changed Euripides' heroine into a suburban wife (Kathleen Chalfant) blaming her fading looks and a culture idolizing youth for the neglect she suffers from a husband, who uses his business trips to deceive her, and for the sexual rejection by her stepson, who masks his latent homosexuality behind his honor in his efforts to debase her.[2] Christine Jones's set materialized Phaedra's painful self-reflection arising from the tension between her domestic prison and smoldering desire by a mirror opening a virtual window onto erotic fantasy and a canopy bed rooted in forest soil.[3] The primitive emotions evoked predate the classic drama and myth which LeCompte also draws on, though like Diamond and Akalaitis she starts from Paul Schmidt's Americanization of Racine's Alexandrine couplets that helps to expose Phèdre as a frazzled bundle. In Diamond's interpretation the Jansenist playwright's moral ban on sexual desire (illicit or other) expels Phaedra (Randy Danson) from Yankowitz's private bedroom into Riccardo Hernandez's monumental set where the queen barely held her ground amidst the dance-like interactions, weakened as she was by the neurasthenia feeding on her shameful sense of sin.[4] LeCompte simultaneously stylized and physicalized the courtly drama by staging it on a badminton court and converting Racine's verbal jousts into literal contests displaying the men's prowess and Phèdre's incapacity. As played by Kate Valk, the queen could not even hold her racket, just as she could not dress, feed or go to the bathroom by herself, and, except for some emotional outbursts and peremptory orders, most of her lines were spoken by a male Reader (Scott Shepherd, doubling as Theramenes) from behind one of several transparent sliding screens. In this theatrical incarnation, the effeteness of the Sun King's self-aggrandizing court[5] and high tragedy's class-based character hemming in its privileged protagonists by a cruel fate and state-sponsored courtly decorum yet valorizing their suffering,[6] automatically make for the queen's debilitation. Incapable even of satisfactorily conveying her adulterous love for her stepson, the woman invited ridicule rather than sympathy. As directed by Akalaitis, Jenny Bacon's high-fevered Phèdre was less undone than set loose, from the play's start, by the shamelessly egotistic, passion-driven life of the rich and famous at the seaside resort into which Gordana Svilar had converted Troezen.[7]

The present article, while not ignoring the particularities of the staging process, develops the gender implications of LeCompte's intertextual method, here limited in the interest of space to the mythical pretext, Euripides' and Racine's adaptations, and selected choreographies by Martha Graham. In 1995, Wooster Group associate Paul Schmidt and translator of Racine's *Phèdre*, wrote the scenario for *Snow on the Mesa: Portrait of Martha*, an homage to the choreographer's life and work, in which Robert Wilson directed the Martha Graham Dance Company. Some of the research carried out on that occasion must have fed into *To You, the Birdie!*. Specific movement patterns drawn from Graham choreographies were video screened and replicated on stage, following the Wooster Group's non-psychologizing and non-identificatory acting practice, on the assumption that individual psychology often masks gender-related social and ideological constructs into which the spectators are forced by the traditional theater's identificatory processes. Moreover, LeCompte's mixing of conservative (Euripides, Racine) with transgressive intertexts (Graham) further challenges the story's underlying patriarchal gender conceptions and invites the audience to refrain from objectifying women or allows for multiple spectatorial positions (active as well as passive), which undermine representations passed off as "natural" by male-dominated power structures. Within their new theatrical context the choreographical subtexts offer a not to be neglected undertow to the drama's ostensible mythical and tragic currents. As such, Phèdre need no longer represent the inevitable victim of tragic fate, a degenerate class, the deterministic guilt culture of a Jansenist religion, or the double standard denying middle-aged women sexual desire, yet allowing Racine a mistress (La Champmeslé, for whom he created the part of Phèdre) or Theseus and the classical male pantheon their sexual escapades. Genre, class, religion, and duplicitous morals: all of these have set up or "framed" both Phèdre and theater audiences into seeing her as a deservedly punished woman, instead of one shamed into repressing her own desire as if it were monstrous, and thus silenced and reduced to an object of exchange in a patriarchal and homosocial world. The Wooster Group exposes and undoes this concerted "frame-up" by reframing Phèdre's story intertextually as well as theatrically through devices like the badminton game, with its arbitrary rules, or the sliding panels, now imposing a focused gaze, now refracting and diverting it by the mirrorings, mediations, and behind the scenes machinations of a male Reader and a female god conceived by men.

Pretext

The play, as is well known, draws extensively on Greek myth. Less familiar and worth recapitulating are the rather unsettling details of the story,[8] particularly the reckless adventures of Phaedra's philandering and negligent husband since they provide a foil to Phèdre's illicit love for her stepson, Hippolytus. Phaedra and her sister, Ariadne, were daughters of Pasiphae and King Minos of Crete. When he refused to sacrifice the bull that Poseidon raised from the ocean to prove Minos' rights to the throne, the god kindled Pasiphae's beastly passion for it. Out of their union was born the Minotaur, kept hidden in the mythical labyrinth at Knossos, which Daedalus had designed, like the contraption that had allowed the queen to couple with the bull. Every year the monster was fed seven boys and seven girls, exacted from the city of Athens in compensation for the killing of Minos' son, Androgeus. To put an end to these sacrifices, Theseus, the son of the Athenian ruler Aegeus, sailed to Crete. After slaying the beast and finding his way back by way of the ball of string provided by an enamored Ariadne, he took her and Phaedra with him when sailing home. However, he abandoned Ariadne on Naxos. In addition, Theseus forgot to change the ship's black sail into a white one, so as to announce his victory to the watchmen, thus causing his father to drown himself before the arrival of his son's fleet. No sooner than he succeeded Aegeus as King of Attica, he again embarked on a series of expeditions that involved the acquisition of women. From that against the Amazons, he returned with Queen Antiope, who bore him a son, Hippolytus, though Theseus repudiated her to marry Phaedra. On a subsequent foray into Sparta, he and his friend Peirithous carried off Helen, who fell to Theseus when the men drew lots. In compensation, he joined his friend into the underworld to abduct Persephone, a hazardous journey from which Hercules had to rescue him.

Euripides

It was during this exploit that Phaedra's incestuous longing for Hippolytus took a turn for the worse, the disastrous consequences of which were dramatized in Sophocles' fragmentarily preserved *Phaedra*, Euripides' lost *Hippolytus Veiled* and the extant *Hippolytus Bearer of the Garland* (428 B.C.). A third play of his, *Stheneboia*, written around the time of the second, also recycles the narrative structure of a woman (Stheneboia) who raises accusations to her husband (Proitos) against the object of her love (her nephew Bellerophon), out of spite for being rebuffed. Figures like Phaedra and Sthenoboai fueled Euripides' reputation as a dramatist who repeatedly depicted bad women making sexual overtures to honorable men, as satirized in Aristophanes' *Thesmophoriazousai* (411 B.C.) and *The Frogs* (405 B.C.).[9] What partly exculpates Phaedra, if not Euripides, as we learn from the opening of his play, is that Aphrodite used her to get back at Hippolytus because he had made a vow of chastity to Artemis, the virginal goddess guarding his prowess as hunter and tamer of horses. The rumors that Theseus' trip into the underworld had cost him his life were only the occasion for Phaedra to break her self-imposed silence and confess her love.

In turn, Hippolytus' Amazon extraction foreshadowed Phaedra's reckless accusation of rape and the ensuing punishments against him (Theseus' curse and Neptune's revenge through the intercession of a sea monster). The ensemble of Greek myths about the horse riding viragos indeed offers a mirror-image of the approved social and heterosexual relations in Greek patriarchal society.[10] These allowed for the ravishment and rape of Antiope in the first place and the victimization of the still virginal Hippolytus as if he were a woman, whose total abstinence is as offensive as Phaedra's illicit lust. The same scenario of male actors committing sexual assaults on passive women is to be found in the gods' amorous pursuits of mortals and the attacks on Greek women by the hybrid Centaurs, half-man, half-horse. The etymological relation between these Centaurs and the Minotaur is no coincidence. For the same reason, Euripides' nurse deliberately recalls the story of Semele's ravishment by Zeus. However, in the contradictory uses of the story — inciting Phaedra to love yet warning against imitating the gods lest she risk death — Euripides also acknowledges the instability of myths, which invite change, both in the telling and the interpretation.

That the story of Semele can be found in "books written in times past"[11] makes it particularly suspicious, given the Greeks' anxieties about writing,[12] confirmed in the calumnious note attached to the wrist of Phaedra's dead body and the equally offensive male report of Hippolytus' crash with his chariot, unequivocally equating the deceitfulness of women with that of writing: Hippolytus cannot be "a villain, not even if the whole female sex should hang itself and all the trees on Ida go to make writing material."[13] These anxieties about writing had to do with the logocentric prejudice according to which speech supposedly guarantees an authentic living presence, as opposed to the secondariness of writing. But as Derrida and poststructuralists have insisted, speech no less than writing is marked by the deferral of language, absence, and mediation. Euripides shows as much, by casting equal doubts on the truthfulness of both. When confronted with Hippolytus' self-defense, Theseus only wishes man had two voices, a natural and an honest one to refute the first should it harbor treachery. Ostensibly, then, Euripides inscribes himself in a revisionist tradition, which simultaneously legitimates and delegitimates his own theatrical enterprise and that of his successors.

To guarantee the story's cultural transmission, Artemis, at the end of Euripides' play, inaugurates a rite of passage with which the divine frame is resumed. On the eve of their wedding virgin girls shall cut their locks in Hippolytus' honor and their mournful songs shall commemorate both him and Phaedra's passion. The grief over Phaedra's and Hippolytus' sorry fate merges with that of the girls over their impending defloration, violence against women sanctioned by patriarchy and abetted by matrimony, institutions normalizing and socializing the uncontainable violence of Phaedra's illicit desire. No wonder the play's final exchanges are reserved for Theseus and his dying son, a prolonged moment in which Hippolytus' absolution of his father reasserts the temporarily disrupted male bond to the exclusion of Phaedra, whose machinations and their outcome an embittered Theseus "shall remember." The closing chorus, too, sings of "great men" lost and mourned. The conclusion, then, evinces Nancy Sorkin Rabinowitz's argument that Euripides' plays seek to relieve male anxieties about the legitimate heirs' expropriation. Through the institution of marriage the heterosexually desiring female, alienating father and son, is turned into an object of exchange that reaffirms the filial tie and thereby covertly gratifies the homosocial desire upon which Greek culture is founded.[14]

Racine

Euripides, in other words, only appears to allocate equal weight to each of his protagonists, first to Phaedra struggling with her love and indecision, then to Hippolytus in his conflict with his father. This may have led Racine to emend his original title, *Phèdre et Hippolyte*, into *Phèdre* (1677), even if the foregrounding of his female protagonist up until her final moments rather than those of her stepson seems weakened by Theseus' final imprecation that "the memory of her appalling misdeeds die with her!"[15] But then the Jansenist Racine admitted in his Preface that he meant his play to serve an edifying purpose by punishing the "aberration" of passions, acted on or intended, despite Phèdre's victimization by fate, a nurse (Enone) goaded by devotion to her Queen and vicarious political ambitions for her legitimate children with Theseus, and the momentary loss of mind that made her accuse her stepson. While the Greeks' double standard still operates in Racine's desire to "spare Theseus"[16] and safeguard the audience's sympathy for him, Hippolytus' friend, Theramenes, immediately singles out Theseus' reputation as a philanderer to explain his year-long absence from Troezen, whereas in Euripides' play Theseus' adulteries are mentioned as one among many possible causes for Phaedra's sickness. As the title, opening, and closing of his play thus indicate, Racine slightly shifts the balance in Phèdre's favor.

Still, it makes little difference whether Euripides has Phaedra hang herself from the "beams of her bridal chamber,"[17] or Racine traces the poison which Phèdre takes to the legendary witchcraft of Theseus' stepmother, Medea, thereby establishing another gender-based generalization in which the false accusation inevitably follows from a split tongue. Enone's abandoning everything to follow Phèdre from Athens to Troezen also invokes Medea, who did not just leave her home country for love of Jason, but betrayed her father and brother to allow her lover to get away with the Golden Fleece. Phèdre and Enone thus become she-devils like Aphrodite a.k.a. Venus, played appropriately in *To You, the Birdie!* by Suzzy Roche, the she-devil from *House/Lights*, now pulling the wool of her cloudy wings over everyone's eyes. Birds of a feather flock together, at least in Euripides' and Racine's dramatic tradition presenting women as fickle and treacherous, the "weaker sex" that needs to be contained by patriarchal authority, their voice silenced, violently if need be. Little wonder that in *To You, the Birdie!* Valk's Phèdre can hardly speak for herself, though she lords it over the domestic help and fusses with plants, shoes, and crown for lack of larger responsibilities, while the *pater familias* is hunting for fairer game.

Paul Schmidt's Translation and the Wooster Group's Reconfiguration of Phèdre/Phèdre

As mentioned, LeCompte relied on the translation Paul Schmidt made for Diamond's 1998 production.[18] In general Schmidt figures translation as an act of ventriloquism that sets up an echo chamber between different parties and their respective languages, between, on the one hand, the playwright, actors, and spectators, and on the other, French and American English.[19] In this sense, textual translation becomes emblematic for the mediations involved in staging a pre-existing text (mythic or dramatic), mediations which Phaedra's letter from Euripides' play characterizes as a deception of sorts and to which LeCompte added visual and choreographic sources, among others. Racine's play no longer features Phaedra's letter but still has Phèdre accuse Hippolytus in veiled terms, rendered duplicitous by the desire that later makes her hide her shameful face. LeCompte may have relied on these figurations—writing, translation, ventriloquism, and veiling—when setting up *To You, the Birdie!* as an echo chamber of intertexts and voices dominated by a male Reader who appropriates Phèdre's utterances, in keeping with the manipulations of Aphrodite and Enone, and Artemis' ultimate subservience to patriarchal institutions. From Schmidt's translation LeCompte removed scenes and characters (Hippolytus' secret love, Aricia, not in Euripides but recycled from Virgil; her friend Ismene; and Phèdre's waiting woman, Panope). The director also allowed for improvised matter like Phèdre's private thoughts, and included Aphrodite's opening address from *Hippolytus*, prior to Phèdre's first entrance. For the audience entering the theater, the story's Greek roots appeared only alluded to in two truncated pillars. However, during the production the plexi sliding panels in Jim Findlay's set made for a baroque confusion that harks back to the extensive symmetries and mirrorings of Euripides' *Hippolytus* and Racine's *Phèdre*. Like the ventriloquism and veiling, literalized in the black gauze head cover hindering Valk's speech upon Theseus' return, these sliding panels problematized identity and human agency. Whenever they threw off reflections, the set fused echoes of the Minotaur's mythical labyrinth with the Sun King's intrigue-infested court, whose abundant spectacles, disguising reality behind blinding appearances, were but one means of disseminating his image.

In the course of the action, *To You, the Birdie!* also evokes a pseudo-classical and conventionally "masculine" complex—palace, acropolis or stronghold with gymnasium pool, locker rooms, semi-public toilets, sauna, and badminton court—a complex which seriously handicaps Phèdre. The god of love has been hoisted high on a video monitor, whereas the badminton referee (Fiona Leaning) and her two line markers (Koosil-ja Hwang and Dominique Bousquet) form a depleted choir, delivering songs built around phrases from the play and compiled on a CD marketed via the Wooster Group's website. If Euripides' female god already frames LeCompte's version of Racine's play, the production is further "greeked" through the gymnasium setting, the physical contest of the badminton games, the skirts the men are wearing, and their parodies of athletes' and classical sculptures' semi-nude poses, like those of Ari Fliakos's Hippolytus when Phèdre declares her love to him. The love songs, performed by Roche, Valk, and Koosil-ja, appearing, for the occasion, as members of the band Drench, translated the emotion-invested lyricism of Phèdre's speeches, already evident in Euripides' assigning Phaedra the kind of lyric part usually reserved for the chorus.[20] Every time the songs from *To You, the Birdie!* are played, the Wooster Group answers Artemis' closing injunction that brides-to-be commemorate Phaedra and Hippolytus on the eve of their wedding night. By marking the girls' sexual initiation and mirroring Hippolytus' resistance to it, this commemorative ritual offered as a compromise speaks of, yet channels Phaedra's desire into marriage sanctioned by patriarchy and functions as a frame breaking epilogue providing a transition to the everyday realm of the fifth-century Athenian audience. In a similar way, Drench's pop songs transcend the Wooster Group's production, in the process reappropriating Phèdre's voice from the male Reader, so it can wend its way into the wider world.

At the same time, LeCompte "outspeaks" Euripides, since in fifth-century Athens well-regulated cults constituted the only public avenue for women, who were a minority even in the theater audience and radically banned from the orchestra. Having her voice digitally transcribed onto an independently produced and distributed audio CD authored by women Phèdre transgresses by speaking and writing out of place, neither in veiled terms nor ventriloquially, i.e. by male proxy.

In this manner the Wooster Group's reconfiguration of *Phèdre* spans two thousand years, from ancient Greece to the postmodern culture industry. It never does so gratuitously but with the effect of exposing reigning power structures from classical patriarchy to the contemporary music industry. Different temporalities and geographies thus intersect and overlap in *To You, the Birdie!*, playing fast and loose with the (neo)classical unities. The Wooster Group's reliance on badminton recalls the courts for ball games or *jeux de paume* where seventeenth century plays were performed before buildings specifically conceived for theater were erected. These improvised spaces in turn conjure the Wooster Group's own Performing Garage, the product of the search for alternative venues by the experimental theaters of the 1960s.

Martha Graham

As an image of how mortals and commoners are caught within the vicious games of the reigning religious and secular authorities, the badminton rackets in *To You, the Birdie!* call to mind the fly swatter from *Brace Up!* (1991), the Wooster Group production based on *Three Sisters*, in which LeCompte's and Chekhov's references to Shakespeare can be complemented with Gloucester's bitter insight that "As flies to wanton boys are we to th' gods,/ They kill us for their sport" (*King Lear* 4.1.36–37). In a similar metaphorical sense, rackets, however, already figured in Martha Graham's section of *Episodes* (1959, New York City Ballet, revived in 1979–80).[21] LeCompte may have seen or come across Graham's work (in collaboration with classical choreographer George Balanchine) when exploring her rendering of *Phaedra* (1962), subsequently reworked into *Phaedra's Dream* (1983), though the 1988 revival, in a double bill with Ariadne's story, *Errand into the Maze* (1947), reverted to the original 1960s creation. In Graham's *Episodes I* Mary Stuart (Sallie Wilson) relives her past prior to her execution February 8, 1587 as a result of her conflict with the reigning Queen Elizabeth (Graham). That battle of wills, one of the most memorable scenes, (resonating with the divine contest between Aphrodite and Artemis in Euripides' *Hippolytus*) is rendered through a veiled ball game, in which gongs and plucked strings marked serves and returns. But unlike *To You, the Birdie!*, where the shuttle's whizz was amplified and undercut by bird twitter, no ball was exchanged. For the rest, the rigidly frontal and stylized performances of the women during the tennis match in *Episodes I*, reminiscent of Japanese Nōh and Kabuki, stand in stark contrast to the overall movement patterns in *To You, the Birdie!*, an eclectic postmodern mix of pomp and ceremony, everyday attitudes, cartoon effects, the explosive gestures of the badminton game, and Graham's modernist dance vocabulary, as copied from the videos. These videos, screened live and occasionally glimpsed by the public in the sliding panels' and monitors' reflections, featured fragments from *Cave of the Heart* (1946), *Seraphic Dialogue* (1955), and *Cortège of Eagles* (1967), based respectively on Medea, Joan of Arc, and Queen Hecuba of Troy. Not used onstage were *Phaedra, Phaedra's Dream*, or *Errand into the Maze* because their gestural vocabulary and rhythms proved less amenable to the new context. All of these Graham choreographies revolving around legendary women further extend the interdisciplinary subtext for the Wooster Group's reinterpretation of *Phèdre*. At the same time they demonstrate Graham's transgressive sexual politics and her dances' formative role for an ever critically reconstituted and diversified spectatorship. Whatever happens on stage, LeCompte, too, always has in "mind these people who will be sitting and watching."[22]

A case in point of LeCompte's investing spectatorship with sexual politics is the already mentioned scene in which a semi-naked Hippolytus (Fliakos) becomes the voyeuristic object of Phèdre's confession, a situation inverting the more common scenario in which woman is silenced and exposed to the male viewer. This voyeurism derives straight from Racine's text, foregrounding verbs of display and the eye-motif,[23] but it was also present in Graham's choreography. The dance critic Anna Kisselgoff has observed that Phaedra's earlier spying on her stepson in the woods was indeed rendered by a sort of striptease, as his body was gradually exposed through the different openings in a Japanese screen.[24] Both voyeuristic scenes are not just about sex but about the denial of women's sexual agency and subject position in a patriarchal society, which presents female desire in illicit or unnatural (incestuous and monstrous) terms. Graham's transgressiveness became clear when Representatives Edna Kelly (NY) and Peter Freylinghuysen (NJ), offended by her overt eroticism and advanced age, denounced the choreography in Congress for being state-subsidized pornography.[25] Particularly offensive must have been Graham's projection of Phaedra's dream of Pasiphae's coupling with the bull and her subsequent enactment of the alleged rape in front of Theseus' very eyes. Euripides' heroine avoids her husband's rage through the subterfuge of the letter read after her death. Racine's Phèdre confronts Theseus but hides her face, expresses her alleged defilement in veiled terms, and quickly leaves. Graham's Phaedra outdoes both of her (neo)classical models when avenging herself on Hippolytus for foiling her advances by provocatively "liv[ing] out — as in a wishful dream — the sexual gratification she so desires"[26] and by doing so in the presence of her philandering husband. By comparison, LeCompte displaces her protagonist's recollected infatuation with Hippolytus onto the inherited family curse, which also "started long ago."[27] At this point, Valk mimics Pasiphae's coupling with the bull, using to great effect one of the performance company's stock-in-trade wheelchairs, its handlebars having been lengthened for the occasion to suggest horns, while a richly layered soundtrack suggestively fills in any imaginative gaps. As Valk backs into the wheelchair-commode, crouched on hands and knees, Phèdre becomes half beast, half machine, rebirthing herself in an act of auto-genesis, penetrated by the monster she felt she had become.

With or without Hippolytus' sword, which she later proffers so he can "kill" her, Phèdre appears prosthetically transformed into the androgynous "woman as phallus" of Man Ray's "Minotaur," which brings in yet another frame, that of the Surrealists. In this famous 1934 gelatin silver print, Lee Miller's beheaded and exposed torso, with her upheld arms petering out in the dark, was made to resemble a bull's horned head. For the Surrealists, the figure of the Minotaur, after which they named one of their journals illustrated with a cover by René Magritte, represented the male "subject lost in the labyrinth of his own desire"[28] and Miller's photographically appropriated female body, turned bull's head, functioned as a projection screen or seat of male fantasies. To the extent that the Wooster Group's stage picture could be said to literalize and recall the Surrealists' iconographic yet sexist image of the Minotaur (also used by André Masson, Pablo Picasso, and Salvador Dalí), it can only do so as a case of Irigaray's mimicry or repetition with a difference, through which female agency and subjecthood are reclaimed.[29] As paraphrased by Susan Rubin Suleiman, "[i]n mimicry, a woman 'repeats' the male — in this case, the male Surrealist — version of 'woman,' but she does so in a self-conscious way that points up the citational, often ironic status of the repetition."[30] Both the citational and differential character of Phèdre's auto-genesis (as performed by Valk) are confirmed by its resemblance to Ariadne's self-engendering in Graham's *Errand into the Maze*, where it results from the confrontation with her own deeper fears and longings,[31] or what Mark Ryder, the second dancer to perform the bull-man, referred to as the "rape" by "one's subconscious" necessary to create.[32] Graham was actually challenged to reassert her (self-authorized) artistic autonomy by the original bull-man, her former partner Erick Hawkins, whose *Stephen Acrobat* (1947) signaled his re-emergence as a choreographer-dancer in his own right.[33] Ariadne's "errand," then, is neither a mistake nor a weakness but an affirmation of the "virile feminine" vision underlying Graham's creative search for primitive otherness[34] and Phèdre's fantasized descent into the labyrinth, the Cretan space of transgression, during her declaration of love in Racine's play.

Graham's and LeCompte's "monsters" should be further distinguished, therefore, from the bull or sea-monster which Theseus' curse conjures, since the latter confirms the patriarchal authority of God and King, guaranteeing its transmission from one generation to the next. After all, Theseus construes the sea-monster's instant apparition as proof that Poseidon is his father, the very god who kindled Pasiphae's monstrous passion to get back at Minos. All of which supports Rabinowitz's thesis that, in Greek culture, women, whose heterosexual desire interceded between men, were turned into objects of exchange which strengthened rather than weakened the homosocial bond. LeCompte lends further credibility to Rabinowitz's thesis by eroticizing some of Hippolytus' encounters with Theramenes and Theseus during which Aricia and Phèdre seem at stake. In the opening of the play, with a set suggesting the locker room of a sports facility, Hippolytus (Fliakos) confesses his love for Aricia while Theramenes' (Shepherd's) hand roams freely underneath Hippolytus' skirt, a scene the audience witnesses voyeuristically on the large, downstage flatscreen monitor behind which both performers sit. And following the cold and brief welcome Phèdre gives Theseus, Hippolytus tries to extricate himself from Theseus' (Willem Dafoe's) intimate embrace in which father and son roll down the stage, while mimicking a movement from Graham.

To counter the male bonding, LeCompte intimates deeper ties between Phèdre and her confidante, Enone. Valk and Sheena See (Frances McDormand in an earlier run) kiss each other on the lips after agreeing on how to cope with Theseus' unanticipated homecoming. By accusing Hippolytus of rape they turn Phèdre's incestuous desire against him, if also against themselves. The strategy tightens the sisterly bond, all the way into death, but it also silences Hippolytus, much as female rape victims have been silenced throughout history through a classic double bind: to keep quiet is to self-destruct, to speak is to invite public censure or shame. Thus, the sisterly pact between Enone and Phèdre not only bespeaks their female desire but remembers and mends what male desire tears apart (the bond between Ariadne and Phèdre as well as that between Phèdre and Enone). Euripides exposes the underlying double standard: Phaedra's (female) honor lies in the courageous silencing of her illicit desire, her not speaking or being spoken of in public, yet (male) honor, as her Nurse speciously points out to elicit Phaedra's confession of love, must be validated by public speech, its courage attested to by others. In Racine's Christianized revision absolution requires confession but confession in this context equals the admission of guilt and the need for punishment. Phèdre's ironical speaking out against rape may have formed LeCompte's strongest reason to rely on the badminton figure. By converting the French *jeux de paume* and Graham's veiled tennis match from *Episodes I* into badminton, the American director prolongs in the shuttle's wake a richly designed intertextual tapestry, reaching all the way to Aristotle's *Poetics* (16.4) and Sophocles' lost *Tereus*. In that play, Philomela, through the "voice of the shuttle," shared with her sister Procne the story of how her brother-in-law raped her and cut out her tongue to prevent discovery. LeCompte's use of the shuttle image joins Phèdre once again to Ariadne, as two siblings equally wronged by Theseus.[35]

Conclusion

Any conclusion to my highly selective, critical trajectory through the intertexts of *To You, the Birdie!* can only be provisional, since its material and conceptual design is composed of many more strands than could be integrated within the scope of the present article. Those touched upon, however, form part of a patriarchal cultural heritage maintained and contested in the two thousand year old stage history of Phaedra, whose revision Euripides invited and each new installment of LeCompte's work in progress reframes. Despite the male Reader's appropriation of Phèdre's voice LeCompte allows it to be heard through the Wooster Group production, in the gap between the character's repressed desire and deferred satisfaction, and in the echo of Drench's *Love Songs*. That there is no end to Phèdre's story should be ascribed less to LeCompte's interpretative call — her company's collective performance tendering the birdie to us as critical spectators— than to the rigidity of these gender constructions and their lingering injustice, requiring that we keep reconfiguring the text and the self.

Notes

1. See Cheryl Black's discussion of JoAnne Akalaitis's *Phèdre* in her article "Transgressive Female Desire and Subversive Critique in the Seventeenth Century Canon: JoAnne Akalaitis's Staging of *Phèdre, The Rover,* and *'Tis Pity She's a Whore*" in this volume.
2. Sharon Friedman, rev. of *Phaedra in Delirium, Women & Performance* 10.1-2 (#19–20) (1999): 297–301.
3. Peter Marks, "A Tragedy Reinterpreted With a Bored Homemaker," *New York Times,* 30 Jan. 1998: E1, 3.
4. Carolyn Clay, rev. of *Phaedra,* dir. Liz Diamond, *Boston Phoenix,* 10–17 Dec. 1998.
5. Ben Brantley, rev. of *To You, the Birdie! (Phèdre),* New York Times, 19 Feb. 2002: E1, 5.
6. Gaby Cody, rev. of *To You, the Birdie! (Phèdre),* Theatre Journal 55.1 (March 2003): 173–5.
7. Wendy Arons, rev. of *Phèdre,* dir. JoAnne Akalaitis, Theatre Journal 55.2 (May 2003): 323–5.
8. Robert Graves, *New Larousse Encyclopedia of Mythology* (London: Hamlyn, 1968 [1959]) 176–179, 198.
9. Richard Rutherford, preface, "Introduction," and annotation, *Hippolytus, Alcestis and Other Plays,* by Euripides, trans. John Davie (Harmondsworth, UK: Penguin, 1996) xxiii, 125–126; Barbara E. Goff, *The Noose of Words: Readings of Desire, Violence and Language in Euripides' Hippolytos* (Cambridge: Cambridge University Press, 1990) 93–95.
10. Froma I. Zeitlin, "Configurations of Rape in Greek Myth," *Rape: An Historical and Social Enquiry,* eds. Sylvana Tomaselli and Roy Porter (Oxford: Basil Blackwell, 1986) 122–151.
11. Euripides 142.
12. Goff 96.
13. Euripides 161.
14. Nancy Sorkin Rabinowitz, *Anxiety Veiled: Euripides and the Traffic in Women* (Ithaca, NY: Cornell University Press, 1993) 173–188.

15. Jean Racine, *Phaedra, in Iphigenia, Phaedra, Athaliah*, trans. John Cairncross (Harmondsworth, UK: Penguin Books, 1970 [1963]) 214.
16. Racine, Preface to *Phaedra* 145.
17. Euripides 150.
18. Jean Racine, *Phèdre*, trans. Paul Schmidt, Theater 30.1 (2000): 102–127.
19. Douglas Langworthy, "*Wordschmidt*," *American Theatre* (Sept. 1993): 16–17.
20. Rutherford xxv.
21. Ernestine Stodelle, *Deep Song: The Dance Story of Martha Graham* (New York: Schirmer Books, 1984) 205–214, 317.
22. Elizabeth LeCompte and Richard Foreman, "Messing Around," *The Village Voice* 10–16 (August 1994): 34.
23. Jean Starobinski, *L'Oeuil Vivant* (Paris: Gallimard, 1961) 69–90.
24. Anna Kisselgoff, rev. of *Phaedra and Errand into the Maze*, New York Times, 13 Oct. 1988.
25. Agnes De Mille, *Martha: The Life and Work of Martha Graham* (New York: Random House, 1991) 354–5.
26. Stodelle 231.
27. Schmidt 107.
28. Hal Foster, *Prosthetic Gods* (Cambridge: MIT Press, 2004) 239.
29. Luce Irigaray, *This Sex Which Is Not One*, trans. Catherine Porter and Carolyn Burke (Ithaca, NY: Cornell University Press, 1985) 76.
30. Susan Rubin Suleiman, *Subversive Intent: Gender, Politics, and the Avant–Garde* (Cambridge: Harvard University Press, 1990) 27.
31. Stodelle 134–135, 151.
32. De Mille 281.
33. Ibid.
34. Mark Franko, *Dancing Modernism/Performing Politics* (Bloomington: Indiana University Press, 1995) 56–57.
35. Patricia Klindienst Joplin, "The Voice of the Shuttle Is Ours," *Stanford Literary Review* 1.1 (1984): 25–53. Also, see Maya Roth's discussion of Philomela and Procne in her article "Myth as Civic Theater: Timberlake Wertenbaker's *The Love of the Nightingale*" in this volume.

III

Nineteenth and twentieth Century Narratives and Reflections: The Romance, the Novel, and the Essay

Outside the Law
Feminist Adaptations of The Scarlet Letter

Lenora Champagne

The tree of knowledge did not stand in the garden of God in order to dispense information on good and evil, but as an emblem of judgment over the questioner. This monstrous irony marks the mythical origin of the law.
— Walter Benjamin, Reflections[1]

There is no law, nor reverence for authority.... [in the child]. None,— save the freedom of a broken law.
— Nathaniel Hawthorne, The Scarlet Letter[2]

During the final decade of the twentieth century, three feminist playwrights, Phyllis Nagy, Suzan-Lori Parks, and Naomi Wallace, turned their attention to the classic American novel, *The Scarlet Letter*.[3] Nathaniel Hawthorne's romance, with its adulterous triangle in which the woman visibly pays for her transgression, proved to be an irresistible template for an examination of hypocrisy in a decade marked by the rise of religious fundamentalism, a backlash against feminism and gay rights, and the culture wars over sexual representation in the arts.[4] The three playwrights under consideration, approaching the novel independently, mine it for implicit relationships of gender and patriarchal authority and, in each case, make them explicit in their dramatic works.

These provocative adaptations are explosions of the classic text that challenge the author's authority by foregrounding his ambivalence about the "feminine" as they focus on the outcast or outsider as seducer, disrupter, and voice of repressed desire in American culture, marked as it is by its Puritan roots. This analysis will explore the liminal, outlaw status of the female characters, who with their witch-like tendencies and unrestrained self-expression in the face of socially normative codes of behavior defy patriarchal power and gender expectations.

Feminist Criticism on The Scarlet Letter: *Puritans, Witches, Women, and Sin*

Feminist literary critics have often seen Hester Prynne as heroic, "a figure of courage, imagination, and passion"[5] and have focused on her agency in her transformation of the symbol of adultery — the letter 'A' — into a more ambiguous and positive sign, such as able, angel, or even art. As Nina Baym argues, "Hester ... endows her letter with many meanings, and with many good meanings."[6] However, apart from Baym, many critics see Hawthorne as ambivalent about Hester's rebellious private thoughts — "The world's law was no law for her mind" — as well as the "feminine" (143). For instance, Judith Fryer observes the narrator's discomfort with Hester's "dark question" regarding the "whole race of womanhood: Was existence worth accepting, even to the happiest among them?" (144). She notes the narrator's qualms about women surmounting these problems through "any exercise of thought."[7] Shari Benstock sees his equation of embroidery with storytelling in his indirect and fanciful autobiographical essay, "The Custom House" as an indication of his anxiety about his own masculinity in the taking up of a woman's tale. She argues that Hester is the victim of male fantasies "ranging from those that concern 'the female body' to the controlling 'fantasy of absolute sexual difference' that lies at the very heart of women's repression and exploitation."[8]

In Hawthorne's nineteenth-century novel, the culture in question is American — seventeenth-century Puritan Massachusetts — for which the forest is not only the edge of town, but the edge of darkness. Nature itself, with its hostile climate, its "savages" and "heathen folk," is seen as a threat to the strict, theocratic, conformist society of the Puritans — a society in which sin is crime. In this codified world, personal expression or deviation from the norm is as threatening as the wilderness.

Enter Hester Prynne, emerging from prison bearing on her breast a red letter beautifully embroidered with gold thread, and in her arms a child with no father's name. As Benstock argues, "The letter A, which is to stand as the sign of sexual fall, escapes by way of Hester's needle the interpretive code it would enforce.... It makes a spectacle of femininity, of female sexuality, of all that Puritan law hopes to repress."[9] Hester's public punishment is meant to shame her; the public spectacle is intended to provide a lesson that interior lives must be repressed.

Of course, the transgression that leads to Hester's public humiliation and

Opposite: Cherise Booth as Hester, La Negrita, *In the Blood* (2002) by Suzan-Lori Parks, produced by New York University's Tisch Graduate Acting Program in collaboration with the Department of Design for Stage and Film, New York. Director: Michael Sexton; Sets: Andromache Chalfant; Costumes: Martin Lopez; Lighting: Michael Brunschwiler. 2002. Photographer: George Mott. Courtesy of NYU Graduate Acting Program.

Reverend Dimmesdale's crippling repression is a sexual act — an outward expression of an internal desire. The perceived dangers of seduction — the public consequences of sexual transgression and, specifically, the expression of female sexuality outside the bonds of marriage — are what force Hester in the novel, and in the adaptations, to the margins of society — to the edge of the forest. And the forest is the place where women deemed witches go to dance with the Devil. As Nina Baym notes,

> The idea of witchcraft is the way in which the Puritans accommodate the ... reality that people ... have interior lives into their worldview.... Their solution ... is to define the inner world as the most exterior world of all: as the alien world of the Forest, the dark, the Black Man, the Other, something that comes upon them from the outside and tempts them away.[10]

Gabriele Schwab, in her analysis of the witch pattern in *The Scarlet Letter*, argues that an internalized pattern of witchcraft was used in the cultural representation of women during Hawthorne's time. "The witch appears ... as other in the cultural production of female subjectivity."[11] Like Baym in her characterization of witchcraft as an expression of interior versus public lives, Schwab observes that

> The witchcraft pattern was also an expression of a cultural relationship to inner nature.... It could absorb ... the male fear of seductive women ... and of strong, independent women.... The pattern was used in the cultural attempt to overcome or subdue nature — be it as wilderness, as native Indian, or as untamed ... women.[12]

As Schwab notes, although Hester Prynne is indicted as an adulteress and not as a witch, and "the drama of seduction has been displaced from a supernatural to a secular stage ... the basic traits of the stereotype remain obvious."[13]

In Schwab's view, Hester, Pearl, her child, and Mistress Hibbens all fit the witch pattern, which includes three types: "the beautiful wild witch," "the "child-woman witch," and "the old or deformed witch ... who comes to represent the inverse of seduction."[14] In the novel, Hester corresponds to the first type, Pearl to the second, and Mistress Hibbins to the third. The three playwrights radically approach the novel by each foregrounding a different character/witch type in their adaptations. Wallace zeros in on Hibbins, Nagy on Pearl, and Parks on Hester.

The Adaptations

In the 1990s, perhaps in response to inroads in American civil life by religious fundamentalists and political conservatives, Naomi Wallace, Phyllis Nagy, and Suzan-Lori Parks responded to the novel with feisty, feminist, complex revisionist adaptations that take the themes of Hawthorne's novel into contemporary cultural debates on gender roles, homosexuality, welfare, and abortion.

Issues related to the surveillance of sexuality alluded to in the novel are named outright in the plays, where gender hierarchy is displayed and, at times, subverted, especially for the women who reside outside the law.

In the adaptations by Wallace and Nagy, two figures circulate outside the law: Hibbins, the witch, and Pearl, the demon child. Hester, though she lives on the outskirts of town and at the margins of society, is marked by the law and therefore a visible sign of it, preventing her from being truly outside it, though she manages, over time, to subvert her symbol. Operating within the recognizable world of the novel, Nagy and, especially, Wallace suggest that, while intelligent and bold at one time, the chastised Hester is less free, and perhaps less interesting, than the female characters who do not live with her constraints or possess her forbearance. The capacity of both Hibbins and Pearl to express pleasure, to act spontaneously, and to challenge authority with provocative questions presents a threat to a community that demands obedience and propriety. They share a marginal status and isolation from the community, and both are more at home in the woods. As disruptive females, they are associated with wildness and darkness.

Wallace and Nagy deconstruct the novel and give these secondary characters prominence. The Wallace play is narrated by Anne Hibbins, the self-acknowledged witch (and sister to Governor Bellingham) in Hawthorne's novel. Repression and subversion cohabit.[15] In Wallace's play, authority is turned upside down and Hibbins has the upper hand. In the Nagy version, Pearl, Hester's impish daughter, played as a sexy child/woman, is narrator of the play.

Both plays are highly theatrical and use various devices to displace or disrupt the narrative and to foreground erotic undercurrents only implied in the Hawthorne, who, after all, did not have Sigmund Freud to draw on for an elucidation of inner lives and erotic drives. For instance, in Nagy's play, Chillingworth, Hester's former husband and Dimmesdale's healer turned tormentor, forces Hester to lick his boots, and becomes explicitly the sadist he is implicitly in the Hawthorne. In Wallace's play, the secret Reverend Dimmesdale represses turns out not to be his desire for Hester, but for Chillingworth.

Wallace and Nagy directly respond to scenes from the novel and feature a New England Puritan setting, replete with anachronistic references. The adaptations parody and play with Hawthorne's characterization of *The Scarlet Letter* as a romance, as is evident in stage directions such as "scary wind" and exaggeratedly passionate characters. Rather than re-create the lush images and romanticism of Hawthorne's novel, both Nagy and Wallace take an ironic approach to the staging of parallel scenes. Choosing a strategy of deliberate knowingness, they establish clear differences with Hawthorne in perspective and tone. They undermine the sobriety of the Puritan world and Hawthorne's serious intentions with levity and disrupt tension with wisecracks and innuendos.

Suzan-Lori Parks's plays *In the Blood* and *Fucking A* are tragic in tone and more focused on Hester, placing her at the very edge of civilization. Parks is more interested in the price society forces Hester to pay for her non-normative behavior. While Parks gives voice to other characters' perspectives (as when, in *Blood*, each of the adults, in direct address to the audience, confesses to having betrayed Hester), her story is principally told from Hester's point of view. These plays are not set in a theatrically-heightened Puritan New England, but in invented, tragic worlds (urban and contemporary in *Blood*; allegorical in *Fucking A*). Parks's plays are angry laments, parables in which language seems to have weight and take up space, and in which Parks indicts a society that blames the poor for their own troubles.

In all the plays, the children are lawless, as Pearl is in the novel. Chillingworth, in Hawthorne's text, observing Pearl inappropriately at play in a graveyard, remarks, "There is no law, nor reverence for authority ... [in the child]" to which Dimmesdale replies, "None, save the freedom of a broken law" (117). Hester's children in the revisionist adaptations all exercise this freedom, with the effect of undermining, at least temporarily, the repression of physical expression and sexual desire that patriarchal Law means to enforce. In Parks's plays, however, not all of the children survive, and the ones that remain behind are unlikely to find freedom on the streets or in the jails that await them.

Naomi Wallace

Naomi Wallace's subversive 1992 adaptation of *The Scarlet Letter* is subtitled: *as told by Anne Hibbins, the Witch* and is set in Salem, rather than in Boston. Mistress Hibbins is a secondary character in the novel, but her perspective becomes central in this revisionist play. The Governor's sister, Anne Hibbins, lives in the bosom of authority, yet, childless and a widow, she has no power in the patriarchal Puritan civil structure. Instead, she attempts to bewitch Hester, as well as Dimmesdale, and convince them to join her on the dark side, in the forest. Wallace's adaptation takes the theme of law breaking beyond heterosexual/adulterous love to subvert the conventional triad of husband/wife/lover. In the course of the play, Wallace references American homophobia and draws on historically documented accounts of events such as the Salem witch trials, where violent punishment was associated with sexual transgression, property disputes, and the repression of difference.[16]

Wallace's play is a pastiche of lines taken verbatim from Hawthorne, historical research on crime and punishment, original songs, anachronistic dialogue, and imaginative theatrical tricks (flying, puppets, smoke and mirrors). Set in an anachronistic 1640s Salem, the stage set for the play is "simple, yet formal." An American eagle "hovers overhead" and is raised and lowered for courtroom scenes; a scaffold is wheeled on and off. The Devil makes an appearance as a traveling-salesman-like character. Early in the play, Anne Hibbins warns the audience in direct address that "her" version of *The Scarlet Letter* is "lewd, crude, and downright rude" (6). While several of Wallace's scenes parallel Hawthorne's narrative, the adaptation bursts with theatricality and polymorphous sexuality and makes provocative connections between the body and property, often instigated by Hibbins. For instance, Hibbins reveals that:

> Bed-talk brings out the witch in me!—so does property. I had a large estate once... Witchcraft suspicions more often than not originated in property disputes. But historically that's never been as exciting as something like this:
> *Anne does a "witch dance," smoke appears.*
> *A wig of long red hair floats down from above.*
> *Anne takes the long wig and puts it on. The hair is bright red....* This is what Anne will wear as Pearl [23].

Wallace's highly theatrical choice to have the same actress play both Hibbins-the-witch and Little Pearl underscores their shared capacity for mischief, disruption, and pleasure. Hawthorne himself links the two by extending the witch pattern to Pearl, especially in his evocation of Pearl's dancing, laughter, and capriciousness. "Pearl laughed and began to dance up and down," Hawthorne writes, "with the humorsome gesticulation of a little imp, whose next freak might be to fly up the chimney" (87). He continues this analogy in Governor Bellingham's hall, when the child is scrutinized by the elders to determine whether Hester has been a fit mother:

> Little Pearl ... laughed, and went capering down the hall, so airily, that old Mr. Wilson raised a question whether even her tiptoes touched the floor. "The little baggage hath witchcraft in her," I profess, said he to Mr. Dimmesdale. "She needs no old woman's broomstick to fly withal!" [102–103].

The traditional image of the old woman with a broomstick corresponds in the novel to Hibbins, of course. Where Pearl dances and capers, Hawthorne describes Mistress Hibbins as sour-visaged. Dancing is linked with devilishness, and the child is aligned with the witch: both act outside the law and are disobedient to authority, and both are drawn to the wilderness that lies beyond the colony.

Wallace connects this wilderness to explicit, active sexuality and subversion of public punishment for sexual transgression. In the opening of her play, we hear voices mocking Hester, interrupted by the sound of Mistress Hibbins' laughter.

> Hibbins: "There's nothing I appreciate more than a nice display of public shame. It's what I like about this community. Everything is public." She goads Hester to reveal her secret. "Who knocked you up? I bet you put your fingers on him first, heh? They say it's usually the lady who makes the first move.... Must be the wilderness in us" [5].

Hibbins knows about making the first move. In a scene that parallels the conclusion of Chapter VIII of the novel, "The Elf-Child and the Minister," when Hester and Pearl (the red wig, trailing in Hester's hand), leave the Governor's house, they encounter Hibbins, who urges Hester to meet her in the forest to sign "the Black Man's book." As in Hawthorne, Hester demurs. Hibbins *"fingers the red wig in Hester's arms"* and asks *"Do you know the color of fire, Hester? I do."* Hibbins runs her hand over Hester's breast, and dares her to *"Say this man's name in your head. Say his name and then kiss me. When you do, you will be kissing through my mouth, the lips of your secret lover."* They kiss, and Hibbins shoves Hester away and exclaims, *"You're a witch!"*

> HESTER: Look who's talking!
> HIBBINS: Be careful, Hester Prynne, or we will take you with us, and from our grasp you will never return.
> HESTER: I will be. For the sake of my Pearl.
> Hester watches Anne fly away in the scary wind [33–34].

The provocative Hibbins pushes the limits. She informs us that, *"in my time, women accused of witchcraft ... were hecklers against the status quo"* (31). But disruptive actions have dire consequences in a rigid society. Ultimately, Hibbins is hanged as a witch. The Governor, who condemns her, declares, *"You have betrayed us. You have rebelled against your natural sex by attempting to access power. Power and women don't mix, Mistress Hibbins"* (106).

His judgment prompts Hibbins to articulate one of Hawthorne's key themes. To the Reverend Wilson who has been "feeling up" the female characters, especially Hester, throughout the play, Hibbins retorts:

> *I may be an outrage. But you are a hypocrite* [106].
> Anne is taken to the scaffold, where the letter 'A' is lowered onto the stage.
> *This 'A' is painted red white and blue.... This 'A' now symbolizes America"* [109].

Although some of Wallace's more political and explicitly feminist points may be somewhat didactic, the theatricality of the play and the fluidity of sexuality and identity are wildly inventive. Desire runs rampant and escapes gender expectations. Everyone is attracted to and tries to seduce everyone else. Hands and mouths are everywhere. Hibbins is a witness to, and an instigator of, several powerfully sexual scenes with other characters.

For instance, in an invented scene, Hibbins encourages Hester to re-enact her seduction of Dimmesdale. Hester refuses, so Hibbins plays the part herself, and propositions the minister. In response, Dimmesdale strikes Anne, prompting Hester to step in and slap him back.

> HESTER: *So I am to be blamed for your desire? But what do you really want, Reverend, right now? Tell us what you want.*
> DIMMESDALE: *Hell, I want hell, And that is you, Hester.*
> HIBBINS: *Listen. Can you hear it? Can you hear the law break when you touch her?*
> He runs his hand over Hester's breast, then he puts his fingers in Hester's mouth....
> She sucks on them, then bites them. He screams [46].

In her play, Wallace pushes the theme of law breaking, particularly with regard to gender roles and expectations. In the scene above, it is Hester who inflicts pain on Dimmesdale, who responds hysterically, with a scream. In the novel, of course, Dimmesdale inflicts pain on himself and remains silent about it, except for the sign of his hand always hovering over his heart. Furthermore, the potential homoeroticism repressed in the novel is foregrounded in her adaptation: Mistress Hibbins tries to seduce both Hester and Dimmesdale, and Dimmesdale and Chillingworth explicitly desire one another.

Critic Scott Derrick, using Eve Sedgwick's formulation of the "erotic triangle" that can "function as a disguise of and conduit for desire between men," has analyzed instances of both homophobia and homoeroticism in *The Scarlet Letter*, which he believes is an important text for understanding the emergence of sexual identity.[17] In reading the novel, we learn that Chillingworth is the betrayed husband, and Dimmesdale was Hester Prynne's illicit lover. However, in the space of the novel, both husband and lover have left her aside and live with each other. Indeed, Chillingworth, in his revenge scheme, concerns himself primarily with Dimmesdale, body and soul. Derrick's reading indicates both homophobic hysteria on Dimmesdale's part as well as homosexual desire on the part of both Dimmesdale and Chillingworth, whose "ghastly rapture" ecstatically "bursts forth" when he voyeuristically uncovers the wound on the sleeping Dimmesdale's chest.[18] The anxious minister has unconsciously subjected himself to "a kind of intimacy" that has grown up between himself and Chillingworth. He has revealed to his tormenter a fitful sleep and a "disorder of the nerves" that opposes a "coherent selfhood" displayed in the controlled persona of the devout pastor. Chillingworth, as Derrick notes, interprets this as unbridled passion: "But see, how passion takes hold upon this man, and hurrieth him out of himself!" He "hath done a wild thing ere now ... in the hot passion of his heart!.... As with one passion, so with another!"[19] Indeed, Derrick argues that "All erotic passion in *The Scarlet Letter* threatens the bodily integrity and rational self-control of its possessor."[20]

In the novel, Chillingworth warns Hester that her unnamed lover "shall be mine!" meaning, apparently, that he shall find him out and take revenge. Wallace takes this declaration in a more explicitly intimate direction. In an invented scene, when Hibbins caresses Dimmesdale's face as he sleeps, it prompts the jealous Chillingworth to complain: "Don't touch him. He belongs to me" (38). When Dimmesdale's feverish illness is at its peak, he grabs Chillingworth's hand and caresses himself with it (41). And in the minister's climactic confession scene on the scaffold, Hester and Chillingworth trade places. At the climax of the play, Dimmesdale proclaims from the scaffold, Chillingworth standing beside him, that Chillingworth betrayed him by loving him: *"By loving me against the rules. Against the rules that sanctify the love between a man and a woman, not the love between a man and a man...."*

> HESTER: *What do you really want right now? ...Spit in the face of your God.... If I learned anything as your martyr, I learned this: You break the law, Dimmesdale, or it breaks you.*

CHILLINGWORTH: *(gently)* What do you want?
DIMMESDALE: Hell. I want Hell. And that's you.
Dimmesdale embraces Chillingworth and begins to unbutton his shirt....
CHILLINGWORTH: We are out of line.
DIMMESDALE: No. We're not. We were between the lines; now we're out front [102–104].

By outing Dimmesdale and Chillingworth, Wallace brings forward what is repressed in Hawthorne's novel: desire that can freely attach itself to bodies, regardless of gender. In Hester's words, we hear both a comment on her function in the story as Dimmesdale's martyr, as the one who takes the blame for his desire, and an echo and extension of "the freedom of the broken law" line spoken by Dimmesdale in the novel:

HESTER: When you break the law, crack, like ice over a pond, you can reach right down into the water ... it's a new world below that surface. And a new world breeds new desire [100].

Wallace cracks the ice in her adaptation, and desire rises.

Phyllis Nagy

Nagy's 1994 adaptation, *The Scarlet Letter*, is wry and ironic; the language is pared down and compressed. Unlike Wallace, whose discursive characters sometimes speak in paragraphs or quote lines directly from Hawthorne's novel, Nagy uses a distilled, contemporary language. Her clean, economical dialogue plays well onstage. In an interview, Nagy discusses her difference from Hawthorne in terms of genre as well as language: "His is a prose language ... not dramatic language. But his language is shot through with a deep sensuality, at times a repressed sensuality.... It seethes with sex and darkness.... My job was to mirror that rather than to mirror a lush, descriptive prose."[21]

Although Nagy compresses and conflates several chapters of the novel, the play parallels the narrative. And while her characters seem very contemporary in their clever, ruthless attitudes, Nagy thinks that "they behave the way the characters in the book behave," though she did insist that Pearl, the narrator, be played by an adult actress as a "constant reminder that she is something quite *other*.[22]

The adaptation is scattered with sexual innuendo; the sexuality and psychology feel contemporary, and are explicitly enacted rather than repressed. Michele Pearce, in her review of the production at Classic Stage Company, noted that "Nagy's adaptation of the classic ... highlights the humor and irony in Hawthorne's writing by translating his dialogue into twentieth-century vernacular."[23] Ben Brantley observed the strategies employed in translating a nineteenth-century text for contemporary theater in terms of subject, tone, and setting:

Symbols, subtext, and contemporary correspondences are scaled up in a way that calls nudging attention to form as well as content.... It is hip, flip, and deeply earnest all at once, shifting between ironic distance and empathetic sincerity. Set largely in an expressionist forest ... the play purports to take us into the deep woods of conflicted erotic impulses behind Hawthorne's Puritan Boston.[24]

Like Wallace, Nagy emphasizes law-breaking and overt sexuality, and includes in her adaptation the scene from the novel in which Mistress Hibbins invites Hester to join her in the forest and sign the Black Man's book. But Nagy sets the scene between Hibbins and Pearl, rather than Hibbins and Hester, thereby reinforcing the idea of Pearl as the embodiment of her mother's darker, rebellious, and disruptive tendencies. It is interesting to note that Schwab, in analyzing the function of the witch pattern in the novel, argues that Hester unconsciously transfers her own witch status/stigma onto Pearl; and that Pearl assumes her witch child identity in collusion with her mother.

Hibbins, who in Nagy's version, is "maddeningly sexy," rather than sour-visaged, finds the whimsical Pearl in a graveyard. "I'm fond of decomposition," the woman/child explains. Recognizing another outsider, Hibbins offers fellowship to the girl:

> HIBBINS: We can be friends.... I can take you with me to the woods.
> PEARL: When?
> HIBBINS: At night.
> PEARL: And who will we meet?
> HIBBINS: My friends. Your mother's friends. The man [26].[25]

Whereas in Wallace's version, as in the novel, Hester declines to accompany Hibbins, because her responsibility to Pearl keeps her from stepping further outside society, all the way into the wilderness, Pearl has no such qualms. Nonetheless, the wary Pearl is suspicious of Hibbins.

Echoing Hawthorne's inquisition scene conducted by the elders in Governor Bellingham's Hall, Hibbins presses Pearl to tell her about the origins of Hester's red letter:

> HIBBINS: It may be special, Pearl, but she got it from somebody. Who gave it to her?
> PEARL: The wind. It came from the wind.
> HIBBINS: It came from the dark man. And who is the dark man?
> PEARL: He lives in the woods.
> HIBBINS: That's right. And he's your father, Pearl [26].

This dialogue is both a subversive, revisionist catechism and a deal: the exchange of knowledge for friendship in the context of surveillance. It suggests that Hibbins is a subversive counterpoint, an alternative authority, to Hawthorne's "venerable pastor" Wilson, who asks Pearl, "Canst thou tell me, my child, who made thee?" with the expectation that she will respond that she is a child of God (99). Instead, Hibbins goads her to admit that she is the devil's child.[26] There is also the suggestion here that Hibbins, as well as Wilson in the originating text, is attracted to Pearl, who represents the broken law and its freedom. Hibbins continues her effort to win Pearl over:

> HIBBINS: *You'll be my special friend.*
> *Hibbins picks a bit of weed from a grave and offers it to Pearl.*
> PEARL: *What's that?*
> HIBBINS: *A gift. From your father.*
> *Pearl grabs Hibbins' hand and bites it.*
> HIBBINS: *Do you always bite your friends?*
> PEARL: *I'm odd. You said so. Do witches bleed?* [26].[27]

The oddly seductive and insightful Pearl detects the vulnerability beneath Hibbins' entreaty as she deconstructs the threatening witch/fragile woman dichotomy. By biting her fingers, she gets back at Hibbins and exposes her vulnerability.

Pearl *is* odd, both unpredictable and not to be trusted; she might hurt you; she's the result of uncontrolled passion, after all. Ben Brantley noted, "There is no doubt that this Pearl is a walking reminder of the moment of illicit carnality in which she was conceived."[28] As Hawthorne's narrator tells us, "The child could not be made amenable to rules. In giving her existence, a great law had been broken, and the result was a being whose elements were perhaps beautiful and brilliant, but all in disorder" (81).

While the scene Nagy stages between the "demon child" and the witch is the playwright's invention, it is a logical development of the parallels and identities in the source text. Whereas Hester has broken the law, she suffers for it. Mistress Hibbins and Pearl simply do not bear the law; they exist alongside it, separate from it, outside it, as though they are free of it. Indeed, in some ways they are. Pearl is too young and Hibbins is too old to bear a child, which is the visible indication of transgression that got Hester her scarlet letter.

Both Wallace and Nagy also include the scene in which Hibbins encounters Dimmesdale after he meets Hester in the woods, a significant point in the novel, when Dimmesdale wants to be released from his sins. He is mortified that he has acknowledged his desires and can no longer repress them. Succumbing to "strange, wild, wicked thing[s]" he even imagines himself "dropping a germ of evil" into the "tender bosom" of a pure maiden in his congregation or "uttering certain blasphemous suggestions" to the "hoary-bearded deacon" (190–191).

In the Nagy play, as in Hawthorne, Dimmesdale is ravenously hungry, filled with temptations; he can no longer completely control his desire to transgress.

> DIMMESDALE: *Have you got any food, Mistress Hibbins?*
> HIBBINS: *I seem to be plum out of food at the moment, Reverend.*
> DIMMESDALE: *Fruit. I'd like some fruit.*

HIBBINS: *You should have picked berries in the woods yesterday.*
DIMMESDALE: *I don't know what you're talking about.*
HIBBINS: *I'm ever so sorry I couldn't be with you. I had another engagement.... But tonight, Reverend, we will all ride again. Together.*
DIMMESDALE: *I really don't want to discuss this.*
HIBBINS: *Awww. I understand. We can speak more freely later. When we're alone in the woods.*
DIMMESDALE: *Slut.*
HIBBINS: *I beg your pardon.*
DIMMESDALE: *Bitch. Whore.*
HIBBINS: *You shouldn't eat peanuts, minister. They clearly have a bad effect.*
DIMMESDALE: *Tramp. Slattern. Witch. Scum. I don't know what's come over me.*
HIBBINS: *I do (she laughs). Till tonight then, Reverend.*
She walks to the scaffold.
DIMMESDALE: *Why did I say those things? Why am I so goddamned hungry?* [37].

Hibbins, with her knowledge of darkness and wildness, knows. Like Wallace, Nagy liberates Hibbins from the sourness and bitterness attributed to witches and supplies her with the physical vitality and irrepressibility of a little Pearl. Dark woman, demon child, wild treasure, truth teller — in every case, the bearer of a body, and of a knowledge, that bespeaks the energy released by the breaking of the law. Others, dancing while they can outside the limits of authority.

Suzan-Lori Parks's Red Letter Plays (In the Blood *and* Fucking A)

In the Parks plays *In the Blood* (1998) and *Fucking A* (2000), the law-breakers are broken. Judgment is harsh and merciless. Unlike Hawthorne's spirited, repentant heroine, Hester is not transformed into a saintly survivor or, ultimately, a respected older woman with wisdom to impart. She is a poverty-stricken black woman who ultimately kills her own child. The Massachusetts woods fall away as the tale is moved to the impoverished urban fringes of *In The Blood*, where Hester's attempts to gain knowledge are thwarted ('A' is the only letter the illiterate Hester has learned to write), and to the allegorical village of *Fucking A* (in which an 'A' branded into Hester's skin marks her as an abortionist). Both of these Hesters reside in liminal spaces outside the law — one under a bridge; the other in a hut that knows blood.

In these bleak plays, Hester is poor, exploited, and betrayed. A single, homeless mother, she does the best she can; her efforts are all for her child(ren). In *In the Blood*, the solitary Pearl has morphed into five treasures, five jewels, five joys, five unruly children by as many fathers—one child is even named Trouble. Hester, La Negrita, is the seductive witch personified: her original sin of sex outside of marriage has multiplied into the threat of uncontained, available sexuality that is a temptation and threat to all and must be repressed so that society can function without disorder. In *Fucking A*, the original crime is economic—Hester's small son steals food and is imprisoned (in prison the Pearl becomes a Monster). As a consequence, Hester loses her job in "the rich girl's house" and takes on the shameful work and symbol of abortionist to earn money to buy her son's freedom.[29] Her branded 'A' represents all the anonymous women saved from having to bear their shame (i.e. a child) by her offices.

In fact, abortion is implicit in *In the Blood*, when the crowd repeatedly says that Hester should not have had so many children. In *Fucking A*, abortion becomes explicit, a necessary, but still shameful, outcome of female sexual transgression. As in Puritan society, and with the most recent Supreme Court decision in twenty-first-century America, the act is both sin and crime.[30]

In *In the Blood*, Park's Hester corresponds to the seductive witch pattern. Everyone whose role should be to help her—doctor, welfare agent, preacher, friend—has had sexual relations with her. Her sexual favors result in her being blamed for her partners' lapses in judgment. Furthermore, they've also all stolen from or tricked her. All five of the adult characters have "confession" monologues—clearly a riff on Dimmesdale's confession on the scaffold in the novel—in which they detail a sexual encounter with and subsequent betrayal and repudiation of Hester. Despite their own transgressions, they judge her as unworthy and strive to clarify and extend the distance between "her kind" and themselves. For instance, the Welfare Lady, in her "confession" to the audience, describes having a "threesome" with her husband and Hester, and concludes with a disavowal of the socially marginal single mother, who is not legitimized by marriage or money:

> *Welfare:*
> *I walk the line*
> *between us and them*
> *between our kind and their kind.*
> ....
> *It was my first threesome*
> *and it won't happen again.*
> *And I should emphasize that*
> *she is a low-class person.*
> *What I mean by that is that we have absolutely nothing in common.*
> *As her caseworker I realize that maintenance of the system*
>   *depends on a well-drawn*
> *boundary line and all parties respecting that boundary.*
> *And I am, after all,*
> *I am a married woman* [61–62].[31]

The Welfare Lady, a woman of color herself, humiliates Hester in order to reinforce the economic and social distance between them and to reinforce her own normative superiority.

In this play, as in the Hawthorne and in the revisions by Wallace and Nagy, hypocrisy is a key theme. The other characters scapegoat and judge Hester rather than bear responsibility for their own desire and its consequences (frequently children). For instance, in Parks's play, the hypocritical preacher, Reverend D, refuses to acknowledge paternity so that he can avoid paying child support. The Doctor, who had sexual relations with Hester and may have fathered one of her children, presses Hester to let him "spay" her; the use of the word underlines Parks's point that the sexually active poor are regarded as animals. In Parks's world, we are all Dimmesdales, fallen sinners who neglect our responsibilities and let someone else bear the consequences of our indiscretions.

In Hawthorne's novel, there is ambiguity about the nature of guilt and sin. With his urgent authorial directive "Be true! Be true! Be true! Show freely to the world, if not your worst, yet some trait whereby the worst may be inferred!" in the conclusion, he urges us to openly accept and bear responsibility for what we do (198). In Parks's plays, there is only blame for those less fortunate and the author's indictment of society for the hypocrisy that characterized the Puritan world and continues to pervade our own. Parks faults society for failing to assist its citizens with the basic needs of food and shelter and for harshly judging those who do not fit within its structures and bounds, its laws and middle-class norms. As J. Cooper Robb observes, "*In the Blood* shows a family that has not so much fallen between the cracks as been completely abandoned."[32] Parks focuses on characters branded as deviant or criminal, a label which prevents them from rising from the bottom, which Brantley interprets as her "brooding sense of individual fate as determined by history."[33] Her depictions of life on the edge, on the margins of a hypocritical society, are bleak. In these liminal areas, the fate of and "bad news" for the children is "in the blood" of the mother. There is no redemption, no grace whatsoever.[34]

Society's contempt for those who survive outside the law is evident from the prologue, where Parks' eschews a light touch and immediately makes her socially-critical perspective clear. As in Hawthorne's first chapter, "The Prison Door," a gossiping crowd is "all clustered together" and judges her in unison.[35]

>All:
>THERE SHE IS!
>WHO DOES SHE THINK
>SHE IS
>THE NERVE SOME PEOPLE HAVE
>SHOULDN'T HAVE IT IF YOU CANT AFFORD IT
>AND YOU KNOW SHE CAN'T
>SHE DON' GOT NO SKILLS
>CEPT ONE
>CAN'T READ CAN'T WRITE
>SHE MARRIED?
>WHAT DO YOU THINK?

> SHE OUGHTA BE MARRIED
> ....
> AND NOW WE GOT TO PAY FOR IT
> ....
> SHE KNOWS SHE'S A NO COUNT
> SHIFTLESS
> HOPELESS
> BAD NEWS
> BURDEN TO SOCIETY
> HUSSY
> SLUT
> PAH!
> ....
> IT WON'T END WELL FOR HER
> ....
> BAD NEWS IN HER BLOOD
> PLAIN AS DAY [5–7]

Hester passes through the crowd and lifts her newborn baby toward the sky: "*My treasure. My joy*" [7].

The Hester of *In the Blood*, unlike Hawthorne's elegant, fallen image of "Divine Maternity" is a mess—hungry, uneducated, utterly without resources or skills. Hawthorne's Hester "incurred no risk of want" because "she possessed an art that sufficed ... to supply food.... It was the art ... of needle-work" (74). But when Welfare suggests to Parks's Hester that she sew to earn money, we see how much more without means this contemporary mother is; she does not even know how to cut the cloth. Her "friend" takes the cloth from her and sells it (no doubt keeping most of the money herself), subverting this unlikely attempt by Hester to become self-sufficient.

Like Wallace, Parks's feminist emphasis highlights class, along with gender, as problematic issues. At one point, paralleling the chapter in Hawthorne in which the narrator reports Hester's thoughts about women's unfair lot ("Was existence worth accepting, even to the happiest among them? (144)") Parks's impoverished, powerless Hester notes:

> *I don't think the world likes women much.*
> WELFARE: *Don't be silly.*
> HESTER: *I was just thinking.*
> WELFARE: *I'm a woman too! And a black woman just like you. Don't be silly*
> [59–60].

In this instance, class trumps race. When Hester puts her hand out for payment for her services, the Welfare Lady stiffs her, as usual.[36]

In *In the Blood*, Parks eschews metaphor and goes for the literal. Hunger isn't a stand-in for desire; Hester is literally starving. The letter 'A' is exactly that — the first letter of the alphabet, the one she is learning to write. "The black man" is her former lover, and her moment of temptation (the equivalent of being asked to sign the Black Man's book in Hawthorne) is her too-good-to-be-true dream of getting married in white to the obsessive, controlling Chilli. But since this dream would mean turning her back on her children, which she will not do, regardless of the temptation, she foregoes this way out of her troubles and remains outside the law.

Hester's attempts are doomed to failure. She repeatedly feels the "five-fingered Hand of Fate" coming down on her, and it does. Scheme after scheme to try to get money to feed herself and her children falls through; no one helps, everyone takes advantage.

Earlier, she begged Reverend D to say her name, to acknowledge her; indeed, there is a fatal struggle around names and naming in the play that parallels the significance of the 'A' in *The Scarlet Letter*. Hester desires recognition of her individual worth. In the end, out of frustration and disappointment, mad with hunger and humiliation, she knocks her son Jabber over the head and kills him dead when he calls her by the name that others have used in contempt: SLUT. When even her eldest turns on her and calls her that name, she loses it and seals her fate and his.

The Hester of *Fucking A* also kills her son, who, like his mother, is called a "bad" name: Monster, a name he "earned" in prison. However, in the fable-like *Fucking A*, the imaginative world of the play is very different from the urban landscape of *Blood*. Whereas in Hawthorne (and in the Wallace and Nagy adaptations) the space outside the law exists in the woods, in dancing and laughter, in *Fucking A*, it exists in language. Women in this world have access to a dialect or patois that is unknown to the men; it allows them a place to discuss sexual secrets. Whereas sex talk in *Blood* is explicit, in *Fucking A* it is mysterious, as in a dark fairy tale. (The playscript provides a translation for this made-up language, but the audience does not have this aid.) What we see of sex in this play is all blood and meat. The passionate romanticism of Hawthorne is ripped away to explore the violent drive to punish and inflict pain on sinners that is implicit in his text, and in both Puritan and contemporary American society.

Fucking A is further from Hawthorne's novel in terms of plot and character parallels than any of the works discussed thus far. However, the figure of the shamed Hester remains a constant. Hester's job as abortionist marks her as the lowest of the low. Whether she bears or aborts children, she is a marked woman. Her plight is complicated by class and race, and there is little hope of survival, much less transformation. Although sought out by women in need, she can offer little in the way of solace. In the end, she kills her own son, who has escaped from prison, when he begs her to do so, in order to spare him the suffering the Hunters will inflict. Hester kills her son painlessly and efficiently, as her boyfriend Butcher showed her how to compassionately kill an animal, then continues with her bloody work, a dead mother of a dead son.

Hawthorne's tale has a happy ending for Pearl. She inherits Chillingworth's wealth when he dies, as he was her mother's legal husband. Pearl travels with

Hester back to England, marries, and, as is implied in Hester's embroidering of baby garments, has a child of her own. But Parks's Hesters were never married; they are poor single black women with fatherless children. There is no way out, no possible happy ending for Hester's offspring in the Parks plays. In *Blood*, Hester kills one child; the others will be orphaned by her prison sentence and will likely be victimized or become criminals themselves in order to survive, as did Hester's child in *Fucking A*. Jailed for stealing food, in prison he becomes a hardened criminal known as "Monster" for the terrible things he learns to do there. The Pearl is ruined by the system.

In contrast to the Wallace and Nagy plays, which are witty feminist deconstructions of the novel, *In the Blood* and *Fucking A* are relentlessly dark. Both plays have the same implication: that for those on the bottom, in marginal lives of poverty and prison, there seem to be no imaginable future or way out of misery. Although Hibbins is hanged in the Wallace play, she has the last word. In both the Nagy and Wallace, the women are disruptive and irrepressible and desire is celebrated. In Parks's *Red Letter Plays*, however, the will to punish wins out; society does its dirty work. There is no redemption, no reconciliation. In *Fucking A*, after her dead son is taken away, Hester picks up her tools and goes back to work, bereft of purpose now. In *Blood*, Hester, jeered at by the others, holds up her hands, as she did in the opening scene, only now, instead of holding a child, they're bloody and empty. Society breaks the lawbreakers, and we're left with that bleak fact.

Notes

1. Walter Benjamin, "On Language As Such and On Human Language," trans. Edmund Jephcott, *Reflections* (New York: Harcourt Brace Jovanovich, 1978) 328.
2. Nathaniel Hawthorne, *The Scarlet Letter* (New York: Penguin Classics, 2003) 117. Additional references in the text.
3. The plays were written between 1992 and 2000: Naomi Wallace, *THE SCARLET LETTER, by Nathaniel Hawthorne, as told by Anne Hibbins, the Witch, and recorded by Naomi Wallace* (1992); Phyllis Nagy, *The Scarlet Letter* (1994); and Suzan-Lori Parks, *In the Blood* (1998) and *Fucking A* (2000). Wallace's play is unpublished, but was given a staged reading in 1994 during the run of the production of Nagy's play at Classic Stage Company (CSC). Parks's plays were both produced at The Public Theatre in New York City. The discussion of these adaptations will be based on the scripts, rather than on productions or staged readings.
4. For an extended discussion of this period, see Steven C. Dubin, *Arresting Images: Impolitic Art and Uncivil Actions* (New York: Routledge, 1994).
5. Nina Baym, "Introduction," *The Scarlet Letter*, by Nathaniel Hawthorne (New York: Penguin Books, 1986) xx.
6. Ibid., xxii.
7. See Judith Fryer's *The Faces of Eve: Women in the Nineteenth-Century American Novel*, qtd. in "What is Feminist Criticism?" *The Scarlet Letter: Case Studies in Contemporary Criticism*, ed. Ross C. Murfin (Boston: Bedford Books of St. Martin's Press, 1991) 282.
8. Shari Benstock, *The Scarlet Letter (a)doree, or the Female Body Embroidered*, in Murfin, 290, 301–302. Also, Benstock qtd. in Murfin, 276.
9. Benstock, 289.

10. Baym, *The Scarlet Letter: A Reading* (Boston: Twayne Publishers, 1986) 55.
11. Gabriele Schwab, "Seduced by Witches: Nathaniel Hawthorne's *The Scarlet Letter* in the Context of New England Witchcraft Fictions," *Seduction and Theory*, ed. Dianne Hunter (Chicago: University of Illinois Press, 1989) 171.
12. Ibid., 172.
13. Ibid., 180.
14. Ibid., 178.
15. Nina Baym maintains that Hawthorne's strategy of "putting the witch and the governor in one house is a narrative economy.... In the symbolic space of the novel Mistress Hibbins represents the other side of the coin of authority" (Baym, *The Scarlet Letter: A Reading*, 56).
16. John D'Emilio and Estelle B. Freedman assert that by "enacting the death penalty for adultery, sodomy, and rape, the colony of Massachusetts Bay equated these acts with capital offenses such as treason, murder, and witchcraft" [*Intimate Matters: A History of Sexuality in America* (New York: Harper & Row Publishers, 1988) 11].
17. Scott Derrick, "'A Curious Subject of Observation and Inquiry': Homoeroticism, the body and Authorship in Hawthorne's *The Scarlet Letter*," *NOVEL: A Forum on Fiction* 28.3 (Spring 1995): 308–309.
18. Ibid., 310–312.
19. Hawthorne, quoted by Derrick in Ibid., 312.
20. Ibid.
21. Douglas Langworthy, "The Violence of Civility," an interview with Phyllis Nagy, *American Theatre* 12.2 (February 1995): 22.
22. Ibid.
23. Michele Pearce, "'A' as in Alternative," rev. of *The Scarlet Letter*, dir. Phyllis Nagy, *American Theatre* 2.10 (November 1994): 13.
24. Ben Brantley, "Magnifying Metaphors in a Work Rich in Them," rev. of *The Scarlet Letter*, dir. Phyllis Nagy, *The New York Times*, 20 Oct. 1994: C18.
25. Nagy, *The Scarlet Letter*, *American Theatre* 12.2 (February 1995). Additional references in the text.
26. In Wallace's play, Pearl's response to Reverend Wilson's question, "Canst thou tell me, my child, who made thee?" is the rude and irreverent, "The Devil farted and out I came." This line plays with Pearl's retort in the novel when she tells the reverend that she was "plucked by her mother off the bush of wild roses, that grew by the prison-door" (99).
27. Pearl's inflicting of pain on Hibbins, who is trying to befriend/seduce her, by biting her hand, is a remarkable parallel to the scene in Wallace, where Hester bites Dimmesdale's fingers after sucking on them. But the oddly seductive Pearl may just want to know what a witch is made of. The action of biting or its resulting marks are used by all three of the adaptors. In Parks's *Fucking A*, Hester recognizes her long-lost son when, as an escaped prisoner who appears on her doorstep, because she marked his arm by biting it with her teeth, and bit an identical mark into her own arm. There is an interesting relationship to pain and passion in the adaptations, as well as in Hawthorne's novel.
28. Brantley, "Magnifying Metphors."
29. By including society's contempt for abortion as a theme in her play, Parks considerably expands her feminist critique of contemporary America.
30. On April 18, 2007, the Supreme Court ruled in favor of *Gonzales v. Carhart*, upholding the so-called Partial-Birth Abortion Ban Act of 2003, which leaves no exception for the health of the mother.
31. Suzan-Lori Parks, *In the Blood, The Red Letter Plays* (New York: Theatre Communications Group, 2001). Additional references in the text.
32. J. Cooper Robb, rev. of *In the Blood*, dir. Suzan-Lori Parks, www.TheaterMania.com, 14 Jan. 2003.
33. Brantley, "A Woman Named Hester, Wearing a Familiar Letter," rev. of *In the Blood*, dir. Suzan-Lori Parks, *The New York Times*, 17 Mar. 2003: E1.
34. Various critics and audience members reacted badly to *In the Blood*, finding it overly

realistic or didactic, simplistic in its indictment of America's hypocrisy and Parks's demand that we regard Hester as a heroine of sorts, a life force repressed by society. I found it to be compelling and relentless, a real tragedy of our time. Fifty-seven percent of the more than 13 percent of Americans living in poverty are women, many of them single women with children. Most of them are poorly educated and have little work experience. Nearly 32 percent of poor women, and nearly 40 percent of poor women who head families, are African American. Another 32 percent of poor women are Hispanic (Source: Ohio State University Extension Poverty Fact Sheet Series: Poverty Among Women). Significantly, the Welfare Reform Act was passed in 1996, suggesting that Parks was responding to anxieties about race and sexualized poor women reflected in this legislation. The combination of low minimum wage and the expense of childcare makes it impractical for these women to succeed at employment, should they find the opportunity to work. Yet the prevailing attitude is to blame the poor for their own sad situations, to continue to regard poverty as akin to vice. If that isn't a legacy of our Puritan origins, what is?

35. Compare this with Naomi Wallace's opening scene: Wallace and Parks both draw analogies with contemporary America and offer an indictment of American society.

> Hester stands frozen. A crowd begins to form around her. They pelt her with garbage. Voices: Will you look at her? The naughty baggage! They should have put a brand of hot iron to her forehead.... Still holds up her head.... Shame on her.... Did you see that child of hers? ...a monster. Burn them both.... Infant poisoned by the crimes of her mother. Expel them. In the name of God.... In the name of America.... In the name of the law [3].

36. In *Blood*, characters can be said to display the gestus of their class, as they do in Brecht's plays. This scene, along with certain others, suggests a possible influence of Brecht's plays, particularly *Mother Courage*, on this one. Examples include the many cases of self-interest in the play-such as Amiga Gringa selling the cloth for Hester (as Yvette bargains for Courage in the Brecht play), the married Welfare woman feeling superior to the single Hester (as Yvette did once she'd married the general, lord it over the unmarried Courage), and Chilli being willing to marry Hester, while being unwilling to take the children (paralleling the Cook offering to take Courage to Utrecht to run the inn, but only if she left Katrin behind). Likewise, *Fucking A*, in some respects resembles the parable or fable form Brecht used in *Good Woman of Szechuan* rather than the more explicitly epic form of *Mother Courage*. In both plays, Parks is, like Brecht, dealing with issues of class and capital.

Expressions of "Lust and Rage"
Shared Experience Theatre's Adaptation of Jane Eyre

Kristin Crouch

Almost immediately after its publication in 1847, Charlotte Brontë's novel *Jane Eyre* was adapted for the stage.[1] Since 1848, Brontë's story of the restless and passionate orphan has continued to be an exceptionally popular subject for stage, film, television, and radio adaptation. H. Philip Bolton records over one hundred different productions of *Jane Eyre* appearing between the years of 1848 and 1998.[2] The adapters have employed various themes from the novel as touchstones for exploring such social issues as education, religion, vocation, class, and marriage. Many of these adaptations, specifically in the nineteenth century, have focused on Jane's dependence on her benevolent master. Others delight in the melodramatic reaffirmation of a victimized but virtuous heroine. In general, these productions have served to reaffirm the patriarchal ideology of Victorian culture, including a particular reverence for representing Jane as the meek, restrained, and longsuffering governess — "angel in the house" of Edward Fairfax Rochester — while demonizing Bertha Mason, Rochester's mad wife of West Indian origin, as a hideous monstrosity. However, an interesting omission from Bolton's list of adaptations is Shared Experience Theatre's 1997–99 production in the U.K. and in tours abroad.[3] This unique production uses physical and expressionist methods to reveal the hidden passions raging beneath the calm exterior of the dutiful governess. Polly Teale, as playwright and director, has created a script that dialogues with the source text, and uses actors' performances and elements of theatrical production to highlight and subvert Victorian gender-based constraints. In the process, the production reveals a deeper layer of meaning — the lust and rage percolating beneath the surface of Jane's prim exterior. Bertha Mason plays a dual role in this production. She appears not only as Edward Rochester's mad wife, the "madwoman in the attic," but also as Jane's alter ego, her more

189

Monica Dolan as Jane and Pooky Quesnel as Bertha in the 1997 production of *Jane Eyre*, Shared Experience, first performed at the Wolsey Theatre, Ipswich, and then in London at the Young Vic Theatre. Photographer: Mike Kwasniak.

passionate and expressive self trapped by the constraints of Victorian behavioral norms for women.

Shared Experience, a London–based theatre company led by Joint Artistic Directors Nancy Meckler and Polly Teale, enjoys an international reputation for re-creating the novel on stage. In addition to their British national tours, the company has appeared in Japan, India, China, Brazil, Israel, Czechoslovakia, Finland, Ireland, and the U.S. Over the past fifteen years, they have adapted many novels such as *Anna Karenina* (1992–93, 1998), *War and Peace* (1996), *Mill on the Floss* (1993–95, 2001), Angela Carter's *The Magic Toyshop* (2001), E.M. Forster's *A Passage to India* (2003), and Mary Webb's *Gone to Earth* (2004). Theatrical productions inspired by women novelists as well as literary figures include Polly Teale's *After Mrs. Rochester* (2003), based on the life of Jean Rhys, author of *Wide Sargasso Sea*, and Teale's recent production of *Brontë* (2005).

Central to the stories of all the adaptations are passionate and intelligent women in conflict with cultural expectations of women particularly among the landed gentry in nineteenth-century English society and the colonies. Jane Eyre, Maggie Tulliver, and Antoinette Cosway/Jean Rhys cry out for liberty, dignity, economic independence, and love, yet they are silenced by the lack of education or opportunity. The Shared Experience productions take a closer look at characters that defy patriarchal convention and subvert the restraints of social acceptability by offering a more explicit representation of female characters' social, emotional, and sexual needs.

Margaret Llewellyn-Jones in "Spectacle, Silence and Subversion: Women's Performance Language and Strategies" suggests the vital need to examine the theatrical strategies and approaches practiced by contemporary women's theater groups, and to document the physical languages used to stage women's lives and experiences.[4] Productions such as *Jane Eyre* have come to fruition through a dynamic and collaborative team of predominantly women directors, adapters, designers, producers, administrators, and movement directors who have worked to uncover the concealed in the protagonists' experiences as rendered by the narrative. Often, these productions emphasize a "split" in the heroine — a division between warring aspects of the character's subjectivity. They explore notions of a split self and repressed desire as they deconstruct and interrogate the heroine's public and private identities. This approach creates avenues for Shared Experience to confront gender-based assumptions and expectations embedded within the cultural history of the text and to reveal hidden tensions and conflicts.

It is not surprising that this British theatre company explores the novel form, given the special, if not revered, place the novel holds in British cultural history. These literary works have contributed to the shaping, negotiating, and challenging of English cultural values and the underlying hierarchies of power, social conventions, class, and gender relations within British society and the empire. These values are continually re-asserted through the presence of the novel on secondary and university-level syllabi throughout the nation and former colonies. Critic Adrienne Rich points out the urgent need for women to re-visit and critique literature as a way of breaking the hold of "traditions" and finding new languages with which to re-build our identities:

> Re-vision — the act of looking back, of seeing with fresh eyes, of entering an old text from a new critical direction — is for us more than a chapter in cultural history: it is an act of survival. Until we can understand the assumptions in which we are drenched we cannot know ourselves.[5]

Feminist critics have been drawn to ambiguities, dichotomies, and gaps in the text of *Jane Eyre* that call for a reinterpretation of the orphaned governess's journey toward maturity, living through temptations for sacrifice to claim self-assertion. Adrienne Rich's "*Jane Eyre*: The Temptations of a Motherless Woman" and Sandra Gilbert's "Plain Jane's Progress" highlight Jane's economically, socially, and sexually vulnerable position within England during the 1840s when the profession of governess was the only source of independence available to the poor and genteel woman.[6] Even more distressing, the governess endured an ambiguous social and economic position within the Victorian home. M.

Jeanne Peterson, in "The Victorian Governess: Status Incongruence in Family and Society," records observations on the "undefined" nature of the status and role of the governess who was "not a relation, not a guest, not a mistress, not a servant — but something made up of all. No one knows exactly how to treat her."[7] Her life was an unpleasant mixture of "mild scorn" and "genteel obscurity."[8] However, this is not the true source of Jane's marginality. Rich suggests that it is Jane's insistence on fulfilling her personal needs — achieving the dignity, respect, and liberty on equal footing with all others — that situates her among other Victorian women who were ruled by unnatural "desires."[9] It is this similarity between the prim, reserved governess and the sexually voracious "monster" hidden away in the attic of Thornfield Hall that has garnered the most consistent attention. Though seemingly dichotomous, both women, notes Gilbert, desperately yearn for freedom from patriarchal bonds, and assert themselves in ways that mark them as dangerous, extreme, and "Other." Although the novel emphasizes her madness and only hints at the ambiguity of her racial status, Bertha's marginality is compounded by her origins as the daughter of a West India planter/merchant and Creole mother. Zohreh T. Sullivan discusses the fear of this monstrous "Other" within the racist, imperialist, and sexist ideology of nineteenth-century British colonialist culture and woven through the text of *Jane Eyre*. She argues that writers of popular fiction "acknowledged the world of Imperial conquest, the colonial, and the colonized female even as they revealed the deepest anxieties of Imperial culture — the loss of manhood, identity, and racial purity." Brontë's Bertha Mason is a product of "English anxieties, primarily about erotic desire and domination, but also about sexually taboo encounters with darker races whose embrace will result in terminal boundary disintegration."[10] In the novel, Rochester roots her insanity in her Creole blood and alludes to her family's wish to marry her off to a person of "good race."[11] Foreign, female, and dark, Rochester's wife represents a dangerous and uncontrollable difference within traditional Victorian society, and threatens to destabilize the ordered and hierarchical world of the patriarch. In Teale's play, Rochester recounts his arranged marriage for fortune and speaks of the "tropical clime" as a lure, and her "true nature" as sexually licentious. A "voice from Europe" whispered in his ear: "Up," it said, "...Take her to England. Confine her at Thornfield then go...."[12] Bertha is represented as wild, erotic, and active; she is everything the "angel in the house" must not be, and, like Jane in her uncontrolled fits of rage, the repulsively assertive monster must be silenced, unsexed, and displaced from sight. The underlying link between the forthright governess and her alter-ego, Bertha, observed by feminist critics, might be gleaned from Queen Victoria's expressed fear that English women who fought for "Women's Rights" "unsexed themselves" and would turn "hateful, heartless — and *disgusting*."[13]

A suggested reading of Bertha as Jane's "dark double" was most famously proposed in literary circles by Sandra Gilbert and Susan Gubar's *The Mad-*

woman in the Attic (1979).[14] These critics argue that such a link between Jane and Bertha is implicit in the story because Bertha's literal imprisonment in the attic parallels Jane's imprisoned "hunger, rebellion, and rage."[15] Subsequent feminist criticism has absorbed this monster-as-alter-ego pairing of Bertha and Jane. Critic Gayle Austin also grounds her article "The Madwoman in the Spotlight: Plays of Maria Irene Fornes" with the theories of Gilbert and Gubar, suggesting the palimpsestic nature of much nineteenth century writing by women. These are "works whose surface designs conceal or obscure deeper, less accessible (and less socially acceptable) levels of meaning."[16] Experiencing an "anxiety of authorship" or a "radical fear that she cannot create, [and] because she can never become a 'precursor,' the act of writing will isolate or destroy her."[17] These women writers adapted conventional genres, "using them to record their own dreams and their own stories in *disguise*." In *Jane Eyre* as well as much subsequent writing by women, a madwoman functions also as the "author's double, an image of her own anxiety and rage."[18] Contemporary playwrights, specifically Maria Irene Fornes, allow renderings of their own madwomen to move from the "metaphorical" to the "social and actual." The madwoman may be silenced and confined, yet she is placed "in the spotlight," and we see her struggle to speak, to escape the imprisonment of patriarchal culture. Austin cites Helene Keyssar's observation that "symbolically at least, and on stage where all things are possible, the woman-as-victim must be killed in her own terms in order to ignite the explosion of a community of women."[19] In Teale's *Jane Eyre*, the alter ego is destroyed so that both women are released. In such a way, women may rebuild themselves, toppling patriarchal bonds, and re-emerging in new images and new identities. As Austin argues, bringing the theater audience into the madwoman's attic and allowing her to speak for herself transform a mere "metaphorical" disturbance into a vision of escape from "form, society, and themselves."[20]

Teale's adaptation of *Jane Eyre* closely follows the overall textual structure and order of the source novel, yet establishes a parallel, feminist space within the mise-en-scène of the production to deconstruct the patriarchal assumptions embedded within the surface layers of the Victorian text. Over the course of thirty-nine brief scenes, it presents Jane's experiences within all five of the major settings of the novel: dependent orphan at Gateshead, charity pupil at Lowood, meek governess at Thornfield, village schoolmistress at Marsh End, and loving wife and companion at Ferndean. Yet, a crucial departure from the structure of the novel is Teale's emphasis on the symbolic connection between Jane Eyre and Bertha Mason Rochester rendered theatrically by Bertha's presence on stage throughout the production. Similar to the theory proposed by Gilbert and Gubar, Teale's split character approach suggests that Jane and Bertha are different aspects of the same woman. Austin, in her discussion of Fornes's plays, usefully explains the practical impact of this dramatic device as the presentation of "a multiple female character" that is "composed of individuals, but, as seen on the stage, a whole that is more than its parts."[21] Polly Teale's production notes for the adapted script of *Jane Eyre* express the multiple subjectivities of the Bertha/Jane union:

> Central to the adaptation is the idea that hidden inside the sensible, frozen Jane exists another self who is passionate and sensual. Bertha (trapped in the attic) embodies the fire and longing which Jane must lock away in order to survive in Victorian England.[22]

Jane is compelled to confront the inner demons of rage and rebelliousness that have haunted her since childhood. As Gilbert and Gubar argue, the "bad animal[s]" locked away in the red room and in the attic represent the fiery spirit "still lurking somewhere, behind a dark door, waiting for a chance to get free."[23]

The mise-en-scène dramatically inteprets both the physical and the emotional landscapes of *Jane Eyre*. The openness of playing space allows for easy flow between one physical location and another, while also reflecting the shifts between layers of Jane's conscious and unconscious desires. The main feature of the scenic design is the massive, burnt-out, skeletal remains of a sweeping staircase, a powerful stage icon signaling the remnants of the patriarchal mansion and foreshadowing its ruin. At the top is a platform with a single door and frame. The door symbolically serves as both entrance into seclusion and containment, and exit towards release and freedom. It is on this platform, imprisoned behind a locked door, that Bertha remains throughout most of the performance, a silent but visible reminder of female constraint. The remainder of the playing space, apart from the staircase, remains open and fluid, allowing for a quick succession of scenes. Scenic designer Neil Warmington created a cloudy "sky" on the vast background scrim to suggest atmosphere, detail, and mood.[24] It helps to define specific locations for indoor and outdoor scenes, yet it can also be lit with a wash of different colors to help reflect the mood of individual scenes. Peter Salem's musical score, characterized by the sumptuous use of electronically-altered and layered sounds of a cello, works together with the scenic designs to suggest the shifting nature of the emotional undercurrents within Jane's inner world.

Both the source novel and Teale's adaptation present Jane as a childhood dependent in her Aunt Reed's home. Scene One establishes Jane's vulnerability as an orphan with prominent images of coldness and dreariness; it is a life deprived of love and nurturing. She sits in the Gateshead library reading a book before being confined in the red room as a punishment for striking back against her abusive cousin, and contemplates running away or starving herself to death, if necessary. Adrienne Rich suggests that it is Jane's determination to be "unalterably herself" that allows her to discover alternatives to potentially destructive temptations, even as a young girl of ten, and ultimately to "survive" patriarchy.[25]

Reading in *Jane Eyre* represents a creative activity that opens her up to other worlds. Taking a cue from the novel, the adaptation highlights the reading of a book as a key event in Jane's transformation into a young woman and ignites her fantasies of another life. Reading, however, is not simply a passive entertainment; it becomes an active challenge to Victorian patriarchal ideology, allowing Jane access to knowledge, expression, ideas, pleasure in language and imagery, and sensual enjoyment. Significantly, Scene One introduces Jane as a divided self, and Jane does not read alone. She and Bertha — her "dark double" and more passionate self — read passages together responding physically to each other and to the images within the book. The novel sets up the reading activity as a solitary escape for Jane. With Bewick's *History of British Birds* for company, Jane revels in the space apart from her vicious cousins: "I mounted into the window-seat: gathering up my feet, I sat cross-legged, like a Turk; and, having drawn the red moreen curtain nearly close, I was shrined in double retirement" (1). It is not until later in the story that we meet Bertha. The adaptation compresses these experiences and recreates parts of Bertha's nature and experience in Jane from our first vision of her. The girls' bodies are intertwined, and their combined responses to the imagery suggest the vital connection between Jane's passion and reason, her private and public selves. The external restraint controlling Jane is emphasized through costume design. Jane appears in a modest and rather prim gray dress, with her hair pulled tightly back from her face. Bertha, on the other hand, appears in a low-cut and sexually provocative red dress. She is barefoot and her hair hangs loosely around her shoulders. Yet, the physical entanglement of the actors' arms and legs suggests their interconnected nature, "as if they are one person" (7).

Jane first chooses to read about the frozen sweep of the Arctic zone, and the girls huddle for warmth before Bertha turns to a page describing the hot and steamy climate of the tropics. Here, the sensory delight of both girls becomes apparent. Jane reads about the fruit, growth, fertility, and colors as both girls laugh and enjoy the fantasy of eating fruit and feeling the warm waters of the island. The movements of the actors suggest Jane's potential for passion even in childhood. Bertha rolls on the ground with open body, luxuriating in the imagined sensuality of the environment reminiscent of her West Indian childhood, and then begins to offer a dance to bring in the rain and storms. The stage directions read: "*They squeal with excitement ... BERTHA stands, her palms turned to the sky and head thrown back. She laughs and begins to dance. JANE watches her with delight and sways slightly in time. BERTHA sings as she dances. The dance becomes wilder and wilder*" (7–8). The passionate feelings, however, are inextricably connected to Jane and cannot be separated from her. Rehearsal activities developed this aspect of Jane's childhood nature. Teale notes:

> Bertha was asked to excite Jane to such a degree that she could not resist reading on. By bringing to life the images from the book she tempts Jane to abandon her reserve and join her in the game. It is as if we are seeing Jane enter the world of her imagination leaving behind the loneliness of her real life.[26]

Bertha's movements are free and sensual, incorporating an aggressive physical closeness with Jane, sexually suggestive dancing, rolling around on her back along the floor, and other fluid and provocative gestures and sounds. However, the scene does not position Bertha as the sexualized and primitive "Other." Jane's participation makes it *jointly* active, loud, exuberant, vocal, and alive.

Jane's imaginative engagement with her book is interrupted by the forceful entrance of John Reed who both demeans and physically attacks her for being an unwanted dependent. Jane and Bertha react jointly to his taunt, Bertha's presence emboldening Jane to resist the tyrant and prompting her to physically retaliate in response to the abuse. Jane is quickly rebuked for having too much "passion" and is promptly shuffled off by Aunt Reed to imprisonment in the red room. There the girls' shared dialogue and physical struggle visibly reveal the strain within Jane's consciousness—a tension between Jane's need to please and her powerful will to strike out against an unwarranted punishment and constraint. In the novel Jane has no sufficient outlet for expression or complaint, and no way to remedy the powerlessness of her situation except through the battle played out within her thoughts:

> "Unjust!-unjust!" said my reason, forced by the agonizing stimulus into precocious though transitory power; and Resolve, equally wrought up, instigated some strange expedient to achieve escape from insupportable oppression — as running away, or, if that could not be effected, never eating or drinking more, and letting myself die [9].

In the play text, her internal conflict is dramatized through a division of spoken lines between the girls and their use of movement to body forth the tensions represented by their respective stances toward the same interaction. Bertha responds to the injustice of the situation, while Jane laments her inability to please others. For example, Bertha voices Jane's anger at the action of her Aunt: "Unjust, unjust." Jane is given the aspects of their alternating monologues that reflect her efforts to please and to obey authority and her fear of revealing her anger. During Mrs. Reed's visit to Jane in the red room, Bertha and Jane together lash out against the cruelty of her aunt. Jane's actions are driven by Bertha's boldness and passion. Here, dialogue from Jane's interaction with the religious ascetic, Helen Burns, at Lowood School to which she is eventually sent is compressed with dialogues from the red room scene, though Jane's retort of righteous indignation is given to Bertha.[27] She begins to stifle Bertha's outbursts:

> JANE: How could you say such things?
> BERTHA: It's true.
> JANE: Look what you've done.
> BERTHA: If good people are always obedient wicked people will have it all their own way....
> JANE: You have made them all hate me [13].

Music, lighting, and particularly gesture become key dramatic elements in this scene, and highlight the vital choice between Jane's need for autonomy and her physical survival. The discordant music and the dark sky that sweeps across the cyclorama illustrate both the strain on Jane's emotional composure and the rage she struggles to suppress. Jane attacks Bertha and tries to smother her mouth: "Shut up, shut up, shut up, shut up..." she begs. She has to physically sit on Bertha to keep her under control. At this point, the separation between Jane and her more passionate self becomes explicit. As a servant pulls Jane out of the red room, Jane and Bertha struggle over the door handle in slow motion. Jane closes the door with her arms stretched out, Bertha pulling it open, while music of the cello underscores this moment of Jane's intense struggle. Jane finally wins, pulling the door shut on Bertha. The symbolism is clear, and the "dark double" is now locked away and does not speak for the remainder of the performance. Although she remains present onstage and is highly visible up on the platform, she is obviously and consciously "contained" and prevented from participating as a strong influence in Jane's daily existence. Teale suggests a possible rationale for Jane's rejection of Bertha at this point: "[Bertha] is both dangerous and exciting. She is passionate and sexual. She is angry and violent. She is the embodiment of everything that Jane, a Victorian woman, must never be."[28] The containment of Bertha and the stifling of Jane's inner passion all suggest the denial of spirit, independence, and sexuality for the ideal woman in Victorian England.[29]

The split between the silenced and imprisoned Bertha in the attic and the dispassionate but free Jane is also a visible reminder of the "social and actual" confinement noted by Gayle Austin in her analysis of a similar stage device used by Fornes in *Sarita* (1984).[30] Teale places Bertha —*highlights her presence*— on the platform. We see more than her metaphorical or symbolic significance. We cannot escape her actuality; we are constantly reminded that this "monster" has been forcibly chained and hidden from public view. We, as audience, view her foreignness, her femaleness, her helplessness, her passion, and her rage.

Although Jane has attempted to lock her away, Bertha's rebellious spirit continues to provoke Jane throughout childhood and into adult life. The adaptation, unlike the source novel, features a continuous and symbiotic thread of experience and response between Jane and Bertha. Bertha continues to communicate, responding to Jane's efforts to conceal her inner self. She pounds on the door, moans, stretches out her hands, or twirls in delight when Jane feels free or loved. In childhood, Bertha reacts for Jane when Jane cannot protect herself or contradict the accusations made against her by her Aunt Reed or by the Draconian Mr. Brocklehurst at Lowood School. Bertha moans loudly as Jane decides to be "useful and pleasant" or cooperative with her oppressors. At other times, when Jane is verbally assaulted, called a "liar" or a young woman with a "tendency to deceit," Bertha bangs on her locked door or whines and murmurs in response to the unfair and punitive judgment. Furthermore, Bertha's response intensifies to reflect whatever extreme emotion Jane experiences or attempts to repress. Each time Jane struggles to remain calm, Bertha acts out Jane's frustration by knocking and making noise at the door.

At times in the novel, Jane breaks from the flow of her story to address the reader and offer a glimpse of her private thoughts. For example, early in her residence as governess at Thornfield, Jane grows discontent with evenings of domestic serenity and tranquility spent with her pupil, Adèle, and the housekeeper, Mrs. Fairfax, and begins to desire "more of practical experience than I possessed; more of intercourse with my kind, of acquaintance with variety of character, than was here within my reach" (100). Climbing up along the battlements or wandering through the corridors of the estate, the restless governess experiences a movement within: Jane's heart "heaved by the exultant movement, which, while it swelled in trouble, expanded it with life." This "movement" opens Jane's "inward ear" to "a tale my imagination created, and narrated continuously." As Jane's restlessness grows, she imagines a wider scope of action than the traditionally feminine duties of "making puddings and knitting stockings" (101).

Teale builds on these reveries by creating monologues for Jane that heighten the emotional tension of these passages and focus on Jane's keenest struggles in these moments. As a performance strategy, Teale has Jane step out of the narrative and speak her thoughts directly in a prayer to God:

> JANE. Oh Lord forgive me. I know that women are supposed to be calm. I know that women should be satisfied with tranquility. But it is not so. Women feel just as men feel. They suffer from stagnation.... They must have action [24].

Her thoughts purged, Jane returns once again to the action of the scene. The use of soliloquy to express interior monologue in the novel is an important theatrical device for a number of reasons, not the least of which involves a means to foster private moments intimately shared between the character and the audience. As performance, the expression of inner thoughts becomes action and provides a concrete, physical depiction of Jane's internal storm and her yearning for occupation, activity, and passion. Moreover, in their disruption of the linear time plot, the monologues offer a clear indication of Jane's inability to release these feelings and utterances in public. Her confessions to God highlight the seriousness of Jane's effort to keep control, to refrain from desire, to yearn for nothing, and to strengthen her resolve to find peace and contentment. The language, however, is often subverted through character action and gesture. Just prior to her plea for God's forgiveness, she picks up Adèle's sampler, begins to unpick the stitches, and "pulls impatiently at the tangled thread making it worse" (24). This underlying anxiety is also revealed through Jane's alter ego. Jane's restlessness is mirrored above by Bertha, "kicking against the floor in a distant room. It is the sound of a caged animal" (24).

Bertha also reacts with Jane as she experiences joy and sexual excitement. During her stay at Thornfield, Jane becomes fiercely attracted to the master of the ancestral home, Mr. Edward Fairfax Rochester. After one particular chance meeting with him, Jane's heart soars with delight. When alone, Jane spins around in circles, demonstrating her excitement; Bertha, upstairs in the attic, spins too, exuding the same thrill. Each time Rochester interacts with Jane her emotions give way and she expresses a semblance of the passion that she shut away in her youth. In Scene Thirteen, after an evening of informal and even affectionate teasing between Rochester and Jane in their drawing room repartee, Jane begins to experience new feelings of happiness as well as the first promptings of desire. We see the corresponding response in Bertha as a kind of return to the freedom and sexual release that characterizes her movements in the rain song from Scene One.

> As soon as [Jane] is alone she touches her face. She feels her features with her fingers. A smile steals across her face. She turns slowly, listening to BERTHA's song. We see BERTHA *above, arms outstretched and head thrown back....* It recalls the rain dance of the first scene but less abandoned. Like a memory of a dance she once knew [33].

Significantly, Jane's next move is to use *"prayer to suppress her feelings of excitement."* In this way, Bertha's physical presence on stage, one of the strongest theatrical devices used by Teale, becomes an emotional barometer for the audience to interpret Jane's conflicting moods. It is an expansive device as well. Bertha's visible delight up in the attic and Jane's kneeling in prayer on the main playing space below create a visual tableaux that reveals the rising tension between Jane's passion and her willful suppression of her inner feelings.

At Thornfield, Bertha also takes on the additional and familiar role of the "madwoman in the attic," while retaining her function as Jane's alter ego. This twofold function has several implications in terms of how Bertha is characterized in the novel and deconstructed in Teale's adaptation. In the novel, Bertha's exotic and ravenous sexuality leads Rochester to reject her as "gross, impure, and depraved" (292). Jane glimpses Bertha's reflection in her mirror on the night before her wedding and sees a monstrous creature with "furrowed brow" and "swollen, dark lips." After the failed wedding ceremony, at which time Bertha's existence is revealed by her brother, she is described as groveling "seemingly on all fours" in the corner of her attic as "some strange wild animal" covered with "dark grizzled hair, wild as a mane" (270, 278). The duality of role within the performance script allows Bertha to continue to reflect Jane's repression of sexual desire associated with "unnatural" women. At the same time, she represents the physical embodiment of the Victorian, patriarchal fear of unrestrained sexuality, the bestial "Other" that must be hidden away.

Scene Fifteen, in which Bertha attempts to set fire to Rochester's bedroom, highlights the deeper significance of the split character device: the tension between lust and rage. At the beginning of the scene, both Jane and Rochester have retired for the evening to separate areas of the stage. As Jane sleeps, her movements and murmuring suggest that she is having a sexual dream: "I want ... I want to ... let me...." (36). As Jane cries out, Bertha steals keys to unlock her door and make her way out of the attic. She carries a candle and descends the stairs towards Rochester's sleeping figure: "*She straddles his sleeping body, bearing down on him in an expression of lust and rage*" (36). Jane's movements echo Bertha's. Bertha then drops the candle and retreats. The resulting fire threatens to burn Rochester in his bed until Jane wakes and douses him with water.

In this scene, the parallel movements and actions of Bertha and Jane emphasize Jane's growing sexual desire for Rochester. Yet, their actions also physicalize the tense battle between the women, as different aspects of Jane's psyche, for control of Jane's sexuality. Bertha's flaming candle, a simple prop, functions as an expression of the burning desire within Jane — one that Jane will not consciously acknowledge. The flames that threaten Rochester's life represent, from his point of view, a devouring sexuality as well as a rejection of patriarchy. The fire, however, also takes on significance as a symbol of rage: Jane's reaction against the inequality of her relationship with Rochester and Bertha's reaction against her confinement to the attic and the subsequent erasure of her marriage and her existence. The water Jane uses to extinguish the flames functions symbolically as well in her attempt to douse the flames of "lust and rage" in her heart and her body.

The symbiosis between Jane and Bertha is repeated in Scene Sixteen of the production in which Bertha enacts Jane's ambivalent response to her growing awareness of sexual desire. In this scene, Mrs. Fairfax describes the beautiful Blanche Ingram — an aristocratic rival for Rochester's affections. As Mrs. Fairfax recounts a story of Blanche and Edward together, the two characters appear on stage as a kind of sub-textual tableau. It is a technique that Teale explores further after Jane has left Thornfield and longs for the presence of Rochester. His character appears on the stage to touch and to kiss Jane, but functions only as a subconscious expression of Jane's yearning. In these "ghost" moments Teale manipulates both time and space by lending physical presence to Jane's tormented imagination. When Jane sees the tableau of Blanche and Rochester, she pushes the imagined characters aside as she retreats to her room, rejecting the image and chastising herself for her misplaced attraction to Rochester. As she does so, Bertha's movements become more "violent and contorted, expressing a sense of sexual guilt and self-hatred" (39).

The apprehension expressed at this moment remains a continuing source of conflict for Jane and is not counterbalanced until Rochester confesses his love and asks for her hand in marriage. Her physical restraint, however, suggests that she is not yet free to express her desires. Bertha does this for her. As Jane accepts the proposal "*the attic door bursts open and BERTHA runs from the room, stripping off her clothes, throwing them to the floor. She runs and runs, finally falling to the ground at JANE's feet, panting and happy*" (57). Bertha's stripping away of her clothing clearly indicates Jane's yearning to be free. However, it is worth noting that even this gesture is not available to Bertha until the moment that Jane accepts Rochester's love. The re-pairing of Bertha and Jane in this scene represents a major departure from the novel. In Teale's interpretive vision, it is Jane and Bertha who are most significantly aligned, subverting the traditional pairing in the novel between Rochester and Jane. Instead, Teale highlights the mutual need between Jane and Bertha. Together, the women may become balanced and whole.

After the marriage proposal, Bertha, as the "madwoman," is again locked up in the attic by Grace Poole, and her internment is inextricably bound up with Jane's sexual and emotional conflicts as she prepares to become a bride. After the wedding ceremony is disrupted, Jane finally stands face to face with Bertha the "strange wild animal," as Rochester reveals the monstrosity that is his wife. Jane, however, recognizes the mad woman "*instantly as the self that she left long ago locked in the red room*" (64). Rochester's rejection and imprisonment of Bertha, the supposed "madwoman," cannot be separated from an implied rejection of Bertha's role as the passionate and sexual extension of Jane's inner, more sensual self.

This intertwining of identities also highlights the inequality and dependence that characterizes Jane's relationship with Rochester at the point of his proposal. Like Bertha, Jane remains the powerless dependent within the Rochester household when Rochester later asks Jane to live with him outside of marriage because of his legal obligation to Bertha. Jane rejects this temptation as well as his needs for comfort and salvation. Despite his pleas to the contrary, Jane sees that taking her place in a long line of mistresses would make her even more dependent both financially and emotionally. Her need to "care for myself," leads her to flee Thornfield penniless and homeless (Brontë 302). When Jane and Bertha stand face to face, the images on stage resonate in a complex interweave of sexual temptation, madness, monstrosity, dependence, and confinement.

Bertha's dual function within *Jane Eyre* also provides an alternative ending to the story. In a departure from the novel, Bertha does not perish in the flames when she sets fire to Thornfield Manor and in the process blinds and maims Rochester. Rather, she is reborn. Again, she is aligned with Jane and remains on stage, expressing both anger and passion. In this last scene she becomes a catalyst to Jane's reunion with Rochester. In Teale's revision, the fire occurs when Jane rejects the prospect of a colorless, lifeless, and loveless marriage to the worthy and virtuous St. John Rivers who asks her to accompany him as a missionary. It is during this time away on her own that Jane reaffirms and accepts her own true desires, refusing to keep "the fire of her nature hidden" any longer (79). At the moment when Jane awakens to her own desires, Bertha breaks free from the ropes restraining her wrists, descends the staircase with a flaming torch, and "becomes" the fire. According to Teale:

This act of burning down the house is a massive act of self-assertion, of protest, it's like tearing apart an enclosed space so that it can never be locked up again. There is a transformation. She's free again, released from that place, no longer a raging spirit.[31]

Through Teale's revisioning, Rochester and Bertha both cry aloud for Jane's return. Only when Jane is reunited with her "secret self," can she form a union with Rochester based on reciprocity, equality, and openness. The final image in the production suggests that the terms of engagement have been reversed. Rochester's dependence upon Jane now allows her to be both a helpmate and an agent of her own life. The scene culminates with all three characters, but this time Bertha guides Rochester to an embrace with Jane.

The artists of Shared Experience create a physical and psychological re-visioning of Charlotte Brontë's *Jane Eyre* that is radical and at times irreverent, casting away some of the demons of traditional assumptions surrounding this narrative. Jane takes the stage not only as a victim, dutiful angel or even as the virtuous governess who follows her heart and her moral convictions, but as a woman who is bold, defiant, passionate — sexual. Through the interweaving of text, gesture, movement, and inventive stage design, Shared Experience reaffirms the stage as a place for rediscovering, exploring, and reconstructing the novel anew.

Notes

1. H. Philip Bolton, *Women Writers Dramatized* (London: Mansell, 2000) 76.
2. Ibid, 76–94.
3. *Jane Eyre* was first performed by Shared Experience Theatre Company at the Wolsey Theatre Ipswich in September 1997 and subsequently at such venues as The Young Vic Theatre, London; The Gaiety Theatre, Dublin, 1999; The Brooklyn Academy of Music, New York, 2000; and Trafalgar Studio, London, 2006.
4. See Margaret Llewellyn-Jones, "Spectacle, Silence and Subversion: Women's Performance Language and Strategies," *Contemporary Theatre Review* 2.1 (1994): 1–9.
5. Adrienne Rich, "When We Dead Awaken: Writing as Re-Vision," *College English* 34.1 (1972): 18.
6. Rich, "*Jane Eyre*: The Temptations of a Motherless Woman," *Critical Essays on Charlotte Brontë*, ed. Barbara Timm Gates (Boston: G.K. Hall & Co., 1990) 142–155; Sandra M. Gilbert, "Plain Jane's Progress," *Critical Essays*, 156–180.
7. Elizabeth Missing Sewell, quoted in M. Jeanne Peterson, "The Victorian Governess: Status Incongruence in Family and Society," *Suffer and be Still: Women in the Victorian Age*, ed. Martha Vicinus (Bloomington: Indiana University Press, 1972) 10.
8. Peterson 4.
9. Rich, "*Jane Eyre*," 149.
10. Zohreh T. Sullivan, "Race, Gender, and Imperial Ideology in the Nineteenth Century," *Nineteenth-Century Contexts* 13.1 (Spring 1989): 26.
11. Charlotte Brontë, *Jane Eyre* (New York: Bantam, 1986) 290. Additional references in the text.
12. Polly Teale, *Jane Eyre* (London: Nick Herne, 1998) 67. Additional references in the text.

13. Rosalind Miles, *The Women's History of the World* (Topsfield, MA: Salem House, 1989) 187.
14. Sandra Gilbert and Susan Gubar, *The Madwoman in the Attic* (New Haven: Yale University Press, 1979) 360.
15. Matthew Arnold, quoted in Ibid., 339.
16. Gilbert and Gubar, quoted in Gayle Austin, "The Madwoman in the Spotlight: Plays of Maria Irene Fornes," *Making a Spectacle: Feminist Essays on Contemporary Women's Theatre*, ed. Lynda Hart (Ann Arbor: University of Michigan Press, 1989) 78.
17. Gilbert and Gubar, quoted in Ibid., 76–77.
18. Gilbert and Gubar, quoted in Ibid., 77–78.
19. Keyssar, quoted in Austin 80.
20. Austin 85.
21. Ibid., 85.
22. Teale 3.
23. Gilbert and Gubar 349.
24. Neil Warmington was the Scenic Designer for the original productions (1997–99). The Scenic Designer for the 2006 revival was Angela Simpson.
25. Rich, "Jane Eyre," 143–44.
26. Teale quoted in Susannah Harding, *Jane Eyre Education Pack* (Shared Experience Theatre Archives, London, 1997) 13.
27. See Chapter 6 of Brontë's *Jane Eyre*, 50. During "play-hour" in the evening, Jane and Helen enjoy companionship as Jane laments the injustices of their treatment at Lowood school.
28. Teale quoted in Harding 10.
29. For further discussion of this "ideal" figure Victorian England, see Vicinus, ed., *Suffer and be Still*.
30. Austin 82.
31. Teale quoted in Harding 21.

A Mystical Place Called Grand Isle
Adapting Kate Chopin's The Awakening

Chiori Miyagawa

It is easy for me to contemplate why I was so attracted to Edna Pontellier in Kate Chopin's 1899 novel *The Awakening* to want to write a theatrical adaptation of the book.[1] Edna is an outsider. She is a Kentuckian who lives among the wealthy Creoles in New Orleans; she is an aloof wife and mother in the company of women utterly devoted to their husbands and children; and she is aware of the gap that exists between her and her surroundings. All of my theatrical characters are outsiders in different ways, because I am one. I don't think I have a choice in the matter; I was not born in the United States, and I did not learn to speak English until I was sixteen. On New Year's Eve, the Japanese reflect on the year that passed and listen to the deep resonant sound of the large bell being rung 108 times at a nearby Buddhist temple — each ring representing a kind of human suffering. Midnight is a serene moment where I come from, and after all these years, I still cannot fathom why the piercing noisemakers usher in the future. I speak with a Japanese accent and I'm frightened of articles — should it be *a* fear or *the* fear or just fear? But part of me is intentionally attached to being an outsider. It allows me to metamorphose into characters that temporarily reside in Bardo, the realm after death and before rebirth, and to think mystically about the next reincarnation. I suspect that my feet are always consciously or unconsciously touching the ancient soil of Japan, and I conjure ghosts of all kinds from my ancestral past. Edna, for one.

> Years have gone by in dreams. Illusions. I might have kept sleeping for a hundred years. How painful it is to wake up to this life. All that I desire will not come true. All that the others demand of me will not be met. There is no place to be alone. There is no beginning, no ending. How strange life is. How very sad and mad and bad it is. How unbearably beautiful it is. Freedom is knowing that none of this stays. It will all pass. As I will.[2]

Awakening, by Chiori Miyagawa, Crossing Jamaica Avenue, Performance Space 122, New York, 2000. Performers (left to right): Charles Parnell, Margi Sharp, Brian Nishii, Sophia Skiles. Photographer: Corky Lee.

I thought about Edna Pontellier's suicide at the conclusion of Kate Chopin's last novel for a long time before I gave this monologue to Edna as she swam out to the deserted winter ocean of Grand Isle. It was impossible not to ascertain Edna's broken heart, but the rejection note — "Good bye — because I love you,"[3] — that Robert Lebrun left her the night before in her house in New Orleans had no lasting meaning in my personal understanding of her journey. Although she still feverishly desires Robert when her foot touches the chilly water, I believed that Edna was on the brink of a true awakening, given her intuition that one day Robert and even the thought of Robert would "melt out of existence, leaving her alone" (139). This line alluded to more than the literal meaning of the inevitable fading of passion between the lovers. It suggested the possibility that Chopin had placed Edna a step away from abandoning the concept of "self" — a fundamental element in Buddhism — abandoning, that is. Buddhism teaches that all human suffering emerges from the delusion of an existence of "self" and that freedom (enlightenment) is obtained through recognizing the truth that all things are interdependent; there is no independent entity. Clinging to the "self" keeps us in samsara — the cyclical life of suffering. Of course, Edna would not have articulated her "awakening" in such a way, and other than this one line, Chopin's text does not support my interpretation either. In fact, I believe that Chopin depicts Edna's awakening as an emergence of her "self," an autonomous individual, from the "vague, tangled, chaotic and exceedingly disturbing" world in which she had been engulfed (35). Edna is becoming an independent thinking person instead of a woman who mechanically participates in the conventions of New Orleans society — its rules governing the receiving of visitors, proper dress for women, bon bons for the children, musical salons, dinner parties, and summers at Grand Isle.

In her late twenties, and after having had two children, sexual desire for her husband Leonce still eludes Edna. She is emotionally provoked by two women whose ways of life do not resemble her own unexamined one — Madame Ratignolle, who is kind and mild in manner, who worries about leaving her husband because he does not enjoy being alone, and worries about making winter clothes for her children when it is still summer; and Mademoiselle Reisz, an eccentric, solitary, and talented pianist, who is brutally honest. After falling in love with Robert at Grand Isle, Edna begins to neglect her social duties when she comes back to New Orleans: She goes out on Tuesdays when she is supposed to be receiving guests at home. She goes to the racetrack with the seductive Alcee Arobin and risks her reputation. She spends all day painting instead of overseeing the cook to make sure that the fish served to Leonce is not scorched. And finally, when Leonce is away on a business trip, she leaves her children with his mother, closes their house, and moves into a small house that she can support with her own money. When Robert returns to her life, she imagines pure happiness, which is beyond his ability to understand: She is a married woman in love with someone other than her husband; he is in love with a married woman. "Good bye — because I love you." By this time, Edna is an outsider in a different way — she has become herself, in Chopin's scenario.

If I were to understand Edna's awakening as merely a resistance to social norms, then the story would be tragic because she dies, unable to stand her ground against prevailing views about the right way of existing. Her solution not to exist would mean defeat. Many literary critics have debated the motives of Edna's suicide. According to Suzanne Wolkenfeld, George M. Spangler regards it "as a pathetic defeat that is inconsistent with the depiction of her previous strength and achievements and accuses Chopin of a lapse from psychological subtlety into banal sentimentality."[4] In contrast, Per Seyersted argues that it is "the crowning glory of her development from the bewilderment which accompanied her early emancipation to the clarity with which she understands her own nature and the possibilities of life as she decides to end it."[5]

In adapting the novel into a play, however, I was not interested in reinterpreting any of the many erudite views already established; rather, I wanted Edna to gain freedom in the end through her realization of the ephemeral nature of all existences. It was personal. My play deconstructs the self/selfless dichotomy that many readers see as fundamental to Edna's dilemma. Instead, I wished to obliterate the category of self; I wanted her to not come back to

Samsara (the suffering of life) after this one, to be dissolved into Nirvana through her recognition of the nature of impermanence, something I wish for all sentient beings, for myself.

Chopin's *The Awakening* is in no need of a feminist revision as it is fundamentally feminist, if we understand feminism to be a defiance of the expectations placed on women by a patriarchal society. My adaptation is feminist in a way that joins Edna with the rest of humanity. I enable a woman to attain what seems elusive, what no male character is capable of in the novel: complete and absolute freedom.

"'Good-bye — because I love you.' He did not know; he did not understand. He would never understand.... It was too late; the shore was far behind her, and her strength was gone" (139). What was it that Edna realized Robert would never understand? Chopin might have been referring to the incident on the previous night when Edna informed the befuddled Robert that she was no man's possession. However, Edna's awareness presents a deeper, more mystical meaning to me, and I prefer to think that Chopin does not provide an explicit answer to what is ultimately out of reach of Robert's comprehension. Instead, I see the ending of the book as magical; Edna hearing random impressionable sounds from her past, the last one being the hum of bees from her Kentucky childhood, as she begins a journey beyond time and place. The monologue that I wrote for Edna, as elusive as it may seem, is my attempt to identify emptiness (enlightenment) that is within Edna's reach at the moment of her death: the cessation of life's suffering, the interconnection of all sentient beings, and the cyclical nature of existence. Nancy A. Walker writes:

> ...we should note that Chopin did not title her novel *Edna's Awakening* or *One Woman's Awakening* but rather *The Awakening*, which suggests that Chopin saw something universal in Edna's experience, and further, that she intended the novel as a general critique of a culture that severely restricted women's opportunities for emotional fulfillment and self-expression.[6]

I wanted to take Edna one step further and drop "The" from my title, therefore suggesting that Edna's experience is not only shared by the entire humanity, but also extends beyond one moment in time. *Awakening*. In any case, my attempt at adapting the novel focused on Edna's spiritual journey. Many scholars have already addressed Edna's developing awareness of her sensuality in terms of her infidelity with Alcee Arobin and her infatuation with Robert. One example of this interpretation is made by Cynthia Griffin Wolff:

> Much of the novel ... is concerned with Edna's quest for a viable and acceptable mode of owning and expressing her sexuality: first by locating the defining boundaries for these feelings and thus being able to define and name what she feels inside herself; second by finding some acceptable social construct which will permit her to enact them in the outside world and to make an appropriate, vital and affirming connection between the "me" and the "not me."[7]

I agree that this is Edna's first step. But in my version, she emerges from her quest knowing the power of another vision of "not me." My interest in the story lay in a question of eternity and the potential for relationships among women beyond individual identities. In my plays women communicate in numinous ways to help each other understand their own strengths. There is an unbroken thread that connects them through history. I set out to demonstrate with my play that Edna's awakening is spiritual, her realization significant for all of us, one hundred years later.

In adapting the novel, I wished to dissolve the author Chopin's disappointment with its scathing reviews,[8] as well as to give Edna a consciousness of emptiness, a different form of consciousness. To achieve these goals, I used three theatrical conventions — the creation of Kate Chopin as a character; minimalist dialogue and action; and what I call "time breaks."

In the play, Kate Chopin lives in 1899 as well as ceaselessly, watches her novel on stage as she writes it, and becomes almost interchangeable with her heroine. Chopin's presence is constant on stage throughout the play. Even though I researched biographical information about Chopin's life, mostly on the period surrounding the publication of the novel, my intention was not to re-create details of her life. By creating the character of Chopin, I opened a door to thinking about life metaphysically; she exists to live and die her own life, which had already happened in real time, but also to live Edna's as time rewinds and fast-forwards in fictional time.

In scene seven of my play, in the summer ocean lit by the moon, Edna discovers that she can swim:

> EDNA: How easy. It is nothing.
> The water shields my solitude,
> dissolves into my body and emerges again
> again and again
> as I reach for the unlimited and lose myself.
>
> *Edna Swims.*
>
> KATE: As I reach for the unlimited and lose myself,
> A wave of loneliness
> threatens to keep me in a haunted chamber.
> I read over my words.
> I know this is my best work.
>
> *Edna has a vision of death.*
>
> EDNA: I have come too far from the shore.
> What if I can't go back to the people I left there?
> Black salt, bitter nausea, memory all consuming my heart.
> Death devours you, your insides burning,
> your tears starved, your hope withered [13].

In this section, I connect Chopin's doubt about the future of the book, the fear that her work will be kept in a "haunted chamber" (locked out from literary history until the 1950s[9]) with Edna's glimpse into death. Edna successfully swims back, but this new insight — the abandoning of self into a "limitless" existence — is the beginning of her awakening that will take her back to the same ocean nine months later. This dialogue is mine except for "How easy it is! It is nothing;" that is Chopin's (49). Throughout the play, the novel is both in the process of being written and already completed. As Edna's discomfort with societal pressure to conform increases, Kate struggles with vicious criticisms of the book that injured her reputation as a writer. But when Edna returns to Grand Isle alone and comes to her final monologue cited at the beginning of this essay, Chopin responds:

> KATE: But I will come back and live again.
> The book will open
> and someone from the next century
> will dream about this story.
> The day will come...
> EDNA: The day will come when Robert too will melt out of existence.
> All things are inevitable.
> My children will grow up without needing to take from me
> the key to the deepest chamber of my soul.
> I will not give up myself [43].

Edna, however, does give up her "self." When she says that "All things are inevitable" she foreshadows her gradual recognition that there is nothing to give up. She is essentially whole, and no husband or children or lover can possess her or dispose of her. There is no need to give up or not to give up. Watching Edna, my Chopin summarizes her life and faces her own death at the end of the play, and like Edna, emerges from the prison of self:

> KATE: I died on August 22, 1904. Five years after *The Awakening*. My last address was 4232 McPherson. I was one of the first in St Louis to get a telephone in 1902. Lindell 1594M. The book is bound with light green linen. There are green and dark red vines printed around the sides. The spine is in the same red. I like red.
> *Kate drops the papers and walks over to Edna and takes her hand* [44].

Her life is distilled to the simplest descriptions as Chopin detaches herself from the emotional journey of the book and from Edna. When she takes Edna's hand, it is not her heroine's hand she is touching; symbolically she is touching the Buddha mind (a universal consciousness from which everything and nothing is born), if I may be so arrogant to suggest.

The dialogue and action in the play are generally distilled. There are certain moments permeated by silence, and a character exits at the end of a prolonged stillness. This is not a realistic exit: it suggests that this character exited sometime during the silence having said some pleasantries, but the audience does not witness it. Of course we know that in life we don't see everything, and that what we see is not everything. But on stage the audience either expects to see all events or to be told about the ones they do not see. I intended to disrupt this expectation with a minimalist aesthetic, and I omitted words and actions from certain parts of the scenes. By doing so, I lifted Edna out of the reality that in the novel remained so compelling to the character until nearly the end of her life.

I used the same minimalist approach to render Edna's emotional expression. When she finds out that Robert is back in New Orleans, her feelings are described by Chopin in two pages of prose, including the following passage that traces the fluctuation of her moods, romantic fantasies, painful regrets, faint hope, and utter hopelessness:

> The morning was full of sunlight and hope. Edna could see before her no denial — only the promise of excessive joy. She lay in bed awake, with bright eyes full of speculation. "He loves you, poor fool." [She is recalling Mme. Reiz's words.] If she could but get that conviction firmly fixed in her mind, what mattered about the rest? She felt she had been childish and unwise the night before in giving herself over to despondency. She recapitulated the motives which no doubt explained Robert's reserve. They were not insurmountable; they would not hold if he really loved her; they could not hold against her own passion, which he must come to realize in time. She pictured him going to his business that morning. She even saw how he was dressed; how he walked down one street, and turned the corner of another; saw him bending over his desk, talking to people who entered the office, going to his lunch, and perhaps watching for her in the street. He would come to her in the afternoon or evening, sit and roll his cigarette, talk a little, and go away as he had done the night before. But how delicious it would be to have him there with her!...
> ...Robert did not come that day. She was keenly disappointed. He did not come the following day, nor the next. Each morning she awoke with hope, and each night she was a prey to despondency... [126–127].

In my play, these two pages become the following brief interaction between Edna and Mademoiselle Reisz that retains Edna's obsessive feelings for all that happens or does not happen:

> REISZ: What are you planning?
> EDNA: I make small bets with myself all day long. If I finish reading the morning paper before the coffee is brewed, I will hear from Robert. If I manage to paint all day without using the color blue, I will run into Robert. If I do all the insignificant aspects of everyday life perfectly, then Robert will appear at my door.
> REIZ: *(sympathetic)* And you call yourself an artist? (38)

Edna's yearnings, dreams, and desolation are transformed into a mystical game, a contest with herself in which she must achieve perfection in order to deserve Robert. Her fate metamorphoses as she does or does not do certain things, and she cannot free herself from the dependent nature of this existence until she releases herself from the delusional burden that is her own creation.

The minimalist approach also gave me the freedom to superimpose Kate on Edna by having them share certain lines. Edna begins a sentence that Kate finishes. Sometimes Edna's thoughts are spoken by Kate. The evening Edna feels death next to her skin in the night ocean, Robert walks her home after the dangerous swim. The sexual tension between Edna and Robert on stage is saturated in the sound of field frogs, but Kate speaks.

> KATE: I write down the tingling of fingertips
> candle lights burning desire
> hearts' tremors
> a night marked with a thirst
> wishing to touch
> wishing to touch
> wishing to touch
> come with me,
> across the ocean and time,
> KATE AND EDNA: come with me [14].

In this shared plea, I connected Edna's physical desire with Kate's desire for her writing to touch the women who will live centuries later: "wishing to touch," "across the ocean and time, come with me." This dialogue might seem too spare for the audience to comprehend, but it resonates with Kate's direct address to women in the next century at other times in the play. She speaks to the audience personified as the future of womankind throughout the play.

The character of Kate acquires knowledge by witnessing Edna's recognition that existence and non-existence are the same in the end — the end which is also the beginning. To set forth this vision, I imagined Edna having multiple identical circular lives; the circles are complete, so her beginning is also her end. These concentric circles do not line up with each other, so at any instance of Edna's life there are other versions of her story in which this particular moment has already happened or has yet to happen. The indication of the multiple dimensions is expressed in "time breaks" when these moments intersect. For example, in scene three A in the play, while Edna and Robert are just getting acquainted, the audience sees a flash from the future in New Orleans. It is a fragment of interaction between Edna and the old pianist Mademoiselle Reisz regarding a letter Robert would write to her from Mexico. Mademoiselle Reisz is a determined outsider; an artist — brilliant, temperamental, and free, she adheres to no social restrictions. Edna grows to admire her fearless personality and befriends her. But that is the future in New Orleans, when the bright summer is already a memory.

> EDNA: Let me see the letter.
> REISZ: No.
> EDNA: Let me see the letter.
> REISZ: What time do you have to be home?
> EDNA: Time doesn't concern me.
> REISZ: It's growing late.
> EDNA: Let me see the letter [7].

When this "time break" happens, the audience does not yet know that Robert will leave Grand Isle suddenly for Mexico because he will no longer be able to hide his desire for Edna, and upon her return to New Orleans, Edna will long for a letter from him, but he will not write. Instead, he will send letters to the pianist, asking her to play Frederic Chopin's *Impromptu* for Edna if she should visit. This brief "time break" is jarring for the audience and is the first signal that life is not what it appears to be. The scene is more fully played out later in its rightful place within the chronological timeline. Scene three A is followed by scene four, back in Grand Isle, when Edna goes to the beach with her friend Adele, the epitome of the perfect wife/mother. Scene four rapidly comes back in a much condensed form as a "time break" immediately in scene four A, as if a video tape is rewound for seconds and the audience is watching a distorted picture of what they have just seen.

In warping time and events, I attempt to show that true awakening comes to Edna when she realizes that the moment of reading Robert's note, "Goodbye — because I love you," has already happened many times, will happen again many more times, and is happening constantly. With that knowledge, she no longer requires her "self" because she has merged with everything there ever is. Inspired by Chopin's foreshadowing of Edna's death with her triumphant night swimming, I begin my play near the ending of the story when Edna's feet touch the water.

> Edna: Let me prolong this moment,
> My last moment of illusion.
> I am a ménage of things lost
> things that cannot be obtained–
> but with this act, I will return to the present,
> to who I am now,
> and release the memory of everything
> all that I suffered
> all that I am yet to suffer [1].

Again, Edna's monologue is purely my invention. Chopin's Edna does not say or think these words in the novel. I pushed Edna forward in her awareness that we would all return to the present, or rather that there was no other time than the present, so she could make a decision to break the cycle of suffering "with this act." When this dialogue is repeated at the end of the play, she adds, "I walk into the ocean. I am awake" (43).

As I reflect on my play, I am ambivalent about having Edna experience something that I personally have not. Furthermore, her action does not completely conform to the Buddhist concept of achieving enlightenment. Her suicide is an obstacle. The ambiguous ending of the novel has prompted many scholars such as Spangler and Seyersted to speculate on her suicide as either positive or negative. In my view it is neither; it simply is. If I were to rewrite Edna's last swim, I would alter it slightly, so that coming back to life would have been an option. In the novel, she was hungry, and she wished to have fish for dinner. Either way, I would still want her to gain knowledge about human existence that I am personally not yet fully convinced of: that there is no separation between sentient beings and that alienation from "the other" that humans play out in discrimination and wars of all kinds is based on a pervasive illusion of "self." And that once Buddha mind is achieved by all, we will not cling to our individual existence, and we will return to the universe. I want to believe this with all my heart, as I want to believe that Chopin knew, at the time she wrote *The Awakening*, that she would come back to live among us again. Although critics chastised the author and her character for *their* immorality, and in 1956, Kenneth Eble called it a "forgotten novel,"[10] Chopin certainly did not need me to rescue her from oblivion. Today, Chopin's name appears in articles and in anthologies in the company of other early modernist writers, such as D.H. Lawrence, Edith Wharton, Henry James, and Willa Cather. Nancy Walker gives a detailed history of the novel's reception that includes praise from numerous scholars who have resurrected, reinterpreted, and preserved her work, especially from feminist perspectives.[11] While being grateful to their work, determining the literary value of the novel was clearly not my intention as a playwright. I wanted Chopin not to have died with a broken heart. I was willing to rewrite history if necessary so that Chopin could have known that she belonged to later generations and that she would live forever.

I realize that I am an amalgamation of contradictions. The book might not have appealed to me had it not been condemned by the critics. I would not have felt akin to Edna were she not an outsider. And if I truly believed in the unity of all sentient beings, what would I do with my sense of outsider-ness that had first injured and then sustained me for all these years? Still, in *Awakening*, I willfully find eternity, the thread that connects me to Kate Chopin and to Edna Pontellier.

> Kate: I write down life in a mystical place called Grand Isle at the mystical hour of 1899.
> When you emerge out of nothing,
> you will remember nothing.
> My words gone my body gone my memory gone,
> there will be no clue.
> Follow the wind to the burial site at sea
> to find me forever,
> to find my book, the last book of my life [41].

Notes

1. *Awakening* was co-produced by Crossing Jamaica Avenue, Dance Theater Workshop, and Performance Space 122, and premiered at PS 122 on November 8, 2000. The production was supported by the Japan Foundation Grant and directed by Sonoko Kawahara, with lyrics by Mark Campbell, music by Daniel Sonnenberg, set by David Korins, costumes by Theresa Squire, lights by Frank DenDanto III, sound by Brian Hallas, and dramaturgy by Judy Cohen. It was performed by Brian Nishii, Charles Parnell, Hope Salas, Margi Sharp, Sophia Skiles, and Dale Soules.

2. Chiori Miyagawa, *Awakening*, production script, November, 2000, 43. Additional references in the text.

3. Kate Chopin, *The Awakening*, ed. Nancy A. Walker (Boston: Bedford/St. Martin's, 2000) 136. Additional references in the text.

4. George M. Spangler cited in Suzanne Wolkenfeld, "Edna's Suicide: The Problem of the One and the Many," *The Awakening*, by Kate Chopin, ed. Margo Culley (New York: W. W. Norton & Company, 1994) 242–243. See George M. Spangler, "Kate Chopin's *The Awakening*: A Partial Dissent," *Novel* 3 (Spring 1970): 249–255.

5. Per Seyersted, qtd. in Wolkenfeld, 242. See Per Seyersted, *Kate Chopin: A Critical Biography* (Baton Rouge: University of Louisiana Press, 1969) 134–163.

6. Nancy A. Walker, "Biographical and Historical Contexts," *The Awakening*, by Kate Chopin, ed. Nancy A. Walker, 19.

7. Cynthia Griffin Wolff, "Un-Utterable Longing: The Discourse of Feminine Sexuality in Kate Chopin's *The Awakening*," *The Awakening*, by Kate Chopin, ed. Nancy A. Walker, 384. Wolff's use of the "me" and "not me" construction is drawn from R.D. Laing, *The Politics of the Family and Other Essays* (New York: Pantheon, 1969) 17–53.

8. See Margo Culley, "Editor's Note: History of the Criticism of *The Awakening*," *The Awakening*, by Kate Chopin, ed. Margo Culley, 159.

9. Nancy A. Walker states that the "overwhelmingly negative reviews effectively removed the novel from wide circulation and influence for fifty years following its publication." Walker, "Biographical and Historical Contexts," 17.

10. Nancy A. Walker, "A Critical History of *The Awakening*," *The Awakening*, by Kate Chopin, ed. Walker, 169–170. See Kenneth Eble, "A Forgotten Novel: Kate Chopin's *The Awakening*," *Western Humanities Review* X (Summer 1956): 261–269.

11. Walker, "A Critical History," 170.

SITI Company's *Room*
Theatrical Performance and/as Feminist Invitational Rhetoric[1]

Sandee K. McGlaun

In classical rhetoric the traditional end of successful communication is persuasion, and the body, when it plays an acknowledged role in that communication, is to be so contained and constrained as to be almost absent. A number of theater practitioners, including Anne Bogart, co-founder of SITI Company, have argued that theater artists influenced by Stanislavski too often follow such a model themselves, privileging psychological expression over the physical, in effect absenting the rhetoric of the body from the stage. Doing so minimizes the full power of the live theatrical moment and, in a sense, runs the risk — as Friedrich Dürrenmatt cautions in a warning oft repeated by Bogart — of turning the theater into a lecture,[2] one that, indeed, persuades us to belief (as an argument or lecture will do), but that may also — as Virginia Woolf cautions us — leave us simply settled back on our cushions in the "common sitting-room."[3] All the more the reason, and challenge, then, for Bogart and SITI Company Associate Artistic Director Ellen Lauren, in their adaptation of Virginia Woolf's *A Room of One's Own*, to take on not simply the original lecture text itself, but to create a stage dialogue between Woolf's essays, the body, and literal and metaphorical space(s), in order to paint a portrait of the creative mind at work.

Commissioned by The Ohio State University's Wexner Center for the Arts, *Room* premiered there in November 2000; Classic Stage Company hosted its New York premiere in 2002. Although *Room* may at first appear to fit neatly into the category of "Bogartian biodrama," one of four production categories theater critic Mel Gussow invented to describe Bogart's work in 1995, it also falls into a second category identified by Gussow: productions that take new approaches to familiar works.[4] *Room* is the second in a series of three SITI Company solo shows, each arguably a biodrama created to explore the imagination of a specific innovative artist.[5] However, in adapting several of Woolf's provocative and self-reflexive essays to the stage, *Room* also gives rise to a new

Ellen Lauren in SITI/Ann Bogart production of *Room*, Classic Stage Company, New York, 2002. Photographer: Dixie Sheridan.

relationship between familiar source texts and their readers/audience. *Room*, much like the Woolf essays from which it is adapted, blurs generic boundaries, defying and revising our rhetorical expectations. Even as it purports to make an argument, it invites self-reflection and collaborative contemplation. In SITI Company's capable and most expressive hands, Woolf's early twentieth-century prose is transformed into a twenty-first century theatrical performance that bodies forth a feminist rhetoric resonant with the complexities of Woolf's essays.

In recent years feminist scholars of rhetoric have questioned the efficacy and desirability of defining successful communication as that which persuades (some say coerces) the audience to surrender thoughtful dialogue and the rich complexities engendered by the exchange of multiple and conflicting points of view to belief in the primacy of a single, right, best viewpoint, action, or solution. Feminist rhetoricians Sonja Foss and Cindy Griffin have proposed instead a model of an invitational rhetoric, a practice of communication that, in their words, "constitutes an invitation to the audience to enter the rhetor's world and to see it as the rhetor does."[6] Both Woolf's original texts and SITI Company's adaptation issue such an invitation, inviting us in to the mind of Woolf, to explore and question the self and the world, and the relationship between the two, with her. As Bogart explains in the director's note in the production program, *Room* is about the "movement of a creative spirit in exquisite crisis ... the room to move, the room to breathe, the room to imagine, emotional room, creative room."[7] Fittingly, in a preview in *The Chicago Sun–Times*, she casts the play's theme, echoing Woolf's central concern, in interrogative form: "I wanted to ask the question: What kind of space does a woman need in order to create, and what shape does that space take today?"[8]

Room: *Source Texts and Adaptation*

Though the adaptation obviously takes its name from Woolf's *A Room of One's Own*, Jocelyn Clarke's *Room* playtext is composed of almost equal parts lengthy excerpts from that essay and Woolf's autobiographical work, "A Sketch of the Past." Additionally, Clarke, who composed the script based on selections Bogart provided, weaves in substantial passages from "Professions for Women" in which Woolf describes the famous "Angel in the House" (the self-sacrificing and sympathetic heroine of Conventry Patmore's Victorian poem who functioned as Woolf's phantom demon, the figure she must slay in order to free herself to write), an essay of literary criticism entitled "Mr. Bennett and Mrs. Brown," as well as smaller excerpts from the essays "A Letter to a Young Poet" and "The Humane Art," published in *Moments of Being*, "Modern Fiction," and "How Should One Read a Book?," which appear in the *Common Reader* series. Very brief fragments from Woolf's letters and diaries appear, as do fragments of Woolf's experimental novel *The Waves* and her last novel, *Between the Acts*. And, although no language from it appears overtly in the playtext, Woolf's *Mrs. Dalloway* is referenced by recurring clock chimes in the production. According to performer Ellen Lauren, the text focuses on Woolf's nonfiction partly to push the audience beyond what they think they already know of Woolf from her novels: "I'm not playing her as the world perceives her," notes Lauren, "as a very eccentric and iconic character ... very little of the text is from her fiction."[9] Instead, the script for *Room* is an intertextual dialogue between Woolf's essays, memoirs, and literary criticism; critics have described it as nonlinear, more "intensely verbal" than previous SITI Company works,[10] and "less plotted and more internal."[11] As such, it effectively captures and reflects the movement of Woolf's writing and thinking.

Woolf's *A Room of One's Own*, arguably the thematic center of *Room*, was first published in 1929. It originated as two lectures delivered at Newnham and Girton Colleges on October 20 and 26, 1928. Asked to speak on the topic of women and fiction, Woolf "offer[ed] ... an opinion on one minor point — a woman must have money and a room of her own if she is to write fiction" (3). The "minor point" is of course not minor at all; the creative "room" Woolf advocates is both literal and metaphorical. Though many earlier critics of Woolf's work dismissed the essay as a simple polemic,[12] later critics such as John Burt suggest that its structure and themes are far more complex.[13] After identifying "the central argument of the book ... in five theses" and an accompanying "underargument composed of three additional theses," Burt concludes — rightfully, I believe — not only that the "argument" in *A Room of One's Own* fails, but that Woolf's text is not really an argument after all; instead, it is "a portrayal of how a mind attempts to come to terms with its world."[14] Laura Marcus notes that *A Room of One's Own* "contains detachable arguments, aphorisms, and ideas" but, at the same time, "its complexity and obliquity render it virtually inexhaustible by interpretation."[15] Woolf herself declares in the opening that her lecture is a sort of offering — perhaps, even, an invitation.

Indeed, the phrasing Foss and Griffin use in their definition of invitational rhetoric — language that "constitutes an invitation to the audience to enter the rhetor's world and to see it as the rhetor does"[16] — echoes a sentence from Woolf's first chapter of *A Room of One's Own* so strongly that one might argue her influence upon it: "One can only show how one came to hold whatever opinion one does hold" (4). Foss and Griffin's definition continues: "Ideally, audience members accept the invitation offered by the rhetor by listening to and trying to understand the rhetor's perspective and then presenting their own."[17] Again, one can hear the echo from Woolf in *A Room of One's Own*: "One can only give one's audience the chance of drawing their own conclusions as they observe the limitations, the prejudices, the idiosyncrasies of the speaker" (4). Despite the fact, then, that the original "performance" of *A Room of One's*

Own was a conventional lecture, typically a one-sided form of communication, Woolf's text actually sets the stage for a conversation; it urges a dialogue.

Woolf's essayistic writing, in general, is marked by invitational rhetorical choices that suggest she was not interested in tightly focused, linear arguments. Mary Gordon identifies a "conversational" tone,[18] while Hermione Lee notes "the essays' tactics of apparently loose, spontaneous form, of interruptive open-endedness."[19] I submit that four specific rhetorical moves contribute to this open-endedness: Woolf frequently raises questions she explicitly declines to answer; constructs detailed fictional narratives that in their literary ambiguity invite multiple interpretations; and makes use of digressions and associative logic. Moreover, she often interjects meta-commentary on her own thinking processes, reflecting self-consciously not only on the ideas themselves but also on how she came to those ideas. Each of these rhetorical moves invites participation from the reader; they create metaphorical and literal interpretative spaces into which the reader may enter.

Catherine Stimpson characterizes *A Room of One's Own* in particular as "an agitating series of gestures that forbids complacency, security, and premature intellectual closure."[20] Woolf opens the essay with a question, posed from the perspective of her reader/audience: "But, you may say, we asked you to speak about women and fiction — what has that got to do with a room of one's own?" Considering the numerous interpretations of her topic, she does not claim to be able to answer the question with a "nugget of pure truth"; rather, she overtly "shirk[s] the duty of coming to a conclusion" and offers only to "try to explain" by "lay[ing] bare" her thinking process (3–4). She goes on to describe the experiences of the fictional Mary Beton at Oxbridge and, in a later chapter of the essay, Shakespeare's invented sister Judith. Both of these fictional narratives provoke the reader into thinking about how the material lives of women thwart their writing, their ability to create; both allow for the reader/listener to imagine her own future for Mary and Judith — and indeed, Woolf explicitly invites the reader at the close of *A Room of One's Own* to "put on the body which [Shakespeare's sister] has so often laid down" (114).

In the autobiographical essay "A Sketch of the Past," the second key source for *Room*, Woolf unsurprisingly relies less on fictional narratives; instead, her meta-commentary is even more abundant, as she repeatedly notes and remarks upon the "difficulties" in the act of composing memoir.[21] Woolf does not attempt to write a neat, seamless history; instead, her internal contemplations invite the reader to wonder about, even fill in, the gaps and omissions endemic to autobiography; she exposes the constructedness of such writing. Digressions figure heavily in this piece as well, as she moves easily from childhood memories of St. Ives to a philosophical "digression" on the problem of capturing the mundanities of daily life, which she refers to as moments of "non-being," in the writing of fiction.[22] Again, such digressions and associative thinking ask the reader to make the connections.

Examples of one or more of the four rhetorical moves (open ended questions, fictional narratives, associative logic, meta-commentary) noted here can be found in most of Woolf's essays. As a result, Hermione Lee notes, Woolf's essays "resist ... definitiveness, closure, and opinionated certainties;"[23] instead, they invite dialogue, collaboration, and (still) opinionated uncertainties. Similarly, Jocelyn Clarke's adaptation of the "interruptive open-endedness" of Woolf's nonfiction in *Room* creates "room" for the reader not only to step into the mind of the "I," but also to participate in that I's making of meaning. Its non-linearity and lack of plot make it challenging to describe the play's structure in traditional terms; aside from the play's opening and closing with selections drawn primarily from *A Room of One's Own*, which gives the play its dramatic and thematic frame, there is no set pattern in the arrangement of the excerpts. Instead, the wavelike structure of the script and its layered multi-vocality extend the invitational rhetorical qualities of Woolf's original works. Instead of answering Bogart's question with a "nugget of pure truth,"*Room* explores the effects of the asking, exposing even more questions, and revealing, through the interweaving of Woolf's personal recollections with her literary theories, how the past and the personal may wash over one's creative energy, serving as both source and obstacle.

Waves and their rhythms figure strongly in Woolf's work, particularly in her experimental novel *The Waves*. Although *Room* draws only one sentence from the novel — "I am telling myself the story of the world from the beginning" — the play owes much to the novel's structure.[24] According to Gillian Beer in *Virginia Woolf: The Common Ground*, "Virginia Woolf said that she wanted in *The Waves* to follow a rhythm, not a plot: the rhythm is figured in the pressure of the waves moving beneath the surface of the sea, humping themselves momentarily at the shore to break in foam. The pattern can express both long continuity and ephemerality, the single and the common life."[25] *Room*, too, seems to follow rhythm as much as plot, and the wavelike pattern is clearly present. Instead of a single dramatic arc with one climactic moment, the play's overall movement is wavelike: within the frame of the lecture, there are several smaller emotional swells that recede, then build again, as we meet our lecturer, listen to her reflect on memory and writing and the nature of reality, as she begins to reveal her past. She focuses for a while on the "unsolved problems" of "woman and fiction" (2), her own struggles with capturing reality in writing, then shifts again into the past, and the waves pick up, breaking harder: first in shame, then in rapture, and then they slowly subside back in to literary theory, some advice, the quiet "peroration." Images and ideas repeat, and each time they reappear, they swell a bit higher, filled with more detail, more emotion.

One image that repeats frequently is that of the waves themselves, which become a featured motif through the playtext. The waves represent Woolf's constant awareness of and fascination with the smallest details of sensory experience; they also might be said to represent the movement of the creative process, the back and forth of ideas that eventually break and splash and, in Woolf's case, sometimes crash over her. Clarke's careful cutting and construction contribute to this effect. The first mention of the waves at St. Ives occurs in the context of a happy memory, a recollection of the "purest ecstasy" of the aliveness of the senses (3). After a digression into a more philosophical contemplation of sensory impressions and the mind (composed of excerpts from four different works of literary criticism), the next appearance of the image of the waves at St. Ives reflects a kind of rolling back, as the excerpt is drawn from an earlier part of "A Sketch of the Past" in which Woolf reflects critically on herself as compared to other people. When St. Ives and the waves return in the script a third time, they follow a lengthy discussion of gender and novel writing excerpted primarily from *A Room of One's Own* and "Professions for Women" in which Woolf laments women writers' straying from "the thing itself," distracted by their need to defend their chosen vocation (9), and explains how she herself had to kill the "Angel in the House." In this context the ecstasy, or "rapture," Woolf describes in sensory experience, the tapestry of "colour and sound memories" from St. Ives, seems both an escape and an effort to ferret out the origins of her need to create. Yet as she "listen[s] to the past," the "rapture" in the sensory shifts to shame, as Woolf recounts her discomfort with her body and her half-brother's molestation of her (11–12). Here the waves crash.

Although Woolf scholars intimately familiar with both essays would no doubt already be aware of the intertextual resonances between the literary theory presented in *A Room of One's Own* and the personal history revealed in "A Sketch of the Past," many in *Room*'s audience would not. Thus, the wavelike motion of Clarke's script, particularly the juxtaposition of Woolf's deeply personal memories with her literary criticism, creates additional space for reflection and adds another layer to Woolf's original, internal meta-commentary. In *A Room of One's Own*, Woolf expresses the need women have for creative freedom and confidence; in "A Sketch of the Past," the creative confidence that for Woolf is rooted in deeply felt sensory experience is compromised by the shame she also connects with sensory experience. This tension leads to the two "wavebreaks" in the play.

When next we hear of the ecstasy of the senses (another recurring motif) that was first connected to listening to the waves, it is in relation to writing, in the context of a description of three "sudden violent shock[s]" she remembers, each of which disrupted the "cotton wool" of Woolf's everyday non-being: a fistfight with her brother Thoby, a flower in the garden at St. Ives, and the moment she learns that a man who had visited St. Ives committed suicide. The two violent incidents made Woolf feel "powerlessness" and "despair;" seeing the flower as a part of a larger whole gave her "satisfaction" (14–15). A self-reflective passage on the role these experiences played in her writing follows the descriptions of the events:

> It is only by putting it into words that I make it whole; this wholeness means that it has lost its power to hurt me; it gives me, perhaps because by doing so I take away the pain, a great delight to put the severed parts together. Perhaps this is the strongest pleasure known to me. It is the rapture I get when in writing I seem to be discovering what belongs to what; making a scene come right; making a character come together [15].

The wavelike structure of the play, the "satisfaction" Woolf recounts in linking flower to earth, her "pleasure" in bringing the "severed parts together ... discovering what belongs to what" in her writing (15) echoes Woolf's contemplation of androgyny in *A Room of One's Own*, the bringing together of the sexes and the easing of repression that emanates from thinking "specially or separately about sex" (99). She proposes this idea in the form of what might best be called a declarative question: "[T]he sight of the two people [a man and a woman] getting into the taxi and the satisfaction it gave me made me also ask whether there are two sexes in the mind corresponding to the two sexes in the body, and whether they also require to be united in order to get complete satisfaction and happiness" (98).

In each of these examples, we see the desire for, the will to create a sense of wholeness; that wholeness is the source of Woolf's "rapture." At the same time, the structure of Clarke's script juxtaposes this desire for wholeness with Woolf's descriptions of her profound sense of disconnection with her own (female) body, her sense of removal from it when gazing in the looking glass. The complexities of the workings of Woolf's mind are made evident in these contradictions: the ecstasy of sensory experience is juxtaposed with Woolf's discomfort in her own body and shame in her experiences in that body. In turn, that *bodily* disconnection and discomfort, which seems a result of an inability to reconcile her "tomboy nature" with the "femininity" that is "very strong in [her] family"(12), is juxtaposed with her desire to bring the sensibilities of the two sexes fully together in her *mind*. As Woolf asserts in *A Room of One's Own*: "It is fatal for anyone who writes to think of their sex" (104). The play reveals a creative spirit both enamored of and utterly overwhelmed by the sensory world; a sensory world that is both at the core of her creativity, *and* somehow less comfortable or accessible than the world of the mind that translates those sensory experiences.

This multiple and contradictory sense of self, emphasized by Clarke's construction of the script, echoes a recurring theme in Woolf's work related to the freedom she deems necessary to create, establishing it as a theme of *Room* as well: people are made up of not just one self, but many.[26] In *Room*, this theme is realized on several levels. First, it is revealed in the repetition of two key sentences in the script which, together, signify the tension Woolf seems to have felt surrounding this realization: "It is so difficult to describe any human being," from "A Sketch of the Past," appears three times.[27] "A self that goes on changing is a self that goes on living," from "Modern Fiction," appears twice; notably, the second iteration immediately follows the third of "It is so difficult to describe any human being."[28] It is, of course, Woolf's awareness of the fact that the self goes on changing — and not simply over weeks or years, but from one moment to the next — that makes it so difficult to describe another, or to know oneself. Woolf's essays reflect this idea, of course, in their questions, digressions, and self-reflections. But Clarke's script possesses its own internal multi-vocality, which resembles a conversation in and of itself: the more formal voice of the literary critic and icon is contrasted with the wry, humble voice of an eternally curious woman wishing to better understand herself and her art, which in turn is juxtaposed against the almost frenzied voice of the artist overwhelmed by senses, memories, all there is to see and notice and record in the world. Here again there seems to be a nod to *The Waves*, in which "the 'eye' and 'I' is multiplied and dissolved."[29]

This multi-vocality, in combination with the digressive structure of the script itself, creates additional spaces for the audience to enter into the conversation, the contemplation. At every "fiercely digressive" swerve, as the play moves associatively from passage to passage, the audience must actively participate in making the interpretative leap.[30] When the script segues from an intellectual observation on the richness of the English language (drawn from "A Letter to a Young Poet"), to a recitation of the nursery rhyme "I was going to St. Ives," to the lush description of Woolf's childhood memory of lying in bed at St. Ives listening to waves roll and break (3), it is left to the audience to fill in the gaps, to make sense of the unspoken connections; and even as we seek to make sense of these particular leaps, we recognize these leaps and shifts as a near universal representation of the mind of an imaginative thinker working at full creative capacity.

In *A Room of One's Own* — in a passage that also appears in the play — Woolf suggests that the realm of the mind is freer than that of the body: "The mind has so great a power of concentrating at any point at any moment that it seems to have no single state of being.... Clearly the mind is always altering its focus, and bringing the world into different perspectives."[31] The freedom of the mind is directly related to the "unity [of the two sexes] in the mind;" in order for the mind to be free, "the whole of the mind must lie wide open," undistracted by an awareness of one's sex, one's body.[32] At the same time, Woolf roots "reality" in the physical, the individual sensory experience: "now ... found in a dusty road, now in a scrap of newspaper in the street, now a daffodil in the sun."[33] Without a profound awareness and experience of the sensory, there would be no experience for the mind to translate; without the body, there would be no ability to share that translation. It is clear, then, that an exploration of the creative mind at work must also bring the body into the conversation. Here we arrive at a slightly different formulation of the question Bogart asks: what room can we give women to create, what room do others allow women, in a world in which our minds are necessarily inscribed (by those selves and others) by our bodies, bodies whose inscriptions may involve alienation, shame, and self-doubt?

Invitational Rhetoric and SITI Company's Process

The process by which SITI Company creates their work also reflects the ideals of a rhetoric of invitation. Typically, the playtexts, like *Room*, are multivocal, constructed from a variety of source texts placed in conversation; often, several company members contribute to the construction of the text. The process of then placing the text(s) in conversation with the performers' bodies and other stage elements is also highly collaborative. Using a movement philosophy referred to as the viewpoints, based on the work of choreographer Mary Overlie, and two other methods called composition and source-work, Bogart and SITI Company quite literally write with the body. Much like the way in which Woolf's writing is rooted in the sensory experience, the viewpoints, the cornerstone of SITI's methods, "encourage actors to root their work in physical realities."[34] Viewpoints of time (such as tempo, duration, repetition, and kinesthetic response) and space (including architecture, topography, spatial relationship, shape, and gesture)[35] contribute to compositions; performance pieces created by company members in and for rehearsals are mined for phrases of movement, expressions of character, and, occasionally, dialogue. Combined with source-work (textual research into relevant historical or biographical information, and the gathering of visual and aural resources such as photographs, objects, and music), the company creates a specific movement vocabulary for a production, from which sequences of movement are choreographed and set as precisely as dances. According to Bogart, the movement of entire scenes may be staged before a word of text for the scene is selected or provided to actors, much less rehearsed.[36] Only later in the process does the company lay text over the movement. To prepare for *Room*, Ellen Lauren studied photographs of Woolf to "learn them the way you learn music or lines of dialogue, learn the tactile, kinetic reality of what they said. We built physical passages from them that gave me a kind of grammar," she explains. "And then I began to meet the words."[37]

This process frees the movement from the text — resulting in an absolute, and intentional, disruption of what I call delivery's classical imperative: the injunction made by classical rhetoricians that, in oral communication, the speaking body must necessarily subject itself to the word or text spoken; movement and gestures must arise out of, support, even be governed by the thought if they (and the speaker) are to be persuasive.[38] The imperative seems to have derived from the fear that the body, if not contained, might prove more persuasive in its own right than the speaker's words, that the body's language might confuse the message.

In this context, it is evident that letting the body have its say could, potentially, redefine the entire art of delivery, and indeed, this is what happens in SITI Company's productions. In *Room* the "grammar" of gestures functions like a second language, each new gesture often first appearing in a relationship to the spoken word that seems natural, that fits the text, but then appearing again later in ways that puzzle, invite question. Bogart describes the result this way: "Theatre begins with the disagreement between what you see and what you hear."[39] It is specifically this disagreement between the body and playtext in performance, as well as their combination/conversation/contradiction with other stage "texts" such as that "of behavior, of acting, of scenography, of blocking," that allow us to re-imagine the relationship of (rhetorical) form to (rhetorical) content.[40] In deliberately creating disjunctions between these various texts, SITI Company literally *embodies* an invitational feminist rhetoric that not only reclaims the role the body plays in the creative act and in communication, but also eschews persuasion for the same kind of exploration, self-reflection, and collaborative contemplation that is invited by Woolf's original essays. Lauren describes the result as "one of the hallmarks of our company. You don't say what it is, you ask what it is."[41]

Room: *In Production*

As *Room* opens, a woman sits perched on the edge of a chair in the house of the theater. If you enter the theater early, you might notice her: the ramrod posture, the intent focus, the almost haughty expression. The audience shuffles in, rustles, settles, and suddenly, with no discernible warning, the woman rises, startled, and walks to the stage, offering a crisp "Good evening." She seems a bit nervous, perhaps a little unnerved that all of you are here, in her room. Though her manner is somewhat stern, even school-marmish, leading you to expect a lecture, the first thing she does is issue an invitation: "Before I begin," she says, "I must ask you to imagine a room. Any room. But it must be your room.... A room of which you are mistress, and where you can close the door to the world outside, and sit and think, and perhaps even write." As the audience takes in the three soaring, bare white walls and the single, simple chair of Neil Patel's set, imagining and projecting their own rooms, perhaps, onto this blank slate, the woman smiles, then notes, "It is our room now" (1).

The woman, of course, is Ellen Lauren, and by opening the play with her seated in the house, the invitation to an exchange is made immediate and intimate; it is not only verbal but also physical: Lauren is, at first, just one of us, a part of the audience. There is no overt contradiction between word and gesture at this point. There is, however, an unspoken question: the woman stands before us clad in a long, gray, twenties-ish sheath, her hair pulled back in a low bun; she physically evokes Woolf in dress and, at first, in stance.[42] Yet, at the same time, Lauren does not "play" Woolf in the sense of imitating her. Instead, the character onstage appears to be a modern woman grappling with what it means to understand, and be, an artist; her performance is "not an impersonation, but an intimation of Woolf's mind at work and the sensibility one encounters when reading her."[43]

In interviews, Lauren uses the word "conduit" to describe her role; she guides us into and through "Woolf's articulated thoughts."[44] This role of the conduit is important, as it reflects the invitational rhetorical trope that Woolf adopts at the beginning of *A Room of One's Own* and in other essays, the fictional persona whom we recognize as both Woolf and not–Woolf: "Here then was I (call me Mary Beton, Mary Seton, Mary Carmichael or by any name you please...)" writes Woolf.[45] Similarly, Lauren embodies both Woolf and not–Woolf in the play: "Call me Emily / Call me Mary / Call me Isa / Or by any name you please, it is not a matter of importance," she echoes. The invocation of multiple, fictional selves—including, in *Room*, Isa, a character from *Between the Acts*—invites the audience to take part in the creation of the narrative, and thus the meaning–making. The physicalization of the narrator as conduit embodies the recurring theme of the multiple selves noted earlier; the dual representation in which Lauren portrays Woolf and comments on her simultaneously also creates an embodied form of the meta-commentary that occurs in Woolf's essays. In *Room*, Woolf's invitational rhetorical practices are bodied forth onstage.

After declaring the shared space "our room," Lauren moves to center stage and begins what initially looks and appears like a formal lecture, the text drawn from the opening of Woolf's *A Room of One's Own*. She stands utterly still, hands clasped behind her back. And yet her body remains so completely motionless for so long that we slowly become aware she is manipulating our expectations of delivery's classical imperative even as she appears to be embodying it. Her gestures begin slowly, smoothly, and at first they seem almost natural, organic: a single hand raised to emphasize a point, dusting her hands together as if to be rid of something vile as she speaks of "throw[ing] the whole of her talk into the wastepaper basket" if we find no truth in it (2). But then the tempo of the dusting gesture slows unexpectedly, she clasps her hands and leans back to the left as chimes sound, and the body and the text are no longer on the same "track."[46] As Lauren leans back, we find ourselves sitting forward, trying to put together what we are hearing and seeing, asking, "Why?"

It is challenging to represent in words a theater so rooted in the body, but I will describe several additional key points in the play with an eye toward making connections between Lauren's gestural vocabulary and the invitational rhetorical tropes already identified in Woolf's and Clarke's texts. Although many of Lauren's gestures are focused in the arms and hands, there is also a series of postures and movements that center around the chair, as well as a few moments when she interacts with the architecture of the floor or walls. Furthermore, Christopher Akerland's lighting design, especially the single "window" projected high on the back wall at different points throughout the play and his use of shadows "explore ... the different and shifting views created by varying angles of perception"—a description scholar Laura Marcus applies to *A Room of One Own*.[47] Darron L. West's evocative soundscape, with its ticking and chiming clocks, rolling surf, falling bombs, and alternately bright and discordant piano music, also contributes to the stage conversation.

As noted in my description of the opening, Lauren's gestures and body placement begin "naturally." Yet even once we begin to notice a change, her movement and gestures remain fairly contained until the first major shifts in text begin. As Lauren/Woolf moves from *A Room of One's Own* into an excerpt from "Professions for Women," remarking on the "novelist's chief desire ... to induce a state of perpetual lethargy," she shifts *out* of a lethargic lean into an upright pose, her hands held low and closed, almost in a fighting stance. This stance contradicts her characterization of the imagination as "that very shy and illusive spirit,"(4) inviting the audience to revise the characterization even as Lauren speaks it: imagination may indeed be "shy and illusive," but her stance suggests it is also tough, a fighter, perhaps even a bully at times.

Throughout most of the long section from "A Sketch of the Past," in which we are literally introduced to "Adeline Virginia Stephen," Lauren stands with her arms held low in front of her torso, arms slightly rounded and crossed at the wrist, the right hand clasped into a fist and the left open, palm flat. The first time we see this gesture in the play, it underscores a passage in which Lauren/Woolf reflects on herself as a source of "fascinating anxiety," a role that brings her both "pleasure" and "disgust." Lauren holds the pose until she asks a question: "Who was I then?"(5). The lights shift to a hot yellow as she moves into a position that reads, for a moment, as if she has been spotlighted and put her hands up for arrest; then we notice she holds her right arm straight out from the shoulder, bent at the elbow in a tight right angle, her hand open, palm facing the audience, while her left hand extends from the shoulder over her head in a gentle curve, her hand still balled into a fist. This pose underscores the actual statement of her given name: "Adeline Virginia Stephen, the second daughter of Leslie and Julia Prinsep Stephen...."(5). In this moment, her hand gestures seem at once to be inviting the audience to know her (the open hand), and threatening us not to get too close (the closed fist), even as her overall body position in conjunction with the lighting continues to suggest someone arrested, or, perhaps in a metaphorical sense, someone trapped or caught. This sense is magnified by the shadow of Lauren projected on to the back wall; it looms over her, its arms raised, both protective and menacing. Though Lauren/Woolf introduces herself with a single name, the texts of body and lighting reveal internal contradictions, multiple selves.

There is still another layer to this gesture, which recurs at different points throughout the play. It recalls a famous metaphor described by Edward P.J.

Corbett in "The Rhetoric of the Open Hand and the Rhetoric of the Closed Fist," in which the open hand represents "persuasive discourse" characterized by "reasoned ... discussion," while the closed fist represents "non-rationale [sic], non-sequential, often non-verbal, frequently provocative means" of persuasion.[48] The gesture, then, quite literally embodies the tension between a rhetoric of words and a rhetoric of the body; as such, it also suggests the tension Woolf experienced between the sensory impressions at the root of her work and the struggle she faced in containing her experience of them and conveying her experience in words.

This gesture reappears later, when a lengthier section from "A Sketch of the Past" appears, introduced, again, by the question "Who was I then?" (12). This scene builds to the two "wave-breaks" of the play, the first a revelation of shame when Woolf/Lauren is unable to bring together mind and body; the second, a moment of rapture, when everything connects for her. Leading up to the first, Lauren holds the "arrested" posture throughout the description of Woolf's discomfort gazing into the looking glass, while Akerlind's lighting again casts a tall shadow of her on the back wall, this time at an angle that creates two additional shadow arms extending from Lauren's waist. A looking glass appears dimly, lit from behind the "window" projected on the back wall, both framing Lauren; with her four arms appearing to push at the boundaries of the looking glass, framed itself by the projected window, the sense of entrapment is heightened. Here the lighting forms a kind of meta-commentary on the words Lauren speaks.

As abstracted as they are, Lauren's gestures at first seem to illustrate her words; as she describes feelings of guilt and dread, she assumes a posture of shame, her back to us, body hunched forward, hands clasped in front of her abdomen. Yet when she states "I must have been ashamed or afraid of my own body"(12), she suddenly turns toward the audience, opens her body up fully, and throws one arm into the air in a kind of victory gesture. Before the audience can decide what to make of this juxtaposition of word and gesture, a chord sounds, chimes come in, and the light shifts. The "shame" posture is repeated a few moments later, after a brief trancelike digression from *Between the Acts*, during which Lauren moves to the chair, clasps her hands in front of her again, and bends over the arm of it sideways. In literally tilting the pose, its meaning shifts as well: although her pose recalls that of a fearful child seeking comfort, it also reveals strength and control. And Lauren's voice is neither contrite nor fearful; it, too, is strong, even angry.

A sequence of several repeated postures, including the "shame" pose, then underscores the climactic ten-sentence description of Woolf's having been molested by her half-brother when she was "very small" (12). Lauren moves among the opening "lecture" pose with hands clasped behind the back; the low version of the open hand/closed fist gesture; both hands held out to the sides as if welcoming an embrace; the hunched-over "shame" posture with hands clasped in front; and another pose that involves sweeping the hand up to her forehead and just above it in a way that disturbingly recalls both a hanging — the jerk of a noose — and swooning. Here again the gestures seem to move from illustrating her shame to a puzzling meta-commentary: does the gesture signify a swoon, and if so, why? Was being molested somehow related to her anxieties about writing? Her desire to end her life? The audience is left to answer the question "Why should I have felt shame then?" for Lauren/Woolf's answer is a simple "I don't know" (13). A good portion of this speech is delivered facing fully or partially upstage, and, again, turning the audience's perspective on a gesture shifts its meaning as well: holding the hands clasped low behind the back recalls a soldier "at ease" — until Lauren turns her back to the audience in the same pose, and suddenly she looks like a prisoner with her hands bound.

When we reach the rapturous wave-break of the play that follows shortly, the movement is almost wholly abstracted from the text. Woolf/Lauren traces the three "sudden violent shocks" noted earlier; as she describes them, she begins to pace, then travel the stage in a grid–like pattern. Her vocal and physical tempos increase steadily as she begins to repeat all the various gestures and poses we have seen thus far in a set sequence. She moves in and out of the chair, leans forward and back, moves her hands and arms, lies on the floor, and gets up again. Her vocal intensity builds to almost a rant, and she moves furiously, faster and faster, as she builds to a revelation:

> From this I reach what I might call a philosophy; at any rate it is a constant idea of mine; that behind the cotton wool is hidden a pattern; that we — I mean all human beings — are connected with this; that the whole world is a work of art; that we are parts of the work of art. Hamlet or a Beethoven quartet is the truth about this vast mass that we call the world. But there is no Shakespeare, there is no Beethoven; certainly and emphatically there is no God; we are the words; we are the music; we are the thing itself. And I see this when I have a shock [15].

At "shock," the music picks up, and Lauren goes silent. She continues to move, again repeating all of the gestures and postures in sequence, but at a slower pace, ballet–like. Whatever gestures or postures might have seemed at least somewhat representative before are now completely abstracted from the words. And this "disagreement between what you see and what you hear" creates unanswered questions for the audience;[49] it leaves gaps of meaning we might choose to fill in with our own narrative through-lines; it produces digressions and manufactures its own reflective meta-commentary. In other words, the conversation among the text(s), the body, and the space in *Room* embodies each of the invitational rhetorical practices in Virginia Woolf's texts. The physical expression of tensions and contradictions enable us to find the conversational space of Woolf's text and enter into a dialogue with it.

Peroration

At the conclusion of the gesture ballet, Lauren sits in the chair and dryly remarks, "All artists I suppose feel something like this" (15). While the wavebreak of shame in *Room* centers around a moment of disconnection, the swell of rapture centers around a moment of profound connection, a recognition of the connection between all people, all artists. Bogart asks, "What kind of space does a woman need to create, and what kind of shape does that space take today?" *Room* suggests that we all must have space in which our words and our bodies might dance; we must have words that move others, and room in which we can move our selves; room to shift perspective. We need physical and emotional space in which to connect mind and body, mental and material. Creative rapture is borne of connection; connection is borne of invitation, conversation.

That room is not always easy to come by. When Woolf wrote *A Room of One's Own* in the early twentieth century, she was concerned with a kind of material freedom for women — "money and a room of one's own" — that allows for a larger psychological freedom necessary to the creative process (4). In the twenty-first century, it is entirely possible for a woman to have achieved the material freedom Woolf refers to but still not experience the psychological freedom she assumed would follow. As the world grows larger, our rooms seem to grow smaller: women's minds are still inscribed by their bodies. In our "postfeminist" world, our awareness of our sex and the ways it both empowers and disempowers is, if anything, heightened. How can women forget their sex in a world in which we actively fight for the right to choose our futures? The same awareness that empowers may, from a Woolfian perspective, alienate as well. We live in a deluge of the sensory input that both inspired Woolf and dogged her; the abrupt, often violent shifts in posture, lighting, and sound in *Room* reflect how the stuff of creative energy may also overwhelm its expression.

The only window in *Room* is an imaginary one, a projection that shifts and changes with our perspective. Are we (only) as free as our imaginations? And though this window does not open, though we only see "out" when the light is just right (and even then we gaze through the hazy scrim of self-perception), the world outside both inspires and encroaches, constantly. If, as Burt writes, *A Room of One's Own* is a "portrayal of how a mind attempts to come to terms with its world," it is also an acknowledgment "that the world is perhaps not a place with which anyone c[an] come to terms," at least not without great vision and imagination.[50] And so we must find time and space to contemplate, to reflect, to both cultivate and escape our self-awareness—to connect with others so that we might imagine a different world.

Room closes with a gentle image. After Lauren/Woolf urges the audience "to write all sorts of books," to do so "for your good and for the good of the world at large,"[51] she reminds us that "there must be freedom and there must be peace.[52] One has only to read, to look, to listen, to remember" (18). She then crosses to sit in the downstage chair, facing upstage, angled so that we can see her profile and her hand resting on the arm of the chair, an iconic Woolfian pose. As she gazes upstage at the lighted window that appears again high on the back wall, her pose seems to invite us to enter her room, to sit and share her gaze. We see these rooms, literal and literary, from her perspective; we contemplate their meanings in and for our selves. "To be present in the theater, in this room, where this mind says, 'be yourself, be free, write books, read books'— that's a very political thing to say onstage in our day and age," claims Ellen Lauren.[53] Together we look at, out, through the window; it is source, shield, slant: the world in a frame. Here we may attempt to come to terms with Woolf's world and ours; here, with Woolf, we may imagine a new world, one still to be written on the blank tablet of this room.

Notes

1. Small portions of this essay first appeared in slightly different form in chapter three of my dissertation, *Re-staging Persuasion: Feminist Theatrical Performance And/As Rhetoric,* The Ohio State University, 2000 (Ann Arbor: University of Michigan, 2000).

2. Mel Gussow glosses this philosophy, which I have heard Bogart reiterate several times, in his essay "Worlds of Bogart," *Anne Bogart: Viewpoints,* ed. Michael Bigelow Dixon and Joel A Smith (Lyme, NH: Smith and Kraus, 1995) 149: "If you go to the theatre and put your hands over your eyes and still understand what is happening onstage, then the play is a lecture. If you put your hands over your ears and still understand what is happening, then it is a slide lecture. It is [Bogart's] credo that theatre begins when there is a tension between the situation and the word, choreography, and psychology."

3. Virginia Woolf, *A Room of One's Own* (Orlando: Harvest/Harcourt, 1989) 113–114. Additional references in the text.

4. Gussow 147.

5. The first show, *Bob,* looks at Robert Wilson, and Score, which followed Room, examines Leonard Bernstein.

6. Sonja Foss and Cindy Griffin, "Beyond Persuasion: A Proposal for an Invitational Rhetoric," *Communication Monographs* 62 (March 1995): 5.

7. Anne Bogart, "Director's Note," *Room* program, Wexner Center for the Arts (Columbus, OH), 1–5 Nov. 2000.

8. Qtd. in Hedy Weiss, "Bogart Gives 'Room' Its Space," *The Chicago Sun–Times,* 18 Apr. 2002, sec. 2:36.

9. Qtd in Michael Grossberg, "A Room of Woolf's Own," *City Talk* (City Theater, Pittsburgh), Jan–Feb 2001: 1–2.

10. Hedy Weiss, "Woolf's 'Room' Filled with Creative Power," *The Chicago Sun–Times,* 21 April 2002: 35A.

11. Christopher Rawson, "'Room' to Roam," *Pittsburgh Post–Gazette,* 19 January 2001, Sooner ed., sec. A&E: 14.

12. See, for example, Ulysses L. D'Aquila, *Bloomsbury and Modernism* (New York: Peter Lang, 1989) and J.K. Johnstone, *The Bloomsbury Group* (New York: Octagon Books, 1978).

13. John Burt, "Irreconcilable Habits of Thought in 'A Room of One's Own' and 'To the Lighthouse,'" *Modern Critical Views: Virginia Woolf,* ed. Harold Bloom (New York: Chelsea House, 1986) 191–206.

14. Burt 192, 194, 197. Burt concludes that the five theses, which trace the oppression of women through to their eventual emancipation —"marked by androgeny"— depend upon

a "progressive view of human history and an optimistic view ... of human nature" (193); the underargument contradicts this hopefulness, suggesting that the "war has destroyed this capacity [for imaginative androgeny] entirely" (194). Thus, the argument fails as argument.

15. Laura Marcus, "Woolf's Feminism and Feminism's Woolf," *The Cambridge Companion to Virginia Woolf*, eds. Sue Roe and Susan Sellers (Cambridge: Cambridge University Press, 2000) 219.

16. Foss and Griffin 5.

17. Ibid.

18. Mary Gordon, "Foreword," *A Room of One's Own* (Orlando: Harvest/Harcourt, 1989) xiii.

19. Hermione Lee, "Virginia Woolf's Essays," *The Cambridge Companion to Virginia Woolf*, eds. Sue Roe and Susan Sellers (Cambridge: Cambridge University Press, 2000) 95.

20. Catherine Stimpson, "Woolf's Room, Our Project: The Building of Feminist Criticism," *Virginia Woolf: Longman Critical Readers*, ed. Rachel Bowlby (New York: Longman, 1992) 164.

21. Virginia Woolf, "A Sketch of the Past," *Moments of Being: A Collection of Autobiographical Writing*, 2nd ed., ed. Jeanne Schulkind (San Diego: Harvest/Harcourt, 1985) 64.

22. Woolf, "A Sketch of the Past," 70.

23. Lee 95.

24. Jocelyn Clarke, adapter, *Room*, unpublished script (Classic Stage Company) 6 May 2002: 7. Additional references in the text. From this point forward, quotations drawn from published versions of Woolf's essays cite the page number of the essay, while quotations referring to Jocelyn Clarke's playtext — which, in some cases, slightly alters Woolf's original text — will indicate the page number corresponding to the script.

25. Gillian Beer, *Virginia Woolf: The Common Ground* (Ann Arbor: University of Michigan Press, 1996) 65. Beer also makes connections between Woolf's work and theories of wave-form emerging in physics at the time.

26. In *Orlando*, Woolf's narrator notes, "A biography is considered complete if it merely accounts for six or seven selves, whereas a person may well have as many as a thousand" (548). In her diary, she also commented on this idea: "But how queer to have so many selves–how bewildering" (4:329).

27. Clarke 3, 4, 16.

28. Clarke 12, 16.

29. Beer 62.

30. Bruce Weber, "When A Writer's Brain is Turned Inside Out," *The New York Times*, 28 May 2002, final ed., sec. Arts/Cultural: 5.

31. Woolf, *A Room of One's Own*, 97; Clarke 5–6.

32. Woolf, *A Room of One's Own*, 97, 104.

33. Woolf, *A Room of One's Own*, 110; Clarke 4.

34. Judith Newmark, "Anne Bogart Puts Act into Acting and Takes the Boredom Out of Theater," *Louisville Courier-Journal*, 3 Feb. 1999, sec. E: 1.

35. This list of viewpoints is representative, not inclusive.

36. Anne Bogart, untitled lecture, with Ellen Lauren and Barney O'Hanlon, Department of Theater, The Ohio State University, 3 Dec. 1999.

37. Qtd. in Misha Berson, "Experimental Theater Troupe Presents a 'ROOM' of its Own," *The Seattle Times*, 28 Sept. 2001: 24H.

38. In classical rhetoric, the insistence on the classical imperative is almost fanatical: according to Quintilian, for example, the head "must receive ... appropriate motions from the nature of the subject on which we speak" (361); the orator's delivery is faulty if so much as the "configuration" of his eyebrows "is at variance" with his words or emotions (363).

39. Qtd. in Jay Weitz, "The Message is the 'Medium,'" rev. of *The Medium*, dir. Anne Bogart, with SITI Company, Wexner Center for the Arts, Columbus, OH, *Columbus Guardian*, 7 Nov. 1996: 14.

40. Richard Schechner, "Theatre Alive in the New Millennium," *The Drama Review*

44.1 (Spring 2000): 5–6. Schechner continues, "Each of these [texts] is autonomous, and can be developed on its own and/or in relation to others" (6).

41. Qtd. in Anna Rosenstein, "Woolf at the Door," *Pittsburgh Post–Gazette*, 12 January 2001, Sooner ed., sec. A&E: 14.

42. *Room*'s costume design was by James Schuette.

43. Thomas Connors, "A 'Room' With a View into Virginia Woolf's World of Words," *The Chicago Tribune*, 17 April 2002, North Sports final ed., sec. Tempo: 3.

44. Siddarth Puri, "Working Solo: Ellen Lauren Gives Virginia Woolf Room of Her Own," *UCLA Daily Bruin*, 30 January 2002: 14.

45. Woolf, *A Room of One's Own*, 50.

46. See Tina Landau, "Source-Work, the Viewpoints, and Composition: What Are They?" *Anne Bogart: Viewpoints*, eds. Michael Bigelow Dixon and Joel A. Smith (Lyme, NH: Smith and Kraus, 1995) 25. Landau compares SITI's process to the separate tracks in a movie; although the sound track and visual track work together, they can be taken apart and reassembled in a variety of combinations with different effects.

47. Marcus 221.

48. Edward P.J. Corbett, "The Rhetoric of the Open Hand and the Rhetoric of the Closed Fist," *CCC* 20.5 (Dec. 1969): 288.

49. Anne Bogart, qtd. in Weitz 14.

50. Burt 197.

51. Although in Woolf's *A Room of One's Own* it is clear that Woolf is specifically urging women to write books, it is less clear in the play whether Lauren/Woolf's statement is directed only to the women in the audience or to everyone.

52. In Woolf's essay, this line refers to "the collaboration ... in the mind between the woman and the man" that is required "if the writer is communicating his experience with perfect fullness" (104). The placement of the line in the play suggests that reading and thinking and conversing will lead us to this "peace" (Clarke 18).

53. Qtd. in Connors 3.

IV

Modern Drama

Deconstructing (A Streetcar Named) Desire
Gender Re-citation in Belle Reprieve

Deborah R. Geis

This essay begins with three intertextual moments of citing/"sighting" Tennessee Williams's *A Streetcar Named Desire*. The first, which closes the main narrative portion of Margaret Atwood's 1985 novel *A Handmaid's Tale*, has Offred, the handmaid, offering the following words as she is delivered to an unknown destiny: "I have given myself over into the hands of strangers, because it can't be helped."[1] In Atwood's novel, Offred's fate runs parallel to that of Moira, the lesbian character. Guilty of what the dystopian regime of Gilead calls "gender treachery," Moira is captured and forced to work at a whorehouse called Jezebel's, where the women can have sex with one another as long as they service men, so that they, too, are perpetually in strangers' hands — or at least until they, like Blanche in *Streetcar*, are driven over the edge and banished from the narrative.

The second, Rosalyn Drexler's 1984 play *Lobby*, is a sequel to *Streetcar* that finds Blanche taking up residence in the Chelsea Hotel with Oscar Wilde as her neighbor and closest confidant. Drexler's Blanche has forsaken the pretensions toward elegance, the histrionics of her past, though she seems to admire these qualities in the equally battle-scarred Oscar. She tells him, "I want to inflate. I want to float above the parade. To be the parade."[2] At the point that we see her, after her release from the mental institution, her greatest struggle is to reconcile with and forgive Stella, her sister. While Oscar ends up in the ER at St. Vincent's, Blanche has a certain triumph in allowing a derelict painter to do her portrait as she narrates, for the first time, the story of her body.

In the third, Tony Kushner's 1993–94 epic play *Angels in America*, bits from *Streetcar* (and other texts) whiz through the air, tempered by the awareness that an AIDS–dominated world affects even the potential for camp inspiration. Belize in Part One, *Millennium Approaches*, scrutinizes Prior in the

Peggy Shaw and Lois Weaver in *Belle Reprieve*, 1990. Photographer: Sheila Burnett.

hospital, telling him, "Stella for star. Let me see. You look like shit, why yes indeed, comme la merde."³ And when an even more ill Prior in Part Two, *Perestroika*, tells Hannah, the sensible Mormon who has brought him to the emergency room, "I have always depended on the kindness of strangers," she replies, "Well that's a stupid thing to do."⁴

The mid–1980s through the mid–1990s, which marked the earliest peak of the AIDS crisis as well as some of the most pivotal dramatic re-interrogations of canonical dramatic texts through the relatively new languages of feminist theory and queer theory, proved to be a fascinating time indeed for invocations of *A Streetcar Named Desire*. Even "straight" revivals of the same period (on Broadway with Jessica Lange and in a TV film with Ann-Margret) called more sympathetic attention to the sexuality of Blanche and other characters. What is striking to me is not simply how often Williams's play (and the subsequent Elia Kazan film) of *A Streetcar Named Desire* has been recycled, so that it has taken on the status of a cultural artifact, but also how deeply these re-citings of Williams's text are caught up in issues of gender and sexuality, as well as issues of performance and the performative. Of queerness and the attachment to cultural objects, Eve Sedgwick writes in *Tendencies*, "We needed for there to be sites where the meanings didn't line up tidily with each other, and we learned to invest those sites with fascination and love."⁵ Perhaps some of the "fascination" of *Streetcar* is the number of these sites—masculinity, femininity, madness, desire—where these slippages of meanings, what Sedgwick would term excesses, tend to occur: where the lines don't fall neatly into place. The trajectory of desire supposedly ends, as Blanche knows, in death (a trope that takes on new significance in the age of AIDS), even though she tells Mitch that the "opposite [of death] is desire": but do the revisited texts extend this trajectory?⁶ Do they make it a circular one? Or do they reject it altogether? And what of the audience, the "desiring bodies"—those strangers upon whose kindness the performers depend, even when that's a "stupid thing to do"?

These, I think, are some of the questions taken up by an explicitly queer, decidedly deconstructive re-vision of *Streetcar* that is my fourth intertext and the focus of this discussion, Bloolips' and Split Britches' collaborative play entitled *Belle Reprieve*. Split Britches was founded in 1980 by New York City performance artists Lois Weaver, Peggy Shaw, and Deb Margolin. Their name, which is taken from a kind of underwear worn by Weaver's ancestors in the Blue Ridge Mountains in Virginia, puns on the garment (which allowed women to stand up and pee when they worked in the fields) and of course on the idea of laughter. They say, "It's a good metaphor for our work: independent and personal bordering on the private ... [and] funny." Their plays, which aim to use and subvert popular culture, "depend on the surprise of transformation rather than the logic of conventional narrative."⁷ Bloolips was a London–based troupe composed mostly of gay male actors; they were known for their highly campy performances and hilarious costumes. In their productions, such as *Lust in*

Space (1981) and *Get-Hur* (1993), they used gender-bending to create critiques of politics and consumerism.[8] Clearly, the two groups — one American and lesbian–identified, the other British and gay–identified, would find *Streetcar* to be a wonderful point of departure for working together.

First presented at London's Drill Hall in January 1991 and then a month later at LaMama in New York, *Belle Reprieve* was co-written and performed by Bette Bourne and Paul Shaw of Bloolips, and Peggy Shaw (no relation, as far as I know) and Lois Weaver of Split Britches. By altering and reversing the gender roles in *Streetcar* (Blanche is played by Bette Bourne as "a man in a dress"; Stanley is played by Peggy Shaw as "a butch lesbian"; Mitch is played by Paul Shaw as "a fairy disguised as a man"; and Stella by Lois Weaver as "a woman disguised as a woman," this theatrical piece creates a Brechtian commentary on the sexual roles and games in Williams's text.[9] *Belle Reprieve*'s intertexts (which include the film version of *Streetcar*), its moments of vaudeville, and the characters' own self-conscious attention to theatricality extend the gendered role-playing into a deconstruction of dramatic role-playing itself. In other words, by showing a constant awareness that characters like Blanche are *performing*, the piece also reminds us of the connections between the theatrical and the everyday "roles" that all of us play. Moreover, we are never really allowed to forget that we are watching not just a drama, but a drama that depends openly on its famous earlier interpretations. Like Heiner Müller's *Hamletmachine* (1978) or like many of Charles Ludlam's works for the Ridiculous Theater (*Big Hotel* (1967), *Bluebeard* (1970), etc.), *Belle Reprieve*'s response to the past, to its theatrical antecedents, is a complex one. Ultimately, the work is less of a parody or an adaptation of *Streetcar* than it is a postmodern refashioning and a "queering" of a play that is already, as C.W.E. Bigsby puts it, about "a culture in a state of crisis, its certainties dislocating, its myths collapsing."[10]

Throughout *Belle Reprieve*, the characters/performers comment on the relationships between the roles of gender and sexuality they play (both in this piece and in "real life"), and the gender/sexuality of Williams's characters. Williams hints throughout *Streetcar*, for instance, at Stella's sensuality: the morning after the "poker night" fight (and tempestuous sexual reconciliation) with Stanley, we are told that as she lies on the bed with a comic book in her hand, "[h]er eyes and lips have that almost narcotized tranquility that is [on] the faces of Eastern idols."[11] The writers of *Belle Reprieve* go one step further and play with the image of Stella's sexual drive as overdetermined and narcissistic. In her opening speech — directed partially at herself, partially at the audience — she asks:

> Is there something you want? What can I do for you? Do you know who I am, what I feel, how I think? You want my body. My soul, my food, my bed, my skin, my hands? You want to touch me, hold me, lick me, smell me, eat me, have me? You think you need a little more time to decide? Well, you've got a little over an hour to have your fill [5].

As the object of Stanley's desire, Stella here has embraced (and refigured) her own role as commodity; moreover, her words call attention to the audience's status as consumers, as hungry to possess the performer, to get their "fill" of her—at least until the (performance) time is up. As if she were aware of Williams's stage directions, *Belle Reprieve*'s Stella explains to Mitch, "Look, I'm supposed to wander around in a state of narcotized sexuality. That's my part" (6). Blanche's visit brings out Stella's quasi-incestuous revelations of her attraction to her sister, as the two don matching cheerleaders' outfits and sing about exploring one another's bodies "under the covers" (14). But we also see the "colored lights" of *Streetcar* enacted in the moments of passion between Stella and Stanley (doubled in Brechtian fashion by the awareness of many audience members in the original performance that Lois Weaver [Stella] and Peggy Shaw [Stanley] were real-life lovers)—particularly when Stella pulls off Stanley's ripped T-shirt as Stanley carries her offstage, thus evoking Marlon Brando's Stanley in the very moment that the audience's attention is called to Peggy Shaw's body. As Elin Diamond puts it, in an often-cited essay on Brechtianism and feminism that has, I think, interesting applications for discussions of queer theater as well, "Brechtian theory imagines a polyvalence to the body's representation, for the performer's body is also historicized, loaded with its own history and that of the character, and these histories ruffle the smooth edges of representation."[12]

In a monologue that Split Britches member Deb Margolin wrote for the play, Stella talks to Cassandra, the seer, asking her for advice on love, and poses and sings "Running Wild" like Marilyn Monroe, after she says to the imaginary Cassandra, "Come sweet prophetess, what is going to happen? Tell me, I'm nailed to this story. Cut me down. I'm in here. Can't you see me?" (22). In this sense, Stella is portrayed as a woman who is entrapped in the limited "part" that has been written for her, yet who makes the best of it by immersing herself in her own desires. She tells Stanley, "I know that your tension is sexual, and it's a desire I share in, but not for your pleasure, for my own" (24). Her words mock Williams's image of Stella as a woman who is willing to sacrifice everything for Stanley's needs (here, even when Blanche is trying to argue Stella out of her attraction to Stanley ["I think he's a fag," she says (27)], Stella is more interested in the taste of the Coke she is drinking, which she conflates with her orgasmic satisfaction: "Pure sugar, liquid sex" [27]). Elizabeth Grosz, in an important essay entitled "Refiguring Lesbian Desire," argues that the traditional psychoanalytic interpretation of desire as based on Freudian and Lacanian "lack" should be replaced with an account of lesbian desire that is full, productive, predicated on presences rather than absences— more, she says, like Gilles Deleuze's characterization of "practices and action" than the Freudian view that links the female with objects, receptacles, emptinesses. It is, in other words, a model based on seeing desire as "positive and productive."[13] *Belle Reprieve*'s Stella is caught between her role as desired object (thus her evocation of Marilyn Monroe), and desiring subject; whereas Williams implies that the characters in *Streetcar* are motivated by desire, by lack — again, the end (or satisfaction) of which is death — the characters in *Belle Reprieve* parody and multiply their desires, making them, in Grosz's terms, "energies, excitations [and] impulses."[14]

It is difficult not to keep Allan — Blanche's first lover in *Streetcar*, who killed himself after Blanche discovered his homosexuality — in mind as we see Mitch in *Belle Reprieve* flirt alternately with Blanche (the drag queen) and with the very butch Stanley. If Mitch, portrayed as a "mama's boy" in Williams's play, is implicitly another Allan, then *Belle Reprieve*'s Mitch is correspondingly only part of the way out of the closet. After he delivers a long speech describing (in intricate detail) a vision of a man with "large bedroom eyes" on a blue feathered throne (16), he engages in a frenzied dialogue of erotic machismo with Stanley (which also evokes some of the homoeroticism of Williams's "poker night" scene). When Mitch gets carried away after he and Stanley arm wrestle — "Bite me! Bite me! Suck on me..." (17) — he has to pretend he is talking about mosquitoes, but the sequence culminates in Stanley's song, "I'm a Man" ("spelled M...A...N" [19]). Mitch woos Blanche by appearing to her above the bathtub, wearing a fairy costume and playing the ukulele. Later, in another one of the piece's tableaulike monologues (parallel, perhaps, to Blanche's confession scene with Mitch, but directed here to the audience) he says:

> I think it all started to go wrong when I wasn't allowed to be a boy scout. There were more important things to be done. Vacuuming, clearing up at home, putting the garbage out.... Then one day I fell in love with a beautiful young man. He came like a messenger from another world bearing a message of simple physical desire. But it was already too late, for me everything about the body was bound up with pain and boredom. I even used to eat fast because I found it so boring. Soon the boy left.... Then I was alone. At night I would lie awake on my bed, and imagine I could hear things [33].

The newsboy in *Streetcar*, referred to by Blanche as the "young man," here becomes the "messenger" of desire for Mitch instead — but again, the invitation is not reciprocated. If Mitch in *Streetcar* is self-conscious about his body (he tells Blanche that he's ashamed of the way he perspires, and that he's afraid his "heavy build" makes him look clumsy)[15], then Mitch in *Belle Reprieve* is, like Stella, both similar to his character in Williams's text and the opposite: he is slight rather than heavy, "bored" with his body, but the effect is to underscore the loneliness and marginalization that both Mitches feel. Williams's Mitch looks on helplessly from the sidelines at the end of *Streetcar* as Blanche is carted off to the asylum — but in *Belle Reprieve* Mitch and Stella join one another in singing that they're not quite the "pushovers" that Williams's text would make them out to be (36).

In *Streetcar*, when Blanche and Mitch return from their date at the amusement park on Lake Pontchartrain (notably bearing, the stage directions say: "a plaster statuette of Mae West"[16]), Blanche remarks to Mitch, "I don't think I've ever tried so hard to be gay and made such a dismal mess of it." She adds, echoing the language of the carnival they have just attended, "I get ten points for trying!"[17] Much, of course, has already been made of the original Blanche as a "coded" gay character. John Clum calls her "in many ways the quintessential gay character in American closet drama"; In a play "without a living homosexual character or overt gay theme," Blanche represents Williams's "protection of his homosexual subtext by hiding it within the actions of a heterosexual female character."[18] David Savran points out, on the other hand, that original impulses to see Blanche as "only" a "female impersonator" have risked creating what he sees as reductive or homophobic interpretations of the play, though not necessarily so.[19] More recently, Anne Fleche has suggested that it might be more useful to see Blanche's character as an example of "the performative, constrained enactment of gender"; Blanche, Fleche argues, "can be viewed as the representation of a woman who finally doesn't pass as a subject, because she does her gender incorrectly, and because her hyperbolic theatricality challenges the masculine/feminine heterosexual codes that enable and constrain gender performativity."[20] That is, Blanche's rather overdetermined and contrary ways of behaving (her conflicted "Southern Belle" hyperfemininity and her taboo nymphomania) combines with her inherently melodramatic/theatrical nature to make it seem that her performance of proper/appropriate/expected womanliness has been thrown off-kilter.

Blanche's identity in *Belle Reprieve* is triply (or perhaps quadruply) embedded: "she" is a woman played by a man who imagines herself not just as Williams's Blanche DuBois, but as Vivien Leigh (like Bette Bourne, a Brit) playing the role of Blanche in Kazan's movie. These multiply visible "texts" of Blanche depend in part on being hyperbolic: just as the "original" Blanche embodies her sexuality through the near-caricatured imagery of the Southern Belle, *Belle Reprieve*'s Blanche has an identity composed of surfaces, of costumes, of performances. When Stanley says that he is going to look through the contents of her trunk to determine who she is, she tells the audience, "And so it was that I set out to prove to the world that I was indeed myself." Stella says, "She threw herself at the feet of an unforgiving world to prove her identity," and Mitch adds, "The answer was somewhere in that trunk" (9). In other words, in a postmodern theatrical universe, "Blanche" is inseparable from the costumes, the odds and ends, the fragments that make up the performance of her "identity." Williams's Blanche, herself, is a consummate actress and role-player; Bigsby, among other critics, has characterized her as "construct[ing] her own drama, costuming herself with care, arranging the set, enacting a series of roles, developing her own scenario."[21] And if Bette Bourne as Blanche in drag is a comment on what Clum and others would see as the original "drag act" of Williams's Blanche, it is worth keeping in mind Judith Butler's argument in *Bodies That Matter* that drag is predicated in part on an awareness of the performance of difference: "What is 'performed' in drag is, of course, the sign of gender, a sign that is not the same as the body it figures, but that cannot be read without it."[22] In *Belle Reprieve*, Blanche describes herself as feeling like "an old hotel. Beautiful bits of dereliction in need of massive renovation" (28). As a "renovation" of the text of *Streetcar*, *Belle Reprieve* itself reassembles the fragments of Blanche into what are still fragments, but ones that allow us to read them (and hence her) differently.

As will be discussed shortly, Stanley's "date with Blanche from the beginning" goes ultimately in a different direction than in Williams's play. As in the original, he argues that Blanche is more like him than she would care to admit, but here he also marks their shared difference for the audience:

> We're in this together, me and you. We've known that from the start. We're the extremes, the stereotypes. We are as far as we can go. We have no choice, me and you. We've tried it all, haven't we? We've rejected ourselves, not trusted ourselves, mirrored ourselves, and we always come back to ourselves. We're the warriors [35].

His words reflect Michel Foucault's sense that power and desire are "linked in a more complex and primary way than through the interplay of a primitive, natural, and living energy welling up from below, and a higher order seeking to stand in its way."[23] To Stanley, in other words, there is a power that comes *from* primitivism, desire, and difference. In Blanche's mind, though, a "higher order" indeed does stand in opposition to, and exerts power over, the animal quality of desire. This is the binarism that Blanche in *Streetcar* attempts to convince Stella exists when she says that he's an "animal" and that we've advanced since the time of the "brute."[24] Blanche says this, no doubt, in her effort to ward off the acknowledgment of her own sexuality, her own desiring body. If Williams's Blanche is rejected by society because her sexual drive is incommensurate with her status both as a woman and as a widow/"spinster," though, the sexuality of *Belle Reprieve*'s Blanche has been affected by the literal linking of sex and death in the AIDS generation. Her song "Beautiful Dream" transforms the first Blanche's pleasure in bathing into a lament for the disappearance of the steam baths in the age of AIDS:

> Thought we'd party 'til the end of time
> But it's over, seems so long ago now
> Down the long parade, see them slowly fade
> As they all leave one by one
> Running out of steam, now the beautiful dream
> Has gone [29].

"I'll always choose applause over death" (29), she adds, though—and Blanche's role-playing as Blanche and as drag queen is laced, continually, with her comments on her desire, yet inability, to resemble Vivien Leigh, for when she hears that music that repeats itself inside her head, she sees "a dark burgundy curtain opening on the stage, and there we are, just me and Vivien" (28). Her constant commentary on her role reflects *Belle Reprieve*'s more general interweaving of its critique of *Streetcar*'s gender roles with the queer appropriation of Brechtian metadrama. The set and props, which consist mostly of exaggerations of selected elements from the set Williams envisioned (at one point, the actors tap dance on stage costumed as giant paper lanterns), underscore the relationship between the theatrical and historical "past" of *Streetcar* and the deconstructive "present" of *Belle Reprieve*. Indeed, in the grand tradition of camp and/or of Ludlam's Ridiculous theater, the outright tackiness of the many slapstick and vaudeville numbers throughout the piece (even including a pie-in-the-face routine) provides the pleasure of acknowledging artifice at the same time that it reminds the spectators of how artifice is clearly a part of Williams's play itself.

By the time the rape scene in *Belle Reprieve* transpires, Blanche — who has just complained that she wants to be in a "real play" ("This is the most confusing show I've ever been in," she says [33]) — tries to resist the apparent inevitability of succumbing to what Williams has dictated (and perhaps what the audience expects) for her character: when Stanley says, "If you want to play a woman, the woman in this play gets raped and goes crazy in the end," she responds, "I don't want to get raped and go crazy, I just wanted to wear a nice frock, and look at the shit they've given me!" (35).

Blanche's resistance is part of the play's larger resistance to narrative closure; Stella taunts the audience, asking, "Did you figure it out yet? Who's who, what's what, who gets what, where the toaster is plugged in? Did you get what you wanted?" (36). The spectators' desires are, like those of the characters, mocked, mimicked, brought to the surface, and rendered both familiar and strange. Blanche's closing words in *Streetcar* form the basis of her opening words in *Belle Reprieve*: she says, from inside of the box she climbs out of at the beginning, "I've always depended on the strangeness of strangers" (6). "Strange" in this case is also a mock-synonym for "queer," but as I remarked in my own opening, the strangers are also the spectators, who may or may not (in these terms) be "strange." In the end, the actors sing, in a vaudevillian encore, "I am madly in love with my art, I love to play my part" (37). The actors/characters of *Belle Reprieve* have managed to show the connections between desire and performance that were always there in *Streetcar*, but here are made wildly, parodically, sensually, and madly evident.

Notes

1. Margaret Atwood, *The Handmaid's Tale* (New York: Fawcett Crest, 1985) 378.
2. Rosalyn Drexler, *Lobby, Transients Welcome* (New York: Broadway Play Publishing, 1984) 31.

3. Tony Kushner, *Angels in America, Part One: Millennium Approaches* (New York: TCG, 1993) 59.
4. Kushner, *Angels in America, Part Two: Perestroika* (New York: TCG, 1994) 141.
5. Eve Kosofsky Sedgwick, *Tendencies* (Durham: Duke University Press, 1993) 3.
6. Tennessee Williams, *A Streetcar Named Desire* (New York: New American Library, 1947) 120.
7. "Split Britches," <http://www.splitbritches.com>, 16 October 2007.
8. "Bloolips," <http://www.nyu.edu/classes/jeffreys/gayandlesbianperformance/sueellentrop/bloolips.html>, 16 October 2007.
9. Bette Bourne, Peggy Shaw, Paul Shaw, and Lois Weaver, *Belle Reprieve*, in Terry Helbing, ed. *Gay and Lesbian Plays Today* (Portsmouth, NH: Heinemann, 1993) 4. Additional references in the text.
10. C.W.E. Bigsby, *A Critical Introduction to Twentieth Century American Drama, Volume Two: Williams, Miller, Albee* (Cambridge: Cambridge University Press, 1984) 16.
11. Williams 62.
12. Elin Diamond, "Brechtian Theory/Feminist Theory: Toward a Gestic Feminist Criticism," *The Drama Review* 32 (Spring 1988): 89.
13. Elizabeth Grosz, "Refiguring Lesbian Desire," in Laura Doan, ed., *The Lesbian Postmodern* (New York: Columbia University Press, 1994) 75.
14. Ibid., 78.
15. Williams 88.
16. Ibid., 85.
17. Ibid.
18. John Clum, *Acting Gay: Male Homosexuality in Modern Drama*, revised ed. (New York: Columbia University Press, 1994) 150–51.
19. David Savran, *Communists, Cowboys, and Queers: The Politics of Masculinity in the Work of Arthur Miller and Tennessee Williams* (Minnesota and London: University of Minnesota Press, 1992) 115.
20. Anne Fleche, "When a Door is a Jar, or Out in the Theatre: Tennessee Williams and Queer Space," *Theatre Journal* 47 (May 1995): 266.
21. Bigsby 61.
22. Judith Butler, *Bodies That Matter* (New York and London: Routledge, 1993) 237.
23. Michel Foucault, *The History of Sexuality, Volume One: An Introduction*, trans. Robert Hurley (New York: Vintage, 1980) 81.
24. Williams 72.

Nora's Journey Through a Century of Feminisms to the Postmodern Stage of *Mabou Mines DollHouse*

Amy S. Green

In the century and a quarter since Nora's slam first reverberated across Europe and abroad, entirely too much ink has been spilled debating whether or not Ibsen intended *A Doll House* to be a feminist play. Whatever his intention, the modern feminist theater debuted with his script. Its production history as a touchstone for women's rights movements in far-flung corners of the world speaks for itself. A wide range of productions and adaptations attest to the play's enduring power as a challenge to patriarchy and other authoritarian systems. Perhaps more important than any labels generations of pundits have applied to or denied the play is the fact that actors, directors, and audiences return to and adapt the script again and again, using it as a pretext to interrogate gender and power across time and place, and in vastly different social and cultural situations.

Ibsen's Feminism

We can begin to dispel any lingering doubts about *A Doll House*'s feminist pedigree by looking at its direct inspiration. Laura Peterson Kieler was one of Ibsen's protégés. In 1878, her husband threw her out, took custody of their children, and had her committed to an insane asylum when he found out she'd forged a note to fund a life-saving trip for him to a warmer climate. Only months earlier, Ibsen had advised a desperate Kieler to "put everything in her husband's hands," assuming, as Nora does, that the man would "bear" the burden of his wife's error.[1] The shocking outcome of the situation led the feminist-leaning playwright to create the first iconic feminist figure in modern

Torvald (performed by Mark Povinelli) and Nora (performed by Maude Mitchell) in *Mabou Mines DollHouse*, St. Ann's Warehouse, Brooklyn, New York, 2003. Courtesy of Mabou Mines. Photographer: Nancy Santos.

drama. Like her rhyming namesake, Nora is trapped in a female predicament. She is defined and delimited by her roles as daughter, wife, and mother. Her climactic decision to leave those roles behind is a choice only a woman can make. Her determination to become a whole person and take an equal place in society is a feminist goal. Hers is a feminist drama.

Fortunately, recent scholars have deftly deflected decades of anti-feminist claims against the play. Such critics as Joan Templeton, Alisa Solomon, Toril Moi, Elaine Hoffman Baruch, and Gail Finney launch a three-pronged attack. First, they debunk the claim that Ibsen's dramatic purpose and imagination transcended social problems. "Critics who deny that *A Doll House* is a feminist play often present their work as part of a corrective effort to rescue Ibsen from an erroneous reputation as a writer of thesis plays," Templeton writes. These same critics wouldn't dream of allowing anyone to think the great Ibsen had "stoop[ed] to 'issues.'"[2] Ibsen's female protagonists are "whisked into metaphoric abstraction" rather than taken as women, explains Solomon, because to celebrate their trials and triumphs as particular to the female half of the human race "is to verge on a feminist reading, and that, these critics contend, is the social concern from which Ibsen requires deliverance most urgently of all."[3]

The anti-feminists base their claim on Ibsen's oft-quoted, late-life remarks to the Women's Rights League that he refused "the honor of having consciously worked for the women's rights movement" because his objective had been to provide "the description of humanity." Yes, Ibsen's larger project was the "description of humanity," and the breadth and variety of his works about the quest for individual freedom attests to his life-long pursuit of that project. But his opus includes several works that clearly focus on the impediments to full human status for women. Humanism and feminism are not mutually exclusive. Nora's trajectory from puppet of patriarchy to agent of her own destiny provides a clear indication that *A Doll House* is founded on humanist ethics. That Ibsen depicts the men as subjected in their own way to the same patriarchal constraints is further argument that he is concerned for the rights of all individuals to be free to develop their potential.

But *A Doll House* is not equally about Nora and Torvald. She is the protagonist. She is the doll. Until her famous exit, her options are subordinate to her husband's will and to a legal system that denies her civic and financial autonomy on the grounds that she is a woman. Nora's humanity is squelched by this system of male privilege. Spectators ride the wave of her increasing desperation over the course of the plot, while her husband remains oblivious to his role in their troubles. His culpability dawns on him only in the final moments of the play. True, Ibsen shows us that Torvald is under pressure to maintain an unrealistic masculine ideal, but he has the power to choose how and when to display his plumage. Nora is subject to his often callous, even cruel, mandates.[4] She can only express her individuality and act upon her own moral choices under cover. The play puts far greater emphasis on the imbalance and unfairness of Nora's condition compared to that of her husband and the other men in the play than it does on the men's burdens of strength and responsibility. Ibsen did not abandon his life-long project of describing humanity when he depicted Nora's plight. He narrowed his beam of illumination on the ways that women in particular are prevented from becoming fully human.

Next, the defenders of Ibsen's feminist agenda refute the tautology that Nora is not a feminist exemplar because she is not really a woman. Unwilling to face the blatant unfairness of Nora's situation or their complicity in it, conservative critics reject her abrupt turnaround as implausible. The dependent child-woman of Acts One and Two could not possibly evolve instantaneously into the intelligent, independent-thinking adult of the final scene. (If only they'd been able to see Claire Bloom's 1973 Nora, whose every glance and gesture was calculated to maintain peace and stability in her home by keeping up her role as Torvald's plaything.) Besides, the critics chided, no real, live woman would leave her children. Nora's "hysterical," unnatural action disqualifies her to represent "normal" womanhood.[5] She is believable, therefore, neither as a woman nor as a character, and the play is dismissed.

On the third front, Ibsen's postmodern defenders conclude that one of the main reasons the play's detractors are so irritated with Nora's decision to leave her family is that it deliberately thwarts the dramaturgical symmetry of the well-made play and its audience's desire for a happy ending. "It makes sense that those who dismiss the obvious critique of women's subjugation in [Ibsen's] plays are the same critics who denigrate their dramatic style," writes Solomon.[6] Nora's exit disrupts the patriarchal uber-narrative in which women exist only as helpmates and mothers and in which a young wife abandoning these roles is unthinkable. At the same time, her departure denies the tidy ending audiences were primed to expect from a well-made play. Until the penultimate scene, Nora is invested in her fantasy of female sacrifice and male rescue, a mainstay of nineteenth century melodrama (and beyond). Just as she hopes for the "wonderful thing" to happen, that Torvald would honor her sacrifice and "bear the burden" of any consequences, the melodramatic conceit that good will triumph over evil demands that the fantasy be fulfilled. Ibsen follows form when he sets us up to expect Torvald's initial fury over Nora's illicit debt. In a typical period melodrama, that would be the climactic scene of the play. The denouement would be the scene of reconciliation in which either the good husband steps in to save his grateful, repentant wife or another hero swoops in to save her from her less-than-heroic mate.

In *A Doll House*, the couple's salvation comes via the *deus ex machina* of Krogstad's letter returning the forged contract. Torvald's relief prompts immediate forgiveness. An audience schooled in and satisfied with the standard melodramatic ending would want Nora to embrace her husband's pardon. Their reconciliation would allow good — in the guise of Nora's sacrifice and Torvald's generosity—to triumph over the evil of Krogstad's threats and a legal system that is emotionally blind.

Of course Ibsen withholds that happy ending. Torvald's offer is too little too late. Nora has seen through his bluster. As Elaine Hoffman Baruch points out, it is "his failure to live up to the chivalric ideal" that prompts Nora's change of heart. "It is disillusionment with Torvald that provides the soil out of which Nora's feminism grows."[7] Solomon sees Ibsen's act of dramaturgical sabotage as an inherently feminist, "implosive critique of dramatic form."[8] The structure of the well-made play rests on specific assumptions of what is right or wrong, good or evil, desirable or repugnant. Ibsen undermines those assumptions when he ends the play with a bold move that he knew most of his audience would find immoral if not impossible. Solomon reminds us that Brian Johnston "insists that the rejection of Ibsen may have seemed like a revulsion toward his dangerous topics, but was really 'the condition of vertigo' instilled by a dramatic style" that pulled the safety net from under its audience's willing suspension of disbelief.[9] Ibsen takes us into Nora's perils and drops us into her abyss. Critics who denigrate the ending of *A Doll House* betray their own lack of imagination and analytical acumen. Instead of trying to answer Goethe's all-important first question in responding to a work of art, "What is the artist trying to do?" they arrogantly underestimate Ibsen's masterful melding of form and content.

So, what was Ibsen trying to do? My reading of the play, in dialogue with pro-feminist Ibsen critics, is that Ibsen dramatizes gender as social performance. He exposes the flimsy construction of the stage upon which it is played, and demonstrates that both men and women are stifled within their strictly disparate roles. More than half a century before sociologist Erving Goffman articulated his theatrical analysis of social discourse and individual identity, Ibsen anticipated his theories. In *The Presentation of Self in Everyday Life* (1959) Goffman demonstrates that all human interactions are carefully calibrated enactments of social roles, tailored to the particular setting, action, cast of characters, and audiences involved in an attempt to elicit a particular response within a shared social framework. What we think of as self is a composite of behaviors that fulfill or resist socially prescribed identities.[10] Ibsen understood that even our most intimate behaviors and relationships are determined and delimited by forces much stronger and potentially more insidious than individual will.

Ibsen shows us that Nora plays her part consciously. Her performance of femininity is precise if not subtle. She "plays" her husband like a violin, to borrow a recent colloquialism. She pretends to be a squirrel; she crawls and crouches at Torvald's feet to get what she wants; she keeps her deviant behaviors out of his range of surveillance. She borrows money on the sly and eats her forbidden macaroons only when Torvald isn't looking. Dancing the tarantella, Nora literally spins around in circles to distract him from learning of her transgressions. Her playacting is effective, but at a terrible cost.

Nora's "sudden" conversion in the final scene is no surprise. Hoffman Baruch argues: "It becomes doubly credible when we realize that her so-called femininity was for much her of life largely an act."[11] By the end of the play, she can no longer sustain the charade. She must remove the wife/mother mask to seek an authentic face. Like an exhausted actor at the end of a strenuous performance, Nora walks off the stage of her marriage, takes off her costume, and stares at herself in the dressing room mirror, wondering who remains when the accoutrements of character are gone, and where can the actor go from here. The ambiguity of Nora's future is crucial. Her new part has not been written. For the first time, she faces the thrilling but daunting prospect of inventing her own script.

Ibsen intentionally left Nora's choices wide open after she closed the door. The disorientation that Nora's unfinished business instilled in its early audiences has inspired receptive women and men ever since to challenge the illusions on which her life was built and to imagine and re-imagine new ways to define themselves and relate to one another as gendered beings. According to the authors of an intercultural production history, "By imaginatively inhabiting the role of Nora, women on the cusp of new social identities were able to explore possible futures and the consequences of possible actions."[12] Nora's business remains unfinished, and the play continues to serve as a touchstone for women's rights and human rights all over the world. As we will see, *A Doll House* has been adapted and re-written many times as we confront new social and political paradigms that force us to question our roles as women, as men, and as citizens of a changing world.

Following a brief survey of culturally diverse adaptations that have paved the way for postmodern experimental productions, this chapter will focus primarily on a single, radical staging that exploits Ibsen's implicit theatricality, his meeting of form and content, the expectations of his audience and ours, and the potential-filled empty space of Nora's future. Director Lee Breuer collaborated closely with actor/dramaturg Maude Mitchell, who plays Nora. They found fertile ground for *Mabou Mines DollHouse* precisely in the tensions between and among the overt and implicit theatrical elements in the play and its groundbreaking iconic status in dramatic literature and in the women's movement. Theirs is a playful postmodern deconstruction of both gender as performance in the Helmer marriage and of Ibsen's use and defiance of melodrama and the well-made play. Whereas Ibsen lured his audience with surface realism that barely contained his own theatricalist agenda, Breuer and company pop the lid off the pressure cooker and release the play's latent theatricality.

Breuer's most daring directorial gesture, the one for which the production became notorious, was casting only tall women and short-statured men. To underscore the ironies in the imbalance of power and oppression on both sides of the marital aisle, the women in the cast are costumed to appear at least six feet tall, while none of the male actors is taller than four foot eleven. Giant Nora, tiny Torvald, and the other over- and under-sized characters deliver tour de force, over-the-top performances of their strict gender roles within a mise-en-scène animated by a live piano score, flashing strobe lights, and emphatic double takes. Mabou Mines makes no pretense about the figurative masks at work in Ibsen's drama. They put them on and take them off the actors, the dramaturgy, and the theatrical conceit. The effect is Brechtian. The spectator is alternately drawn into the characters' emotions and dilemmas and pushed back to a critical distance from which we can see the artifice of gender in theatrical and everyday performance.

Twentieth-Century Adaptations of A Doll House

Internationally, *A Doll House* has been appropriated to advocate for various women's and political causes in places like Republican China and the Islamic Republic of Iran. In their book *Women's Intercultural Performance*, Julie Holledge and Joanne Tompkins argue that intercultural translations of "women-centered narratives" invite "an interactive engagement with gendered subjects in their new audiences" and assume "a symbolic importance in wider political struggles." In particular, Nora's search for "subjective freedom" in the form of social, legal, and economic autonomy invites her intercultural interpreters and spectators to consider "possible identities that are tested out by spectators during the performance, either through analysis and observation, or directly through an empathic relationship" to the character on the stage. To fully appreciate just what is transmitted or transmuted in the shift from culture to culture, Holledge and Tompkins caution us to be "aware of the universalizing tendencies in western feminism and seek to avoid automatic assumptions concerning the meanings these narratives hold in their new contexts." We must be especially careful not to apply western standards of "progress" to non-western adaptations. Such a myopic view, they caution, suggests that "the 'west' inhabits the present, while the 'rest' are locked in the past."[13]

Holledge and Thompkins discuss a 1935 Chinese adaptation as a case in point. In the early decades of the twentieth century, emerging leftist periodicals debated the status of Chinese women. The journal *New Woman* promised to import and interpret "the 'latest American and European literature'" that dealt with women and feminism. Western humanist feminism that advocated for women's rights as individuals was popular in the 1920s and early 1930s but fell out of favor as the Chinese began to doubt "whether capitalism could 'lead human beings to attain their true freedom.'" With the rise of competing socialist and communist ideas came a desire to "reconcile women's emancipation with traditional values of motherhood, sacrifice, loyalty, and honour." In 1934, a young Communist activist was released from prison and turned up on the Shanghai theater scene. Jiang Qing would later be known to the world as Madame Mao, but in 1935 she was cast as Nora in a production that drew so much attention that it set off "The Year of Nora" in the city. Stanislavskian director Zhang Min strove to present western plays "in ways that maximized their positive influence on Chinese society." In Nora, Jiang Qing claimed that "she had discovered the woman–rebel," a revolutionary icon that attracted and enthralled her audience. In this incarnation "the text became a displacement for a local political struggle, but this time the model from the west was presented as outmoded." At this time "the open expression of pro-communist sentiments" was forbidden, so the production functioned as allegory. Jiang Qing's rebel Nora became "a symbol of their own revolutionary thinking," a thinly veiled Communist who walks out of her retrograde home to help construct a new, egalitarian society.[14]

In Iran, a literally veiled Nora was the subject of a 1994 film, *Sara*, written and directed by Dariush Mehrjui. As Holledge and Tompkins observe, the film looks at women's lives under the Islamic regime, where "discussions regarding the position and role of women are still framed through interpretations of the Qur'an."[15] Islamic scripture dictates discrete rights and responsibilities for women and men. Mehrjui purged the text of western ideas that would conflict with or offend Islamic sensibilities. Gone are the "notion that the law is man-made," all references to sex, and the tarantella. It is Hessam (Torvald) who dances in this sex-segregated film — with the other men at his promotion party, "while the women sit and watch." Sara, played by Niki Karimi, is seen "gently swaying to the music as a tear falls from her eye." Mehrjui is not interested in Sara's access to education or career, both crucial to Ibsen's "modernist subjectivity." According to Holledge and Tompkins, "It is not the gender division within the Islamic world that is problematised, rather it is the specific relationship between Hessam and Sara and their inability to reach equality within their different roles." However, Holledge and Tompkins detect at least one plea for women's rights in the fact that Sara takes her daughter with her when she goes (back to her father's house). They see this as a "challenge to Iranian child custody laws," that overwhelmingly privilege fathers. Furthermore, their analysis of the clothing in the film leads them to infer a deeper critique of the separate but equal basis of Islamic gender roles. Sara's traditional *hejab* severely restricts her movement, while Hessam wears western clothes, a symbol of his increasing clout as a result of the promotion. The difference between the ways their clothes facilitate or impede their lives "seems to suggest that women will never achieve equality while they are excluded from the secular world of Iranian modernity."[16]

The contemporary western audience — a not so distant relative of Ibsen's own in terms of middle-class mores, comforts, and aspirations — might dismiss Nora's near-total domestic dependence as a relic. Nora's original audiences saw in her a "new or 'modern' woman," a "representative of the middle class women who were agitating for financial independence, the vote, equality before the law, access to education, and a place in the workforce."[17] There may no longer be blatant legal impediments to those rights, but Elaine Hoffman Baruch cautions us not to fall under delusion that constructions of gender no longer oppress or that the play has nothing to tell us about the status of women today. The conflicted "claims of marriage and motherhood on one hand and those of the self, on the other, provide an irreconcilable conflict" both for Nora and the women who come later.[18] Who is more likely to be the victim of domestic abuse, whether verbal, emotional, physical, or financial? Whose bodies are subject to greater scrutiny and regulation? Nora's issues may now be expressed in less egregious inequalities, but they still loom large in our public and private lives. In fact, we may have merely traded one set of oppressions for another. So valid still is Ibsen's concern for the ways that gender expectations entrap and oppress men, women, and children that it is possible to imagine him cringing as we pat ourselves on the back for having made so much progress since Nora's day.

That said, Nora's modern, western audience may have a hard time relating her specific circumstances to their own lives, and postmodern directors and audiences may bristle at the confines of the well-made form. If theater artists and audiences are no longer roused by Nora's claim to human status, if her anthem seems dated, if we find Ibsen's first-wave feminism both strident and old hat, if women's studies has shifted to gender studies, what revisionist approaches to the text might reveal fresh insights into the legacy of middle-class gender oppression from Ibsen's time to our own?

In the last few decades, playwrights and directors have attempted to update the play to address contemporary perspectives on feminism and gender. They use a wide variety of approaches, from minimal edits and staging innovations to total deconstructions of the play. For example, in the mid–1980s, Emily Mann took a step toward reading the marriage as a double tragedy. In a pared down, less cluttered and more modern looking set, she moved the exit scene to the bedroom where a vulnerable Torvald sits forlornly on the bed. Mann wanted to divide the audience's empathy between both victims of patriarchy, wife and husband.[19] At one end of the spectrum of *A Doll House* adaptations are what Robert Brustein labeled "similes."[20] They are based on the premise that the new setting is enough like the original that it is possible to transpose the action from one to the other, implying similarities and differences without disrupting the veneer. This strategy can help to bridge the perception of a gulf between a dead playwright and his era and the world of a later audience, but its reach is limited to making the old play feel relevant. For example, Timothy Near directed *An American Doll's House* at the Alliance Theater in Atlanta in 1987. Near moved the action to a suburb in the American South in the 1950s. The cast was majority African American.[21] Bad-boy German director Thomas Ostermeier furthered the impulse to modernize the setting. In the production, brought to the Brooklyn Academy of Music in 2004, he moved the play to a spiffy high rise apartment and handed Nora a gun which she used to kill Torvald on her way out the door.

Playwright Rebecca Gilman wrote a new version of the play, set in a not-yet-gentrified Chicago neighborhood where Nora and "Terry" live with their children but aspire to a more upscale part of town. Her *Dollhouse* debuted at Chicago's Goodman Theater in 2005. Gilman shifts the blame for Nora's restless unhappiness from the authoritarian patriarchy that subsumes Ibsen's heroine to the updated couple's rampant consumerism. Nora sneaks fancy truffles and shops at Crate and Barrel and Pottery Barn. The kids must be driven to classes at My Gym. Trapped on a treadmill of material acquisition, Gilman's Nora is obsessed with clothes and furniture and the right schools for her children as means to achieve higher social status, but the pursuit ultimately leaves her empty and disillusioned. Her epiphany dawns with the realization that she can live without the brand names and designer accessories. Still, Gilman's despairing wife doesn't spend long on the other side of the door. She reenters after a "long pause," demands a thank you for having saved Terry's life, then waits for him to fetch the champagne glasses so they can toast to "new beginnings."[22] It's hard to predict whether they'll be tossing the Restoration Hardware catalog into the marble-mantled fireplace any time soon.[23]

At the other end of the spectrum are postmodern adaptations that deconstruct familiar works. These are more likely to force a radical reexamination of the original text; its theoretical, historical, and dramaturgical underpinnings; and our perceived notions about it, about ourselves, and about the theater. Neuroscientist-turned-theater-director Yelena Gluzman used *A Doll House* as the basis for an original deconstruction called *I'm So Sorry for Everything* at The Performing Garage in 2002. The "science experiment," as it was publicized, featured two Noras, both engulfed in "enormous bird-heads."[24] As the performance unfolded, more Noras arrived, including one who impersonates a dog. The Noras sign among themselves a subtext that betrays what they say to the other characters. Kristine is played by a man and sound technicians hummed "I've Been Workin' on the Railroad" while Torvald complained of Nora's profligate spending. Gluzman fractured the role and the plot, she says, to get beyond its oversimplified binaries — good woman or bad, stay or go, etc. "The text presents choices so clearly, and does not allow for the presence of choices it can't describe,"[25] she told an interviewer, who commented that "Gluzman's multiple Noras convey what it feels like for a woman to partition and maneuver her complex identity within a society that remains endemically sexist."[26]

Size Matters: A Graphic Critique of Gender in Mabou Mines DollHouse

Mabou Mines DollHouse begins as what Brustein calls a "metaphor" production because it concretizes images and intentions in the text.[27] Breuer's set is a miniature doll house. His Nora moves, talks, and dresses like a doll, albeit a rather tall one. The exaggerated height differential between the female and male actors is graphic evidence of the imbalances in their relationships and personalities. But the production moves beyond metaphor to a total deconstruction of the text, its cultural baggage, and the preconceptions the contemporary audience brings to its depiction of women and gender. Breuer fractures Ibsen's decorous veneer with exaggerated, stagy melodramatics, defying us not to reconsider what we think we know about Ibsen's classic. The production began in workshop in 2002, opened at St. Ann's performance space in Brooklyn Heights in 2003, and toured nationally and internationally through 2008. It was filmed for French television in the fall of 2007.

Breuer's iconoclastic classical deconstructions (such as *Gospel at Colonus*, 1985, and his gender-reversed *Lear*, 1988, which starred Ruth Maleczech as an irascible, aging queen) are predicated on a "what if" question. For *DollHouse*, Breuer and Mitchell asked: what if Nora were literally the bigger of the two spouses, if her larger spirit and yearning were made concrete in the person of a large woman? And if Torvald's stunted vision, compassion, and maturity were similarly made manifest by casting an actor of short stature in the part? What if all the women and men were big and small, respectively? What if the house in which the action unfolds were built to his scale rather than hers? And what if the underlying melodrama in Ibsen's script were turned loose on the stage? How would stagy theatrics intensify or diminish the characters and the issues at the center of the play? The validity of Breuer's invention rests on the fact that he adds nothing that is not already present or implied in the text.

The potential danger of basing a directorial conceit on these "clever ideas" is that they risk one-dimensional interpretation.[28] A production could become an extended one-liner that blots out the richness, nuance, and emotional truth at the core of the subject text. The beauty of Breuer's staging is that he uses his highly entertaining gestures to explicate and interrogate the text. Height is not just a sight gag in Breuer's *DollHouse*; it is an ironic metaphor for the distorted, disfiguring impact of patriarchy on the women and men who live in its grasp. Breuer doesn't let a line go untouched. His constant invention seeks every opportunity to take the questions further, to give them a new twist, and to keep challenging his audience.

DollHouse is set in a doll house — a brightly colored and ornamented miniature home (designed by Narrele Sissons) whose collapsible walls open and close to barely contain the oversize histrionics that unfold on stage.[29] If Ibsen's depiction of gender is exaggerated and his use of the well-made play subversive, so Breuer's mise-en-scène exploits the melodrama embedded in the script for its full theatrical and ironic potential. Just as Ibsen subverted his audience's happy expectations of a tidy resolution, Breuer explodes our knee-jerk belief that we know the play, its form, and its familiar critique of women's inequality. He supplants Victorian decorum with bawdiness and surface realism with self-conscious special effects. These postmodern interjections liberate what is neatly tucked into the original, well-made frame and animate dormant theatrical impulses. They allow us to see beneath the veneer to the underlying structure of the play and the social scaffold around which it was constructed. Likewise, by startling the audience out of complacency, the production challenges us to see how we perpetuate the myths and abuses that we thought Nora vanquished when she slammed the door behind her.

From the red velvet curtain that begins and ends each act to the live piano score (adapted by Eve Beglarian from Edvard Grieg), dramatic lighting, frenetic movement, to the presence of the tall women and small-statured men, and their comical accents and vocal inflections, Breuer continually surprises his audience, finding humor in Ibsen's politeness and flaunting the faux-suspense created by the fact that we all know the ending before the play begins. Built into the downstage left corner of the stage floor is the surreally exaggerated lid of a grand piano. Below that is a real piano upon which Ning Yu, in formal gown, accompanies the dialogue with sweeping crescendos and silent-movie trills. Mary Louise Geiger's angular, heavily shadowed lighting augments the self-conscious, melodramatic effect and hits the big moments with strobes and lightening flashes. The casts speaks a parody version of the Norwegian accent. Torvald calls his wife "Nyooora."

Moving around this theatrically-charged metaphoric space are seemingly enormous female characters and tiny men. Maude Mitchell, who plays Nora and collaborated closely with Breuer, is only 5' 4" in bare feet, but her exaggerated costume and teased blonde wig make her look much bigger on stage. Her seemingly endless limbs flutter and flail as she prances and skips and talks in a baby voice. She is more Raggedy Ann than Barbie–wife. The house and its scaled-down furniture are too small for the women they contain. The women are too big for the world they are forced to inhabit. Nora, Kristine, and Helene must duck to get through doors and squeeze themselves into delicate settees. Like Goldilocks, however, the men find the house and its furnishings just right. Mark Povinelli who plays Torvald stands about 3'6". Torvald's macho strut, compacted into his diminutive frame, makes him seem like a little boy crudely rehearsing manhood. The interactions between Mitchell/Nora and Povinelli/Torvald are visually comical. In order to cajole Torvald, Nora paddles over on all fours and crouches at his knee. She is not quite groveling, but enacting some grotesque, flirtatious approximation. The image is humiliating, maddening, and funny.

We are taught from early childhood not to stare at physical difference, but

Breuer and his cast of over- and under-sized characters and exaggerated effects elicit an almost lurid gaze. We bear witness to Nora's need to diminish herself — to literally stoop — to place herself below Torvald's gaze. We challenge our notions of virility and masculinity and the places we expect to find them when the men are sexually aggressive. There's something of the caricature about it all — distorted, transgressive, and irresistible to watch. We don't want to stare at what startles us in the men's and women's dimensions, but they are on display for the purpose of making us look. By physicalizing the gender paradigm in this way, the production critiques and ridicules our prejudices about size and power and sexual prowess. Breuer keeps us on the edges of our seats — amused, eager for the next surprise — but he also keeps us on our critical toes. You thought you knew this play? Sit back. We're going to show you stuff you probably never noticed before. Mabou Mines looks at Ibsen's play through a postmodern kaleidoscope that in turn challenges us to dissect how we see ourselves.

We have seen how early critics of *A Doll House* mistook radical dramaturgy for ineptitude. Ibsen cloaked his theatrically and thematically subversive script in the familiar garb of well-made melodrama; Breuer's bold directorial strategy rips away the realistic veneer that hoodwinked the playwright's contemporaries and risks making the play a relic now. The logic of Breuer's adaptation is that he doesn't have to dig far below that surface to pull up and exploit the text's latent theatrical potential.

Toril Moi makes the case that *A Doll House* has a "theatricalist agenda." She points to the tarantella rehearsal scene as a prime example of Ibsen's metatheatricality. Nora dances wildly, her husband complains, "as if [her] life depended on it," and she readily admits that he is right. Her dervish–like movement exceeds the bounds of both Torvald's propriety and that of the late nineteenth-century stage. She threatens to careen right out of her domestic arrangements, her society, her psyche, and her play. In addition, Moi reminds us, Nora dances for multiple on- and off-stage audiences. Torvald watches as her husband and teacher, Rank as unrequited admirer, and Kristine (originated by the smoky-voiced Honora Fergusson), who is putting together the clues to these complex relationships, watches them watch. The audience takes an even longer view and sees the whole, layered dynamic. This show-stopping flamboyance, Moi says, "reminds us that we are in a theatre" and reflects Ibsen's "sense that we need theater — I mean the actual art form — to reveal to us the games of concealment and theatricalization in which we inevitably engage in everyday life."[30]

The Helmers self-theatricalize, playing to the hilt the script of husband and wife. Ibsen wants us to catch our own reflection and take note of how we play gender and what impact it has on ourselves and our relationships. Are we also self-deceivers, pretending to enjoy the show? The playwright winks and nods at us from below the surface of his realism. So does Breuer, except that he does not hide behind the dramaturgical mask. Isn't it funny how they used to tell these stories?—Breuer's overtly theatrical staging asks. But we're not off the hook; so much of it still applies.

The tarantella rehearsal that ends the first half of the production ends with a classic silent-movie effect. The music blares, lights flash blue and white and black, and the characters twirl and fall like the passengers of a ship in a storm. The staccato lights make their movements appear jerky, robotic, and puppet-like. The thunderous score drowns out the dialogue. White sheets imprinted with the characters' lines in curlicue font unfurl and drop from above. The stage goes black and silent. We hear Nora whisper, "only thirty more hours to live." Blackout. Melodrama's mandatory, pre-intermission cliffhanger is revved to almost farcical intensity. Yet the images haunt. We are left aching for Nora, the pretty, increasingly hysterical damsel in distress, whose tempest-tossed, constructed domesticity is about to shatter. Likewise, Nora's Showdown with Krogstad is lit in icy blue. Glaring footlights cast huge shadows of the conspirators against the back wall of the set. Krogstad roars his agony and his threats of blackmail. He might as well be the stock, mustachioed landlord who threatens that the beleaguered heroine "must pay the rent."

Breuer reaches beyond stock melodramatic effects as well. In the penultimate scene, Torvald reads Krogstad's blackmail letter informing him of Nora's forgery. This *petit tyrant* of a husband goes on a rampage, screaming and striking at her. She cowers in a downstage corner, loading rocks into the pockets of her cloak, as she prepares to drown herself. Torvald's furious antics and shortness make him seem like a child throwing a tantrum. His testosterone-fueled outburst leaves him spent and whimpering. He falls to the floor beside her. Nora cradles and rocks him in her lap until he is quiet. This invocation of the Pieta reverses the power dynamic. Torvald's strutting masculinity is exposed as a shallow façade that crumbles at the first threat. But Nora's nurturing "femininity" is strong enough to endure his weakness. The image foreshadows the end of the play. Nora will survive this turmoil. Torvald may not.

In the midst of this highly charged, emotional scene, Nora defends her illicit financial activities by explaining to Torvald that she only borrowed the money out of love for him. Torvald's typical male dismissal of her "excuse" becomes a pivotal moment in the production. "No more melodrama!" he commands. Nora and Torvald do a long take directly to the audience. They recognize the in-joke and allow themselves to titter, then laugh out loud. Breuer's parodic, postmodern version of the Brechtian gestus breaks the tension in the scene and the audience's emotional involvement in the quarrel. Removed from emotional identification, the audience is invited to wonder: Are we to take this seriously? Are gender politics this ludicrous and artificial? Are we still pretending to enjoy these games? Have things really changed?

The director uses similar comic devices throughout the production to manipulate the audience's identification and critical attention. Unlike Ibsen, Breuer is not interested in dramaturgical subterfuge. He doesn't want his audience to be fooled, to suspend disbelief and live vicariously in the Victorian era for a couple of hours. He keeps us on guard, punctuating the performance with self-conscious theatrical humor to point the finger back at us. We may not see ourselves as Noras and Torvalds, he implies, but we harbor and perpetuate our own damaging myths and rules about gender, family, love, and sexuality.

Evidence of our continued struggle with the gender binary emerged during a touring performance of *DollHouse* in a small college town in South Carolina. Maude Mitchell recalls hearing a male voice ring out from the audience when she tore off her poufy blonde wig and threw it to the ground in the final scene to reveal her own close-cropped hair. "Jesus H. Christ! It's been a man the whole goddamn time!" exclaimed the triumphant, middle-aged gentleman. Mitchell also drops her pitch at this point to speak in her natural register. When she came back onstage after the curtain call for a Q&A with the audience, Mitchell heard the same voice equivocate, "It's a woman? It's a man? Who are these people? They're too weird."[31] His confusion made him angry. We like our gender categories clear cut and reliable.

One of the most audacious elements of Breuer's production is in the way it exploits the comic potential of its male actors' short stature. On the surface, their height symbolizes the ways that patriarchy diminishes both men and women. It reflects the stunted psychological and emotional condition that results from having to sustain an unmitigated burden of strength, certainty, and responsibility. On a deeper level, it challenges us to confront our own narrow definitions of masculinity and virility.

Mark Povinelli's Torvald is a throwback to a pre–Mann, less egalitarian reading of the play. His Torvald is unsympathetic — a blustering, hyper-masculine, psychological, and emotional midget with a Napoleon complex. While the size of the house and furniture may suit him fine, the set seems to be booby trapped for him. After the party, a tipsy Torvald demonstrates for Nora and Kristine how to make an effective exit. He walks downstage center, pivots to face directly upstage and heads in the direction of the French doors that form the primary entrance to and exit from the set. In a vainglorious flourish, he attempts to leap over the bed that sits stage center, but his little legs cannot hoist him high enough, and he does a dignity-deflating pratfall over it. The slapstick laugh is intensified when, true to character, Povinelli rights himself, keeping his back to both the women in the scene and the theater audience, straightens his clothing, and moves on, as if nothing had happened.

Earlier in the scene, he sits on Kristine's knitting needles, jumps off the settee, and implores her to take up embroidery. He uses the offending implements to demonstrate the inelegance of knitting. "There's something Chinese about it," he concludes with revulsion. Breuer takes advantage of Torvald's racist insult to remind us of yet another area in which we may overestimate how far we are from Ibsen's time. When Torvald speaks disparagingly of the "Chinese," pianist Ning Yu slams the piano keys, gets up, and crosses below the stage to exit in protest. Seeing her, and realizing what has happened, the cast freezes. They stare at her. She stares at them. "It's in the text," Maude Mitchell apologizes sheepishly. Ning pauses again and reverses direction to return to the keyboard. Late-Victorian aesthetes like Torvald might have felt empowered to make blanket racial denunciations, but we don't want to offend. Then again, the sequence suggests, we are willing to tolerate and make excuses when someone else makes an impolitic remark. And we expect the offended party to comply with this unspoken agreement. On tour, Mitchell makes her comment in the local language. She reports that the moment consistently gets the biggest laugh in the show.[32]

Torvald's height prompts another gag in one of the production's signature moments. After Torvald reads Krogstad's second letter, forgiving Nora's debt and relinquishing the threat of blackmail, the recently weeping man–child literally walks on air. Hoisted aloft by a taller, black-clad performer, Povinelli climbs a wall and somersaults gleefully in midair. He could be a Bunraku puppet floating across the stage over his handler's head, feet dancing, eyes shining, a grotesque (and ironic, given that we know what's coming) grin of relief on his face. Ibsen's Torvald has at least a chance to recover his dignity when he reverts to his role as all-protecting and forgiving husband. Povinelli's dancing puppet doesn't have a prayer.

While these visual jokes about being short or tall elicit laughter, it is clear that Breuer is not poking fun at his actors. Like cross-gender or cross-ethnic casting, the intentional display of height differences offers a fresh lens on familiar characters and situations. The purpose is not to ridicule the actors but to take a jab at the perverse gender system of which their bodies are symbolic. He prompts his audience to examine further their own prejudice about size and sexuality as he unleashes the libidinal tensions that under-gird Ibsen's delicate references to intimacy. In the text, Torvald wants "to be with" Nora after the party. Kristine will "do anything" to prove her love to Krogstad. Breuer takes the delicacy out of Ibsen's innuendo and makes desire explicit on the stage. Nora and Krogstad move in for a kiss when they discover they have both considered suicide, then veer away in frightened recognition. When the Helmers come home after Nora has danced the tarantella, Torvald pursues her like a bullfighter. He waves his cape. She charges. He dodges in teasing foreplay. They romp and wrestle until Kristine makes her presence known. Rank's arrival follows close on the heels of her departure and again interrupts the couple's antics. Torvald, annoyed and embarrassed, must adjust himself before inviting his friend to enter.

After Rank leaves, having delivered his coded message to Nora that he is "certain" to die very soon, she is devastated. Torvald's desire, however, is unabated. He insists that they continue what they had started and pushes her onto the bed ferociously. Because he cannot overpower her with physical mass, he uses intimidation and violence to get her to submit. Given the size differential, Nora could probably fend him off with a good whack. But she doesn't. Instead, she begs him to stop. "I don't want to," she wails. When he finally desists, she falls to the floor and crawls away, tugging her tussled skirts over her naked legs. Her near-submission to marital rape is the more pitiful because she does not use her size advantage to protect herself. The topsy-turvy physical dynamic intensifies the brutality of sexual ownership.

Breuer and company take a comic jab at sex in the context of romance in the love scene between Kristine and Krogstad. Their long-desired reconciliation seems too good to be true. Krogstad cannot trust Kristine's declarations. He needs proof. Stripped to his long-johns, he seems reassured by her blow job. After that, they dance a seated, simulated-intercourse ballet with arching backs, grand arabesques, and an earth-quaking climax accompanied by the flashing chandelier. The humor of their size difference is compounded by the silliness of the dance as it mimics and distorts our illusions about the beauty, grace, and nobility of making love.

Breuer brings us back to the potential solipsism of male desire in the final scene. Nora has gone off to change out of her costume. Torvald, left alone on stage, relieved that the crisis is over, jumps under the covers and masturbates to his rhapsody of how much more he will love his wife now, knowing that she is even weaker, more naïve, and needier than he thought before. The fantasy of her complete dependence thrills him and intensifies his self-stimulation. He thrusts and climaxes to his reverie, then drops off to sleep. Satisfied at last, he is snoring, oblivious, when Nora returns to announce her momentous decision. Her moment has arrived. He couldn't care less.

Breuer's final *coup de théâtre* takes place shortly after Torvald opens his eyes and realizes that his wife is saying something important. Nora's declarations have come down to us as one of the inaugural anthems of the struggle for women's rights. Breuer emphasizes its historical status. Maude Mitchell drops her high-pitched baby-talk voice when she begins to speak. Nora is not a child any more. As she launches, contralto, into her speech, a recorded military tattoo swells, setting the rhythm and the momentum of her speech. She is leading the march, taking the first, declarative step in the campaign for women's equality. She tells her husband that she is not unique, that "thousands" of women and couples live under the same pitiful delusions. The dollhouse frame flies out. The velvet curtains part to reveal eighteen rectangular boxes, each populated by a marionette couple, miniature Noras and Torvalds who watch and replicate the couple's painful reckoning.

When speech is no longer adequate to convey the epic proportions of Nora's seriousness and intensity, she switches to opera. Mitchell lip-syncs her speech to a recorded aria. Eventually, Torvald raises his baritone in duet as he attempts to make sense of what she tells him. One of the benefits of the production's long shelf-life is that its creators have had time to mull things over and make changes. Originally, the female voice was a soprano, but Mitchell came to feel that the difference between the couple's voices was too stark. She wanted them to make some progress, to come in closer range by the end of the song. For their performance at the 2007 Edinburgh Fringe Festival and subsequent taping for French television, they re-recorded the sung passages with a contralto and a tenor.[33]

Over the years, audiences and critics have had predictably mixed reactions to *Mabou Mines DollHouse*, whose very title demands the company's license to reframe Ibsen's text. The mixed-bag responses echo those the play received in its earliest incarnations. Spectators who latched on to Breuer's tongue-in-cheek ironies admired the production's audacity, insight, and theatrical verve. Those who didn't found it superficial and annoying, even insulting to its male cast. Still others toggled between skepticism and appreciation.[34]

Mabou Mines DollHouse won two OBIE's in 2004, one for direction and the second for Maude Mitchell's performance. Between 2005 and 2008, it played throughout the U.S. and at festivals in Germany, France, Israel, China, Australia, Spain, Canada, Italy, Thailand, Scotland, Poland, Colombia, and England. Lyn Gardner reviewed the Edinburgh performance for *The Guardian*. The production ends, she writes:

> In an astonishing, confounding moment, Mitchell tosses off her corset and blonde wig to reveal herself completely naked and entirely hairless. She looks at once Amazonian and desperately vulnerable, like a newborn babe about to stride out into the world. It is a stunning moment in a stunning show, which concludes with the eerie image of Nora's young daughter sitting astride the nursery rocking-horse, riding into her future. Like that final glimpse of her mother, it is an ambivalent representation that suggests this tot might indeed carve a new role for herself in the world, but also hints at how, a century after Nora slammed the door, many men and women are content to remain in the doll's house, where they will always be vulnerable.[35]

Breuer's breathless directorial conceit titillates and illuminates, whisking Ibsen's modern masterpiece onto the postmodern stage and reminding us that theatrical treasure lies waiting to be mined in even the most stalwart and familiar old chestnuts.

Notes

1. Joan Templeton, "The Poetry of Feminism," *Ibsen's Women* (New York: Cambridge University Press, 2001) 135–36.
2. Templeton 137.
3. Alisa Solomon, "The New Drama and The New Woman: Reconstructing Ibsen's Realism," *Re-dressing the Canon: Essays on Theater and Gender* (New York: Routledge, 1997) 49.
4. Templeton reminds us that Ibsen corresponded admiringly with leading feminists, railed at the Scandinavian Club in Rome when the members refused to allow women to be candidates or vote for club librarian, and lobbied the Norwegian Parliament to enact a bill allowing married women separate property rights (126–7). Gail Finney supposes that Ibsen did not mean to deny the feminist orientation of his plays but to refuse the imposition of

being labeled a card-carrying anything. (*"Ibsen and Feminism," The Cambridge Companion to Ibsen*, ed. James McFarlane (Cambridge: Cambridge University Press, 1994) 90.
  5. Templeton 112–14.
  6. Solomon 49.
  7. Elaine Hoffman Baruch, *"Ibsen's A Doll House: A Myth for Our Time," Yale Review* 70 (1980): 378.
  8. Solomon 53.
  9. Brian Johnston, *The Ibsen Cycle* (Philadelphia: University of Pennsylvania Press, 1992) 370, qtd. in Solomon, 53.
  10 Erving Goffman, *The Presentation of Self in Everyday Life* (New York City: Anchor Books, 1959).
  11 Baruch 381.
  12 Julie Holledge and Joanne Tompkins, *Women's Intercultural Performance* (London and New York: Routledge, 2000) 15.
  13 Holledge and Tompkins, 19–24.
  14 Ibid., 32–36.
  15 Ibid., 38.
  16 Ibid., 38–42.
  17 Ibid., 21.
  18 Baruch 383.
  19 Janice Paran, "Redressing Ibsen: Directors Fornes, Near and Mann Emancipate His Proto-Feminist Plays From Their Victorian Bonds," *American Theater* (November 1987): 15–20.
  20 Robert Brustein, "Reworking the Classics: Homage or Ego Trip?" *The New York Times*, 6 November 1988, sec. Arts and Leisure: H5.
  21 Interestingly, audiences and critics went along with the move to an Eisenhower-era Southern suburb but balked at the racial profile of its middle-class characters.
  22 Rebecca Gilman, *Dollhouse*, 115–117.
  23 Of course, Gilman is not the first to leave Nora in the house. Ibsen was confronted by the threat that the producers of the first German production, where he had no copyright protection, would write their own ending. Afraid of the potential bowdlerizing, Ibsen wrote his own happy ending in which "Helmer forces Nora to the door of the children's bedroom and tells her that, if she leaves, they will be motherless. This convinces her to stay." (Baruch, 380).
  24 Theresa Smalec, "Yelena Gluzman's *I'm So Sorry for Everything*," *The Drama Review* 47.3 (2003): 137.
  25 Smalec 138.
  26 Ibid.
  27 Brustein H5.
  28 Ibid.
  29 London-based Shared Experience also set their 2000 production of the play in a doll house, but theirs was life-size. Nora's first entrance was from within a toy doll house tucked into a corner of the set. When she left at the end, a whole wall flew out to let her escape.
  30 Toril Moi, "'First and Foremost a Human Being': Idealism, Theatre, and Gender in *A Doll's House*," *Modern Drama* 49.3 (Fall 2006): 272.
  31 Maude Mitchell, telephone interview with the author, 31 July 2007.
  32 Mitchell 2007.
  33 The second of at least twenty-five venues that *Mabou Mines DollHouse* played on its intermittent international tour was the Ibsen International Stage Festival in Oslo in 2004. Theirs was one of six productions of the play to be performed. Mitchell was eager to compare notes with other Noras. She asked the festival organizers to arrange a meeting. To her astonishment, they refused, citing scheduling difficulties. She found it ironic that the voices of the women who gave voice to Nora's *cris de coeur* were not provided a forum. Mitchell is now collaborating on a book of interviews with women who have played the part.
  34 Writing for *The New York Times*, Ron Jenkins called the staging a "wonderland of

mismatched proportions." (Jenkins, "Men are the Real Dolls in this House of Ibsen," *The New York Times*, 16 November 2003, sec. 2.) Margo Jefferson, in the same paper, inferred that the audience's response to Breuer's "extravaganza of nineteenth-century theater conventions" was "the laughter of pained recognition (who hasn't seen a woman make a fool of herself to get something she needs from a powerful man?) and of chagrin (we've all had to admit that someone we loved turned out to be an emotional dwarf)." In sum, Jefferson concluded, "The whole experience is so fascinating — thrilling here, confounding there — that it must be seen." (Jefferson, "Funhouse Proportions Turn Dominance Upside Down," *The New York Times*, 24 November 2003.) Not surprisingly, Ibsen champion (and sometime Breuer collaborator) Alisa Solomon, in *The Village Voice*, appreciated Breuer's deconstruction of the playwright's theatrical idiom. "To make these hoary devices visible to spectators some hundred years later," she wrote, "Breuer campily quotes melodramatic gestures and contrivances." Although "at first, such theatrical italicizing seems too much," Solomon feared, she found the production "surprisingly moving," its Nora "tragically lost in her drawing room." (Solomon, "Growing Pains: Lee Breuer's 'Little Woman' Takes Revenge in Her Dollhouse," *The Village Voice*, 26 November–2 December 2003.) Elinor Fuchs in *Theatre Journal* recounts a controversy surrounding the casting of the short men. "A few left the theater outraged," she reports. But she concluded that "Breuer ridiculed a smug male world that held women down because it couldn't see above their waists, yet regarded these same males with evident compassion. The identification with the male point of view, which Breuer has said was one of his intentions in the production, carried over to artistic respect for the three strong actors as well" (Fuchs, "Mabou Mines DollHouse," *Theatre Journal* 56.3 (2004): 498–500).

35 Lyn Gardner, *Mabou Mines DollHouse, The Guardian Unlimited*, 27 August 2007.

Bibliography

Adlard, John, ed. *The Debt to Pleasure: John Wilmot, Earl of Rochester, in the Eyes of His Contemporaries and in His Own Poetry and Prose*. Cheshire, UK: Carcanet Press Ltd, 1974.
Altaba-Artal, Dolors. *Aphra Behn's English Feminism*. Selinsgrove, PA: Susquehanna University Press, 1999.
Andreach, Robert J. "Ellen McLaughlin's *Iphigenia and Other Daughters*: A Classical Trilogy from a Contemporary Perspective." *Comparative Literature Studies* 35.4 (1998): 379–392.
Arons, Wendy. Rev. of *Phèdre*, dir. JoAnne Akalaitis. *Theatre Journal* 55.2 (May 2003): 323–5.
Aston, Elaine. *An Introduction to Feminism and Theatre*. New York: Routledge, 1995.
_____. *Feminist Theatre Practice: A Handbook*. New York: Routledge, 1999.
_____. *Feminist Views on the English Stage: Women Playwrights 1990–2000*. Cambridge, UK, and New York: Cambridge University Press, 2003.
_____, and Janelle G. Reinelt. *The Cambridge Companion to Modern British Women Playwrights*. New York: Cambridge University Press, 2000.
_____, and Geraldine Harris, eds. *Feminist Futures?* Houndmills, Basingstoke, and Hampshire: Palgrave Macmillan, 2006.
Atwood, Margaret. *The Handmaid's Tale*. New York: Fawcett Crest, 1985.
Austin, Gayle. *Feminist Theories for Dramatic Criticism*. Ann Arbor: University of Michigan Press, 1990.
_____. "The Madwoman in the Spotlight: Plays of Maria Irene Fornes." *Making a Spectacle: Feminist Essays on Contemporary Women's Theatre*. Ed. Lynda Hart. Ann Arbor: University of Michigan Press, 1989.
Barthes, Roland. "From Work to Text." *Image, Music, Text*. New York: Hill & Wang, 1977.
Baruch, Elaine Hoffman. "Ibsen's A Doll House: A Myth for Our Time." *Yale Review* 70 (1980): 374–387.
Bassnet, Susan. "The Politics of Location." *Cambridge Companion to Modern British Women Playwrights*. Eds. Elaine Aston and Janelle Reinelt. Cambridge: Cambridge University Press, 2000.
Bayley, Clare. "Women in Shakespeare." *Royal Shakespeare Company Magazine* (Spring 1994): 16–19.
Baym, Nina. "Introduction." *The Scarlet Letter*. New York: Penguin Classics, 2003 (1983).
_____. *The Scarlet Letter: A Reading*. Boston: Twayne Publishers, 1986.
Beer, Gillian. *Virginia Woolf: The Common Ground*. Ann Arbor: University of Michigan Press, 1996.
Belli, Angela. *Ancient Greek Myths and Modern Drama: A Study in Continuity*. New York: New York University Press, 1969.
Benjamin, Walter. "On Language As Such and On Human Language." *Reflections*. Trans. Edmund Jephcott. New York: Harcourt Brace Jovanovich, 1978.

_____. "Theses on the Philosophy of History." *Illuminations*. Ed. Hannah Arendt. Trans. Harry Zohn. New York: Shocken Press, 1969.
Bennett, Susan. *Performing Nostalgia: Shifting Shakespeare and the Contemporary Past*. London: Routledge, 1996.
_____. *Theatre Audiences: A Theory of Production and Reception*. London: Routledge, 1990.
Benstock, Shari. "*The Scarlet Letter* (a)doree, or the Female Body Embroidered." *The Scarlet Letter: Case Studies in Contemporary Criticism*. Ed. Ross C. Murfin. Boston and New York: Bedford Books of St. Martin's Press, 1991.
Berger, John. *Ways of Seeing*. London: BBC and Penguin, 1972.
Bigsby, C.W.E. *A Critical Introduction to Twentieth Century American Drama, Volume Two: Williams, Miller, Albee*. Cambridge: Cambridge University Press, 1984.
Black, Cheryl. "A Visible Oppression: JoAnne Akalaitis's Staging of John Ford's '*Tis Pity She's a Whore*." *Theatre Studies* 40 (1995): 5–16.
Blunt, Alison, and Gillian Rose, eds. *Writing Women and Space: Colonial and Post-Colonial Geographies*. New York: Guilford Press, 1994.
Bolton, H. Philip. *Women Writers Dramatized: A Calendar of Performances from Narrative Works Published in English to 1900*. London: Mansell, 2000.
Bourne, Bette, Peggy Shaw, Paul Shaw, and Lois Weaver. *Belle Reprieve*. In *Gay and Lesbian Plays Today*. Ed. Terry Helbing. Portsmouth, NH: Heinemann, 1993.
Brecht, Bertolt. *Brecht on Theatre*. Ed. and Trans. John Willett. New York: Methuen, 1964.
Brontë, Charlotte. *Jane Eyre*. New York: Bantam, 1986.
Brown, Janet. "Feminist Theory and Contemporary Drama." *The Cambridge Companion to American Women Playwrights*. Ed. Brenda Murphy. New York: Cambridge University Press, 1999.
Brunner, Cornelia. "Roberta Sklar: Toward Creating a Women's Theatre." *The Drama Review: TDR* 24.2 (June 1980): 23–40.
Bryant-Bertail, Sarah. "Gender, Empire and Body Politic as Mise en Scène: Mnouchkine's *Les Atrides*." *Theatre Journal* 46.1 (March 1994): 1–30.
Burt, John. "Irreconcilable Habits of Thought in 'A Room of One's Own' and 'To the Lighthouse.'" *Virginia Woolf: Modern Critical Views*. Ed. Harold Bloom. New York: Chelsea House, 1986.
Butler, Judith. *Antigone's Claim: Kinship Between Life and Death*. New York: Columbia University Press, 2000.
_____. *Bodies That Matter: On the Discursive Limits of "Sex."* New York and London: Routledge, 1993.
Callaghan, Dympna. *Woman and Gender in Renaissance Tragedy*. Atlantic Highlands, NJ: Humanities Press, 1989.
Campbell, John. *Questioning Racinian Tragedy*. Chapel Hill: University of North Carolina Press, 2005.
Canaday, John. *Mainstreams of Modern Art*. Chicago: Holt, Rinehart, and Winston, 1981.
Canning, Charlotte. *Feminist Theaters in the USA: Staging Women's Experience*. London and New York: Routledge, 1996.
_____. "Constructing Experience: Theorizing a Feminist Theatre History." *Theatre Journal* 45 (1993): 529–540.
Carlson, Susan. "Cannibalizing and Carnivalizing: Reviving Aphra Behn's *The Rover*." *Theatre Journal* 47. 4 (1995): 517–539.
_____. "Issues of Identity, Nationality and Performance: The Reception of Two Plays by Timberlake Wertenbaker." *New Theatre Quarterly* 9.35 (1993): 267, 267–89.
Case, Sue-Ellen. *Feminism and Theatre*. New York: Routledge, 1988.

_____. *Performing Feminisms: Feminist Critical Theory and Theatre.* Baltimore: London and Baltimore, 1990.
_____. "Technologies of Gender." *Technologies of Gender: Essays on Theory, Film, and Fiction.* Bloomington: Indiana University Press, 1987.
_____. "Toward a Butch-Femme Aesthetic." *Making a Spectacle: Feminist Essays on Contemporary Women's Theatre.* Ed. Lynda Hart. Ann Arbor: University of Michigan Press, 1989.
Chinoy, Helen Krich, and Linda Walsh Jenkins. *Women in American Theatre.* New York Theatre Communications Group, 1987.
Chodorow, Nancy. "Gender, Relation, and Difference in Psychoanalytic Perspective." *The Future of Difference.* Eds. Hester Eisenstein and Alice Jardine. Boston: G.K. Hall, 1990.
Chopin, Kate. *The Awakening.* Ed. Nancy A. Walker. Boston: Bedford/St. Martin's, 2000.
Claycomb, Ryan. "Re-Performing Women and Reconstructing the Audience: Paula Vogel's *Desdemona* and Post-modern Feminist Parody." *Text and Presentation* 20 (1999): 87–93.
Clement, Susan, and Ellen Donkin. *Upstaging Big Daddy: Directing Theater as if Gender and Race Matter.* Ann Arbor: University of Michigan Press, 1993.
Clover, Carol. *Men, Women, and Chainsaws: Gender in the Modern Horror Film.* Princeton: Princeton University Press, 1992.
Clum, John. *Acting Gay: Male Homosexuality in Modern Drama.* New York: Columbia University Press, 1994.
Cody, Gaby. Rev. of *To You, the Birdie! (Phèdre). Theatre Journal* 55.1 (March 2003): 173–5.
Corbett, Edward P.J. "The Rhetoric of the Open Hand and the Rhetoric of the Closed Fist." *CCC* 20.5 (Dec. 1969): 288–296.
Coss, Clare, Sondra Segal, and Roberta Sklar. "Notes on the Women's Experimental Theatre." *Women in Theatre: Compassion and Hope.* Ed. Karen Malpede. New York: Drama Book Publishers, 1983.
Cott, Nancy. *The Grounding of Modern Feminism.* New Haven, CT, and London: Yale University Press, 1987.
Cousin, Geraldine. *Women in Dramatic Place and Time: Contemporary Female Characters on Stage.* London: Routledge, 1996.
Curb, Rosemary K. "Re/cognition, Re/presentation, Re/creation in Woman-Conscious Drama: The Seer, The Seen, The Scene, the Obscure." *Theatre Journal* 37 (1985): 302–316.
Curran, Beverley. "Mingling and UnMingling Opposites: Bending Genre and Gender in Ann-Marie MacDonald's *Goodnight Desdemona (Good Morning Juliet)." He Said, She Says: An RSVP to the Male Text.* Madison, NJ: Associated University Press, 2001.
Cutter, Martha. "Philomela Speaks: Alice Walker's Revisioning of Rape Archetypes in *The Color Purple.*" *MELUS* 25.3/4 (Autumn-Winter 2000): 161–180.
D'Aquila, Ulysses L. *Bloomsbury and Modernism.* New York: Peter Lang, 1989.
Davies, Oliver Ford. *Playing Lear: An Insider's Guide from Text to Performance.* London: Nick Hern Books, 2003.
De Grazia, Victoria. *How Fascism Ruled Women: Italy 1922–1945.* Berkeley: University of California Press, 1992.
DeJean, Joan. "Fictions of Sappho." *Critical Inquiry* 13.4 (1987): 787–805.
de Lauretis, Teresa. *Feminist Studies/Critical Studies.* Bloomington: Indiana University Press, 1986.
_____. *Technologies of Gender: Issues on Theory, Film, and Fiction.* Bloomington, Indiana University Press, 1987.

———. "Upping the Anti [sic] in Feminist Theory." *Conflicts in Feminism*. Eds. Marianne Hirsch and Evelyn Fox Keller. New York: Routledge, 1990.
Demers, Patricia. *Women's Writing in English: Early Modern England*. Toronto and Buffalo: University of Toronto Press, 2005.
De Mille, Agnes. *Martha: The Life and Work of Martha Graham*. New York: Random House, 1991.
DeRitter, Jones. "The Gypsy, The Rover, and The Wanderer: Aphra Behn's Revision of Thomas Killigrew." *Restoration* 10 (1986): 82–92.
Derrick, Scott S. "A Curious Subject of Observation and Inquiry: Homoeroticism, the Body and Authorship in Hawthorne's *The Scarlet Letter*." *NOVEL: A Forum on Fiction* 28.3 (Spring 1995): 308–326.
Diamond, Elin. "Brechtian Theory/Feminist Theory: Toward a Gestic Feminist Criticism." *The Drama Review: TDR* 32 (Spring 1988): 82–94.
———. "Mimesis, Mimicry and the True-Real." *Modern Drama* 32 (1989): 58–72.
———. *Unmaking Mimesis: Essays on Feminism and Theater*. New York: Routledge, 1997.
Dickinson, Peter. "Duets, Duologues, and Black Diasporic Theatre: Djanet Sears, William Shakespeare, and Others." *Modern Drama* 45:2 (Summer 2002): 188–208.
DiGaetani, John L. "Interview with Timberlake Wertenbaker." *A Search for a Postmodern Theater*. New York: Greenwood Press, 1991.
Dixon, Michael Bigelow, and Joel A. Smith, eds. *Anne Bogart: Viewpoints*. Lyme, NH: Smith and Kraus, 1995.
Dolan, Jill. *The Feminist Spectator as Critic*. Ann Arbor: UMI Press, 1988.
———. "In Defense of the Discourse: Materialist Feminism, Postmodernism, Poststructuralism...and Theory." *Presence and Desire: Essays on Gender, Sexuality, and Performance*. Ann Arbor: UMI Press 1993.
Drexler, Rosalyn. *Lobby*. In *Transients Welcome*. New York: Broadway Play Publishing, 1984.
Dubin, Steve. *Arresting Images: Impolitic Art and Uncivil Actions*. New York: Routledge, 1994.
Dusinberre, Juliet. *Shakespeare and the Nature of Women*. London: Macmillan, 1985.
Dymkowski, Christine. "'The Play's the Thing': The Metatheatre of Timberlake Wertenbaker." *Drama on Drama: Dimensions of Theatricality on the Contemporary British Stage*. Ed. Nicole Boireau. New York: St. Martin's Press, 1997.
Eble, Kenneth. "A Forgotten Novel: Kate Chopin's *The Awakening*." *Western Humanities Review* X (Summer 1956): 261–269.
Euripides. *Alcestis and Other Plays*. Trans. John Davie. Harmondsworth, UK: Penguin, 1996.
Evan, Raima. "Women and Violence in *A Mouthful of Birds*." *Theatre Journal* 54.2 (2002): 263–284.
Evans, Greg. "Iphigenia and Other Daughters." *Variety*, 13 February 1995.
Ferris, Lesley. *Acting Women: Images of Women in Theatre*. London: Macmillan, 1990.
———, ed. *Crossing the Stage: Controversies on Cross-Dressing*. London: Routledge, 1993.
Fetterley, Judith. *The Resisting Reader: A Feminist Approach to American Fiction*. Bloomington: Indiana University Press.
Finney, Gail. "Ibsen and Feminism." *The Cambridge Companion to Ibsen*. Ed. James McFarlane. Cambridge: Cambridge University Press, 1994.
Fischlin, Daniel, and Mark Fortier, ed. *Adaptations of Shakespeare: A Critical Anthology of Plays from the Seventeenth Century to the Present*. London: Routledge, 2000.
Fleche, Anne. "When a Door is a Jar, or Out in the Theatre: Tennessee Williams and Queer Space." *Theatre Journal* 47 (May 1995): 253–67.
Foley, Helene. "Bad Women: Gender Politics in Late Twentieth-Century Performance and Revision of Greek Tragedy." *Dionysus Since 69: Greek Tragedy at the Dawn of*

the Third Millennium. Eds. Edith Hall, Fiona Macintosh, and Amanda Wrigley. Oxford: Oxford University Press, 2004.

———. *Female Acts in Greek Tragedy*. Princeton, NJ: Princeton University Press, 2001.

———. "Tragedy and Democratic Ideology: The Case of Sophocles' *Antigone*." In *History, Tragedy, and Theory*. Ed. Barbara Goff. Austin: University of Texas Press, 1995.

Ford, John. Introduction. *'Tis Pity She's a Whore*. Ed. Lisa Hopkins. London: Nick Hern Books, 2003.

Forte, Jeanne. "Focus on the Body: Pain, Praxis and Pleasure in Feminist Performance." *Critical Theory and Performance*. Eds. Janelle Reinelt and John Roach. Ann Arbor: UMI Press, 1992.

———. "Women's Performance Art: Feminism and Postmodernism." *Performing Feminisms: Feminist Critical Theory and Theatre*. Ed. Sue-Ellen Case. Baltimore: Johns Hopkins University Press, 1990.

Foss, Sonja, and Cindy Griffin. "Beyond Persuasion: A Proposal for an Invitational Rhetoric." *Communication Monographs* 62 (March 1995): 2–18.

Foster, Hal. *Prosthetic Gods*. Cambridge: MIT Press, 2004.

Foucault, Michel. *History of Sexuality: Volume One*. New York: Vintage Books, 1990.

Franko, Mark. *Dancing Modernism/Performing Politics*. Bloomington: Indiana University Press, 1995.

Friedman, Sharon. "Feminist Revisions of Classic Texts on the American Stage." *Codifying the National Self: Spectators, Actors, and the American Dramatic Text*. Eds. Barbara Ozieblo and Lola Narbona. Brussels: Peter Lang, 2006.

———. Rev. of *Phaedra in Delirium*. *Women & Performance* 10.1–2 (#19–20) (1999): 297–301.

Fuchs, Elinor. "Mabou Mines DollHouse." *Theatre Journal* 56.3 (2004): 498–500.

Galinsky, G. Karl. *Ovid's Metamorphosis*. Berkeley: University of California Press, 1975.

Gay, Penny. "Changing Shakespeare: New Possibilities for the Modern Actress." *The Cambridge Companion to the Actress*. Eds. Maggie B. Gale and John Stoke. Cambridge: Cambridge University Press, 2007.

Gibson, Wendy. *Women in Seventeenth-Century France*. New York: St. Martin's Press, 1989.

Gilbert, Sandra M. "Plain Jane's Progress." *Critical Essays on Charlotte Brontë*. Ed. Barbara Timm Gates. Boston: G.K. Hall, 1990.

———, and Susan Gubar. *The Madwoman in the Attic: The Woman Writer and the Nineteenth-Century Literary Imagination*. New Haven: Yale University Press, 1979.

Goff, Barbara E. *Readings of Desire, Violence & Language in Euripides' "Hippolytos."* Cambridge: Cambridge University Press, 1990.

Gohlke Sprengnether, Madeline. "'I Wooed Thee with My Sword': Shakespeare's Tragic Paradigms." *Othello*. By William Shakespeare. Ed. Alvin Kernan. New York: Signet Classic, 1998.

Goodman, Lizbeth. *Contemporary Feminist Theatres: To Each Her Own*. London: Routledge, 1993.

———. "Women's Alternative Shakespeares and Women's Alternatives to Shakespeare in Contemporary British Theatre." *Cross-Cultural Performances: Differences in Women's Re-Visions of Shakespeare*. Ed. Marianne Novy. Urbana: University of Illinois Press, 1993.

———, ed. *Mythic Women/Real Women: Plays and Performance Pieces by Women*. London: Faber and Faber, 2000.

———, and W.R. Owens, eds. *Shakespeare, Aphra Behn and the Canon*. London: Routledge, 1996.

Graves, Robert. *The Greek Myths*. London: Penguin, 1993.

———. *New Larousse Encyclopedia of Mythology*. London: Hamlyn, 1968 [1959].
Green, Amy. *The Revisionist Stage: American Directors Reinvent the Classics*. Cambridge and New York: Cambridge University Press, 1994.
Greenblatt, Stephen. *Renaissance Self-Fashioning*. Chicago: University of Chicago Press, 1980.
———. *Will in the World: How Shakespeare Became Shakespeare*. New York: W.W. Norton, 2004.
Greene, Gayle, Carolyn Ruth Swift Lenz, and Carol Thomas Neely, eds. *The Woman's Part*. Urbana: University of Illinois Press, 1980.
Griffin, Gabriele, and Elaine Aston, eds. *Herstory: Plays by Women for Women*. Vol. 1. Sheffield: Sheffield Academic Press, 1991.
Griffin Wolff, Cynthia. "Un-Utterable Longing: The Discourse of Feminine Sexuality in Kate Chopin's *The Awakening*." *The Awakening*. By Kate Chopin. Ed. Nancy A. Walker.
Grosz, Elizabeth. "Refiguring Lesbian Desire." *The Lesbian Postmodern*. Ed. Laura Doan. New York: Columbia University Press, 1994.
Gussow, Mel. "Worlds of Bogart." *Anne Bogart: Viewpoints*. Eds. Michael Bigelow Dixon and Joel A. Smith. Lyme, NH: Smith and Kraus, 1995.
Hamburger, Kate. *From Sophocles to Sartre*. New York: Frederick Ungar Publishing, 1969.
Hamilton, Edith. *Mythology: Timeless Tales of Gods and Heroes*. Boston: Little, Brown, 1942.
Harding, Susannah. *Jane Eyre: Education Pack*. London: Shared Experience Theatre Archives, 1997.
Harris, Geraldine. *Staging Femininities: Performance and Performativity*. Manchester, NH: Manchester University Press, 1999.
Hart, Lynda, ed. *Making a Spectacle: Feminist Essays on Contemporary Women's Theatre*. Ann Arbor: University of Michigan Press, 1989.
Hartigan, Karelisa V. *Greek Tragedy on the American Stage: Ancient Drama in the Commercial Theatre, 1882–1994*. Westport, CT: Greenwood Press, 1995.
Hawthorne, Nathaniel. *The Scarlet Letter*. New York: Penguin Classics, 2003.
Hersh, Allison. "'How Sweet the Kill': Orgiastic Female Violence in Contemporary Revisions of Euripides' *The Bacchae*." *Modern Drama* 35.3 (1992): 409–423.
Holledge, Julie, and Joanne Tompkins. *Women's Intercultural Performance*. London and New York: Routledge, 2000.
Huggan, Graham. "Philomela's Retold Story: Silence, Music and the Post-Colonial Text." *Journal of Commonwealth Literature* 25 (1990): 12–23.
Hughes, Derek, and Janet Todd. *The Cambridge Companion to Aphra Behn*. Cambridge: Cambridge University Press, 2004.
Irigaray, Luce. *This Sex Which Is Not One*. Trans. Catherine Porter and Carolyn Burke. Ithaca, NY: Cornell University Press, 1985.
Iizuka, Naomi. "What Myths May Come: Can We See the Future in the Mirror of Our Storied Past?" *American Theatre* 16.7 (September 1999): 78–80.
Johnson, Paul. *A History of the Jews*. New York: Harper and Row, 1987.
Johnstone, J. K. *The Bloomsbury Group*. New York: Octagon Books, 1978.
Joplin, Patricia Klindienst. "The Voice of the Shuttle Is Ours." *Stanford Literary Review* 1.1 (1984): 25–53.
Kahn, Coppélia. "The Absent Mother in *King Lear*." *Rewriting the Renaissance: The Discourses of Sexual Difference in Early Modern Europe*. Eds. Margaret Ferguson, Maureen Quilligan, and Nancy J. Vickers. Chicago: University of Chicago Press, 1986.
———. *Man's Estate*. Berkeley: University of California Press, 1981.
Kaplan, E. Ann. *Women and Film*. New York: Methuen, 1983.

Kernan, Alvin, ed. *Othello.* By William Shakespeare. New York: Signet Classic, 1998.
Keyssar, Helene. "Feminist Theatre of the Seventies in the United States." *The Cambridge Companion to American Women Playwrights.* Ed. Brenda Murphy. Cambridge: Cambridge University Press, 1999.
_____, ed. *Feminist Theatre and Theory.* New York: St. Martin's Press, 1996.
Kimball, Gayle, ed. *Women's Culture: Renaissance of the Seventies.* Metuchen, NJ, and London: The Scarecrow Press, 1981.
Klett, Elizabeth. "'O, How This Mother Swells Up Toward My Heart': Performing Mother and Father in Helena Kaut-Howson's Cross-Gender *King Lear.*" *Shakespeare Bulletin* 22 (September 2005): 53–73.
Knowles, Ric. "Othello in Three Times." *Shakespeare in Canada: 'a world elsewhere'?* Eds. Diana Brydon and Irena R. Makaryk. Toronto: University of Toronto Press, 2002.
Kolin, Philip C. *Shakespeare and Feminist Criticism: An Annotated Bibliography and Commentary.* New York: Garland, 1991.
Koppen, Randi S. "'The Furtive Event': Theorizing Feminist Spectatorship." *Modern Drama* XXXV.3 (September 1992): 378–394.
Krasner, David. Rev. of *In the Blood.* Dir. Suzan-Lori Parks. *Theatre Journal* 52.4 (December 2000): 565–567.
Krauss, Rosalind. *L'Amour Fou.* New York: Abbeville Press, 1985.
Kruger, Loren. "The Dis-play's the Thing: Gender and Public Sphere in Contemporary British Theatre." *Theatre Journal.* 42:1 (March 1990): 27–47.
Kuhn, Annette. *The Power of the Image: Essays on Representation and Sexuality.* London: Routledge, 1985.
Kushner, Tony. *Angels in America, Part One: Millennium Approaches.* New York: Theater Communications Group, 1993.
_____. *Angels in America, Part Two: Perestroika.* New York: Theater Communications Group, 1994.
Laing, R.D. *The Politics of the Family and Other Essays.* New York: Pantheon, 1969.
Landau, Tina. "Source-Work, the Viewpoints, and Composition: What Are They?" Eds. Michael Bigelow Dixon and Joel A. Smith. Lyme, NH: Smith and Kraus, 1995.
Langridge, Natasha, and Heidi Stephenson. *Rage and Reason: Women Playwrights on Playwriting.* London: Methuen Drama, 1997.
Langworthy, Douglas. "Wordschmidt." *American Theatre* (Sept. 1993): 16–20.
_____. "The Violence of Civility: An Interview with Phyllis Nagy." *American Theatre* 12.2 (February 1995).
Leavitt, Dinah. *Feminist Theatre Groups.* Jefferson, NC: McFarland, 1980.
Lee, Hermione. "Virginia Woolf's Essays." *The Cambridge Companion to Virginia Woolf.* Eds. Sue Roe and Susan Sellers. Cambridge: Cambridge University Press, 2000.
Leverenz, David. "Mrs. Hawthorne's Headache: Reading *The Scarlet Letter.*" *The Scarlet Letter: Case Studies in Contemporary Criticism.* Ed. Ross C. Murfin. Boston and New York: Bedford Books of St. Martin's Press, 1991.
Llewellyn-Jones, Margaret. "Spectacle, Silence and Subversion: Women's Performance Language and Strategies." *Contemporary Theatre Review* 2.1 (1994): 1–9.
Lupu, Michael, and Belinda Westmaas Jones, eds. *The Rover Study Guide.* Minneapolis: The Guthrie Theater, 2004.
Mack, Sara. *Ovid.* New Haven, CT: Yale University Press, 1988.
Malnig, Julie, and Judy C. Rosenthal. "The Women's Experimental Theatre: Transforming Family Stories into Feminist Questions." *Acting Out: Feminist Performance.* Eds. Lynda Hart and Peggy Phelan. Ann Arbor: UMI Press, 1993.
Marcus, Laura. "Woolf's Feminism and Feminism's Woolf." *The Cambridge Companion to Virginia Woolf.* Eds. Sue Roe and Susan Sellers. Cambridge: Cambridge University Press, 2000.

Marder, Elissa. "Disarticulated Voices: Feminism and Philomela." *Hypatia* 7.2 (1992): 148–66.
Marrero, Maria Teresa, and Caridad Svich, eds. *Out of the Fringe*. New York: Theatre Communications Group, 2000.
Martin, Carol, and Saviana Stanescu, ed. *Global Foreigners*. London, New York, and Calcutta: Seagull Press, 2006.
Matthews, J. H. *Eight Painters: The Surrealist Context*. Syracuse: Syracuse University Press, 1982.
McDonald, Marianne. "The Atrocities of *Les Atrides*: Mnouchkine's Tragic Vision." *Theatre Forum* 1.1 (Spring 1992): 13–19.
McLaughlin, Ellen. "Iphigenia and Other Daughters." *The Greek Plays*. New York: Theatre Communications Group, 2005.
Michelakis, Pantelis. "Greek Tragedy in Cinema: Theatre, Politics, History." *Dionysus Since 69: Greek Tragedy at the Dawn of the Third Millennium*. Ed. Edith Hall, Fiona Macintosh, and Amanda Wrigley. Oxford: Oxford University Press, 2004.
Miller, Jonathan. *Subsequent Performances*. New York: Viking Penguin, 1986.
Moi, Toril. "'First and Foremost a Human Being': Idealism, Theatre, and Gender in *A Doll's House*," *Modern Drama* 49.3 (Fall 2006): 256–284.
Muir, Kenneth. "Introduction." *The Arden Shakespeare: King Lear*. London: Methuen, 1969.
Mulvey, Laura. *Visual and Other Pleasures*. Bloomington: Indiana University Press, 1989.
_____. "Visual Pleasure and Narrative Cinema." *Screen* 16.3 (1975): 6–18.
Muratore, Mary Jo. *Expirer Au Féminin: Narratives of Female Dissolution in French Classical Texts*. New Orleans: University Press of the South, 2003.
Murphy, Brenda, ed. *The Cambridge Companion to American Women Playwrights*. Cambridge: Cambridge University Press, 1999.
Nagy, Phyllis. *The Scarlet Letter*. *American Theatre* 12.2 (February 1995): 22–39.
Neely, Carol Thomas. "Remembering Shakespeare, Revising Ourselves." *Women's Re-Visions of Shakespeare: On the Responses of Dickinson, Woolf, Rick, H.D., George Eliot and Others*. Ed. Marianne Novy. Urbana: University of Illinois Press, 1990.
Newman, Karen. "'And wash the Ethiop white': Femininity and the Monstrous in *Othello*." *Shakespeare Reproduced*. Eds. Jean E. Howard and Marion O'Connor. New York: Methuen, 1987.
Novy, Marianne, ed. *Cross-Cultural Performances: Differences in Women's Re-Visions of Shakespeare*. Urbana: University of Illinois Press, 1993.
_____. *Engaging with Shakespeare: Responses of George Eliot and Other Women Novelists*. Athens: University of Georgia Press, 1994.
_____. "Introduction." *Transforming Shakespeare: Contemporary Women's Re-Visions in Literature and Performance*. New York: Palgrave, 2000.
Orlando, Francesco. *Toward a Freudian Theory of Literature with an Analysis of Racine's Phèdre*. Trans. Charmaine Lee. Baltimore and London: The Johns Hopkins University Press, 1978.
Ovid. *Metamorphoses*. Trans. A.D. Melville. Oxford: Oxford University Press, 1988.
Paran, Janice. "Redressing Ibsen: Directors Fornes, Near and Mann Emancipate His Proto-Feminist Plays from their Victorian Bonds." *American Theater* (November 1987): 15–20.
Parks, Suzan-Lori. *The Red Letter Plays: In the Blood* and *Fucking A*. New York: Theatre Communications Group, 2001.
Parrish, Sue. "Forward: The Power of Tradition." *The Glass Ceiling*. London: The Sphinx, 1991.
Pearce, Michele. Rev. of *The Scarlet Letter*. Dir. Phyllis Nagy. *American Theatre* 2.10 (November 1994): 13.

Pechter, Edward. *Othello and Interpretive Traditions*. Iowa City: University of Iowa Press, 1999.
Peterson, M. Jeanne. "The Victorian Governess: Status Incongruence in Family and Society." *Suffer and Be Still: Women in the Victorian Age*. Ed. Martha Vicinus. Bloomington: Indiana University Press, 1972.
Phelan, Peggy. *Mourning Sex: Performing Public Memories*. London: Routledge, 1997.
Quintilian. *Institutes of Oratory*. Trans. John Selby Watson. London: George Bell and Sons, 1876.
Rabey, David Ian. "Defining Difference: Timberlake Wertenbaker's Drama of Language, Dispossession and Discovery." *Modern Drama* 33.4 (1990): 518–28.
Rabinowitz, Nancy Sorkin. *Anxiety Veiled: Euripides and the Traffic in Women*. Ithaca, NY: Cornell University Press, 1993.
Rabkin, Gerald. "Is There a Text on this Stage: Theatre/Authorship/Interpretation." *PAJ 26/27* IX.2 and 3 (1985): 151–152.
Racine, Jean. *Iphigenia, Phaedra, Athaliah*. Trans. John Cairncross. Harmondsworth, UK: Penguin Books, 1970 [1963].
———. *Phèdre*. Trans. Paul Schmidt. *Theater* 30.1 (2000): 102–127.
Rayner, Alice. "The Audience: Subjectivity, Community and the Ethics of Listening." *Journal of Dramatic Theory and Criticism* 7.2 (1993): 3–24.
Rea, Charlotte. "Women for Women." *Drama Review* 18 (December 1974): 77–87.
———. "Women's Theatre Groups." *Drama Review* 16 (June 1972): 79–89.
Reinelt, Janelle. "Navigating Postfeminism: Writing Out of the Box." *Feminist Futures?* Eds. Elaine Aston and Geraldine Harris. Houndmills, Basingstoke, and Hampshire: Palgrave Macmillan, 2006.
Reinhart, Nancy S. "New Directions for Feminist Criticism in the Theatre and the Related Arts." *A Feminist Perspective in the Academy: The Difference It Makes*. Eds. Elizabeth Langland and Walter Gove. Chicago: University of Chicago Press, 1981.
Rich, Adrienne. "*Jane Eyre*: The Temptations of a Motherless Woman." *Critical Essays on Charlotte Brontë*. Ed. Barbara Timm Gates. Boston: G.K. Hall, 1990.
———. "When We Dead Awaken: Writing as Re-Vision." *College English* 34.1 (1972): 18–30.
Richlin, Amy. "Reading Ovid's Rapes." *Pornography and Representation in Greece and Rome*. New York: Oxford University Press, 1992.
Roe, Sue, and Susan Sellers, eds. *The Cambridge Companion to Virginia Woolf*. Cambridge: Cambridge University Press, 2000.
Rogers, K.M. *Feminism in Eighteenth-Century England*. London: Harvester Press, 1982.
Rotman, Brian. *Signifying Nothing: The Semiotics of Zero*. Stanford: Stanford University Press, 1993.
Rudakoff, Judith. *Fair Play: Twelve Women Speak: Conversations with Canadian Playwrights*. Toronto: Simon & Pierre, 1990.
Savran, David. *Communists, Cowboys, and Queers: The Politics of Masculinity in the Work of Arthur Miller and Tennessee Williams*. Minnesota and London: University of Minnesota Press, 1992.
Schafer, Elizabeth. *Ms-Directing Shakespeare: Women Direct Shakespeare*. New York: St. Martin's Press, 2000.
Schechner, Richard. "Theatre Alive in the New Millennium." *The Drama Review: TDR* 44.1 (Spring 2000): 5–6.
Schor, Naomi. "Feminist and Gender Studies." *Introduction to Scholarship in Modern Languages and Literatures*. Ed. Joseph Gibaldi. New York: MLA, 1992.
Schroeder, Patricia R. "American Drama, Feminist Discourse and Dramatic Form: A Defense of Critical Pluralism." *Theatre and Feminist Aesthetics*. Ed. Karen Laughlin and Catherine Schuler. Madison, NJ: Fairleigh Dickinson University Press, 1995.

Schwab, Gabriele. "Seduced by Witches: Nathaniel Hawthorne's *The Scarlet Letter* in the Context of New England Witchcraft Fictions." *Seduction and Theory*. Ed. Dianne Hunter. Chicago: University of Illinois Press, 1989.

Scott, Joan. "Gender: A Useful Category of Historical Analysis." *Gender and the Politics of History*. New York: Columbia University Press, 1999.

Sedgwick, Eve Kosofsky. *Tendencies*. Durham: Duke University Press, 1993.

Segal, Sondra and Roberta Sklar. "The Women's Experimental Theatre." *Women in American Theatre*. Eds. Helen Krich Chinoy and Linda Walsh Jenkins. New York: Crown Publishers, 1987.

Seyersted, Per. *Kate Chopin: A Critical Biography*. Baton Rouge: University of Louisiana Press, 1969.

Sharrock, Alison. "Gender and Sexuality." *Cambridge Companion to Ovid*. Cambridge: Cambridge University Press, 2002.

Showalter, Elaine, ed. *Speaking of Gender*. New York and London: Routledge, 1989.

Singh, Jyotsna. "The Interventions of History: Narratives of Sexuality." *The Weyward Sisters: Shakespeare and Feminist Politics*. Eds. Dympna Callaghan, Lorraine Helms, and Jyotsna Singh. Oxford: Blackwell, 1994.

Sklar, Roberta. "*Sisters* or Never Trust Anyone outside the Family." *Women and Performance* 1.1 (Spring-Summer 1983): 58–70.

Slavitt, David R., trans. *The Metamorphosis of Ovid*. Baltimore: Johns Hopkins University Press, 1994.

Smalec, Theresa. "Yelena Gluzman's 'I'm so Sorry for Everything.'" *The Drama Review: TDR* 47.3 (2003): 136–142.

Smith, Iris. "Mabou Mines's *Lear*: A Narrative of Collective Authorship." *Theatre Journal* 45 (1993): 279–301.

Snyder, Susan. "Beyond Comedy: *Romeo and Juliet*." *The Tragedy of Romeo and Juliet*. By William Shakespeare. Ed. J.A. Bryant, Jr. New York: Signet Classic, 1998.

Solomon, Alisa. "The New Drama and the New Woman: Reconstructing Ibsen's Realism." *Re-Dressing the Canon: Essays on Theater and Gender*. London and New York: Routledge, 1997.

_____, and Framji Minwalla, eds. *The Queerest Art: Essays on Lesbian and Gay Theater*. New York: New York University Press, 2002.

Spangler, George M. "Kate Chopin's *The Awakening*: A Partial Dissent." *Novel* 3 (Spring 1970): 249–255.

Starobinski, Jean. *L'Oeuil Vivant*. Paris: Gallimard, 1961.

Steadman, Susan M. *Dramatic Re-Visions: An Annotated Bibliography of Feminism and Theatre, 1972–1988*. Chicago: American Library Association, 1991.

Still, Judith, and Michael Wortin. Introduction. *Intertextuality: Theories and Practices*. Manchester: Manchester University Press, 1990.

Stimpson, Catherine. "Woolf's Room, Our Project: The Building of Feminist Criticism." *Virginia Woolf (Longman Critical Readers)*. Ed. Rachel Bowlby. New York: Longman, 1992.

Stodelle, Ernestine. *Deep Song: The Dance Story of Martha Graham*. New York: Schirmer Books, 1984.

Suleiman, Susan Rubin. *Subversive Intent: Gender, Politics, and the Avant-Garde*. Cambridge: Harvard University Press, 1990.

Sullivan, Esther Beth. "Women, Woman, and the Subject of Feminism: Feminist Directions." *Upstaging Big Daddy: Directing Theatre as if Gender and Race Matter*. Eds. Ellen Donkin and Susan Clement. Ann Arbor: University of Michigan Press, 1993.

Sullivan, Zohreh T. "Race, Gender, and Imperial Ideology in the Nineteenth Century." *Nineteenth-Century Contexts* 15.1 (1989): 19–32.

Suntree, Susan. "Women's Theatre: Creating the Dream Now." *Women's Culture: The*

Women's Renaissance of the Seventies. Ed. Gayle Kimball. Meteuchen, NJ, and London: Scarecrow Press, 1981.
Svich, Caridad, ed. *Divine Fire: Eight Contemporary Plays Inspired by the Greeks*. New York: Backstage Books, 2005.
Teale, Polly. *Jane Eyre*. London: Nick Hern Books, 1998.
Templeton, Joan. "The Poetry of Feminism." *Ibsen's Women*. New York: Cambridge University Press, 2001.
Todd, Janet. *The Secret Life of Aphra Behn*. New Brunswick, NJ: Rutgers University Press, 1996.
Tomaselli, Sylvana, and Roy Porter, eds. *Rape: An Historical and Social Enquiry*. Oxford: Basil Blackwell, 1986.
Vicinus, Martha. Ed. *Suffer and Be Still: Women in Victorian Society*. Bloomington: Indiana University Press, 1972.
Vickery, John. *Myth and Literature*. Lincoln: University of Nebraska Press, 1966.
_____. *Myths and Texts: Strategies of Incorporation and Displacement*. Baton Rouge: Louisiana State University, 1983.
Von Hendy, Andrew. "The Modernist Contribution to the Construction of Myth." *Modern Myths*. Amsterdam: Rodopi, 1993.
Wagner, Jennifer. "Formal Parody and the Metamorphosis of the Audience in Timberlake Wertenbaker's *The Love of the Nightingale*." *PLL Papers on Language and Literature* 31.3 (1995): 227–54.
Wandor, Michelene. *Carry On, Understudies: Theatre and Sexual Politics*. London: Routledge, 1986.
_____. *Understudies*. London: Methuen, 1981.
Wertenbaker, Timberlake. *Plays One*. London: Faber and Faber, 1996.
Williams, Tennessee. *A Streetcar Named Desire*. New York: New American Library, 1947.
Wilmer, Steve. "Women in Greek Tragedy Today: A Reappraisal." *Theatre Research International* 32. 2. Cambridge: Cambridge University Press, 2007. 106–118.
Winston, Joe. "Re-Casting the Phaedra Syndrome: Myth and Morality in *The Love of the Nightingale*." *Modern Drama* 38.4 (1995): 510–19.
Wittig, Monique. "The Point of View: Universal or Particular." *Feminist Issues* (1983): 63–69.
Wolkenfeld, Suzanne. "Edna's Suicide: The Problem of the One and the Many." *The Awakening*. By Kate Chopin. Ed. Margo Culley. New York: W. W. Norton, 1994.
Women's Theatre Group and Elaine Feinstein. *Lear's Daughters*. In *Adaptations of Shakespeare: A Critical Anthology of Plays from the Seventeenth Century to the Present*. Eds. Daniel Fischlin and Mark Fortier. London: Routledge, 2000.
Woolf, Virginia. *Between the Acts*. New York: Harcourt, Brace and Company, 1941.
_____. *The Common Reader: First Series*. New York: Harcourt, Brace and World, 1925.
_____. *The Common Reader: Second Series*. New York: Harcourt, Brace and World, 1932.
_____. *The Death of the Moth and Other Essays*. New York: Harcourt, Brace and Company, 1942.
_____. *The Diary of Virginia Woolf*. Ed. Anne Olivier Bell. New York: Harcourt Brace Jovanovich, 1977.
_____. *Mr. Bennett and Mrs. Brown*. Norwood, PA: Norwood Editions, 1978.
_____. *Moments of Being: A Collection of Autobiographical Writings*. Ed. Jeanne Schulkind. San Diego, CA: Harvest/Harcourt, 1985.
_____. *Orlando*. San Diego, CA: Harvest/Harcourt, 1973.
_____. *A Room of One's Own*. Orlando: Harvest/Harcourt, 1989.
_____. *The Waves*. New York: Harcourt, Brace and Company, 1931.
Wyckoff, Elizabeth. *Sophocles I*. Ed. David Greene. Chicago: University of Chicago Press, 1970.

Yarbro-Bejarano, Yvonne. "Chicanas' Experience in Collective Theatre: Ideology and Form." *Feminist Theatre and Theory.* Ed. Helene Keyssar. New York: St. Martin's Press, 1996.

Zeitlin, Froma. *Playing the Other: Gender and Society in Classical Greek Literature.* Chicago and London: University of Chicago Press, 1996.

Zimmerman, Mary. "The Archaeology of Performance." *Theatre Topics.* 15.1 (2005): 25–35.

About the Contributors

Cheryl Black is associate professor of theatre and director of graduate studies at the University of Missouri–Columbia, book review editor of *Theatre History Studies* and secretary of the American Theatre and Drama Society. She is the author of *The Women of Provincetown* (2002) and has published articles on women's and feminist theatre in *Theatre Survey*, *Theatre Studies*, *Theatre History Studies*, *The Journal of American Drama and Theatre*, and the *Journal of Dramatic Theory and Criticism*. She is also an actress, director, dramaturg, and the author of eight plays and dramatic adaptations.

Johan Callens teaches at the Vrije Universiteit Brussel. He edited and introduced *The Wooster Group and Its Traditions* (2004), to which he also contributed an essay on The Builders Association's *Jump Cut (Faust)*. His research on Sam Shepard resulted in essays on his adaptation of Marlowe's *Doctor Faustus* for *The Cambridge Companion to Sam Shepard* (2002), on Robert Altman's screen version of *Fool for Love* for *American Literature and the Arts* (1991), and the critical study *From Middleton and Rowley's "Changeling" to Sam Shepard's "Bodyguard": A Contemporary Appropriation of a Renaissance Drama* (1997). His book *Existentialist Inspiration and Generic Experimentation in the Early Work of Jack Richardson* (1993) also contains a chapter on *The Prodigal*, a re-vision of Aeschylus' *Oresteia*.

Lenora Champagne is a playwright, solo performer, director and occasional essayist. She is also professor of drama studies at Purchase College, SUNY. Champagne is the recipient of numerous fellowships for her playwriting (NYFA and NEA). In 1999, she and composer Daniel Levy received the Richard Rodgers Award from the American Academy of Arts and Letters for *THE SINGING: A CYBERSPACE OPERA*. In addition, she was artistic associate at Classic Stage Company. Her performance writing has been published in *Performing Arts Journal*, *Women and Performance Journal*, *Performance Research*, and in her edited collection, *Out from Under: Texts by Women Performance Artists* (1990).

Kristin Crouch is the literary director for the Milwaukee Repertory Theater. Prior to her move up north, Kristin served as assistant professor of drama at Trinity University in San Antonio, Texas. Recent directing credits include Shakespeare's *Much Ado About Nothing*, Rebecca Gilman's *Boy Gets Girl*, and Caridad Svich's *Alchemy of Desire/Dead Man's Blues*. Her current research focuses on physical theater, narrative adaptations, and British and Scottish contemporary theatre. Other articles on Shared Experience include "Inside Out: The Creative Process of Shared Experience" for *TheatreForum*.

Lesley Ferris is a director and a scholar, and she has chaired departments of theater at Middlesex University, London, University of Memphis, Louisiana State University, and Ohio State University. Her books include *Acting Women: Images of Women in Theatre* (1990) and *Crossing the Stage: Controversies on Cross-Dressing* (1993) and she has

279

written numerous essays on women's performance. She has directed nearly fifty plays internationally. In 2003, she directed Adrienne and Adam P. Kennedy's *Sleep Deprivation Chamber* at Ohio State that experimented with digital animation, interactive computer interfaces, and real-time visual effects. Her most recent project was co-curating *Midnight Robbers: The Artists of Notting Hill Carnival*, an exhibition that opened in London in 2007.

Sharon Friedman is associate professor in the Gallatin School of New York University where she teaches literary forms, dramatic literature and criticism, and (with Julie Malnig) "Text and Performance." Her essays have appeared in *American Studies*; *New Theatre Quarterly*; *Women and Performance*; *New England Theatre Journal*; *Contemporary Authors Bibliographical Series: American Dramatists*; *TDR*; *Susan Glaspell: Essays on Her Theater and Fiction*; and *Codifying the National Self: Spectators, Actors, and the American Dramatic Text*. She is co-author (with Stephen Steinberg) of *Writing and Thinking in the Social Sciences* (1989).

Deborah R. Geis is associate professor in the English Department at DePauw University in Greencastle, Indiana, where she teaches courses in contemporary drama, postmodern literature, and film studies. She is author of *Postmodern Theatric(k)s: Monologue in Contemporary American Drama* (1993), co-editor (with Steven F. Kruger) of *Approaching the Millennium: Essay on Angels in America (1997)*, and editor of *Considering MAUS: Approaches to Art Spiegelman's "Survivor's Tale" of the Holocaust* (2003). Her most recent book, *Digging (Up) History: The Drama of Suzan-Lori Parks*, is forthcoming from the University of Michigan Press.

Amy S. Green is associate professor of speech, theater, and media studies and chair of the Women's Studies Committee at John Jay College of Criminal Justice (CUNY) in Manhattan. Professor Green is the author of *The Revisionist Stage: American Directors Reinvent the Classics* (1994) and two original testimonial dramas, *Girlz in Blue* (about female officers of the NYPD) and *What Happened: The September 11th Testimony Project*. She has received numerous citations for directing from the Kennedy Center/American College Theatre Festival and is currently serving her second term as regional chair of the National Critics Institute.

Julie Malnig is associate professor in the Gallatin School of Individualized Study at New York University where she teaches courses in performance criticism, history, and theory. She is the author of *Dancing Till Dawn: A Century of Exhibition Ballroom Dance* (1995) and *Ballroom, Boogie, Shimmy Sham, Shake: A Social and Popular Dance Reader* (2008). Her numerous articles on contemporary performance, performance art, and gender and performance have appeared in Hart and Phelan's *Acting Out: Feminist Performances* and Dils and Albright's *Moving History/Dancing Cultures*, and other publications. She has served as an editor of *Women & Performance: A Journal of Feminist Theory* and *Dance Research Journal*.

Carol Martin is associate professor of drama at Tisch School of the Arts, New York University, and general editor of "In Performance," a series of international plays and contexts (Seagull Books). She was also the guest editor of a recent issue of *TDR* devoted to the subject of documentary theatre. Her books include *Documentary Theatre on World Stages* (forthcoming 2008); *Global Foreigner* (co-edited with Saviana Stanescu, 2007); *Brecht Sourcebook* (co-edited with Henry Bial, 1999); *A Sourcebook of Feminist Theatre: On and Beyond the Stage* (1996); and *Dance Marathons: Performing American Culture of* *the 1920s and 1930s* (1994). She is a contributing editor to *TDR* and *Assaph: Studies in the Theatre*.

Sandee K. McGlaun is associate professor of English and director of the writing center at Roanoke College in Salem, Virginia. She has been following the work of Anne Bogart and SITI Company since interning at Actors Theatre of Louisville in 1993, and her research frequently explores intersections between rhetoric, composition, and theatre. Her dissertation, "Re-Staging Persuasion: Feminist Theatrical Performance and/as Rhetoric," was completed at The Ohio State University. Her essays have appeared in publications such as *Dialogue* and *Southern Discourse*. She is also the writer and performer of the one-woman show *What a Doll*.

Chiori Miyagawa's plays have been produced Off Broadway, at renowned performance spaces in New York City, and regionally. Six of her plays have been published in anthologies, including *Woman Killer* in *Plays and Playwrights, 2002*; *Nothing Forever* in *Positive/Negative: Women of Color and HIV/AIDS*; and *Jamaica Avenue* in *Tokens? The Asian American Experience on Stage*. She is a recipient of numerous fellowships and grants including New York Foundation for the Arts Playwriting Fellowship and McKnight Playwriting Fellowship. She is a resident playwright of New Dramatists, co-artistic director of Crossing Jamaica Avenue, playwright-in-residence under director JoAnne Akalaitis at Bard College, and serves on the board of ART/NY.

Andrea J. Nouryeh is associate professor of dramatic literature and theater history at St. Lawrence University. She has been the university's resident dramaturg since 1992 and has assisted directors with many productions, including *Midsummer Night's Dream*, *Medea Myth*, *Getting Out*, and *Cloud Nine*. She is co-author of *Drama and Performance* (1996), and has contributed chapters to *Foreign Shakespeare*, ed. Dennis Kennedy; *Black Theatre*, ed. Paul Carter Harrison; and *Interrogating America through Theatre and Performance*, eds. William W. Demastes and Iris Smith Fischer. Her articles appear in encyclopedias, bibliographies, and such journals as *Theatre Topics*, *New England Theatre Journal*, *Shakespeare on Film Newsletter*, *On-Stage Studies*, *Black American Literature Forum*, *Research in African Literatures*, and *Encyclopedia of the Harlem Renaissance*.

Maya E. Roth is assistant professor of theater and performance studies at Georgetown University, where she served as the Davis Center's first artistic director and shepherded a new major that integrates critical and creative studies. Her specializations include civic theater, feminist performance, the plays of Timberlake Wertenbaker, and space-based criticism. Her book *International Dramaturgy: Translation and Transformations in the Theatre of Timberlake Wertenbaker*, co-edited with Sara Freeman, is forthcoming from Peter Lang Press. Roth also coordinates the Jane Chambers Playwriting Contest for feminist playwrights, a joint project of WTP and ATHE.

Index

Page numbers in **_bold italics_** refer to illustrations.

Aeschylus: *Agamemnon* 21; *The Eumenides* 21; *The Libation Bearers* 21; *Oresteia* 21, 23, 26, 29, 32, 33, 80, 102–3
African Solo (Sears) 127
Agamemnon (Aeschylus) 21
Agamemnon (Euripides) 33
Akalaitis, JoAnne: *Phèdre* 153; and seventeenth-century classics 135, 136, 148–49; *'Tis Pity* 137 138
Akerland, Christopher 227
America Dreaming (Miyagawa) 86
American Repertory Theatre 153
Andoh, Adjoa 102
Andreach, Robert 34
Angels in America (Kushner) 237
Anouilh, Jean 82
Antigone (Anouilh) 82
Antigone (Demirel) 82
Antigone (Sophocles) 79, 80–85, 88, 91; feminist readings of 81, 84; other readings of 81, 82–83, 89–90
Antigone: A Cry for Peace (Koundouros) 82–83
Antigone a tí druhi [*Antigone and the Others*] (Karvas) 82
Antigone Arkhe (Svich) 79, 91
Antigone Furiosa (Gambaro) 82
Antigone Prism (Suntree) 83–84
Antigone Project (Women's Project) 79, **_80_**, 81–82, 85–91, 92n2
Apuleius 64
Argentina, Dirty War in 48
Aristophanes: *The Frogs* 156; *Thesmophoriazousai* 156
Aristotle 103; *Poetics* 163; views on women 93n17
Arons, Wendy 148
Artaud, Antonin 26, 83, 117
The Ash Girl (Wertenbaker) 43
Astell, Mary 140
Aston, Elaine 5, 104
ATHE, Woman and Theatre Program 1
Atwood, Margaret (*A Handmaid's Tale*) 237
Austin, Gayle 115, 193, 197
The Awakening (Chopin): Miyagawa's adaptation of 204–14

The Bacchae (Euripides) 45, 50
Bacon, Jenny 147–48, 154

Bakhtin, Mikhail 8
Balanchine, George 160
Barfield, Tanya (*Medallion*) 79, **_80_**, 87–89
Barthes, Roland 117
Bassnet, Susan 51, 52
Bay Street Theatre **_114_**
Bayes, Christopher 141
Baym, Nina 171, 172
"Beautiful Dream" (song) 244
Beauvoir, Simone de 141
Bedford, Brian 99
Beer, Gillian (*Virginia Woolf: The Common Ground*) 220
Beglarian, Eve 258
Behn, Aphra 99; *The Rover* 135, 136, 140–45
Bell, Monica **_22_**, 23
Belle Reprieve **_238_**, 239–45
Belli, Angela 14n9
Benjamin, Walter 131
Bennett, Larry 82
Bennett, Susan 117; *Performing Nostalgia* 116, 131n11
Benstock, Shari 171
Berger, John 98
Berry, Gabriel 143
Between the Acts (Woolf) 218
Bigsby, C.W.E. 240
Bloolips 239–40
Bloom, Claire 250
The Bluest Eye (Morrison) 52
Bodies that Matter (Butler) 243–44
Bogart, Anne: and *Room* 215, **_216_**, 217, 220, 223, 225, 230; and SITI Company 215, 224, 225; on Stanislavski method 215
Bogartian biodrama 215
Boileau, Nicolas 145
Boland, Eavan 50, 52
Bolton, H. Philip 189
Booth, Cherise **_170_**, 171
Bourne, Bette 240, 243
Bousquet, Dominique 159
Brando, Marlon 241
Brantley, Ben 1, 97, 178, 180, 183
Brecht, Bertolt: *Good Woman of Szechuan* 188n36; influence of 7, 28, 44, 83, 103, 121, 240, 241, 245, 253; *Mother Courage* 188n36
Breuer, Lee 101, 252, 257–64

283

Brill, Fran *114*
Brontë, Charlotte (*Jane Eyre*) 189–203
Brooklyn Academy of Music 256
Brown, Janet 8, 62
Brunschwiler, Michael 171
Brustein, Robert 255, 257
Burnett, Sheila, photo by *238*
Burt, John 218
Butler, Judith 84, 85; *Bodies That Matter* 243–44

Callaghan, Dympna 2
Campbell, John 145
Canaday, John 139
Canning, Charlotte 6, 24, 25
Carlson, Susan 43, 55, 57, 143
Case, Sue Ellen 23, 24, 30, 93n17
Cather, Willa 213
Cavendish, Margaret 140, 141
Chaikin, Joseph 26
Chalfant, Andromache 171
Chalfant, Kathleen 34, 153
Chambers, Janys 102
Chautauqua Theatre Company *22*, 23
Chekhov, Anton 160
China, feminism in 253
Chirico, Georgio de 137, 138, 139
Chodorow, Nancy 27
Chopin, Kate: *The Awakening*, Miyagawa's adaptation of 204–14; as character in Miyagawa's play 208–9; immortality of 213
Churchill, Caryl 15n15
Civil War 129
Clarke, Jocelyn (*Room* playtext) 217, 220–23, 226
Classic Stage Company, New York 31, 153, 178, 215, 216
Clum, John 243
collage style 2
Collins, Joey *80*
The Color Purple (Walker) 52
Common Reader series (Woolf) 217
Conklin, John 136, 137
Corbett, Edward P. J. 227–28
Coss, Clare 23, 25, 27, 29, 30
Cott, Nancy 90
Cousin, Geraldine 50, 55, 57
Crossing Jamaica Avenue 79, 205
Curran, Beverly 122
Cutter, Martha 52

Dafoe, Willem 163
Dalí, Salvador 162
Daly, Mary 36
Danson, Randy 153
Darfur 48
The Daughters Cycle (WET) 26, 27
Davies, Oliver Ford 99–100
Davis, Viola 144
De Grazia, Victoria 137
DeJean, Joan 146

de Lauretis, Teresa: on feminist theory 25, 26, 30, 38n17; *Technologies of Gender* 6
Deleuze, Gilles 241
Demirel, Kemal (*Antigone*) 82
Derrick, Scott 177
Derrida, Jacques 157
Desdemona (Vogel) 113, *114*, 116, 118–22, 127
Diamond, Elin 241
Diamond, Liz (*Phaedra*) 153, 158
Dianeira (Wertenbaker) 43
Dickinson, Peter 127
DiGaetani, John L. 56
Dixon, Beth *22*, 23
Dolan, Jill 3, 24, 25, 114
Dolan, Monica *190*
A Doll House (Ibsen) 249–53; and audience expectations 250–51, 252, 258; in cultural context 253–56; and feminist agenda 247, 249–52, 255, 257; and *Mabou Mines DollHouse* *248*, 252–53, 257–64; on tour 261, 262, 264; twentieth-century adaptations of 253–56
Drench (band) 159, 163
Drexler, Rosalyn (*Libby*) 237
Dürrenmatt, Friedrich 215
Dusinberre, Juliet 105, 106, 107
Dymkowski, Christine 50

Eble, Kenneth 213
Edinburgh Fringe Festival 264
Electra (McLaughlin) 34–35
Electra (Sophocles) 27–29, 33
Electra Speaks (WET) 27–30; and *The Daughters Cycle* 26, 27; feminist agenda in 23, 24, 25–26, 27, 30, 31, 33, 34, 36; and the *Oresteia* myth 23, 29, 32, 33
Electronic Seminar Series Archive 37n2
Eliot, T. S. 152
Episodes (Graham) 160, 163
Epstein, Alvin 99
Erincin, Serap 92n11
Errand into the Maze (Graham) 160, 162
The Eumenides (Aeschylus) 21
Euripides 21; *Agamemnon* 33; *The Bacchae* 45, 50; *Hippolytus* 45, 145, 152, 154, 156–57, 158–60, 161, 163; *Iphigenia in Aulis* 31, 33, 34; *Iphigenia in Tauris* 31; *Stheneboia* 156
Eurydice (Ruhl) 77n28
Evans, Christine (*Trojan Barbie: A Car-Crash Encounter with Euripides' Trojan Women*) 1

Falls, Robert 99
Fascism 137–38, 139
Feinstein, Elaine 102
feminism: in cultural context 253–56; as defiance of expectations 207; and democracy 90; and gender studies 5–6; humanist 253; and Ibsen's *A Doll House* 247, 249–52, 255, 257; liberal, bourgeois 5, 23–24; materialist (socialist) 5, 23, 24; as movement

90; and the performer's body 241; pioneers of 140, 141; and race 117; radical (cultural) 5, 23, 24, 32; second wave (1970s) 26–27, 28, 116, 117; sexual equality sought by 90, 192; splintered movement of 33–34; trajectory of 23–25; transnational thinking in 5, 253–54
feminist theater 1–8; avant-garde 1; breaking sexual taboos in 5; challenging heterosexuality as norm 5; collaborative process in 72–75; emergence of 4; and feminist theory 4–7, 114–15; and Greek tragedy 83–85; intertextuality in 1–2; postmodern productions in 2; re-visioning classical works in 1, 2–3, 116, 127; theatrical styles in 7–8; use of term 61
feminist theater criticism 4–5; and creativity 114; and feminist theories 5, 25; on *Jane Eyre* 191–92, 193; on *Othello* 116–17, 118; on *Phèdra* 146; playwright as critic 122, 131; on *The Scarlet Letter* 171–72; shifting focus of 31
feminist theory: de Lauretis on 25, 26, 30, 38n17; and feminist theater 4–7, 114–15; and re-visioning classic theatrical works 1; Shakespeare rewritten in 113
Fergusson, Honora 259
Fetterley, Judith 122
Findlay, Jim 159
Finney, Gail 249, 264n4
Fischlin, Daniel 2, 8–9, 98, 102, 110
Fleche, Anne 243
Fliakos, Ari 159, 161, 163
Foley, Helene 27, 34, 82
Ford, John: life of 136–37; *Patriarcha* 137; *'Tis Pity She's a Whore* 135, 136–40, **136**, 141, 145, 147
Fornes, Maria Irene 193; *Sarita* 197
Fortier, Mark 2, 8–9, 98, 102, 110, 127, 131
Foss, Sonja 217, 218
Foucault, Michel 135, 244
Fragments of a Trilogy (Serban) 2
French, Marilyn (*Shakespeare's Division of Experience*) 106
Freudian theory 26, 173, 241
Freylinghuysen, Peter 161
The Frogs (Aristophanes) 156
Fryer, Judith 171
Fucking A (Parks) 173–74, 181, 182, 185–86
Fugard, Athol (*The Island*) 82

Gambaro, Griselda (*Antigone Furiosa*) 82
Gamel, Mary-Kay 37n2
Gardner, Lyn 264
Garvey, Marcus 129
Gearhart, Mary (photo by) **153**
Geiger, Mary Louise 258
gender: ambiguity of 106, 107; androgyny 222; and casting 99–102, 106; and class 120–21, 184; and commerce 109, 138; and culture 121, 128, 190–91, 207, 252, 255; and genre 117; and identity 243–44, 245; and power 101, 103, 108, 110, 116, 176; and race 117, 127, 129; and sexuality 239, 240–42; as social performance 251; theatrical artifice of 253; unity based on 90; use of term 40–41n62, 43; and writing 193, 221
gender studies, rise of 5–6, 255
Gibson, Wendy 145
Gilbert, Sandra 191, 192–93, 194
Gilman, Rebecca 256
Gluzman, Yelena (*I'm So Sorry for Everything*) 256
Goethe, Johan Wolfgang von 251
Goffman, Erving (*The Presentation of Self in Everyday Life*) 251
Gone (King) 83
Good Woman of Szechuan (Brecht) 188n36
Goodman Theater, Chicago 256
Goodnight Desdemona (MacDonald) 113, 116, 117, 122–26, 127
Gordon, Mary 219
Goreau, Angeline 141
Graham, Martha 154, 160–63; *Episodes* 160, 163; *Errand into the Maze* 160, 162; *Phaedra's Dream* 160; and *Snow on the Mesa: Portrait of Martha* 154; and *To You, the Birdie!* 154, 160, 162–63
Greco, Loretta 81–82
Green, Amy 2, 6, 67
Greenblatt, Stephen 127; *Will in the World* 110
Greer, Germaine 106
Grieg, Edvard 258
Griffin, Cindy 217, 218
Griffin, Gabriele 104
Grosz, Elizabeth ("Refiguring Lesbian Desire") 241, 242
Gubar, Susan 192–93, 194
Gussow, Mel 215, 231n2

The Hair Net (Man Ray) 139
Hall, Edward 97
Hamilton, Edith, *Mythology* 64, 65, 69
Hamlet (Shakespeare) 99
Hamletmachine (Müller) 240
A Handmaid's Tale (Atwood) 237
Hang Ten (Hartman) 79, 86–87
Hara, Doug **63**
Hardwick, Lorna 37n2
Harlem Duet (Sears) 113, 117, 126–31
Harlem Renaissance 129
Harrel, Dana Iris 80
Harris, Geraldine 4, 6, 8
Hart, Lynda (*Making a Spectacle*) 6, 8, 119
Hartigan, Karelisa V. 92n5
Hartman, Karen (*Hang Ten*) 79, 86–87
Hawkins, Erick 162
Hawthorne, Nathaniel: "The Custom House" 171; hypocrisy as theme of 176, 183; *The Scarlet Letter* 169–88
Hegel, Georg Wilhelm Friedrich 84

Herman, Claudia 64
Heroides (Ovid) 145
Hillman, James (*A Blue Fire*) 70
Hippolytus (Euripides): and Phaedra myth 145, 152, 154, 156–57, 158, 160, 161, 163; and Philomela myth 45
Hitchcock, Alfred (*The 39 Steps*) 1
Hoffman Baruch, Elaine 249, 251, 252, 255
Holledge, Julie 253, 254
Hopkins, Lisa 137
Hoppe, Marianne 100, 106
House/Lights (LeCompte) 152, 158
Howard, Jean E. 116
Hoyle, John 142
Huggan, Graham 52
Hughes, Gwenda 102
Hume, Lindy 44
Hunter, Kathryn 100, 106

Ibsen, Henrik: *A Doll House* 247, 249–53; feminist agenda of 247, 249–52, 255, 257; and Women's Rights League 249
Iizuka, Naomi 54; *Polaroid Stories* 52, 53
I'm So Sorry for Everything (Gluzman) 256
In the Blood (Parks) **170**, 171, 173–74, 181–85, 186
intertextuality 1–2
Iphigenia and Other Daughters (McLaughlin) **22**, 28, 31–36; and the *Oresteia* myth 23, 29, 32, 33
Iphigenia in Aulis (Euripides) 31, 33, 34
Iphigenia in Aulis (McLaughlin) 34
Iphigenia in Tauris (Euripides) 31
Iphigenia in Tauris (McLaughlin) 35–36
Iran, feminist theater in 254
Iraq, war in 37, 85
Irons, Jeremy 144
Irvin, Polly 102
The Island (Fugard) 82

Jackson, Jesse 129
James, Henry 213
Jane Eyre (C. Brontë) 189–203; in British cultural history 191, 192; nineteenth-century adaptations of 189; Shared Experience's adaptation of 189–203, **190**; soliloquy in 198; Victorian culture depicted in 189–93, 195, 197
Jiang Qing 254
Johnston, Brian 251
Jones, Ann Rosalind 131n10
Jones, Cherry **114**
Jones, Christine 153
Jones, Felicity **63**

Kahn, Coppélia 102–3, 109
Kalke, Celise 146
Kane, Sarah 146
Karimi, Niki 254
Karvas, Peter (*Antigone a tí druhi* [*Antigone and the Others*]) 82

Kaut-Howson, Helena 100
Kazan, Elia 239, 243
Keach, Stacy 99
Kelly, Edna 161
Keyssar, Helene 4–5, 7, 8, 114, 193
Kieler, Laura Peterson 247
Killigrew, Thomas (*Tomaso, The Wanderer*) 140
Kilmer, Val **136**
King, Cathy (*Gone*) 83
King, Martin Luther 128, 129
King Lear (Shakespeare) 98–102, 160; difficulty of Lear role 100; Fool's role in 106; love and power in 109; women in Lear role 99–102, 106
Kisselgoff, Anna 161
Kline, Kevin 99
Knowles, Ric 117, 122, 127
Koosil-ja Hwang 159
Koundouros, Nikos: *Antigone: A Cry for Peace* 82–83; *The Photographers* 82–83
Kruger, Loren 61
Kushner, Tony: *Angels in America* 237; *Millennium Approaches* 237; *Perestroika* 239

Lacan, Jacques 84
La Mama E.T.C. 99
Lamb, Charles 98
Lamson, Louise 71
Lapine, James 99
Lapotaire, Jane 99
Lauren, Ellen: and *Room* 215, **216**, 218, 224–29, 230–31
Lawrence, D. H. 213
Leaning, Fiona 159
Lear (Mabou Mines) 100–102, 257
Lear's Daughters (WTG) **98**, 102–10; collaborative process in 102; Fool's role in 105–8, 110; Kahn's reading of 102–3; money as theme in 107–9; as reinvention 102
Leavitt, Dinah 4
LeCompte, Elizabeth 152; *House/Lights* 152, 158; *To You, the Birdie! (Phèdre)* 153–54, 157–64
Lee, Hermione 219, 220
Leigh, Vivien 243, 244
The Libation Bearers (Aeschylus) 21
The Living Theatre 26
Llewellyn-Jones, Margaret 191
Lopez, Martin 171
The Love of the Nightingale (Wertenbaker) 42–60, **44**; activist street theater in 55; adapted as opera 46; audience as participants in 47, 48, 49, 53, 54–55; auditory space activated in 50; interrogatory form of 50; myth of 43, 44–45, 47, 48, 51, 52–57; play-within-the-play 45; popularity of 46; staging post-colonial feminism in 47–51, 55; storytelling in 50; structure and content of 43, 44–46; war as subject of 48, 49–50, 56

Ludlam, Charles 240
Lum, Mary 29
Luther, Martin 94n45

Mabou Mines 135; *DollHouse* **248**, 252–53, 257–64; *Lear* 100–102, 257
MacDonald, Ann-Marie: comparisons with 128, 129, 130, 131; *Goodnight Desdemona* 113, 116, 117, 122–26, 127
Mack, Sara 64–65
The Madwoman in the Attic (Gilbert and Gubar) 192–93
Magritte, René 162
Making a Spectacle (Hart) 6, 8, 119
Malcolm X 129
Maleczech, Ruth 101, 257
Malina, Judith 83
Mandela, Nelson and Winnie 128
Mann, Emily 255
Marcus, Laura 218, 227
Marder, Elissa 52
Margolin, Deb: and *Belle Reprieve* 239, 241; and *Electra Speaks* 25, 36–37; and Split Britches 239
Martha Graham Dance Company 154
Martini, Alberto 137, 138
Marvel, Elizabeth 144
Masson, André 162
Matthews, Emma **44**
Maycock, Hazel **98**, 102
McDonald, Marianne 37n2
McKellan, Ian 99
McLaughlin, Ellen: *Electra* 34–35; *Iphigenia and Other Daughters* 22, **23**, 24–25, 28, 31–36; *Iphigenia in Aulis* 34; *Iphigenia in Tauris* 35–36; postmodernism of 33–34, 36; radical reorganization of the original plays by 32–33
Meckler, Nancy 190
Medallion (Barfield) 79, **80**, 87–89
Mehrjui, Dariush 254
Metamorphoses (Ovid) 43, 52, 53, 61–62, 64–67, 70, 71, 72, 75
Metamorphoses (Zimmerman) 61–78, **63**; anachronism in 67–68; collaboration in 72–75; family drama in 67–68; female narrators in 62, 65–68; humanist themes in 62, 75; myth redefined in 67, 68; source text for 53, 64–65, 66, 69, 70, 72; transformation in 68–72; water as setting/metaphor in 71–72, 73
Millennium Approaches (Kushner) 237
Miller, Arthur 152
Miller, Jonathan 23, 99
Miller, Lee 137, 162; *Nude* 138
Mills, Richard 44
Mrs. Dalloway (Woolf) 218
Mitchell, Maude, and *DollHouse* **248**, 252, 257, 258, 261, 262, 263–64
Miyagawa, Chiori 204–14; *America Dreaming* 86; and *Antigone Project* 79, 85, 92n2; and Chopin's *Awakening* 204–14, **205**; and Japanese culture 204, 213; minimalist approach of 209–11; objectives of 206–8; as outsider 204, 213; *Red Again* 79, 85–86; time breaks used by 211–12
Mnouchkine, Ariane (*Les Atrides*) 33
Modleski, Tania 115
Moi, Toril 249, 259
Moments of Being (Woolf) 217
Monks, Aoife 3
Monroe, Marilyn 241, 242
Morrison, Toni (*The Bluest Eye*) 52
Mother Courage (Brecht) 188n36
Mott, George 171
Muir, Kenneth 106
Müller, Heiner (*Hamletmachine*) 240
Muratore, Mary Jo 146, 147
Mythology (Hamilton) 64, 65, 69
myths: of Africa 52; anachronistic redefinition of 67; emotionalism of 55; engaging 52–54; and *Love of the Nightingale* 43, 44–45, 47, 48, 51, 52–57; as performance texts 65; phallocentrism of 55; re-seeing 64; transforming 54–57; transnational 52

Nagy, Phyllis (*The Scarlet Letter*) 169, 172–73, 178–81, 182–83, 186
Naylor, Gloria (*The Women of Brewster Place*) 52
Near, Timothy 255
Neely, Carol 113
New York Shakespeare Festival **136**
Newman, Karen 128, 130
Nightwood Theatre, Toronto 122, 126–27
Ning Yu 258, 261–62
Nishii, Brian **205**
Nottage, Lynn (*A Stone's Throw*) 79, 89
Novy, Marianne 116, 117, 119
Nunn, Trevor 99

O'Connor, Marion 116
Olivier, Sir Laurence 127
O'Neill, Eugene 152; *Mourning Becomes Electra* 2
Open Theatre 26
Oresteia (Aeschylus) 21, 26; and *Antigone* 80; and *Electra Speaks* 23, 29, 32, 33; and *Iphigenia and Other Daughters* 23, 29, 32, 33; and *King Lear* 102–3; other feminist-oriented adaptations of 33
Oresteia myth 23, 29, 32, 33
Orlando (Woolf) 232n26
Ostermeier, Thomas 255–56
Ostling, Daniel 73
Othello (Shakespeare) 113, 116, 118–34; gender issues in 116, 120, 127; handkerchief in 121, 129–30; MacDonald's adaptation of 113, 116, 117, 122–25, 127; race issues in 129; resistant reading of 126, 127, 131; Sears's prequel to 113, 117, 127–31; Vogel's adaptation of 113, **114**, 116, 118–22

Our Country's Good (Wertenbaker) 43
Overlie, Mary 224
Ovid: *Heroides* 145; and immortality 75; as masterful storyteller 64–65, 68; *Metamorphoses* 43, 52, 53, 61–62, 64–67, 70, 71, 72, 75

Packer, Tina 99
Parks, Suzan-Lori: *Fucking A* 173–74, 181, 182, 185–86; *In the Blood* **170**, 171, 173–74, 181–85, 186; *Red Letter Plays* 169, 172, 173–74, 181–86
Parnell, Charles **205**
Parrish, Sue 97–98
Patel, Neil 225
The Patriot Act 85
Pearce, Michele 178
Peck, Sabrina 79
Perestroika (Kushner) 239
The Performing Garage 26, 160, 256
Performing Nostalgia (Bennett) 116, 131n11
Pershing, John Joseph 88
Peterson, M. Jeanne 192
Phaedra (Diamond) 153, 158
Phaedra (Sophocles) 156
Phaedra in Delirium (Women's Project) 153
Phaedra in Delirium (Yankowitz) 153–54
Phaedra's Dream (Graham) 160
Phaedre (Seneca) 145
Phèdre (Akalaitis) 153
Phèdre (Phaedra) story: contemporary adaptations of 153–55, 160–64; in Euripides' *Hippolytus* 145, 152, 154, 156–57, 158, 160, 161, 163; and Graham 154, 160, 162–63; pretext 155; Racine's play 135, 136, 145–49, 152, 154, 157–58, 159, 161, 162, 163; and *To You, the Birdie!* 153–55, 157–59, 160–63
Phèdre (Wertenbaker) 146
Phelan, Peggy 84
The Photographers (Koundouros) 82–83
Picasso, Pablo 162
Plummer, Christopher 99
Poetics (Aristotle) 163
Polaroid Stories (Iizuka) 52, 53
postmodernism, stylistic 8
postmodernist critical theory, rise of 5, 6
Poulter, Lizz 102
Povinelli, Mark **248**, 258, 261, 262
power: and desire 244; and gender 101, 103, 108, 110, 116, 176; and language 51; and love 103, 109; might as right 49; and money 107–9; relationships based on 53
The Prayer (Man Ray) 138
The Presentation of Self in Everyday Life (Goffman) 251
Propeller Company 97
Public Theatre 99

queer theater 241, 245
queer theory, rise of 5–6
Quesnel, Pooky **190**

Rabey, David Ian 57
Rabinowitz, Nancy Sorkin 157, 163
Racine, Jean (*Phèdre*) 135, 136, 145–49, 152, 154, 157–58, 159, 161, 162, 163
radical theater 4
Ray, Man 137; *The Hair Net* 139; "Minotaur" 162; *The Prayer* 138; *Tears* 139
Red Again (Miyagawa) 79, 85–86
Red Letter Plays (Parks) 169, 172, 173–74, 181–86
Reeve, Christopher 144
Reinelt, Janelle 8
Renaissance 107, 119
Restoration 99, 140, 141, 142, 143
re-vision, use of term 8–9
rhetoric: classical 215, 232n38; feminist 217, 225; invitational 217, 218–20, 224–25, 226, 229
Rich, Adrienne 36, 191, 194
Ridiculous Theater 240
Riefenstahl, Leni 139
Rilke, Rainer Maria 68
Robb, J. Cooper 183
Robeson, Paul 129
Roche, Suzzy 158, 159
Rochester, John Wilmot, earl of 142
Rogers, Katharine 141
Romeo and Juliet (Shakespeare) 99, 125–26, 137
Room (SITI) 215–33, **216**; collaborative process in 224–25; movement vocabulary of 224–25; peroration 230–31; in production 225–29; source texts and adaptation 217–24; Woolf represented in 225–26, 228–29
A Room of One's Own (Woolf) 141, 215, 217–23, 226–27, 230
Rothe, Lisa **22**, 23
Rotman, Brian (*Signifying Nothing: The Semiotics of Zero*) 109
The Rover (Behn) 135, 136, 140–45
Royal Shakespeare Company 43, 99, 144
Rubens, Peter Paul (*Tereus Confronted with the Head of His Son*) 55
Ruhl, Sarah (*Eurydice*) 77n28
Rungé, Philip Otto 139
Ryder, Mark 162

Sainer, Arthur 4
St. Ann's Warehouse, Brooklyn 153
Salem, Peter 194
Salem witch trials 174, 176
Sanders, Leslie 129
Sappho (*A l'aimee*) 145
Sara (film) 254
Savran, David 243
The Scarlet Letter (Hawthorne) 169–88; ambiguity in 183; feminist criticism on 171–72; language in 178; lawlessness in 172, 174, 180; Parks's *Red Letter Plays* 169, 172, 173–74, 181–86; Puritan roots of 169,

171–72, 173, 183; revisionist adaptations of 172–74; transformation in 181; witchcraft pattern in 172, 176, 179, 182
The Scarlet Letter (Nagy) 169, 172–73, 178–81, 182–83, 186
The Scarlet Letter (Wallace) 169, 172–73, 186; class issues in 184; hypocrisy in 182–83; and lawlessness 172, 176, 180; and sexuality 175–78, 179, 180–81; and witchcraft 174–76, 179
Schafer, Elizabeth 100
Schmidt, Paul 146–47, 153, 154, 158–59
Schor, Naomi 5
Schroeder, Pat 62
Schwab, Gabriele 172, 179
Scofield, Paul 100
Scott, Joan 43
Sears, Djanet: *African Solo* 127; *Harlem Duet* 113, 117, 126–31; *Testifyin* 127
Sedgwick, Eve 177, 239
See, Sheena 163
Segal, Sondra 23, 25, 27, 28, 29, 30, 36–37
Seneca (*Phaedre*) 145
Serban, Andre (*Fragments of a Trilogy*) 2
seventeenth century: feminist writing in 141; Puritanism in 174, 183; transgressive sexual desires in 135–36, 177, 178, 180; witchcraft in 172, 174, 176, 179, 182
Sexton, Michael 171
Seyersted, Per 206, 212
Shakespeare, William: gender absolutism in works of 106; gender in casting of 99–100; *Hamlet* 99; Judith as invented sister of 219; *King Lear* 98–102, 160; *Othello* 113, 116, 118–34; reading and writing back to 117, 118; *Romeo and Juliet* 99, 125–26, 137; sources for 122; *Taming of the Shrew* 97; theatrical adaptations of his plays 97–99, 115–17, 118, 127, 131, 160; *Titus Andronicus* 52, 55
Shakespeare and Company 99
Shakespeare's Division of Experience (French) 106
Shared Experience Theatre: collaborative teamwork in 191, 202; *Jane Eyre* adapted by 189–203, **190**; reputation of 190; theatrical productions of 190–91
Sharp, Margi **205**
Sharrock, Alison 67
Shaw, Paul 240
Shaw, Peggy **238**, 239, 240, 241
Shepard, Sam (*Silent Tongue*) 52
Sher, Anthony 106
Siddons, Sarah 99
Signifying Nothing: The Semiotics of Zero (Rotman) 109
Silent Tongue (Shepard) 52
Singh, Jyotsna 119
Sissons, Narrele 257
Sister/Sister (WET) 26
SITI Company: biodramas produced by 215;

collaboration in 217, 224–25; comparisons with 218; *Room* 215–33, **216**
Skiles, Sophia **205**
Sklar, Roberta 23, 25, 26, 27, 28, 29, 30
Slavitt, David R. 61
Smith, Iris 101
Smith-Cameron, J. **114**
Snow on the Mesa: Portrait of Martha 154
Snyder, Susan 124
Solomon, Alisa 46, 249, 250, 251
Sophocles 21; *Antigone* 79, 80–85, 88, 89–90, 91; *Electra* 27–29, 33; *Phaedra* 156; *Tereus* 55, 163
Sourvinour-Inwood, Christiane 82
South African Truth and Reconciliation Commission 59n27
Spangler, George M. 206, 212
spectatorship, male 5
Split Britches 239, 240, 241
Sprengnether, Madeline Gohlke 132n16
Stanislavski method 215, 254
Steadman, Susan 5
Stein, Gertrude 152
Stheneboia (Euripides) 156
Still, Judith 115
Stimpson, Catherine 219
A Stone's Throw (Nottage) 79, 89
Stratford Shakespeare Festival (Canada) 99
A Streetcar Named Desire (film) 239, 240, 243
A Streetcar Named Desire (Williams) 237–46; adaptations of 239, 244; and *Belle Reprieve* **238**, 239–45
Suleiman, Susan Rubin 162
Sullivan, Esther Beth 25
Sullivan, Zohreh T. 192
Summers, Alison 153
Suntree, Susan (*Antigone Prism*) 83–84
Surrealism 137, 138, 162
Svich, Caridad (*Antigone Arkhe*) 79, 91

Taming of the Shrew (Shakespeare) 97
Tanguy, Yves 137, 138
Tate, Nahum 98
Teale, Polly: and *Jane Eyre* 189–202
Tears (Man Ray) 139
Technologies of Gender (de Lauretis) 6
Templeton, Joan 249
Tennant, Emma 52
Tereus (Sophocles) 55, 163
Tereus Confronted with the Head of His Son (Rubens) 55
Testifyin (Sears) 127
Thesmophoriazousai (Aristophanes) 156
The 39 Steps (Hitchcock) 1
Thompson, April Yvette **80**
'*Tis Pity* (Akalaitis) 137, 138
'*Tis Pity She's a Whore* (Ford) 135, 136–40, **136**, 141, 145, 147
Titus Andronicus (Shakespeare) 52, 55
To You, the Birdie! (*Phèdre*) [LeCompte] 153–54, **153**, 158–64

Tolstoy, Leo 98
Tomaso, the Wanderer (Killigrew) 140
Tompkins, Joanne 253, 254
Tripplehorn, Jeanne **136**, 139
Trojan Barbie: A Car-Crash Encounter with Euripides' Trojan Women (Evans) 1
Tsypin, George 143
Tyrrell, Blake 82

universalism 93–94n43

Valk, Kate **153**, 154, 158, 159, 162, 163
Victoria, queen of England 192
Virginia Woolf: The Common Ground (Beer) 220
Vogel, Paula: comparisons with 123, 127, 129, 131; *Desdemona* 113, **114**, 116, 118–22

Wagner, Jennifer 50, 53
Walker, Alice (*The Color Purple*) 52
Walker, Nancy A. 207, 213
Wallace, Naomi (*The Scarlet Letter*) 169, 172–73, 174–78, 179, 180, 182–83, 184, 186, 188n35
Wandor, Michelene 7, 23, 72
Warmington, Neil 194
The Waves (Woolf) 1, 218, 220, 223
Weaver, Lois **238**, 239, 240, 241
Wellman, Mac 83
Wertenbaker, Timberlake: *The Ash Girl* 43; *Dianeira* 43; dislocations in plays of 44; *The Love of the Nightingale* 42–60, **44**; *Our Country's Good* 43; *Phèdre* 146; as postcolonial writer 51
West, Darron L. 227
Wexner Center for the Arts, Ohio State University 215
Wharton, Edith 213
Wilde, Oscar 237
Wilder, Thornton 152
Will in the World (Greenblatt) 110
Williams, Tennessee: homoeroticism in works of 242, 243–44; stage directions of 241, 245; *A Streetcar Named Desire* 237–46
Williamstown Theatre 144
Wilmer, Steve 83
Wilson, Robert 100, 154
Wilson, Sallie 160
Winston, Joe 45
Wittig, Monique 8
Wolff, Cynthia Griffin 207
Wolkenfeld, Suzanne 206
women: control and commodification of 138, 158; cultural expectations of 93n17, 121, 128, 190–91, 207, 252, 255; and double standard 89, 141, 163; freedom and space for 223, 230; language of 185; and patriarchy 34, 154, 158–59, 207; performance art of 120; and poverty 188n34; problems of theater professionals 99, 106, 110, 152; and race 127; and rape 141, 144, 163; reactionary violence by 145; rights of 192; selfhood of 122; status of 140, 252; and succession 145; traditional roles of 119, 122, 140, 249, 250, 252, 255; as victims 193; writers 193, 219, 221, 230
The Women of Brewster Place (Naylor) 52
Women's Ensemble 83
Women's Experimental Theatre (WET) 25–27; acting technique in 30; *The Daughters Cycle* 26, 27; *Electra Speaks* 23, 24, 25–26, 27–30, 31, 32, 33, 34, 36; founders of 23, 25; groundbreaking work of 24; Matrilineage 27; *Sister/Sister* 26
Women's Intercultural Performance (Holledge and Tompkins) 253, 254
Women's Project and Productions: *Antigone Project* 79, **80**, 81–82, 85–91, 92n2; mission of 81; *Phaedra in Delirium* 153
Women's Rights League 249
Women's Theatre Group (WTG): *Lear's Daughters* **98**, 102–10
Woolf, Virginia: on androgyny 222; and the "Angel in the House" 217, 221; *Between the Acts* 218; *Common Reader* series 217; creative mind of 215, 217, 219, 222–23, 230; "How Should One Read a Book?" 217; "The Humane Art" 217; "A Letter to a Young Poet" 217, 223; letters and diaries 217; *Mrs. Dalloway* 218; "Mr. Bennett and Mrs. Brown" 217; "Modern Fiction" 217, 222; *Moments of Being* 217; multi-vocality of 222–23; *Orlando* 232n26; "Professions for Women" 217, 221, 227; represented in *Room* production 225–26, 228–29; rhetorical moves of 219–21, 225, 226, 229; *A Room of One's Own* 141, 215, 217–23, 226–27, 230; "A Sketch of the Past" 217, 219, 221, 222, 227, 228; *The Waves* 1, 218, 220, 223
Wooster Group 152, 154–55, 158–62, 164
Worton, Michael 115
Wright, Garland 33

Yankowitz, Susan (*Phaedra in Delirium*) 153–54
Yaw, Sandra 102
Yellow Earth Theatre 112n27

Zeitlin, Froma 21, 30
Zhang Min 254
Zimmerman, Mary: collaboration with 72–75; *Metamorphoses* 53, 61–78, **63**; transformation of 69, 70; women as focus in work of 61, 65–68; as writer and director 72–73

www.ingramcontent.com/pod-product-compliance
Lightning Source LLC
Chambersburg PA
CBHW051210300426
44116CB00006B/514